UQ HOLDER!

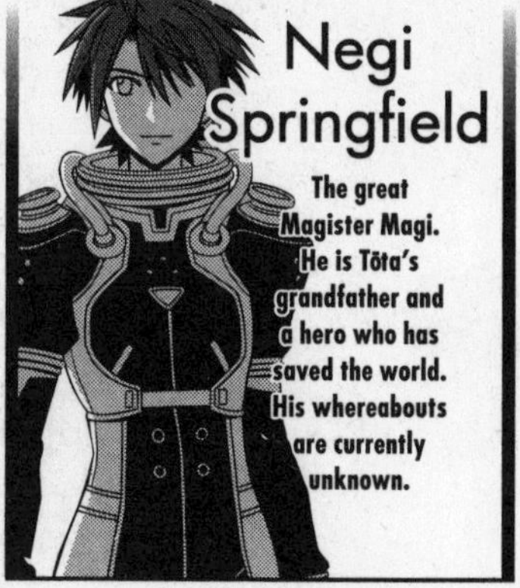

Negi Springfield
The great Magister Magi. He is Tōta's grandfather and a hero who has saved the world. His whereabouts are currently unknown.

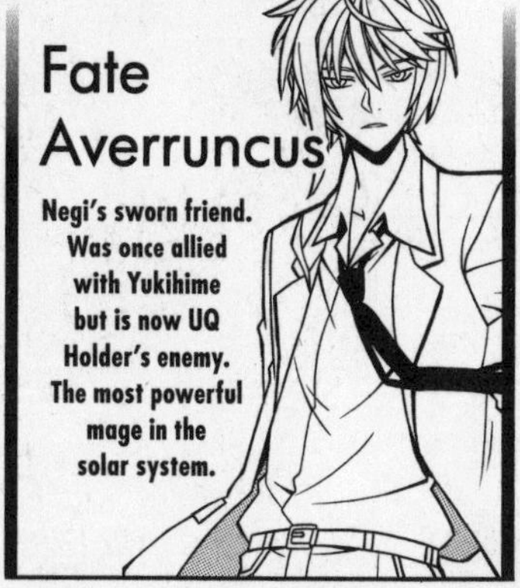

Fate Averruncus
Negi's sworn friend. Was once allied with Yukihime but is now UQ Holder's enemy. The most powerful mage in the solar system.

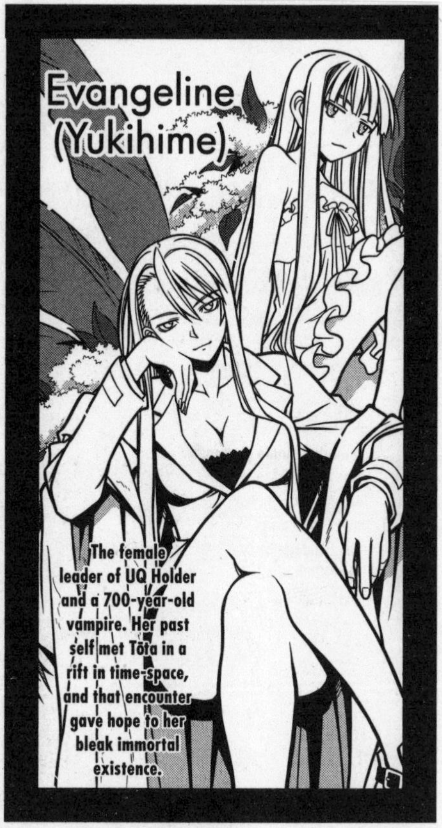

Evangeline (Yukihime)
The female leader of UQ Holder and a 700-year-old vampire. Her past self met Tōta in a rift in time-space, and that encounter gave hope to her bleak immortal existence.

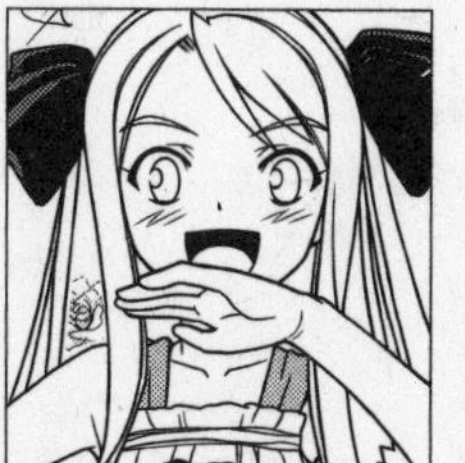

MIZORE YUKIHIRO

Heiress to the Yukihiro Conglomerate. She has decided that Tōta will be her husband.

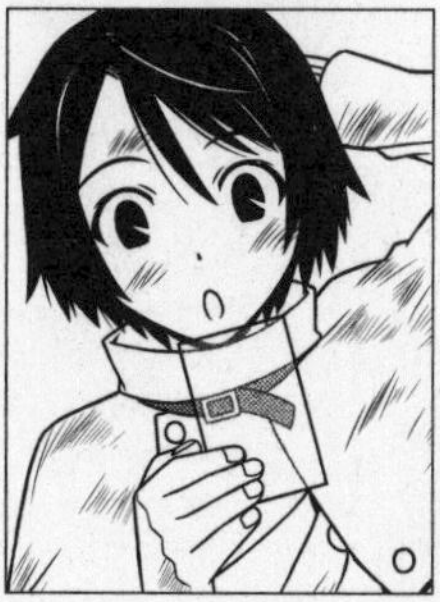

SHINOBU YŪKI

Met Tōta earlier in our story, when he was en route to the capital. Loves machines. Her dream is to leave her village and participate in the grand race around the solar system.

THE STORY SO FAR

Account of the Battle(?) Over Tōta.

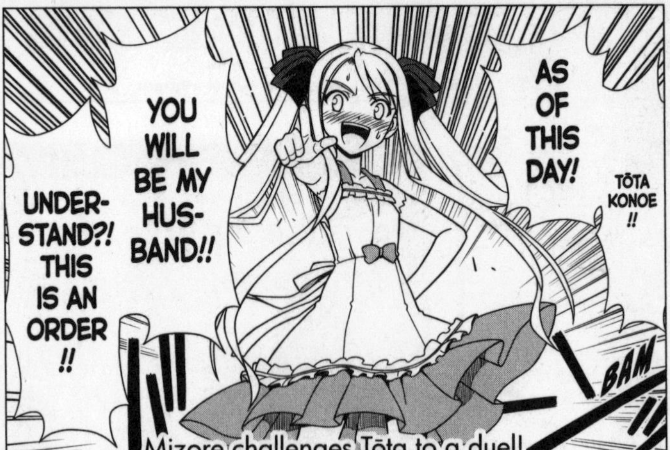
TŌTA KONOE !!
AS OF THIS DAY!
YOU WILL BE MY HUS-BAND!!
UNDER-STAND?! THIS IS AN ORDER !!
BAM

Mizore challenges Tōta to a duel!
She loses and declares her love...

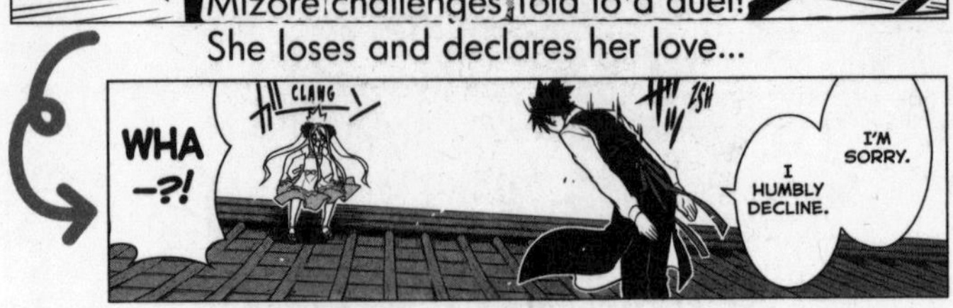
I'M SORRY.
I HUMBLY DECLINE.
ZSH
CLANG
WHA —?!

...and is shot down.

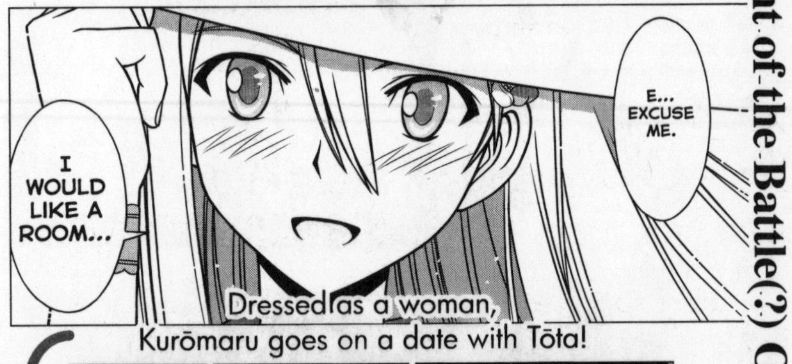
E... EXCUSE ME.
I WOULD LIKE A ROOM...

Dressed as a woman,
Kurōmaru goes on a date with Tōta!

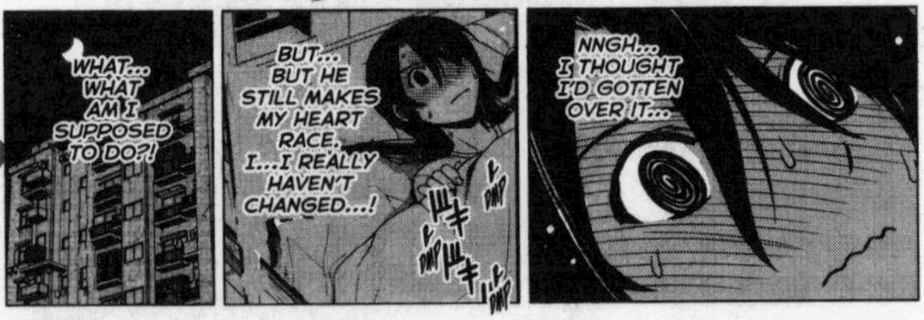
NNGH... I THOUGHT I'D GOTTEN OVER IT...
BUT... BUT HE STILL MAKES MY HEART RACE. I...I REALLY HAVEN'T CHANGED...!
DMP
WHAT... WHAT AM I SUPPOSED TO DO?!

But is not over it.

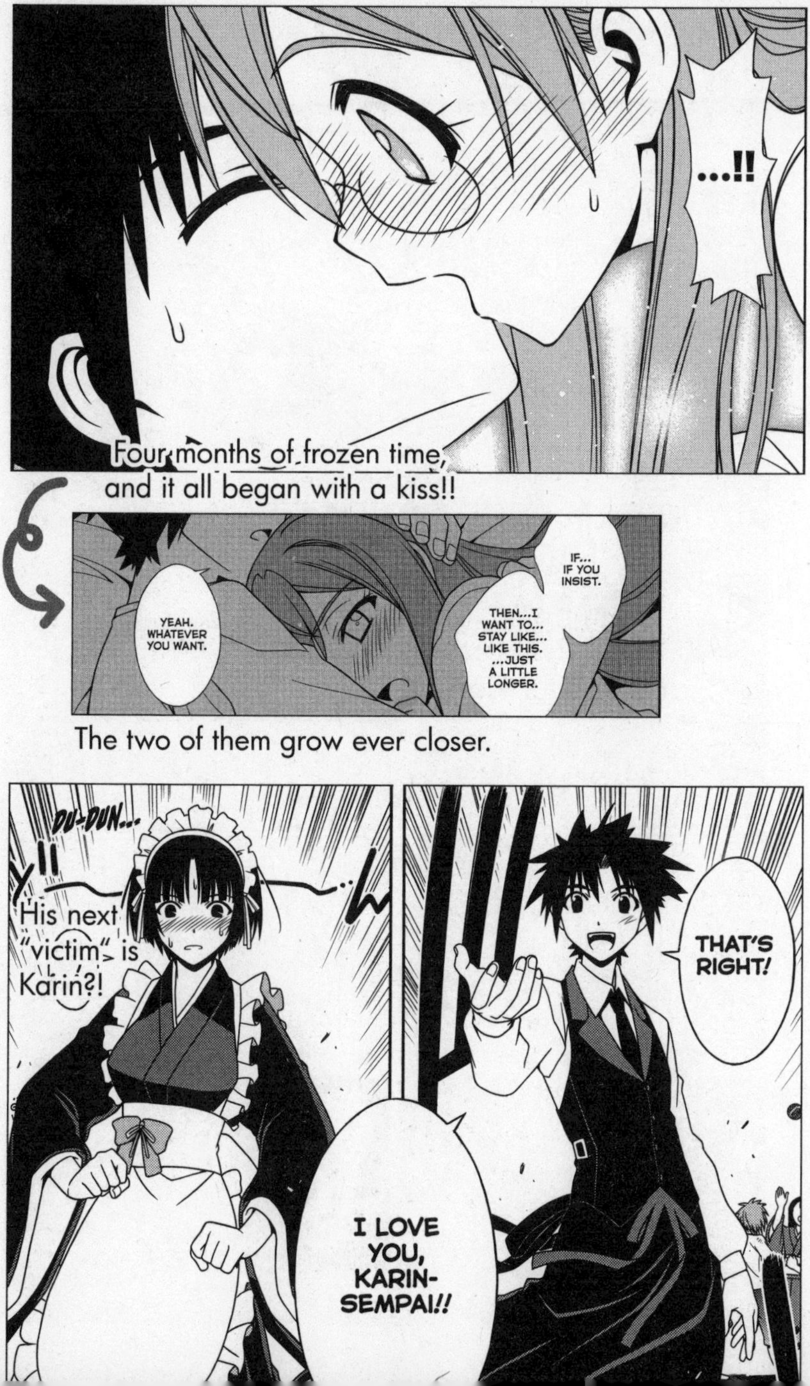
...!!
Four months of frozen time, and it all began with a kiss!!
IF... IF YOU INSIST.
THEN...I WANT TO... STAY LIKE... LIKE THIS. ...JUST A LITTLE LONGER.
YEAH. WHATEVER YOU WANT.
The two of them grow ever closer.
THAT'S RIGHT!
I LOVE YOU, KARIN-SEMPAI!!
DU-DUN...
His next "victim" is Karin?!

CONTENTS

Stage.108 ENTER THE LADY-KILLER 7

Stage.109 THE DANGERS OF HONESTY 23

Stage.110 YUKIHIME'S CONFESSION 39

Stage.111 GATHERING FOR THE MAHORA MARTIAL ARTS TOURNAMENT ... 57

Stage.112 THE STUDENTS OF MAHORA ACADEMY CLASS 3-A ... 73

Stage.113 LET'S GO WITH THE FORCEFUL METHOD................89

Stage.114 FOR NEGI 105

Stage.115 BRAIN FUNCTION STOPS. EVERTHING STOPS.... 123

Stage.116 THE SOLUTION 139

Stage.117 YOU ACTIVATE IT BY................................157

Stage.118 THE FACE OF THE ENEMY 173

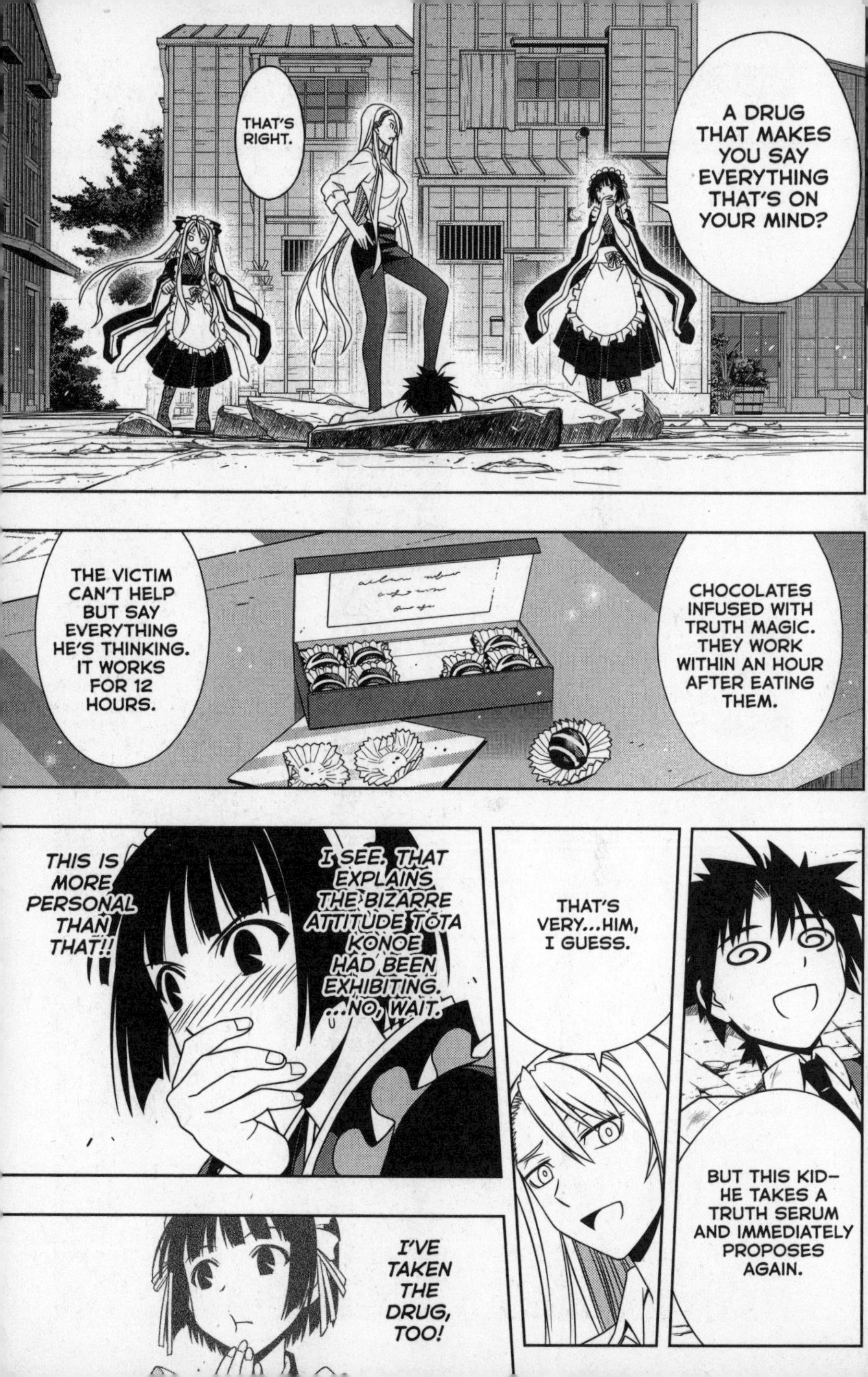
A DRUG THAT MAKES YOU SAY EVERYTHING THAT'S ON YOUR MIND?
THAT'S RIGHT.
CHOCOLATES INFUSED WITH TRUTH MAGIC. THEY WORK WITHIN AN HOUR AFTER EATING THEM.
THE VICTIM CAN'T HELP BUT SAY EVERYTHING HE'S THINKING. IT WORKS FOR 12 HOURS.
BUT THIS KID— HE TAKES A TRUTH SERUM AND IMMEDIATELY PROPOSES AGAIN.
THAT'S VERY...HIM, I GUESS.
I SEE. THAT EXPLAINS THE BIZARRE ATTITUDE TŌTA KONOE HAD BEEN EXHIBITING. ...NO, WAIT.
THIS IS MORE PERSONAL THAN THAT!!
I'VE TAKEN THE DRUG, TOO!

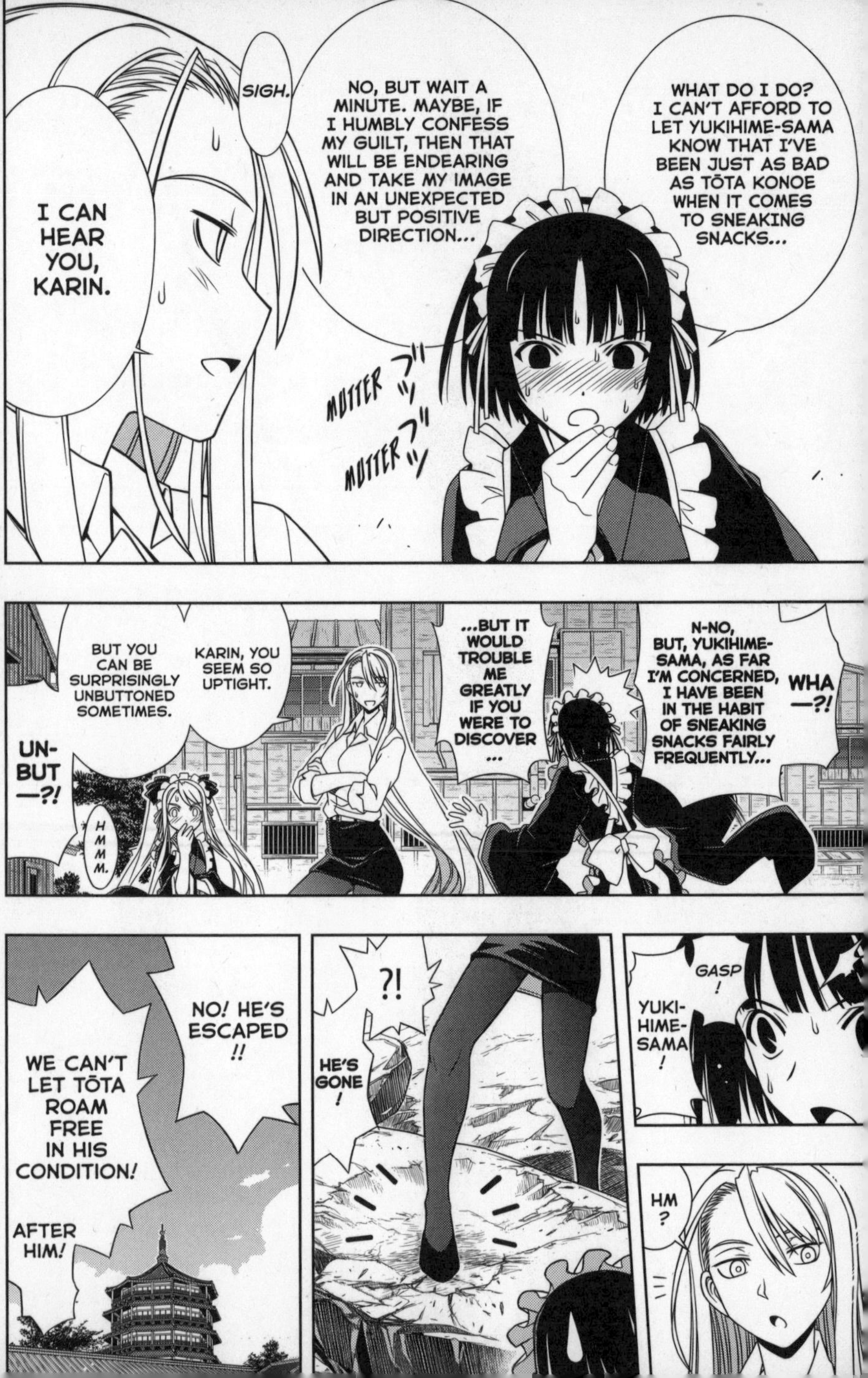
WHAT DO I DO? I CAN'T AFFORD TO LET YUKIHIME-SAMA KNOW THAT I'VE BEEN JUST AS BAD AS TŌTA KONOE WHEN IT COMES TO SNEAKING SNACKS...
NO, BUT WAIT A MINUTE. MAYBE, IF I HUMBLY CONFESS MY GUILT, THEN THAT WILL BE ENDEARING AND TAKE MY IMAGE IN AN UNEXPECTED BUT POSITIVE DIRECTION...
SIGH.
MUTTER MUTTER
I CAN HEAR YOU, KARIN.
WHA—?!
N-NO, BUT, YUKIHIME-SAMA, AS FAR I'M CONCERNED, I HAVE BEEN IN THE HABIT OF SNEAKING SNACKS FAIRLY FREQUENTLY...
...BUT IT WOULD TROUBLE ME GREATLY IF YOU WERE TO DISCOVER...
KARIN, YOU SEEM SO UPTIGHT.
BUT YOU CAN BE SURPRISINGLY UNBUTTONED SOMETIMES.
UN-BUT—?!
HMMM.
GASP!
YUKI-HIME-SAMA!
HM?
?!
HE'S GONE!
NO! HE'S ESCAPED!!
WE CAN'T LET TŌTA ROAM FREE IN HIS CONDITION!
AFTER HIM!

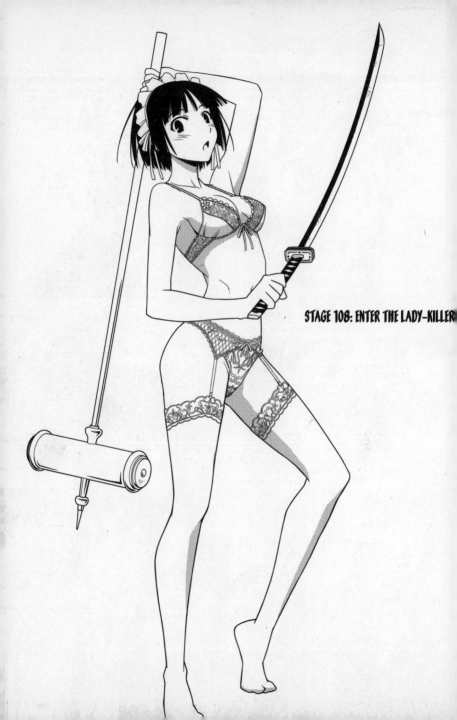

STAGE 108: ENTER THE LADY-KILLER

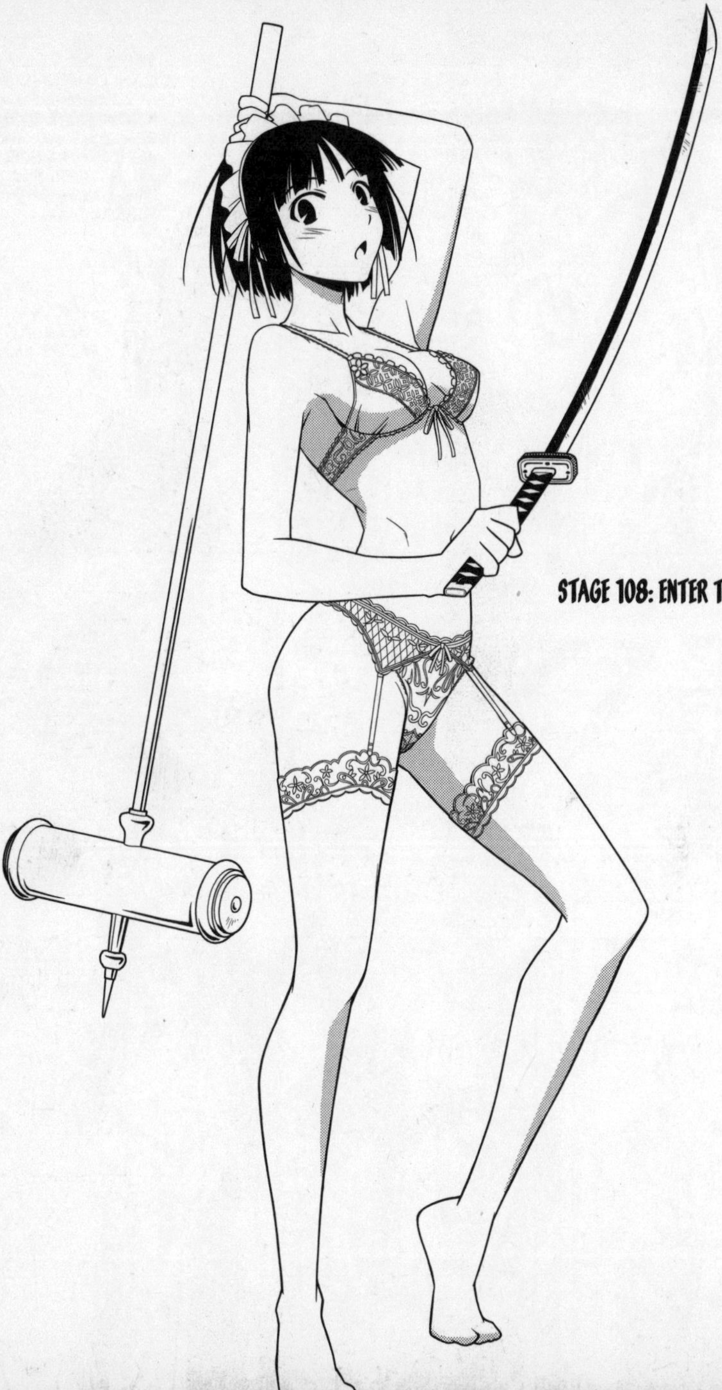

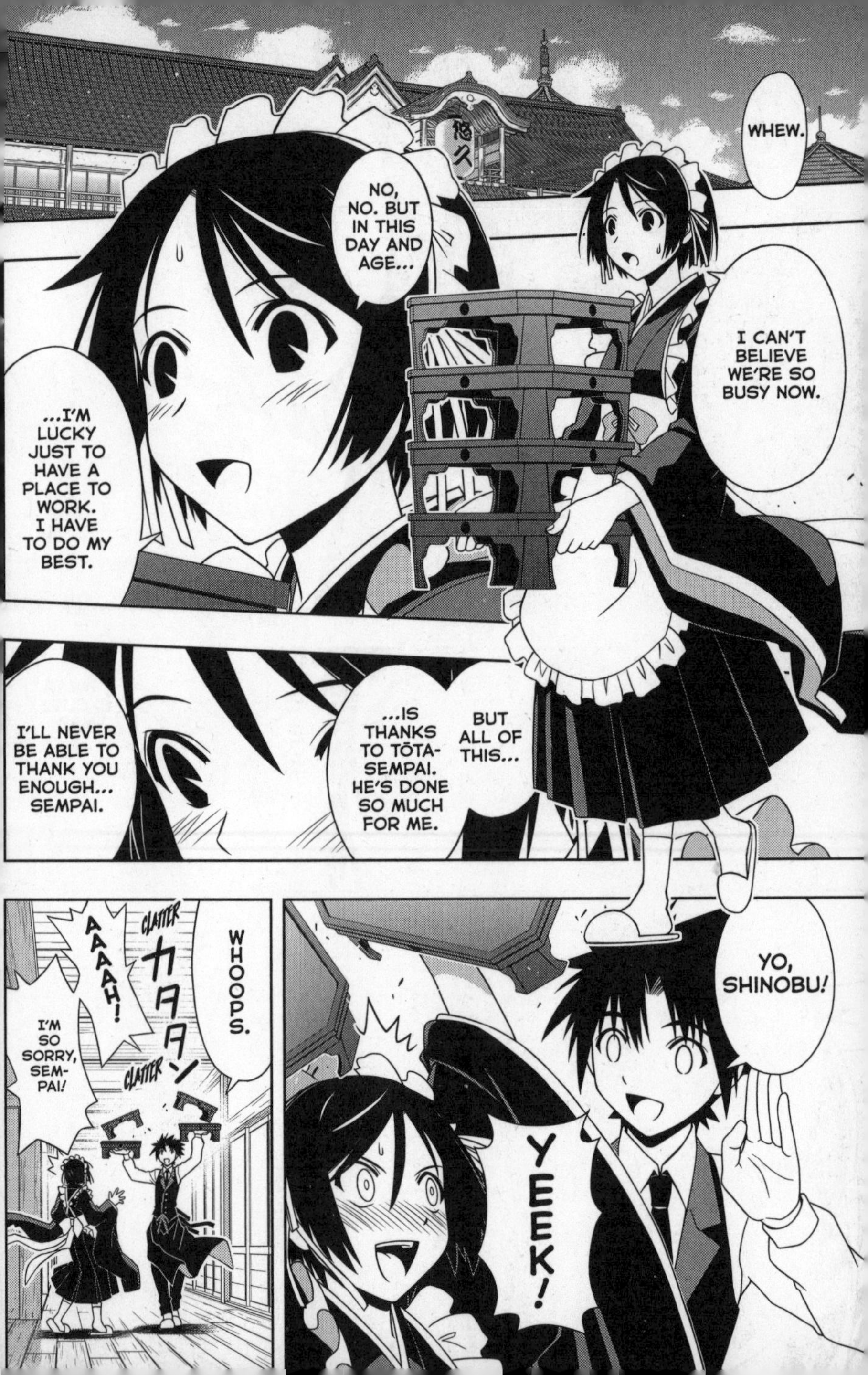
WHEW.
I CAN'T BELIEVE WE'RE SO BUSY NOW.
NO, NO. BUT IN THIS DAY AND AGE...
...I'M LUCKY JUST TO HAVE A PLACE TO WORK. I HAVE TO DO MY BEST.
BUT ALL OF THIS...
...IS THANKS TO TŌTA-SEMPAI. HE'S DONE SO MUCH FOR ME.
I'LL NEVER BE ABLE TO THANK YOU ENOUGH... SEMPAI.
YO, SHINOBU!
YEEK!
WHOOPS.
CLATTER
カタタン
AAAAH!
CLATTER
I'M SO SORRY, SEMPAI!

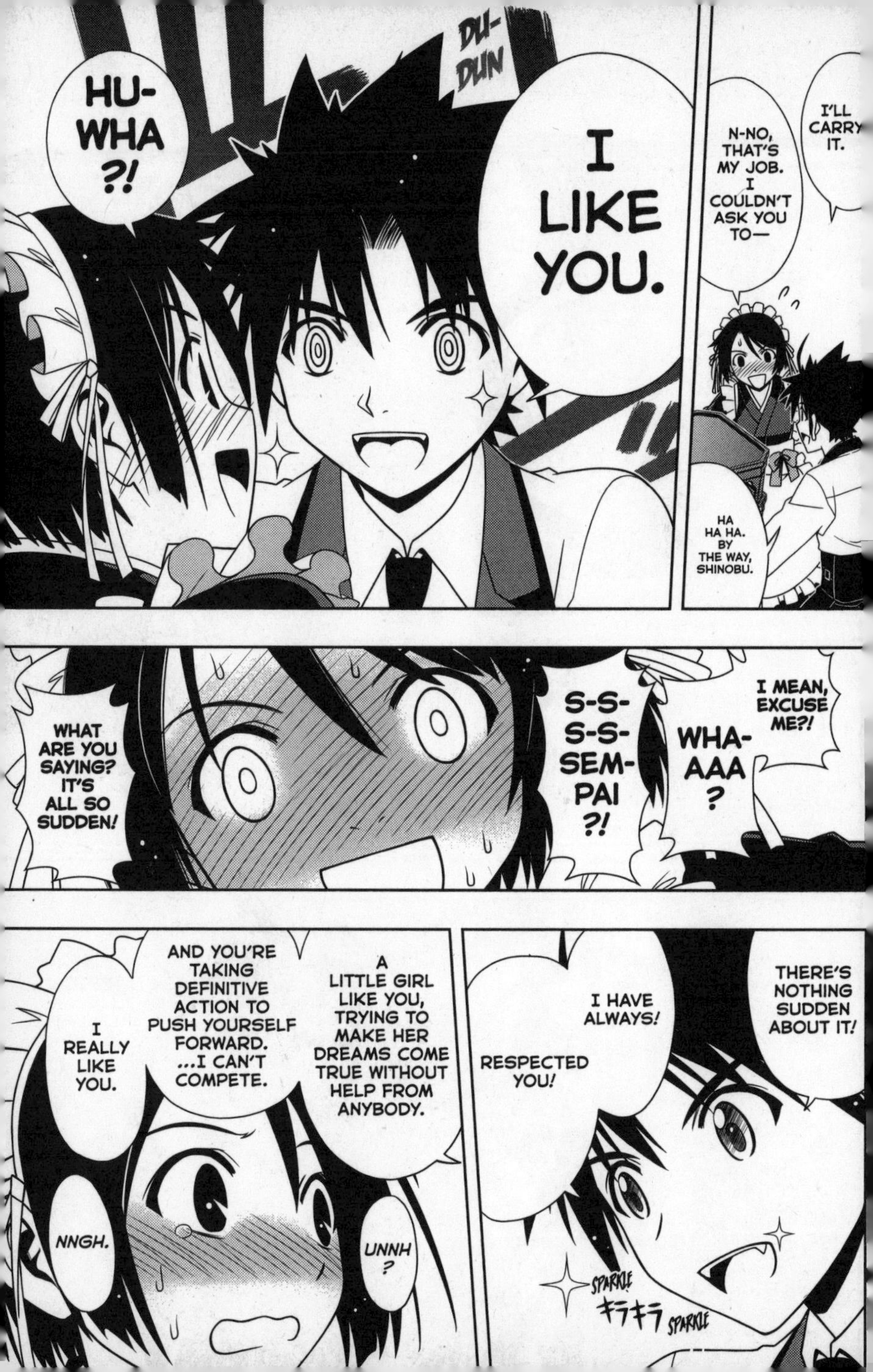
I'LL CARRY IT.
N-NO, THAT'S MY JOB. I COULDN'T ASK YOU TO—
HA HA HA. BY THE WAY, SHINOBU.
DU-DUN
I LIKE YOU.
HU-WHA?!
I MEAN, EXCUSE ME?!
WHA-AAA?
S-S-S-S-SEM-PAI?!
WHAT ARE YOU SAYING? IT'S ALL SO SUDDEN!
THERE'S NOTHING SUDDEN ABOUT IT!
I HAVE ALWAYS!
RESPECTED YOU!
SPARKLE
キラキラ
SPARKLE
A LITTLE GIRL LIKE YOU, TRYING TO MAKE HER DREAMS COME TRUE WITHOUT HELP FROM ANYBODY.
AND YOU'RE TAKING DEFINITIVE ACTION TO PUSH YOURSELF FORWARD. ...I CAN'T COMPETE.
I REALLY LIKE YOU.
UNNH?
NNGH.

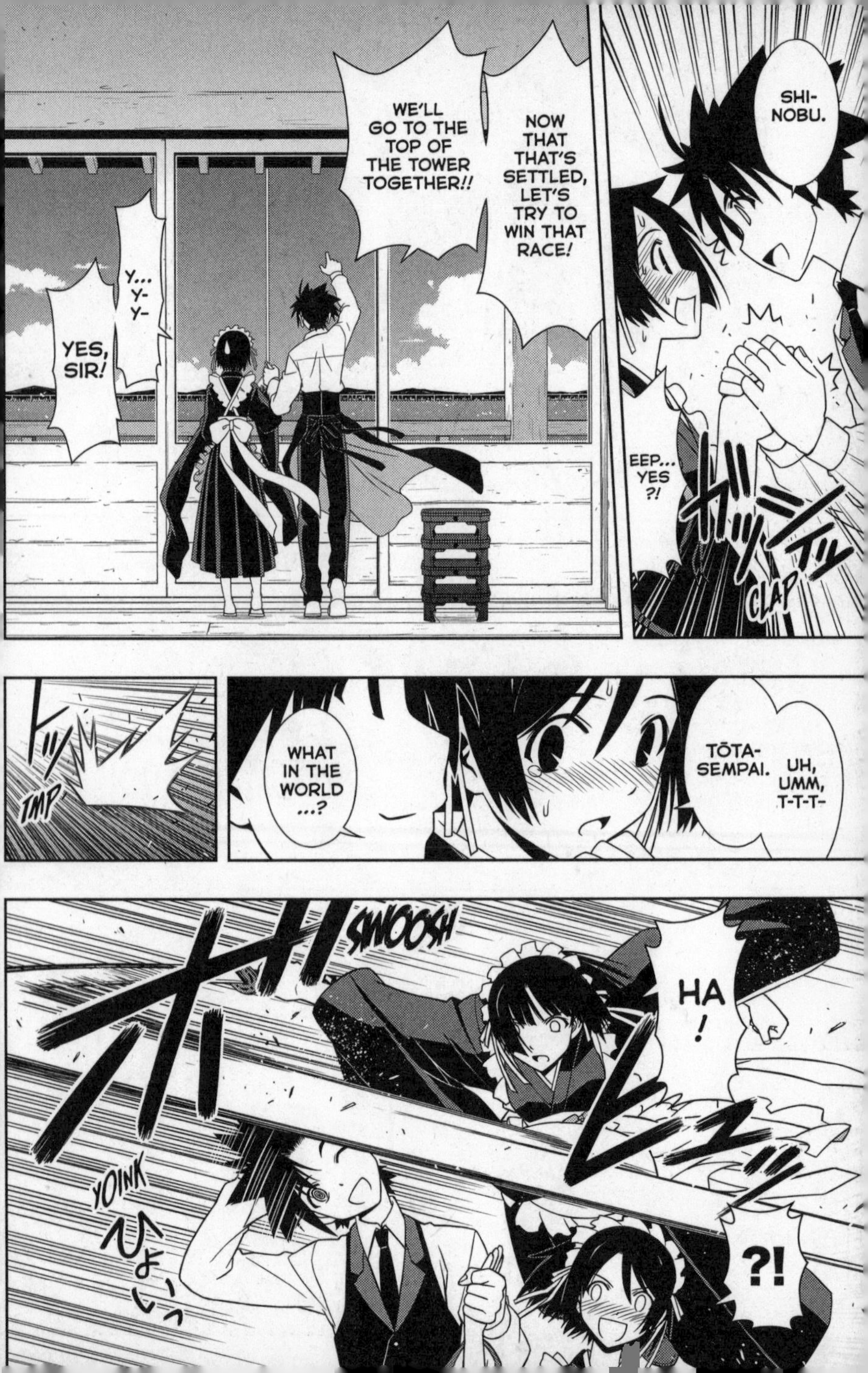
SHI-NOBU.
EEP... YES ?!
CLAP
NOW THAT THAT'S SETTLED, LET'S TRY TO WIN THAT RACE!
WE'LL GO TO THE TOP OF THE TOWER TOGETHER!!
Y... Y- Y-
YES, SIR!
UH, UMM, T-T-T-
TŌTA-SEMPAI.
WHAT IN THE WORLD ...?
TMP
HA!
SWOOSH
?!
YOINK

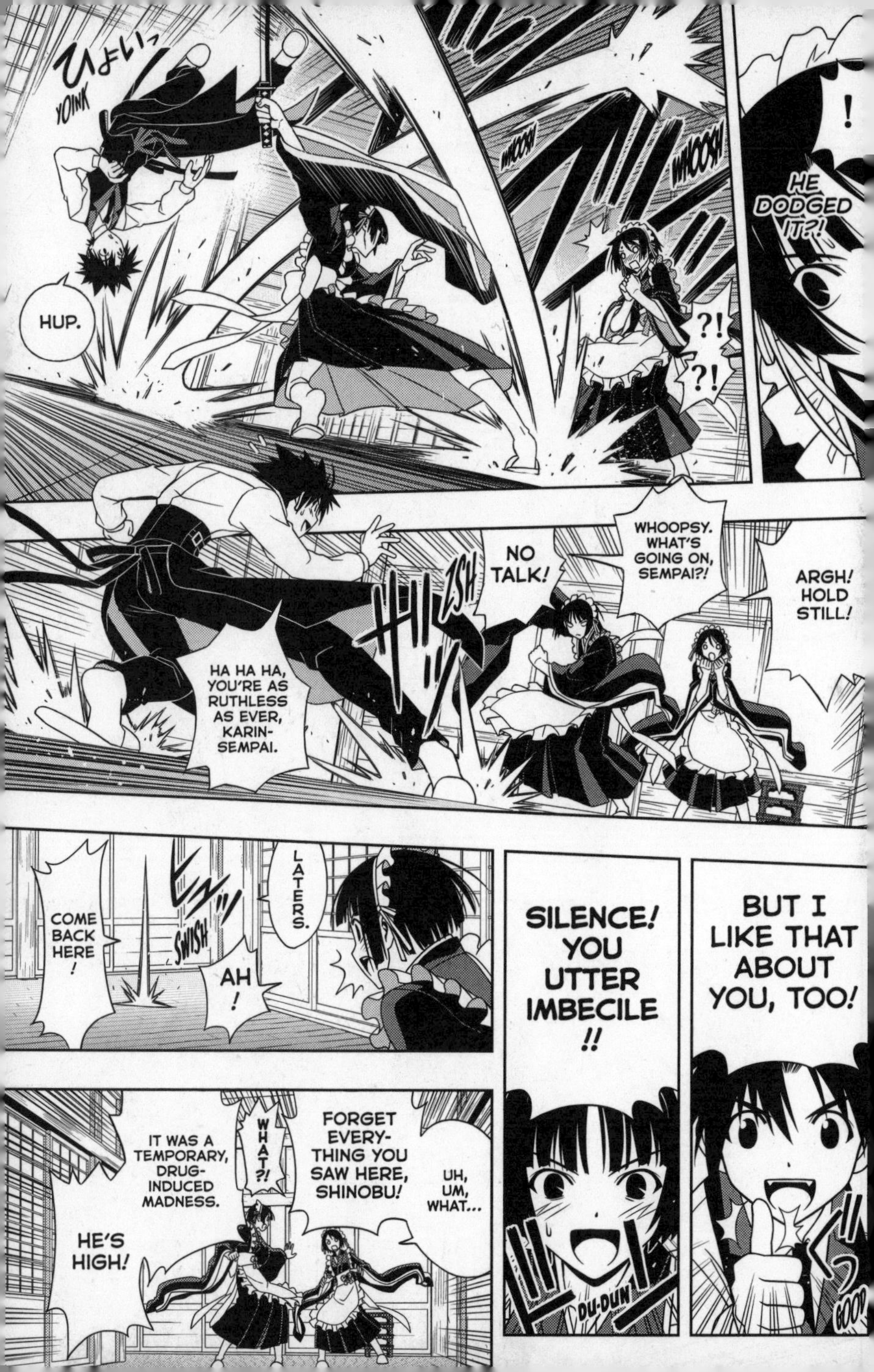
!
HE DODGED IT?!
WHOOSH!
WHOOSH!
?!
?!
ひょいっ
YOINK
HUP.
ARGH! HOLD STILL!
WHOOPSY. WHAT'S GOING ON, SEMPAI?!
NO TALK!
ZSH
HA HA HA, YOU'RE AS RUTHLESS AS EVER, KARIN-SEMPAI.
BUT I LIKE THAT ABOUT YOU, TOO!
くっ
GOOD
SILENCE! YOU UTTER IMBECILE!!
DU-DUN
LATERS.
AH!
SWISH
COME BACK HERE!
FORGET EVERY-THING YOU SAW HERE, SHINOBU!
UH, UM, WHAT...
WHAT?!
IT WAS A TEMPORARY, DRUG-INDUCED MADNESS.
HE'S HIGH!

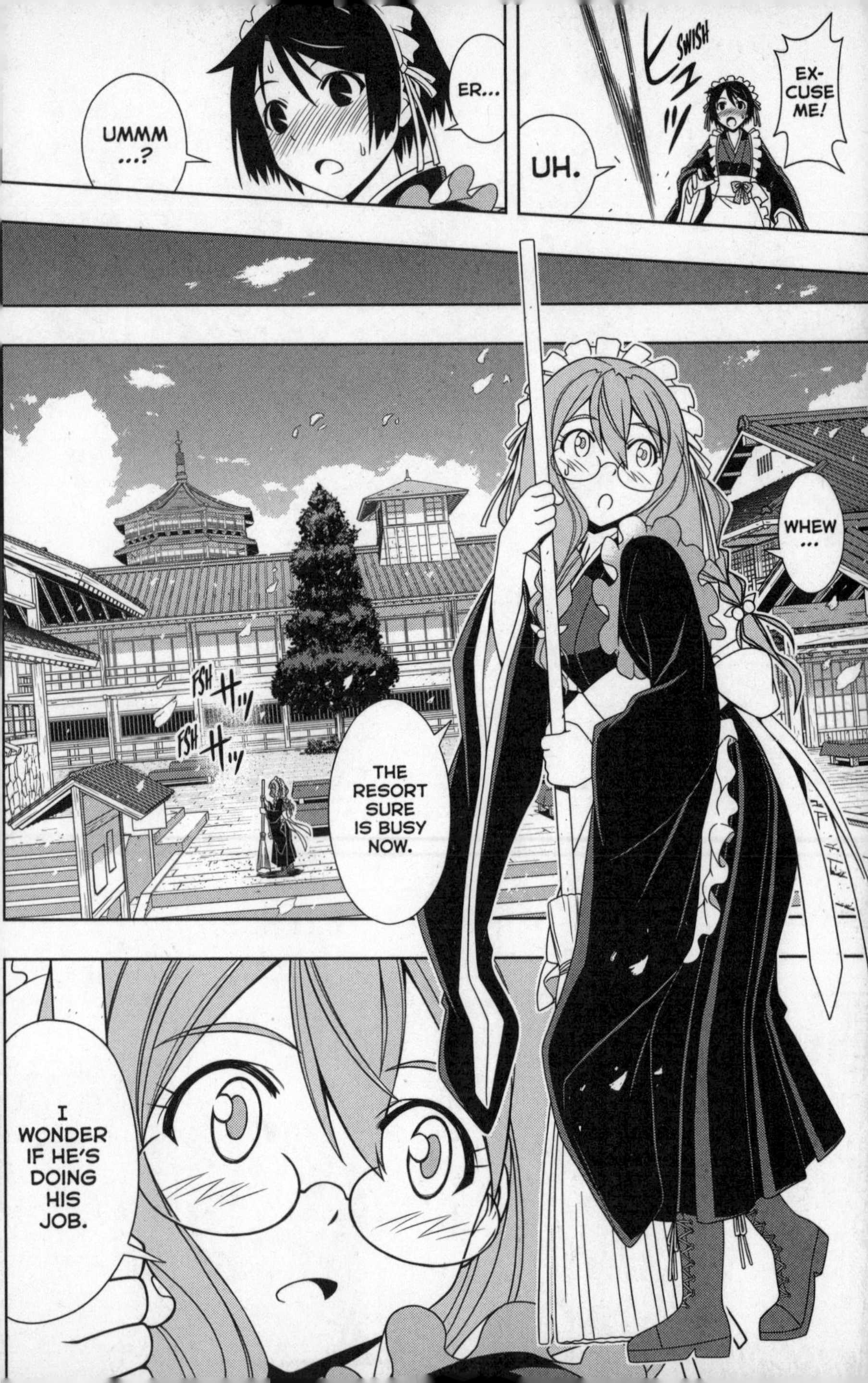
EX-
CUSE
ME!
SWISH
UH.
ER...
UMMM
...?
WHEW
...
FSH
FSH
THE
RESORT
SURE
IS BUSY
NOW.
I
WONDER
IF HE'S
DOING
HIS
JOB.

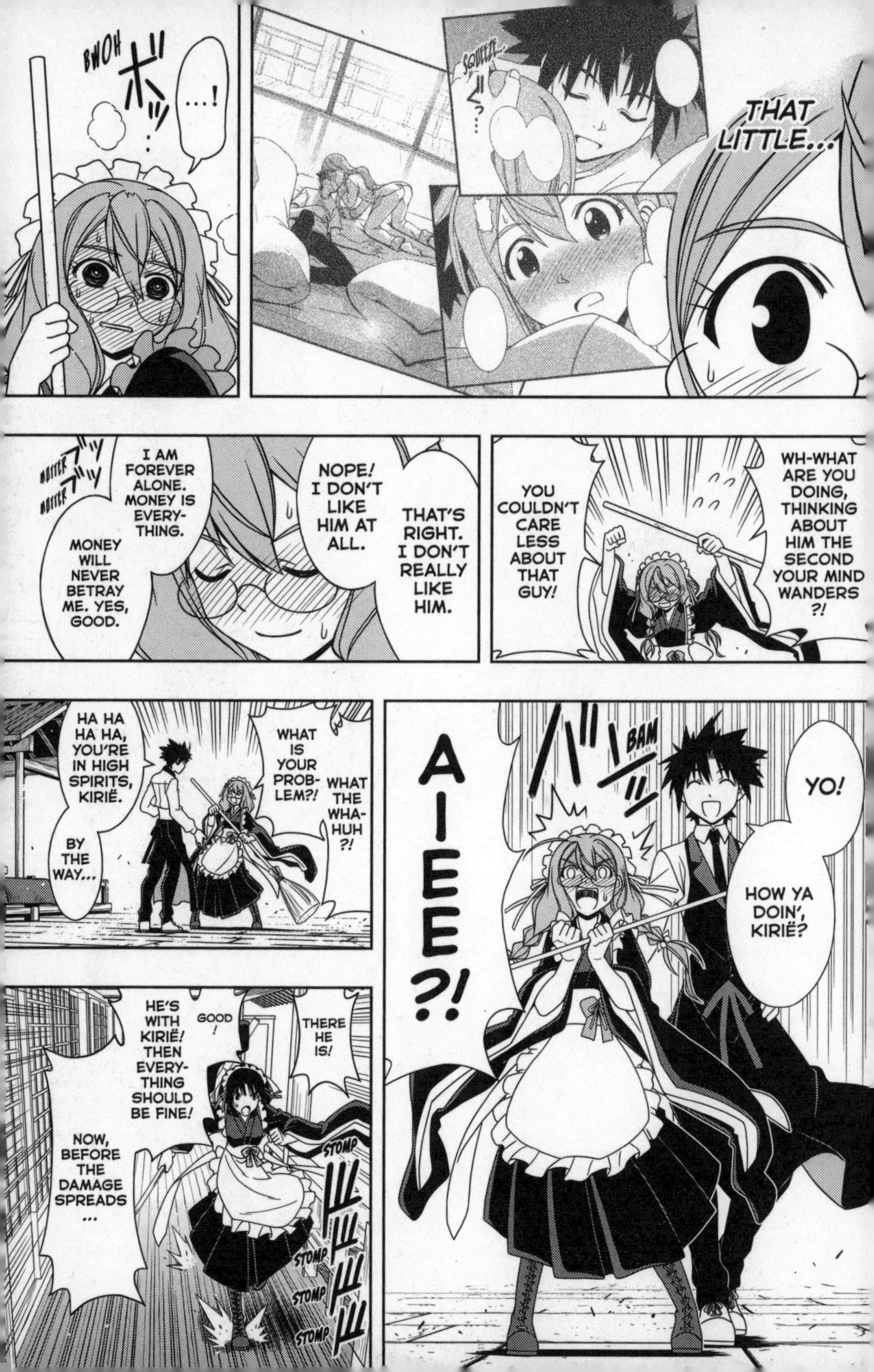
THAT LITTLE...
SQUEEZE...
BWOH
...!
WH-WHAT ARE YOU DOING, THINKING ABOUT HIM THE SECOND YOUR MIND WANDERS?!
YOU COULDN'T CARE LESS ABOUT THAT GUY!
NOPE! I DON'T LIKE HIM AT ALL.
THAT'S RIGHT. I DON'T REALLY LIKE HIM.
I AM FOREVER ALONE. MONEY IS EVERY-THING.
MONEY WILL NEVER BETRAY ME. YES, GOOD.
MUTTER MUTTER
YO!
HOW YA DOIN', KIRIË?
BAM
AIEE?!
WHAT THE WHA-HUH?!
WHAT IS YOUR PROB-LEM?!
HA HA HA HA, YOU'RE IN HIGH SPIRITS, KIRIË.
BY THE WAY...
THERE HE IS!
GOOD!
HE'S WITH KIRIË! THEN EVERY-THING SHOULD BE FINE!
NOW, BEFORE THE DAMAGE SPREADS...
STOMP
STOMP
STOMP
STOMP

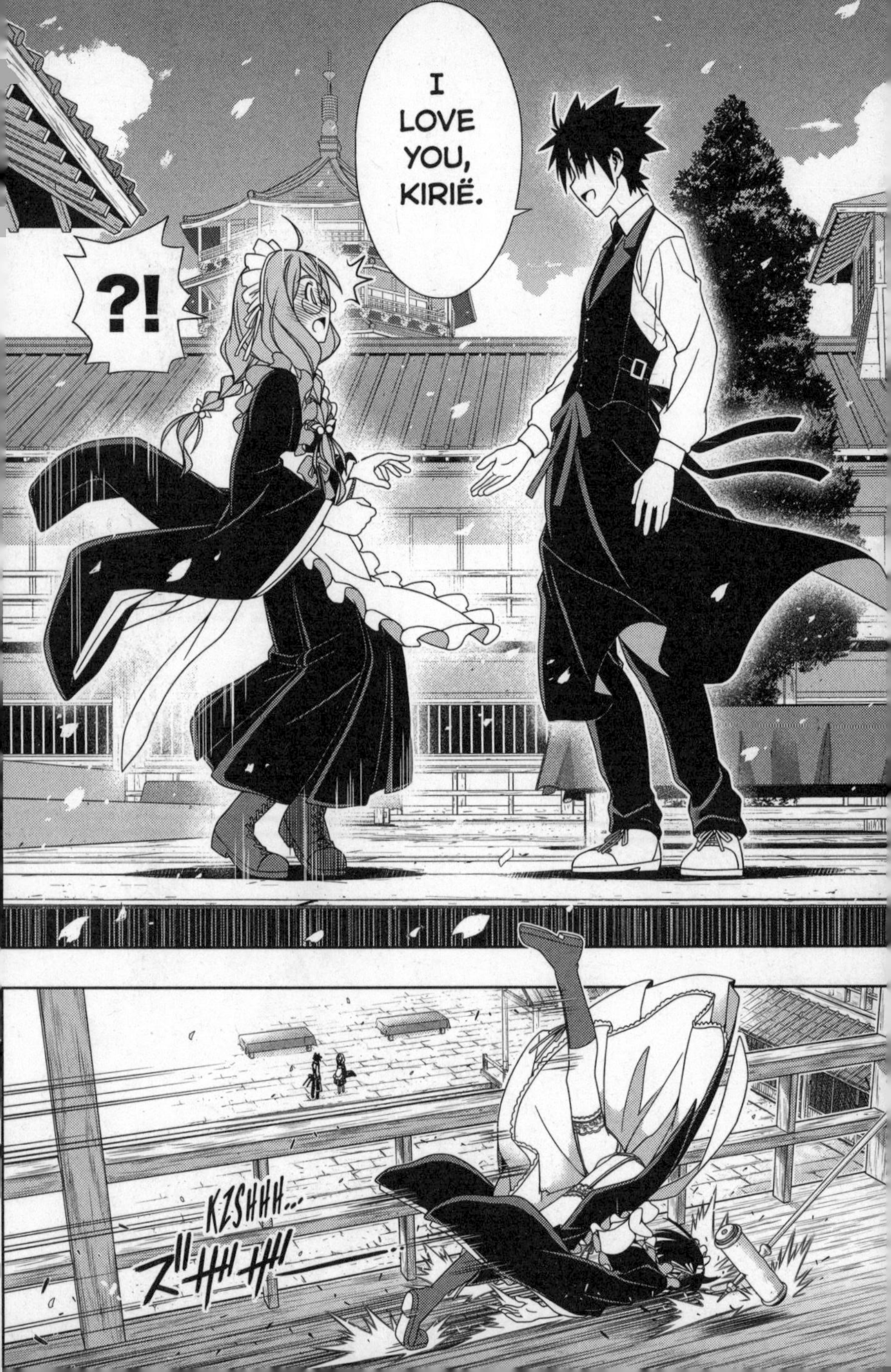
I LOVE YOU, KIRIË.
?!
KZSHHH...
ズザザ

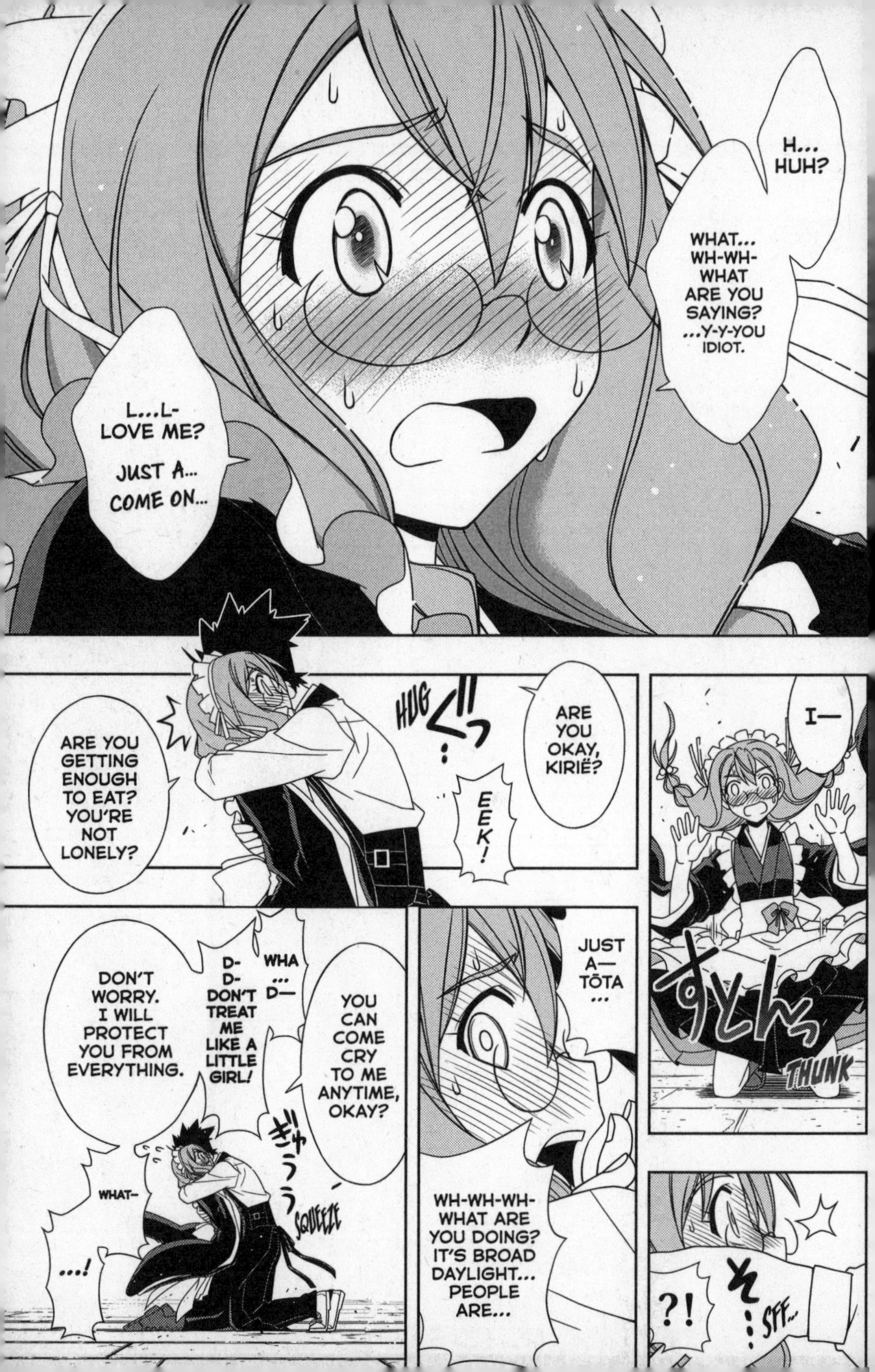
H... HUH?
WHAT... WH-WH-WHAT ARE YOU SAYING? ...Y-Y-YOU IDIOT.
L...L-LOVE ME?
JUST A... COME ON...
I—
すとん
THUNK
?!
そ
SFF...
ARE YOU OKAY, KIRIË?
ぐっ
HUG
EEK!
ARE YOU GETTING ENOUGH TO EAT? YOU'RE NOT LONELY?
JUST A— TŌTA...
WH-WH-WH-WHAT ARE YOU DOING? IT'S BROAD DAYLIGHT... PEOPLE ARE...
YOU CAN COME CRY TO ME ANYTIME, OKAY?
WHA... D—
D-D-DON'T TREAT ME LIKE A LITTLE GIRL!
DON'T WORRY. I WILL PROTECT YOU FROM EVERYTHING.
ぎゅうう
SQUEEZE
WHAT-
...!

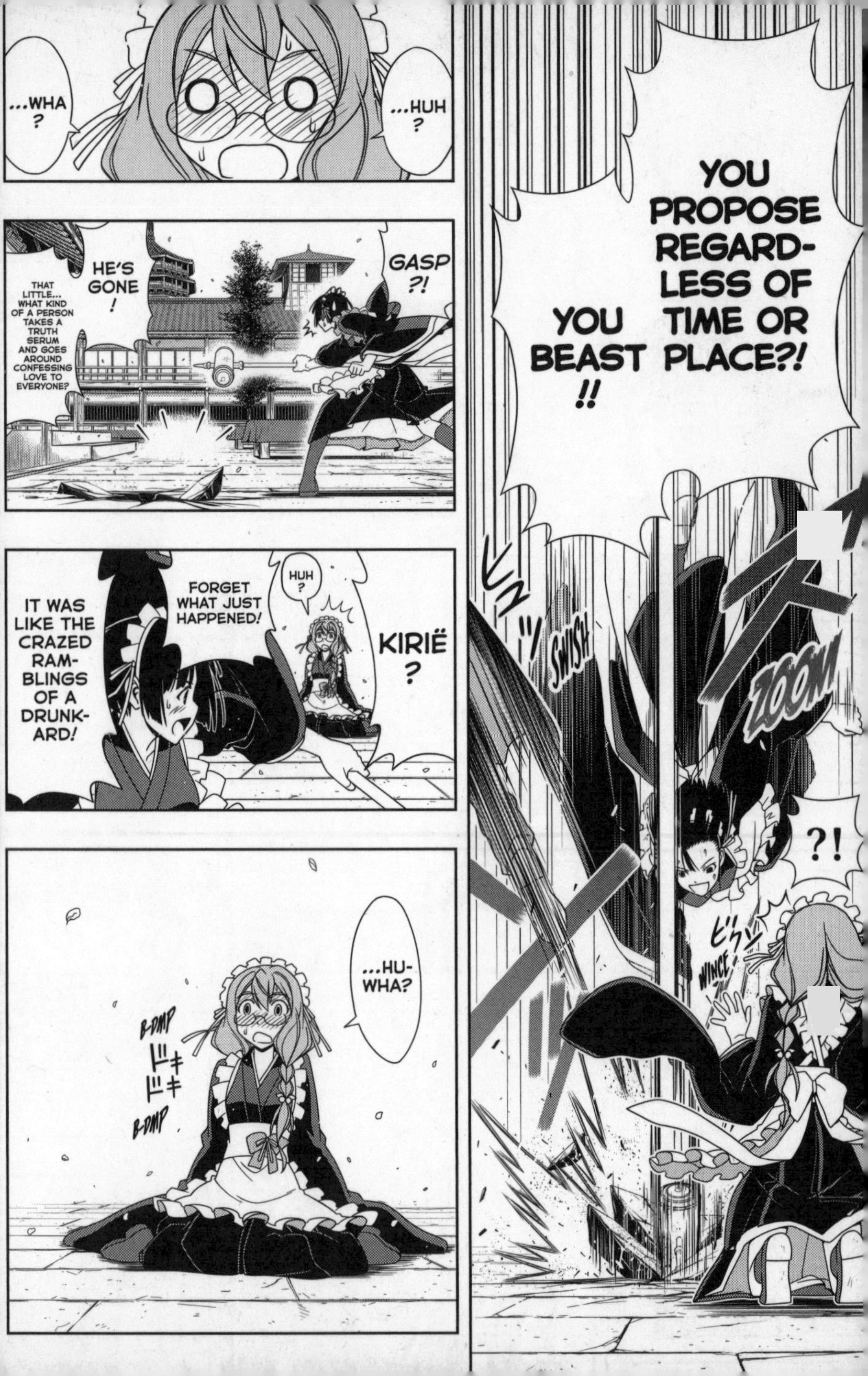

YOU PROPOSE REGARDLESS OF TIME OR PLACE?!
YOU BEAST !!
ZOOM
SWISH
?!
WINCE
...HUH ?
...WHA ?
GASP ?!
HE'S GONE !
THAT LITTLE... WHAT KIND OF A PERSON TAKES A TRUTH SERUM AND GOES AROUND CONFESSING LOVE TO EVERYONE?
KIRIË ?
HUH ?
FORGET WHAT JUST HAPPENED!
IT WAS LIKE THE CRAZED RAMBLINGS OF A DRUNKARD!
...HU-WHA?
B-DMP
ドキ
ドキ
B-DMP

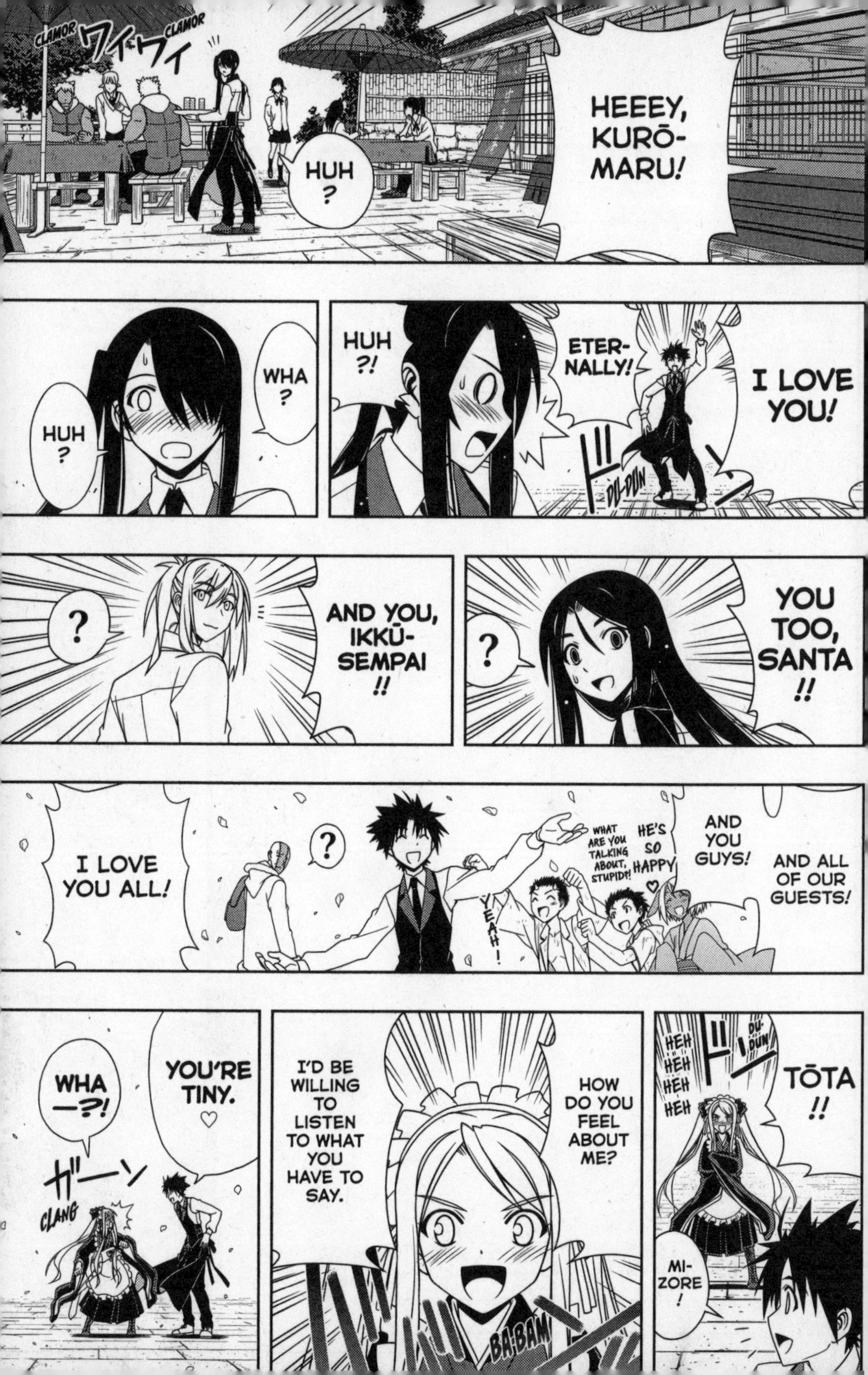
HEEEY, KURŌ-MARU!
CLAMOR
ワイワイ
CLAMOR
HUH?
I LOVE YOU!
ETERNALLY!
DU-DUN
HUH?!
WHA?
HUH?
YOU TOO, SANTA!!
?
AND YOU, IKKŪ-SEMPAI!!
?
AND ALL OF OUR GUESTS!
AND YOU GUYS!
HE'S SO HAPPY
WHAT ARE YOU TALKING ABOUT, STUPID?!
YEAH!
?
I LOVE YOU ALL!
TŌTA!!
DU-DUN
HEH HEH HEH HEH
MI-ZORE!
HOW DO YOU FEEL ABOUT ME?
I'D BE WILLING TO LISTEN TO WHAT YOU HAVE TO SAY.
BA-BAM
YOU'RE TINY.
WHA—?!
ガーン
CLANG

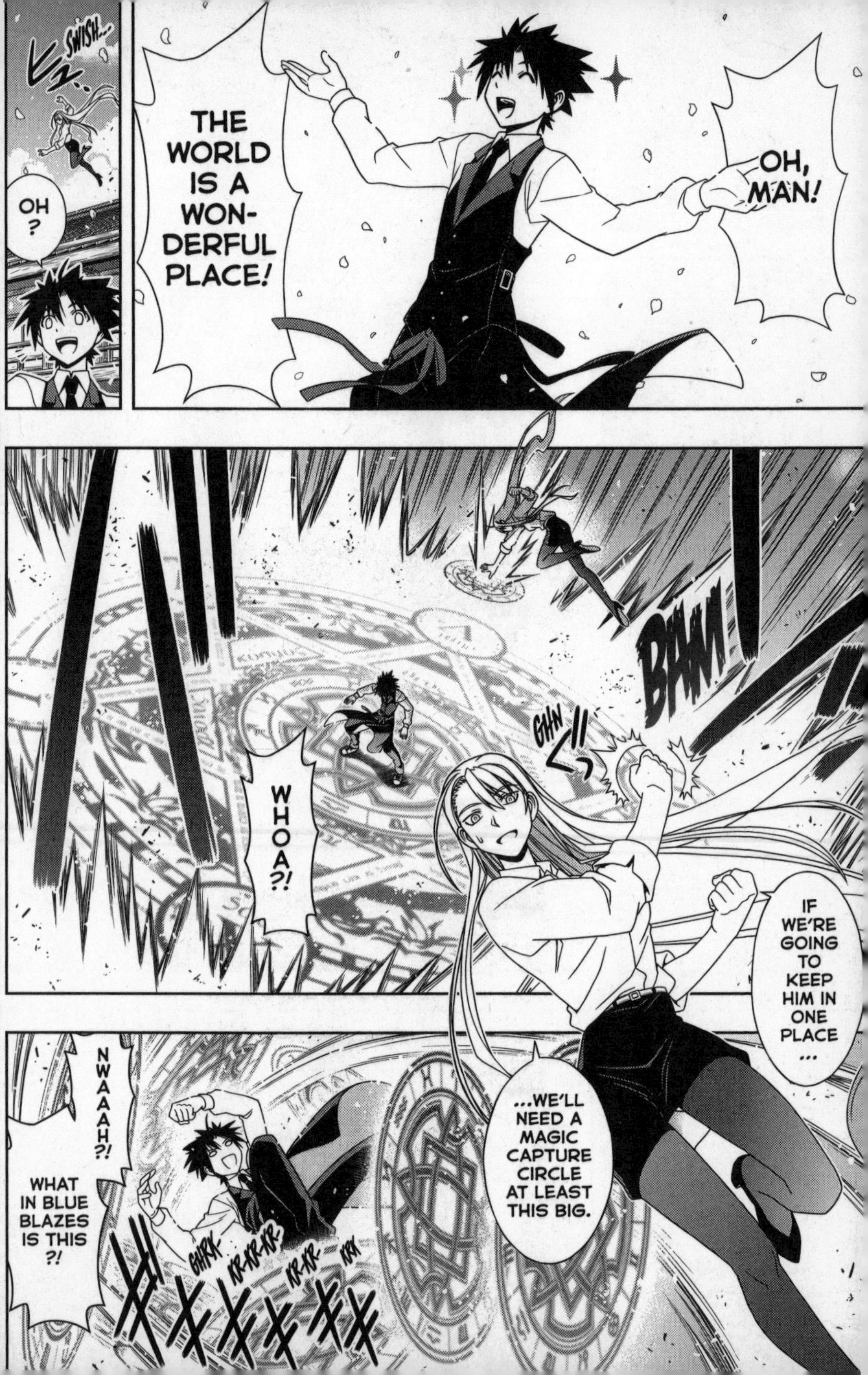
OH, MAN!
THE WORLD IS A WON-DERFUL PLACE!
SWISH...
OH?
BAM
GHN
WHOA?!
IF WE'RE GOING TO KEEP HIM IN ONE PLACE...
...WE'LL NEED A MAGIC CAPTURE CIRCLE AT LEAST THIS BIG.
NWAAAAH?!
WHAT IN BLUE BLAZES IS THIS?!
GHRK
KR-KR-KR
KR-KR
KRK

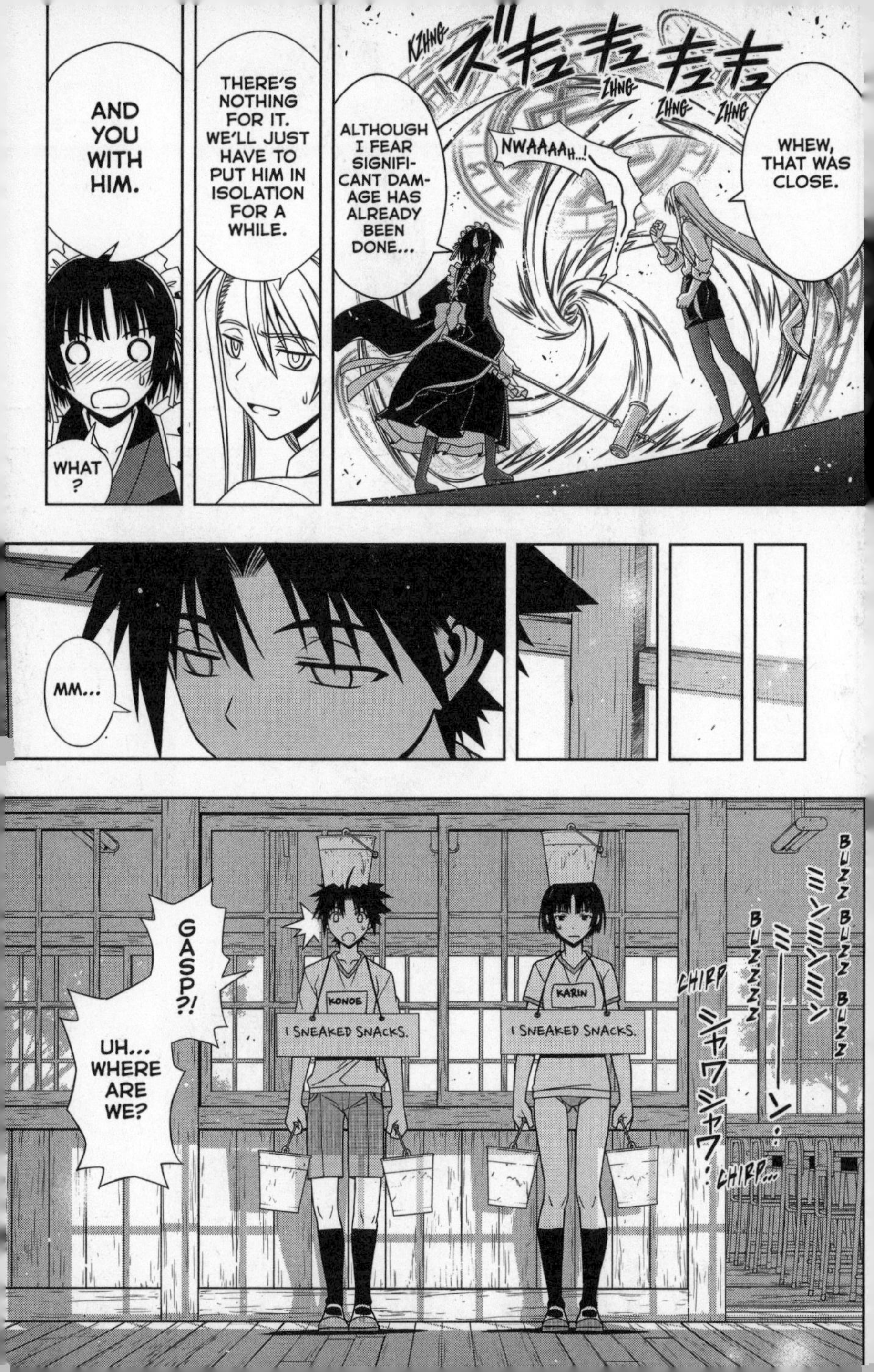
WHEW, THAT WAS CLOSE.
KZHNG
ズキュキュキュキュ
ZHNG
ZHNG
ZHNG
NWAAAAH...!
ALTHOUGH I FEAR SIGNIFICANT DAMAGE HAS ALREADY BEEN DONE...
THERE'S NOTHING FOR IT. WE'LL JUST HAVE TO PUT HIM IN ISOLATION FOR A WHILE.
AND YOU WITH HIM.
WHAT?
MM...
BUZZ BUZZ BUZZ
ミンミンミン
ミーーーン...
BUZZZZ
CHIRP
シャワシャワ...
CHIRP...
KARIN
I SNEAKED SNACKS.
KONOE
I SNEAKED SNACKS.
GASP?!
UH... WHERE ARE WE?

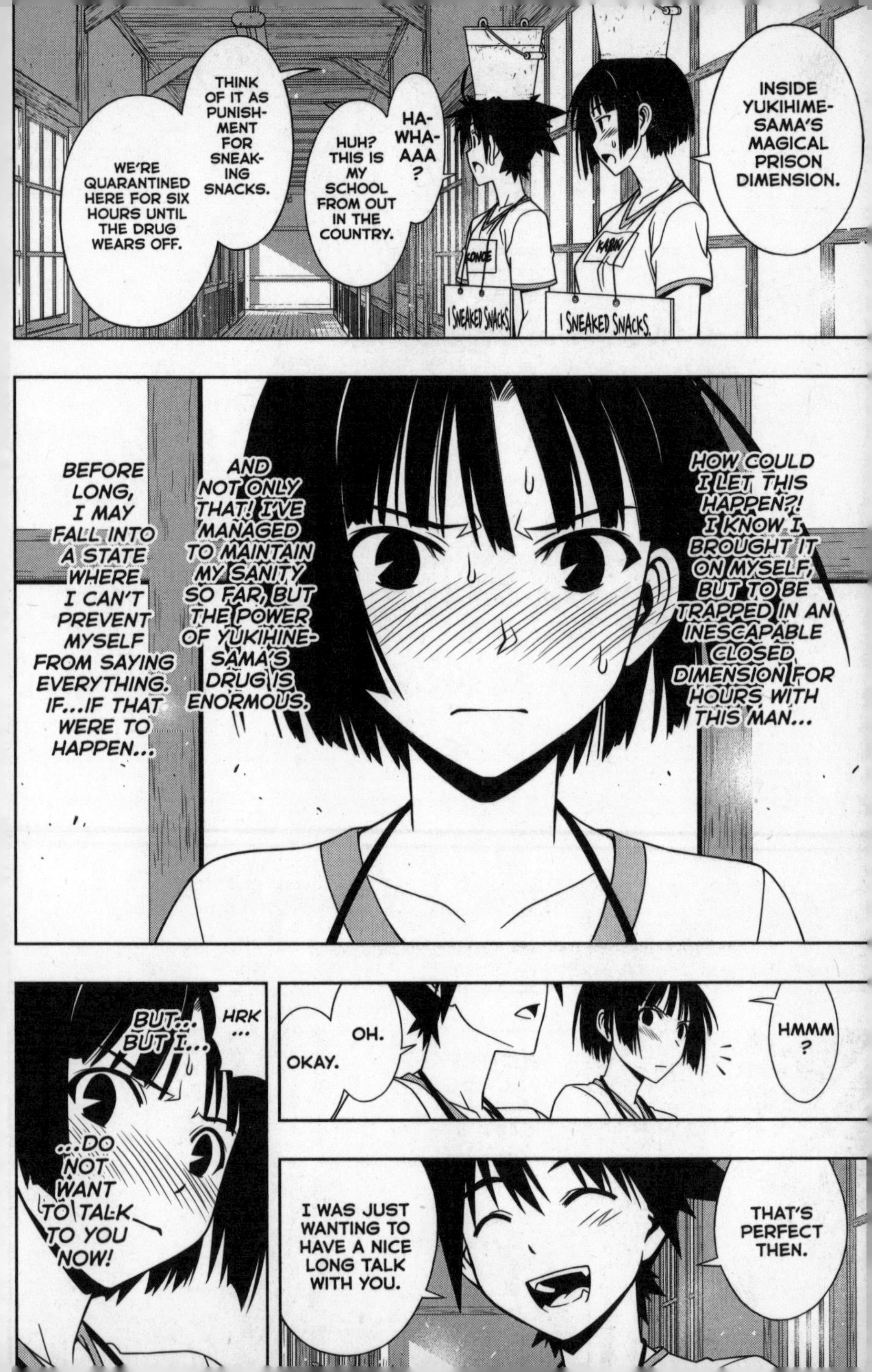
INSIDE YUKIHIME-SAMA'S MAGICAL PRISON DIMENSION.
HA-WHA-AAA?
HUH? THIS IS MY SCHOOL FROM OUT IN THE COUNTRY.
THINK OF IT AS PUNISHMENT FOR SNEAKING SNACKS.
WE'RE QUARANTINED HERE FOR SIX HOURS UNTIL THE DRUG WEARS OFF.
I SNEAKED SNACKS.
I SNEAKED SNACKS.
HOW COULD I LET THIS HAPPEN?! I KNOW I BROUGHT IT ON MYSELF, BUT TO BE TRAPPED IN AN INESCAPABLE CLOSED DIMENSION FOR HOURS WITH THIS MAN...
AND NOT ONLY THAT! I'VE MANAGED TO MAINTAIN MY SANITY SO FAR, BUT THE POWER OF YUKIHIME-SAMA'S DRUG IS ENORMOUS.
BEFORE LONG, I MAY FALL INTO A STATE WHERE I CAN'T PREVENT MYSELF FROM SAYING EVERYTHING. IF...IF THAT WERE TO HAPPEN...
HMMM?
OH.
OKAY.
THAT'S PERFECT THEN.
I WAS JUST WANTING TO HAVE A NICE LONG TALK WITH YOU.
HRK...
BUT... BUT I...
...DO NOT WANT TO TALK TO YOU NOW!

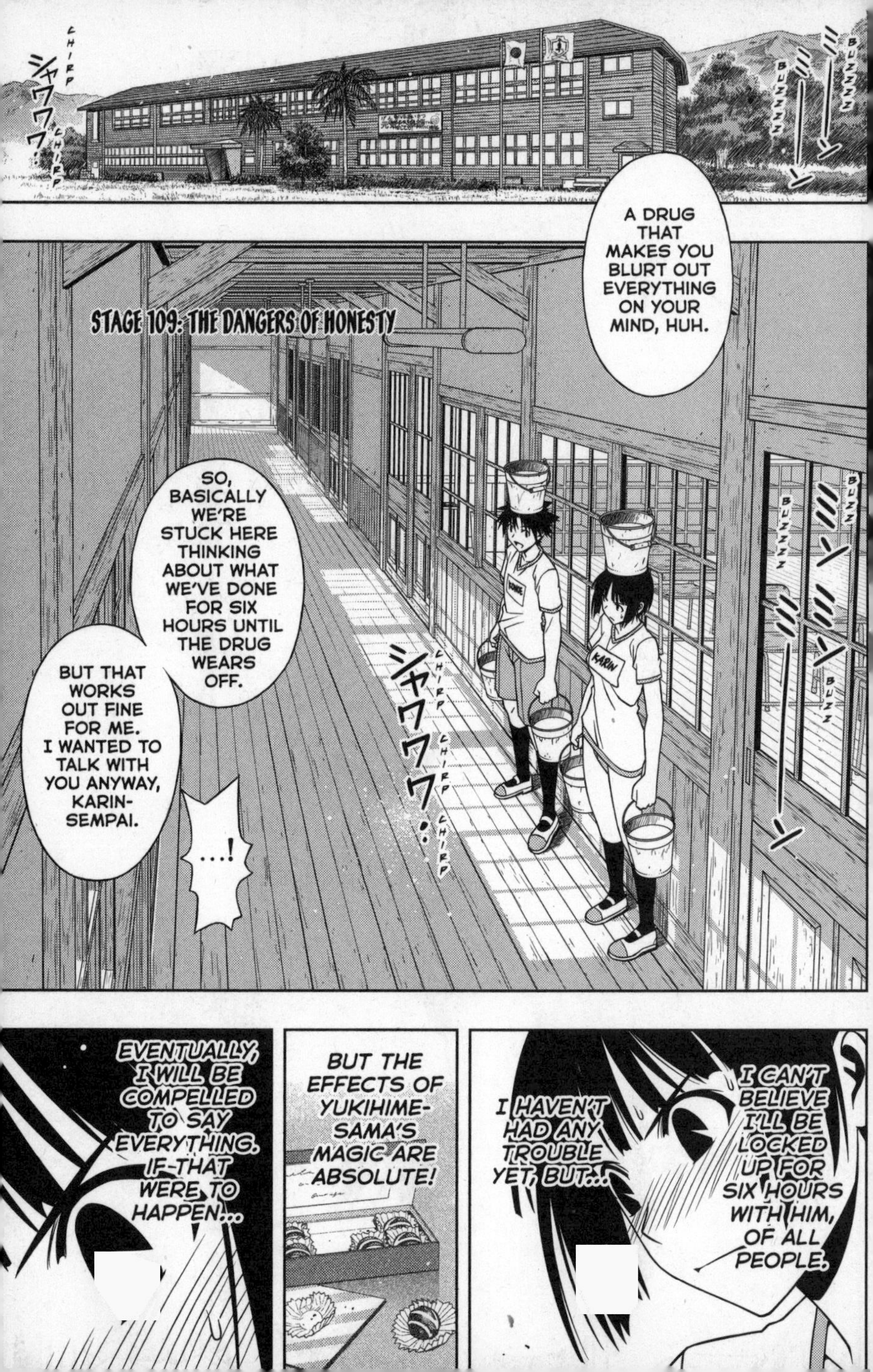
BUZZZZ BUZZZZ
ミーン
CHIRP CHIRP
シャワワ
STAGE 109: THE DANGERS OF HONESTY
A DRUG THAT MAKES YOU BLURT OUT EVERYTHING ON YOUR MIND, HUH.
BUZZ BUZZZZ
BUZZ BUZZ
ミンミンミーン
CHIRP CHIRP CHIRP
シャワワ
KARIN
SO, BASICALLY WE'RE STUCK HERE THINKING ABOUT WHAT WE'VE DONE FOR SIX HOURS UNTIL THE DRUG WEARS OFF.
BUT THAT WORKS OUT FINE FOR ME. I WANTED TO TALK WITH YOU ANYWAY, KARIN-SEMPAI.
...!
I CAN'T BELIEVE I'LL BE LOCKED UP FOR SIX HOURS WITH HIM, OF ALL PEOPLE.
I HAVEN'T HAD ANY TROUBLE YET, BUT...
BUT THE EFFECTS OF YUKIHIME-SAMA'S MAGIC ARE ABSOLUTE!
EVENTUALLY, I WILL BE COMPELLED TO SAY EVERYTHING. IF THAT WERE TO HAPPEN...

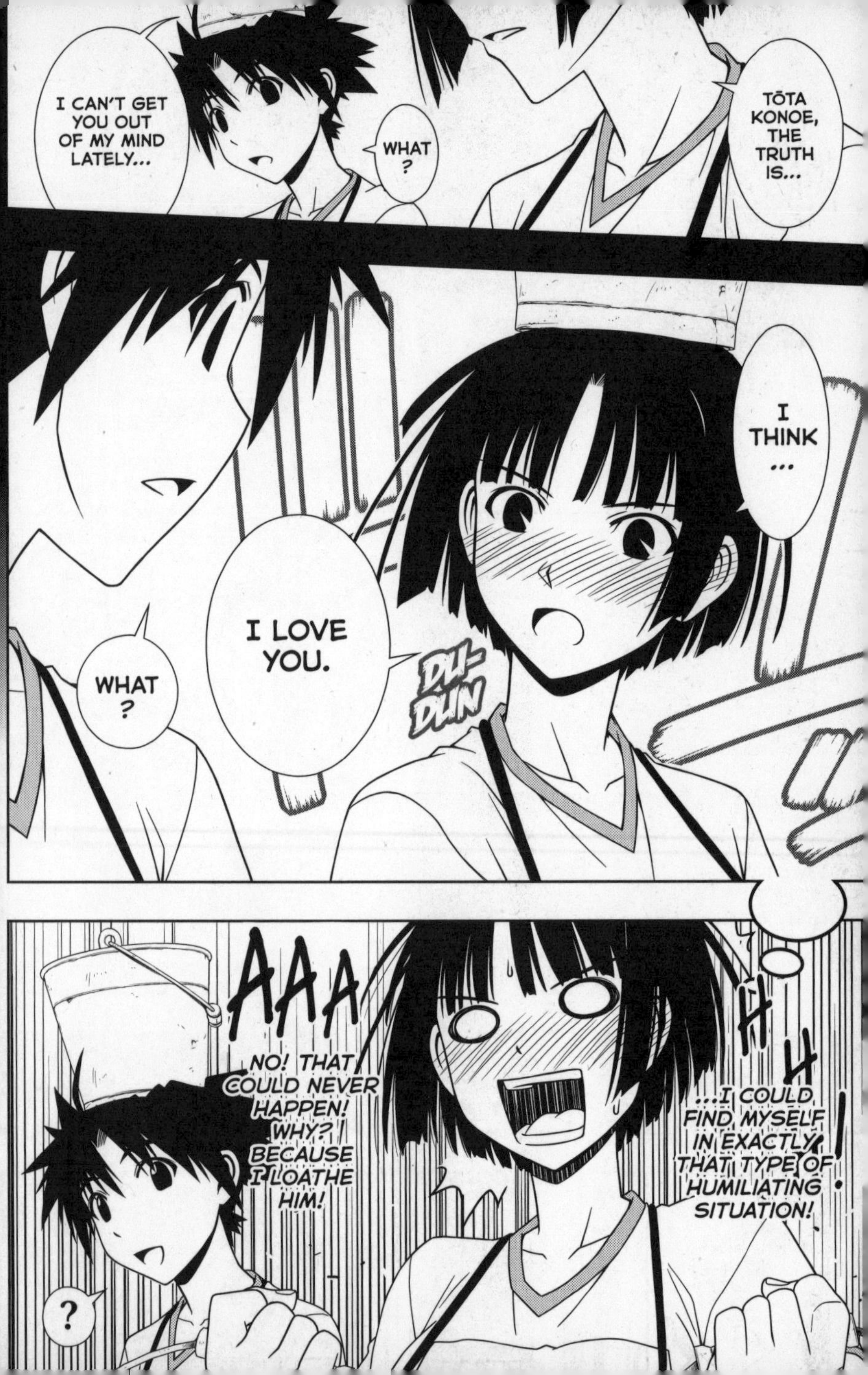
TŌTA KONOE, THE TRUTH IS...
WHAT?
I CAN'T GET YOU OUT OF MY MIND LATELY...
I THINK...
I LOVE YOU.
DU-DUN
WHAT?
AAAHH!
...I COULD FIND MYSELF IN EXACTLY THAT TYPE OF HUMILIATING SITUATION!
NO! THAT COULD NEVER HAPPEN! WHY? BECAUSE I LOATHE HIM!
?

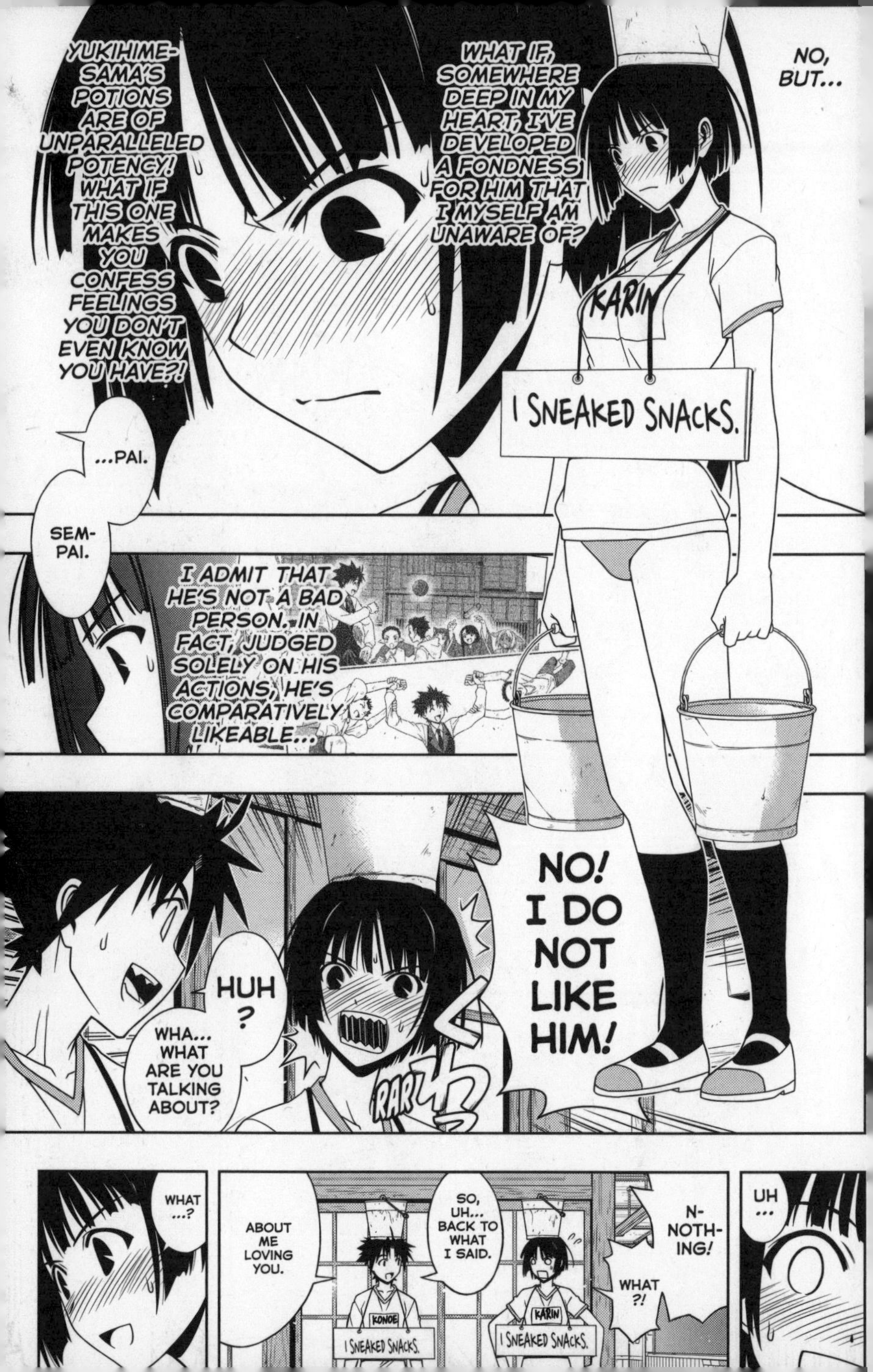
NO, BUT...
WHAT IF, SOMEWHERE DEEP IN MY HEART, I'VE DEVELOPED A FONDNESS FOR HIM THAT I MYSELF AM UNAWARE OF?
KARIN
I SNEAKED SNACKS.
YUKIHIME-SAMA'S POTIONS ARE OF UNPARALLELED POTENCY! WHAT IF THIS ONE MAKES YOU CONFESS FEELINGS YOU DON'T EVEN KNOW YOU HAVE?!
...PAI.
SEM-PAI.
I ADMIT THAT HE'S NOT A BAD PERSON. IN FACT, JUDGED SOLELY ON HIS ACTIONS, HE'S COMPARATIVELY LIKEABLE...
NO! I DO NOT LIKE HIM!
RAR
HUH?
WHA... WHAT ARE YOU TALKING ABOUT?
UH...
N-NOTHING!
SO, UH... BACK TO WHAT I SAID.
ABOUT ME LOVING YOU.
WHAT?!
KARIN
I SNEAKED SNACKS.
KONOE
I SNEAKED SNACKS.
WHAT...?

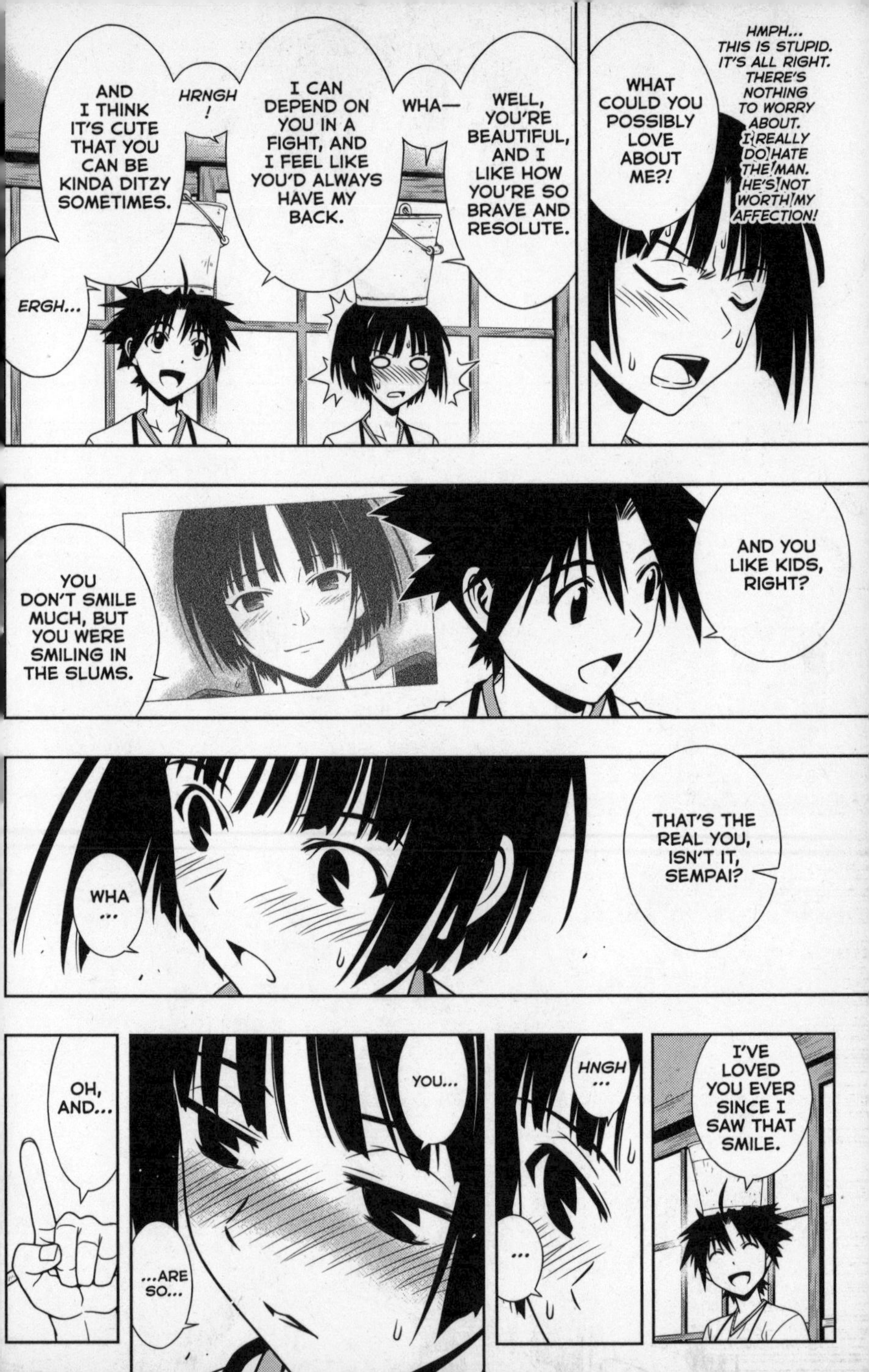
HMPH... THIS IS STUPID. IT'S ALL RIGHT. THERE'S NOTHING TO WORRY ABOUT. I REALLY DO HATE THE MAN. HE'S NOT WORTH MY AFFECTION!
WHAT COULD YOU POSSIBLY LOVE ABOUT ME?!
WELL, YOU'RE BEAUTIFUL, AND I LIKE HOW YOU'RE SO BRAVE AND RESOLUTE.
WHA—
I CAN DEPEND ON YOU IN A FIGHT, AND I FEEL LIKE YOU'D ALWAYS HAVE MY BACK.
HRNGH!
AND I THINK IT'S CUTE THAT YOU CAN BE KINDA DITZY SOMETIMES.
ERGH...
AND YOU LIKE KIDS, RIGHT?
YOU DON'T SMILE MUCH, BUT YOU WERE SMILING IN THE SLUMS.
THAT'S THE REAL YOU, ISN'T IT, SEMPAI?
WHA...
I'VE LOVED YOU EVER SINCE I SAW THAT SMILE.
HNGH...
...
YOU...
...ARE SO...
OH, AND...

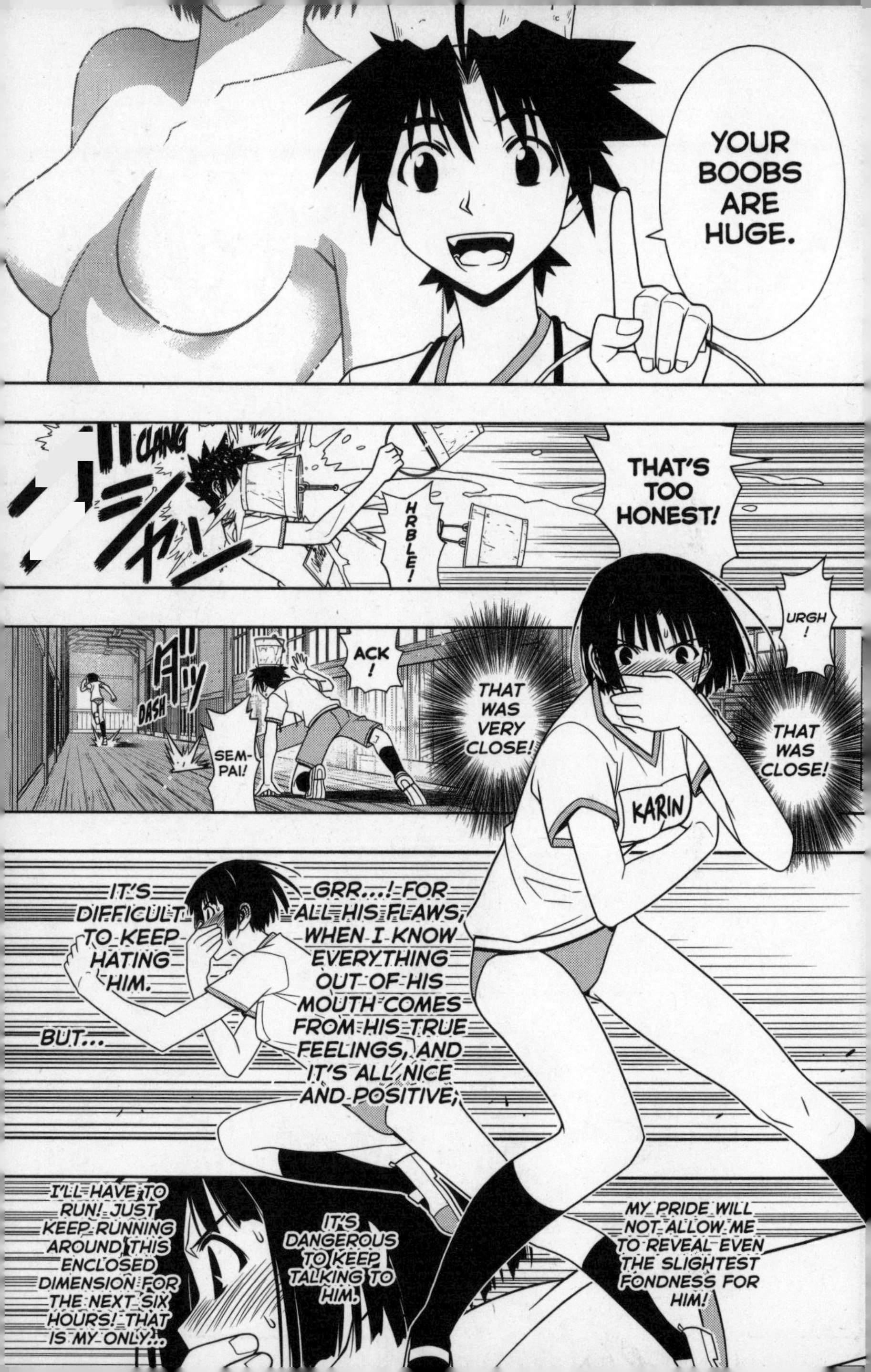
YOUR BOOBS ARE HUGE.
THAT'S TOO HONEST!
HRBLE!
CLANG
URGH!
THAT WAS CLOSE!
THAT WAS VERY CLOSE!
KARIN
ACK!
SEM-PAI!
DASH
GRR...! FOR ALL HIS FLAWS, WHEN I KNOW EVERYTHING OUT OF HIS MOUTH COMES FROM HIS TRUE FEELINGS, AND IT'S ALL NICE AND POSITIVE,
IT'S DIFFICULT TO KEEP HATING HIM.
BUT...
MY PRIDE WILL NOT ALLOW ME TO REVEAL EVEN THE SLIGHTEST FONDNESS FOR HIM!
IT'S DANGEROUS TO KEEP TALKING TO HIM.
I'LL HAVE TO RUN! JUST KEEP RUNNING AROUND THIS ENCLOSED DIMENSION FOR THE NEXT SIX HOURS! THAT IS MY ONLY...

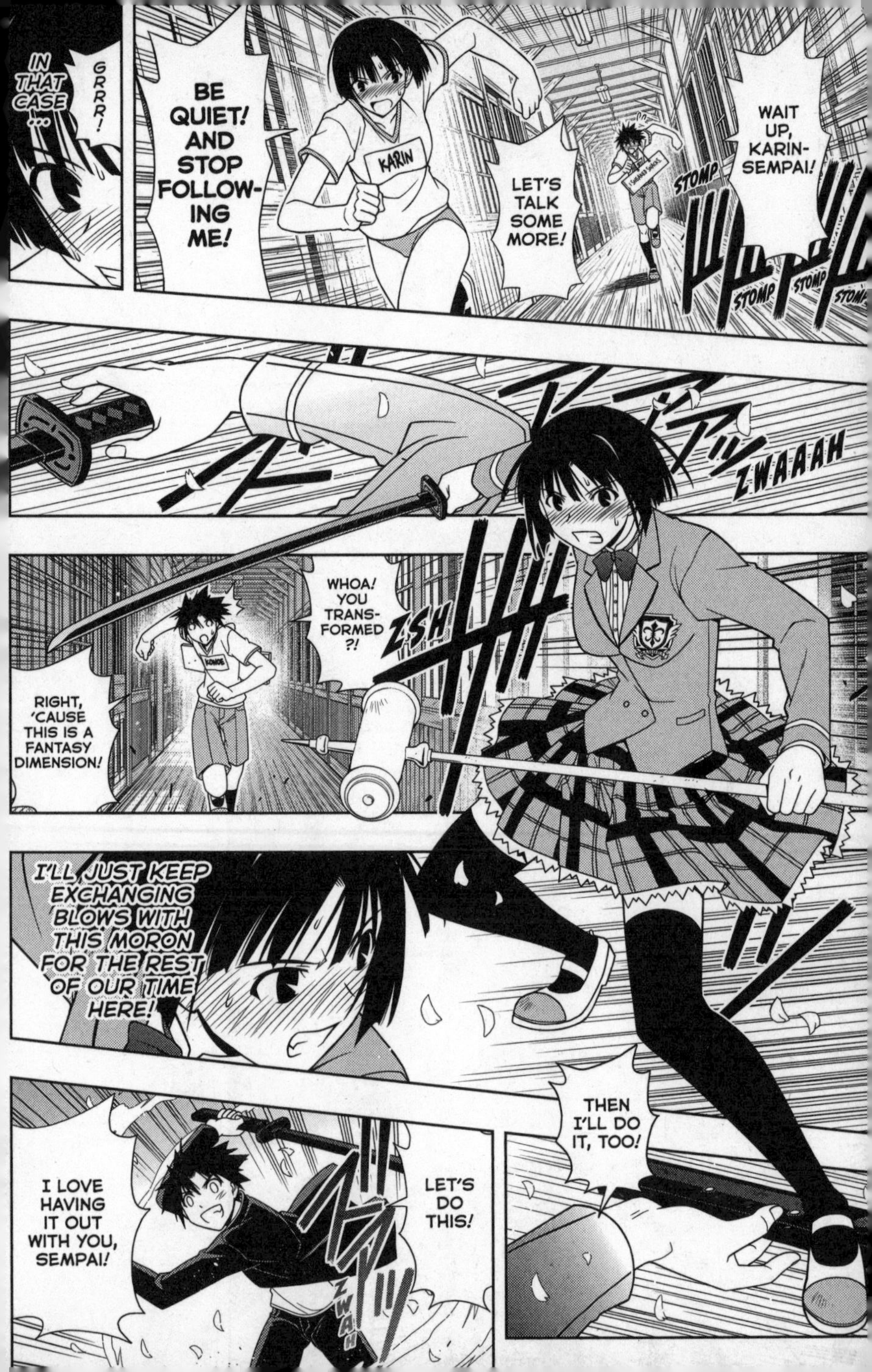
WAIT UP, KARIN-SEMPAI!
LET'S TALK SOME MORE!
STOMP
STOMP STOMP STOMP
BE QUIET! AND STOP FOLLOWING ME!
KARIN
GRRR!
IN THAT CASE...
ZWAAAH
WHOA! YOU TRANSFORMED?!
RIGHT, 'CAUSE THIS IS A FANTASY DIMENSION!
ZSH
I'LL JUST KEEP EXCHANGING BLOWS WITH THIS MORON FOR THE REST OF OUR TIME HERE!
THEN I'LL DO IT, TOO!
LET'S DO THIS!
I LOVE HAVING IT OUT WITH YOU, SEMPAI!
ZWAH

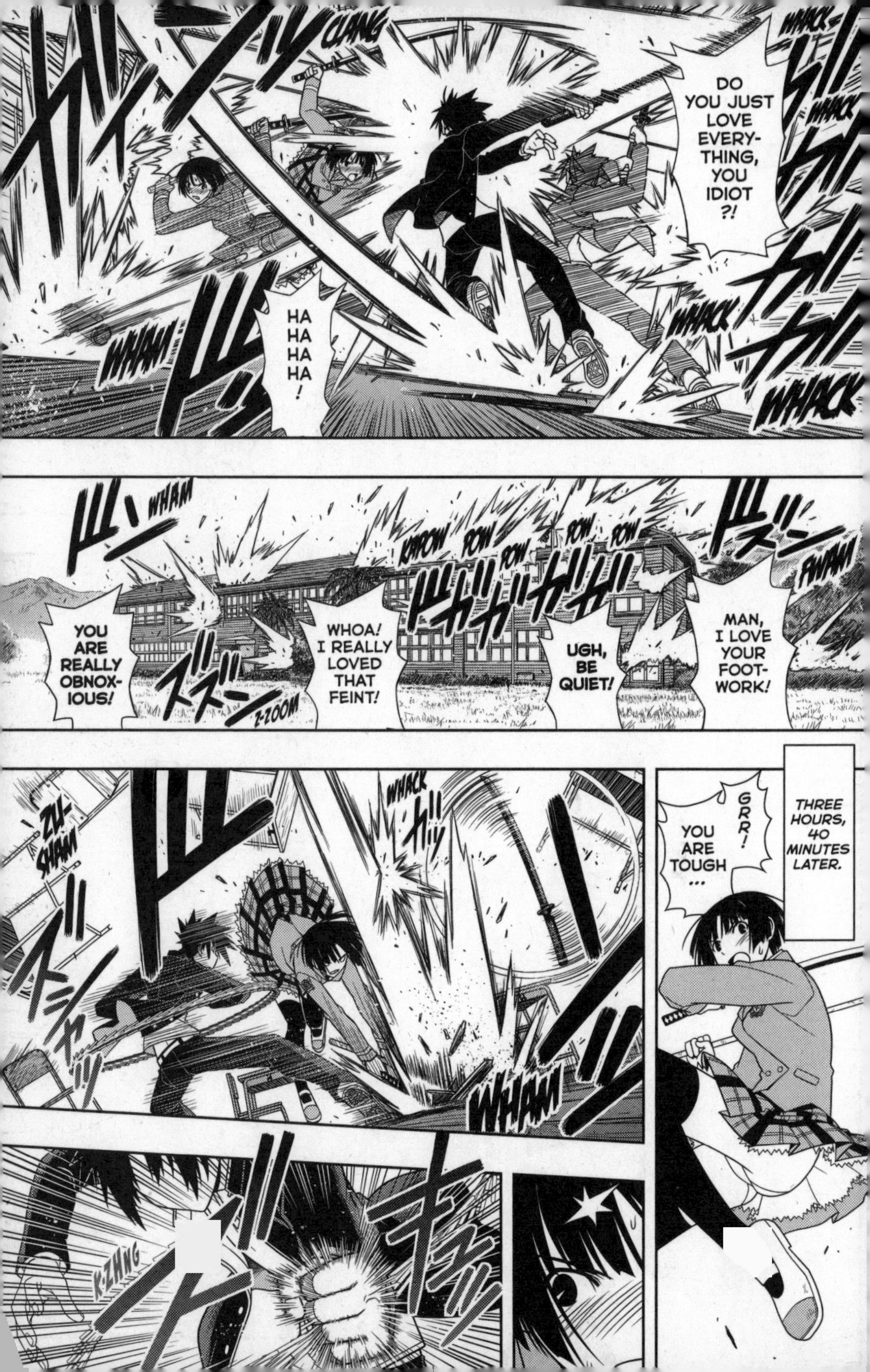
WHACK
WHACK
DO YOU JUST LOVE EVERY-THING, YOU IDIOT ?!
CLANG
WHACK
WHACK
HA HA HA HA!
WHAM
FWAM
MAN, I LOVE YOUR FOOT-WORK!
POW
POW
POW
KAPOW
UGH, BE QUIET!
WHOA! I REALLY LOVED THAT FEINT!
WHAM
Z-ZOOM
YOU ARE REALLY OBNOX-IOUS!
THREE HOURS, 40 MINUTES LATER.
GRR!
YOU ARE TOUGH...
WHACK
WHAM
ZU-SHAM
K-ZHNG

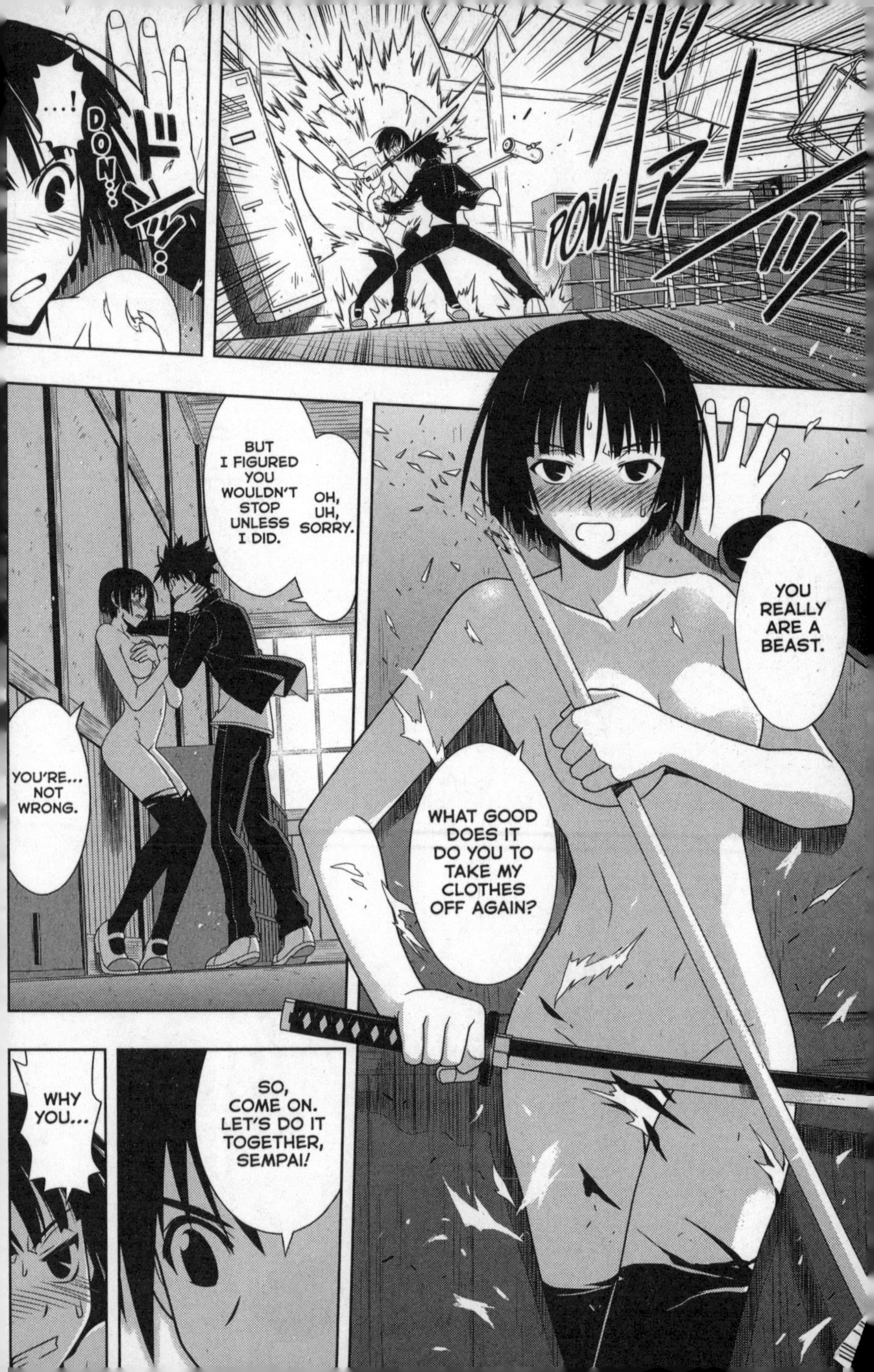
POW
...!
DON
YOU REALLY ARE A BEAST.
WHAT GOOD DOES IT DO YOU TO TAKE MY CLOTHES OFF AGAIN?
OH, UH, SORRY.
BUT I FIGURED YOU WOULDN'T STOP UNLESS I DID.
YOU'RE... NOT WRONG.
SO, COME ON. LET'S DO IT TOGETHER, SEMPAI!
WHY YOU...

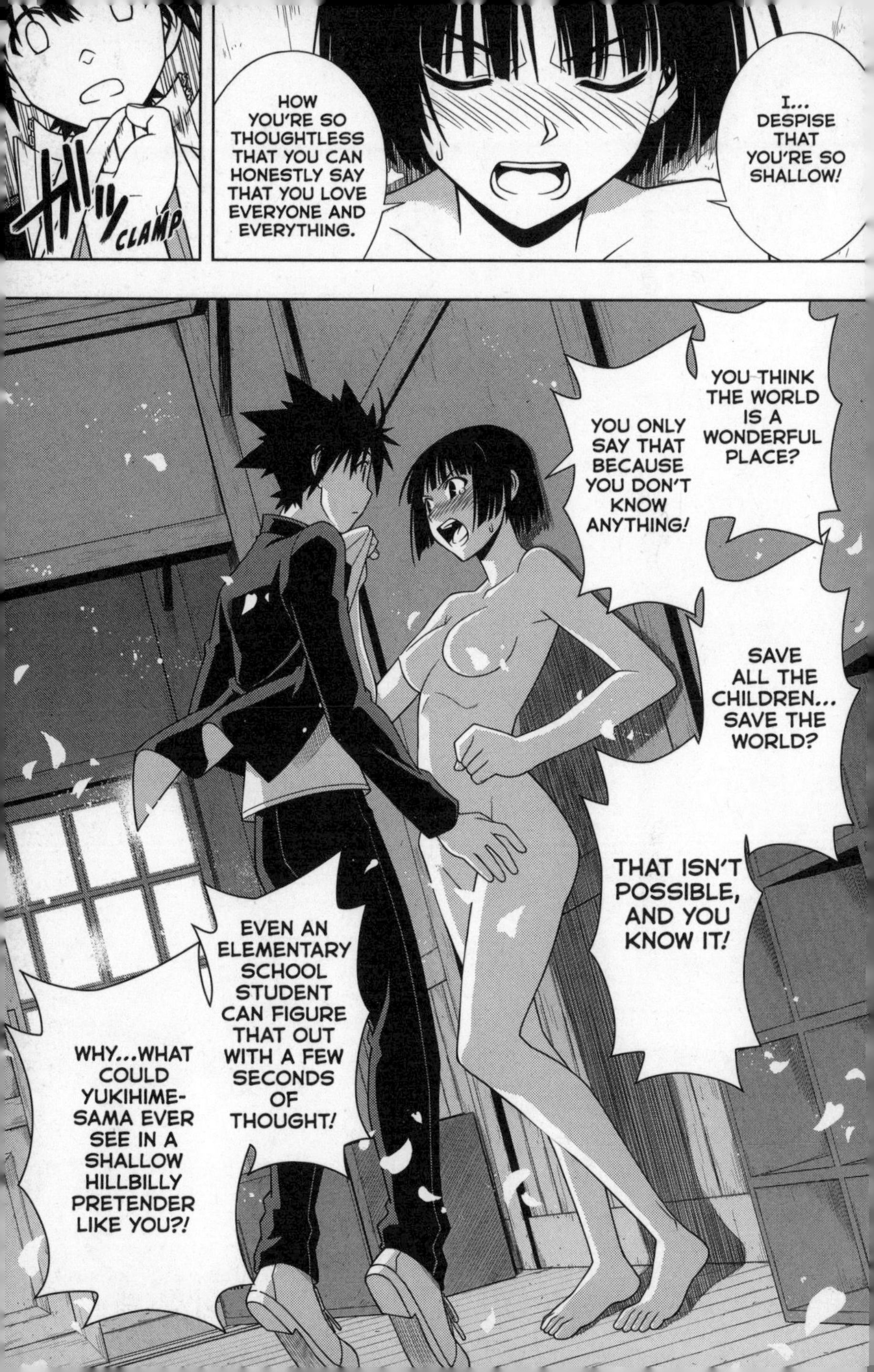
I... DESPISE THAT YOU'RE SO SHALLOW!
HOW YOU'RE SO THOUGHTLESS THAT YOU CAN HONESTLY SAY THAT YOU LOVE EVERYONE AND EVERYTHING.
CLAMP
YOU THINK THE WORLD IS A WONDERFUL PLACE?
YOU ONLY SAY THAT BECAUSE YOU DON'T KNOW ANYTHING!
SAVE ALL THE CHILDREN... SAVE THE WORLD?
THAT ISN'T POSSIBLE, AND YOU KNOW IT!
EVEN AN ELEMENTARY SCHOOL STUDENT CAN FIGURE THAT OUT WITH A FEW SECONDS OF THOUGHT!
WHY...WHAT COULD YUKIHIME-SAMA EVER SEE IN A SHALLOW HILLBILLY PRETENDER LIKE YOU?!

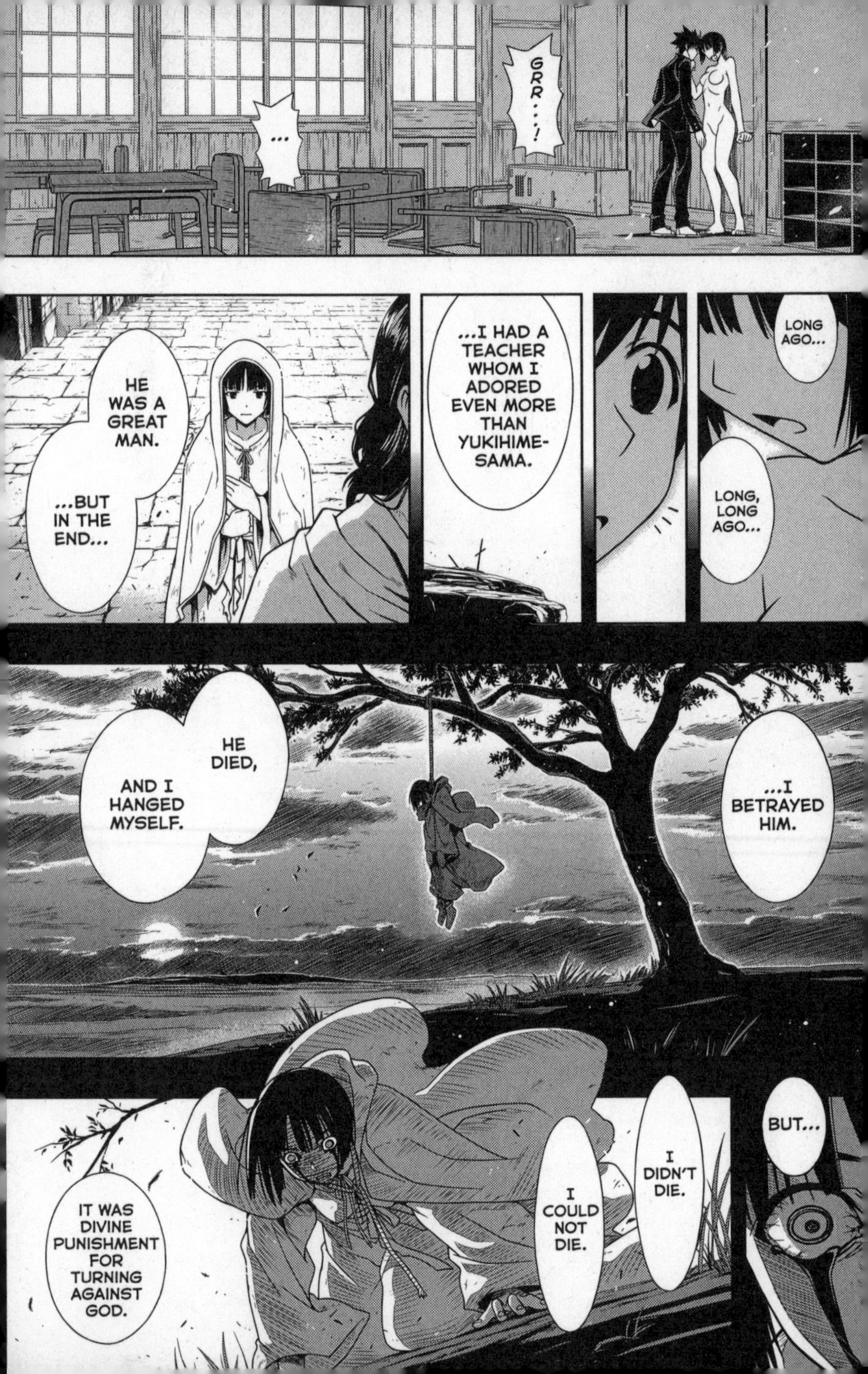
GRR...!
...
LONG AGO...
LONG, LONG AGO...
...I HAD A TEACHER WHOM I ADORED EVEN MORE THAN YUKIHIME-SAMA.
HE WAS A GREAT MAN.
...BUT IN THE END...
...I BETRAYED HIM.
HE DIED,
AND I HANGED MYSELF.
BUT...
I DIDN'T DIE.
I COULD NOT DIE.
IT WAS DIVINE PUNISHMENT FOR TURNING AGAINST GOD.

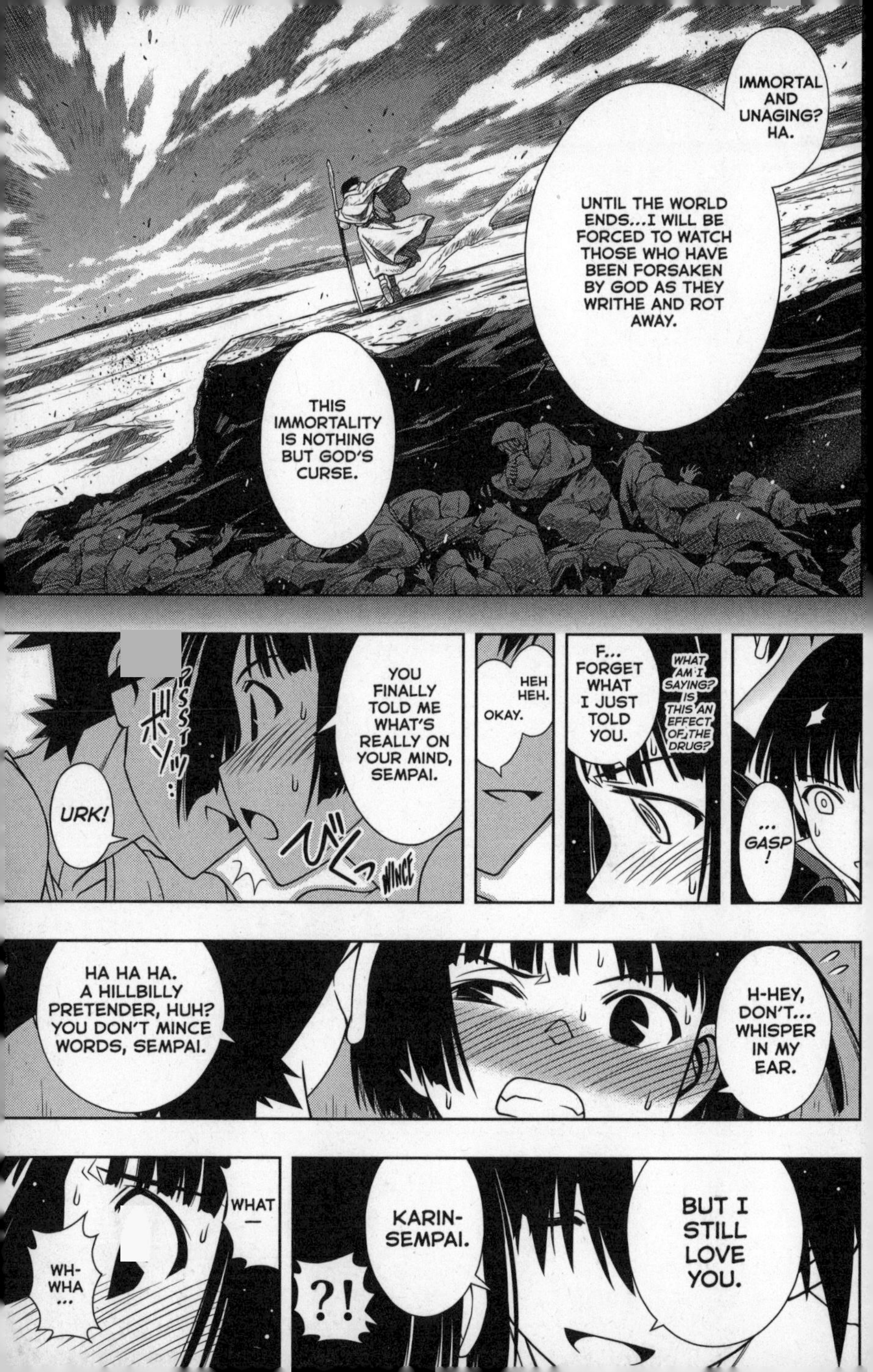

IMMORTAL AND UNAGING? HA.
UNTIL THE WORLD ENDS...I WILL BE FORCED TO WATCH THOSE WHO HAVE BEEN FORSAKEN BY GOD AS THEY WRITHE AND ROT AWAY.
THIS IMMORTALITY IS NOTHING BUT GOD'S CURSE.
...GASP!
F... FORGET WHAT I JUST TOLD YOU.
WHAT AM I SAYING? IS THIS AN EFFECT OF THE DRUG?
HEH HEH.
OKAY.
YOU FINALLY TOLD ME WHAT'S REALLY ON YOUR MIND, SEMPAI.
PSST
URK!
WINCE
H-HEY, DON'T... WHISPER IN MY EAR.
HA HA HA. A HILLBILLY PRETENDER, HUH? YOU DON'T MINCE WORDS, SEMPAI.
BUT I STILL LOVE YOU.
KARIN-SEMPAI.
?!
WHAT—
WH-WHA...

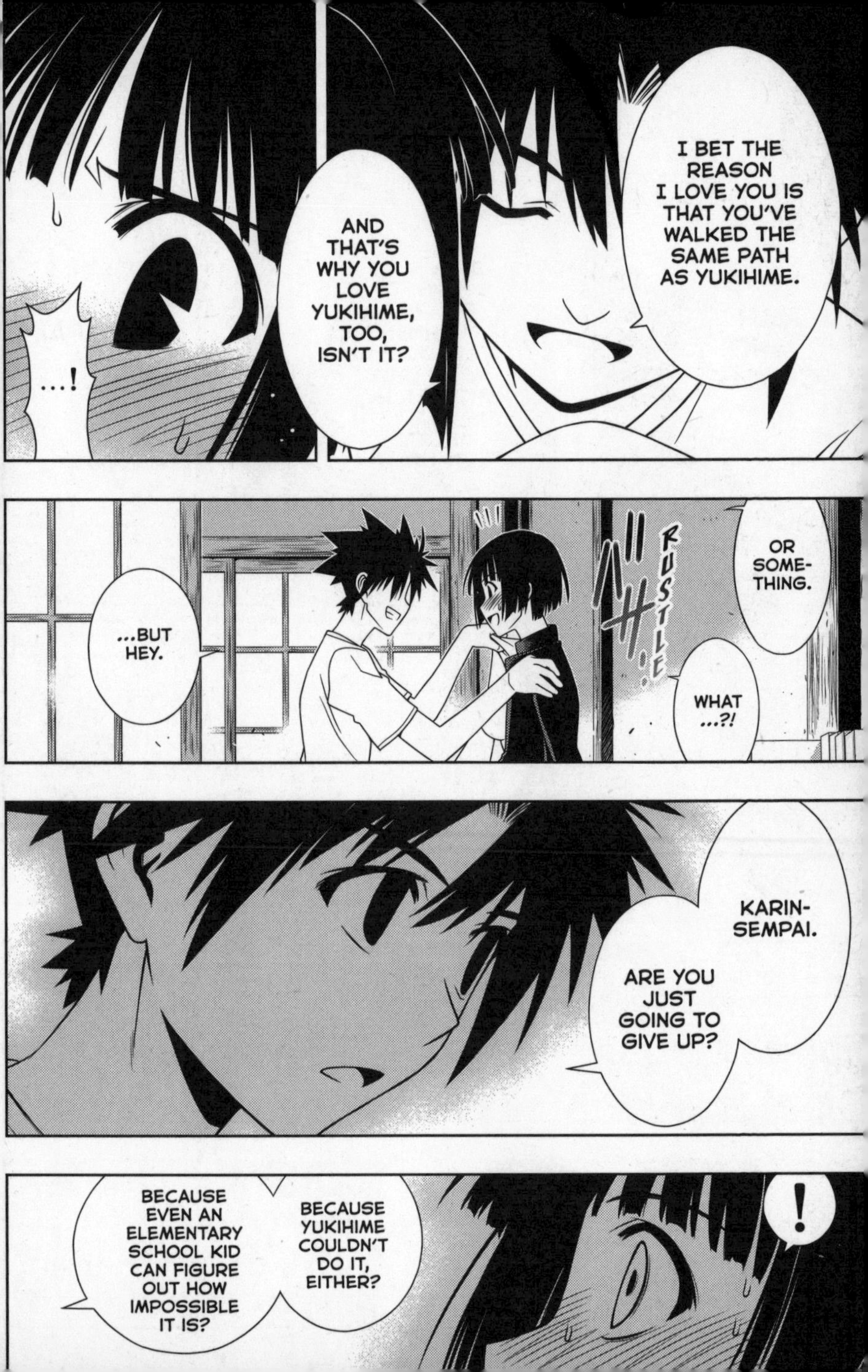
I BET THE REASON I LOVE YOU IS THAT YOU'VE WALKED THE SAME PATH AS YUKIHIME.
AND THAT'S WHY YOU LOVE YUKIHIME, TOO, ISN'T IT?
...!
OR SOME-THING.
RUSTLE
WHAT ...?!
...BUT HEY.
KARIN-SEMPAI.
ARE YOU JUST GOING TO GIVE UP?
!
BECAUSE YUKIHIME COULDN'T DO IT, EITHER?
BECAUSE EVEN AN ELEMENTARY SCHOOL KID CAN FIGURE OUT HOW IMPOSSIBLE IT IS?

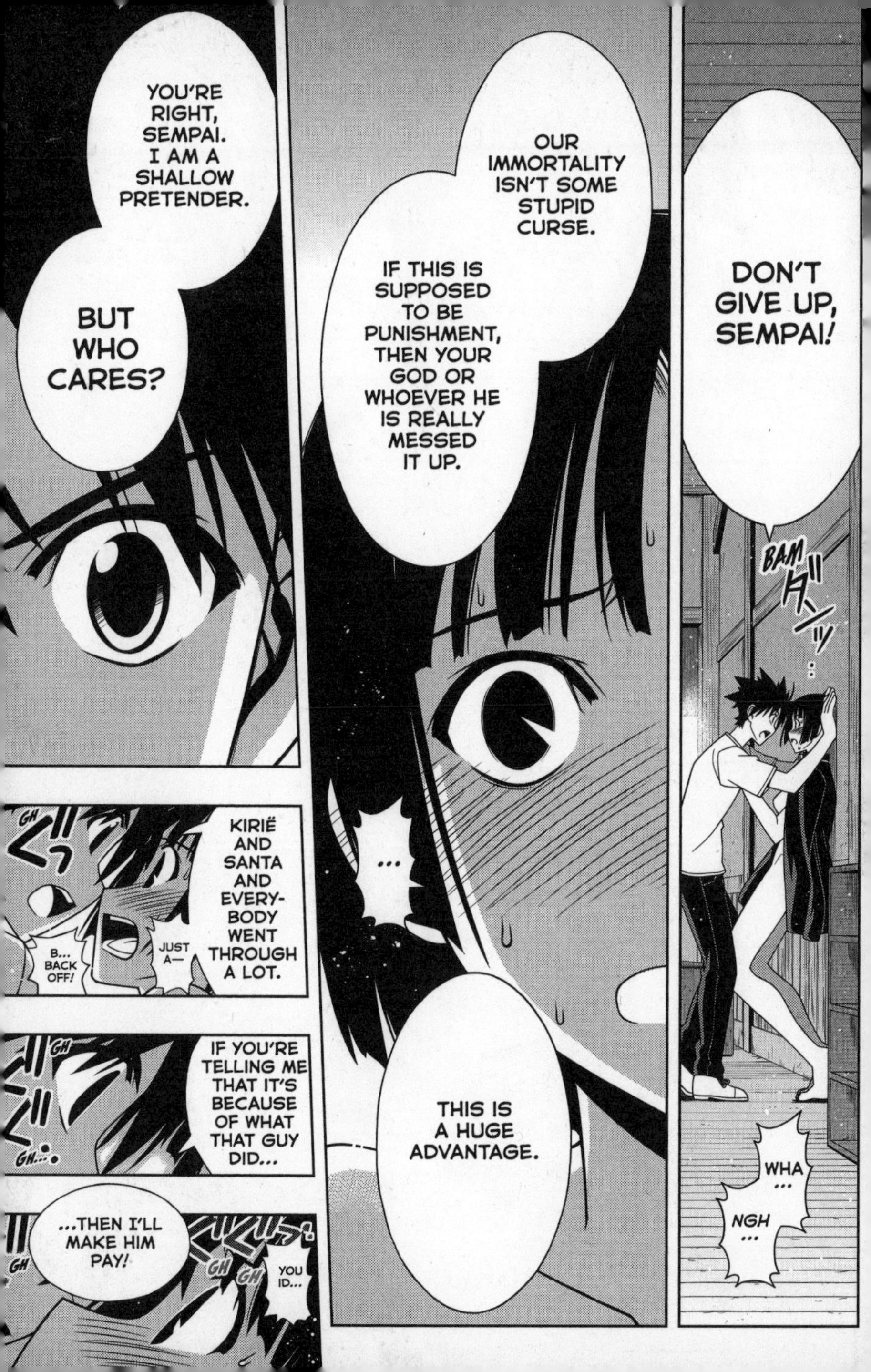
DON'T GIVE UP, SEMPAI!
BAM
WHA...
NGH...
OUR IMMORTALITY ISN'T SOME STUPID CURSE.
IF THIS IS SUPPOSED TO BE PUNISHMENT, THEN YOUR GOD OR WHOEVER HE IS REALLY MESSED IT UP.
...
THIS IS A HUGE ADVANTAGE.
YOU'RE RIGHT, SEMPAI. I AM A SHALLOW PRETENDER.
BUT WHO CARES?
GH
KIRIË AND SANTA AND EVERY-BODY WENT THROUGH A LOT.
JUST A—
B... BACK OFF!
GH
IF YOU'RE TELLING ME THAT IT'S BECAUSE OF WHAT THAT GUY DID...
GH...
GH
GH
YOU ID...
...THEN I'LL MAKE HIM PAY!
GH

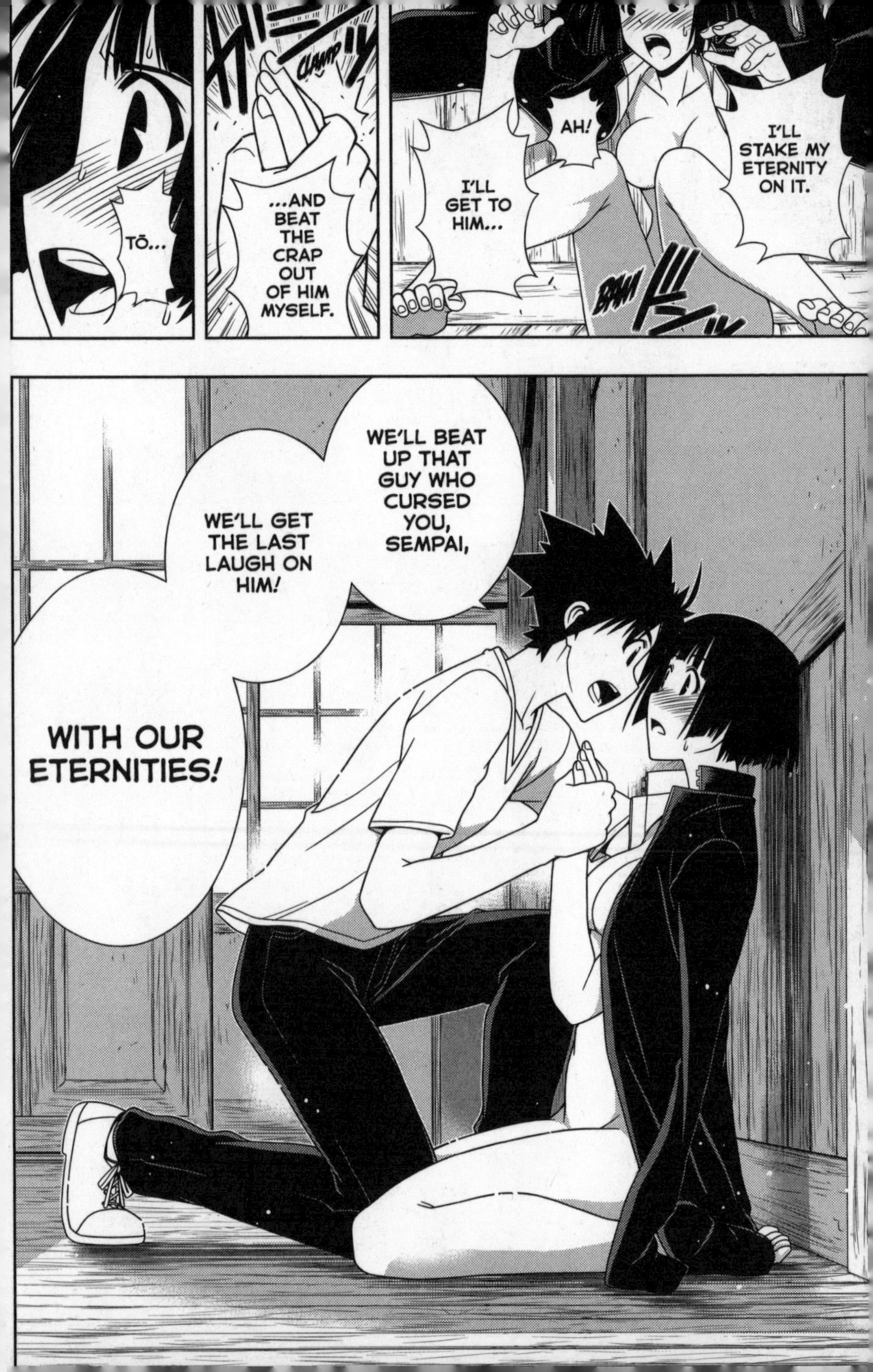
I'LL STAKE MY ETERNITY ON IT.
AH!
I'LL GET TO HIM...
BAM
...AND BEAT THE CRAP OUT OF HIM MYSELF.
CLAMP
TŌ...
WE'LL BEAT UP THAT GUY WHO CURSED YOU, SEMPAI,
WE'LL GET THE LAST LAUGH ON HIM!
WITH OUR ETERNITIES!

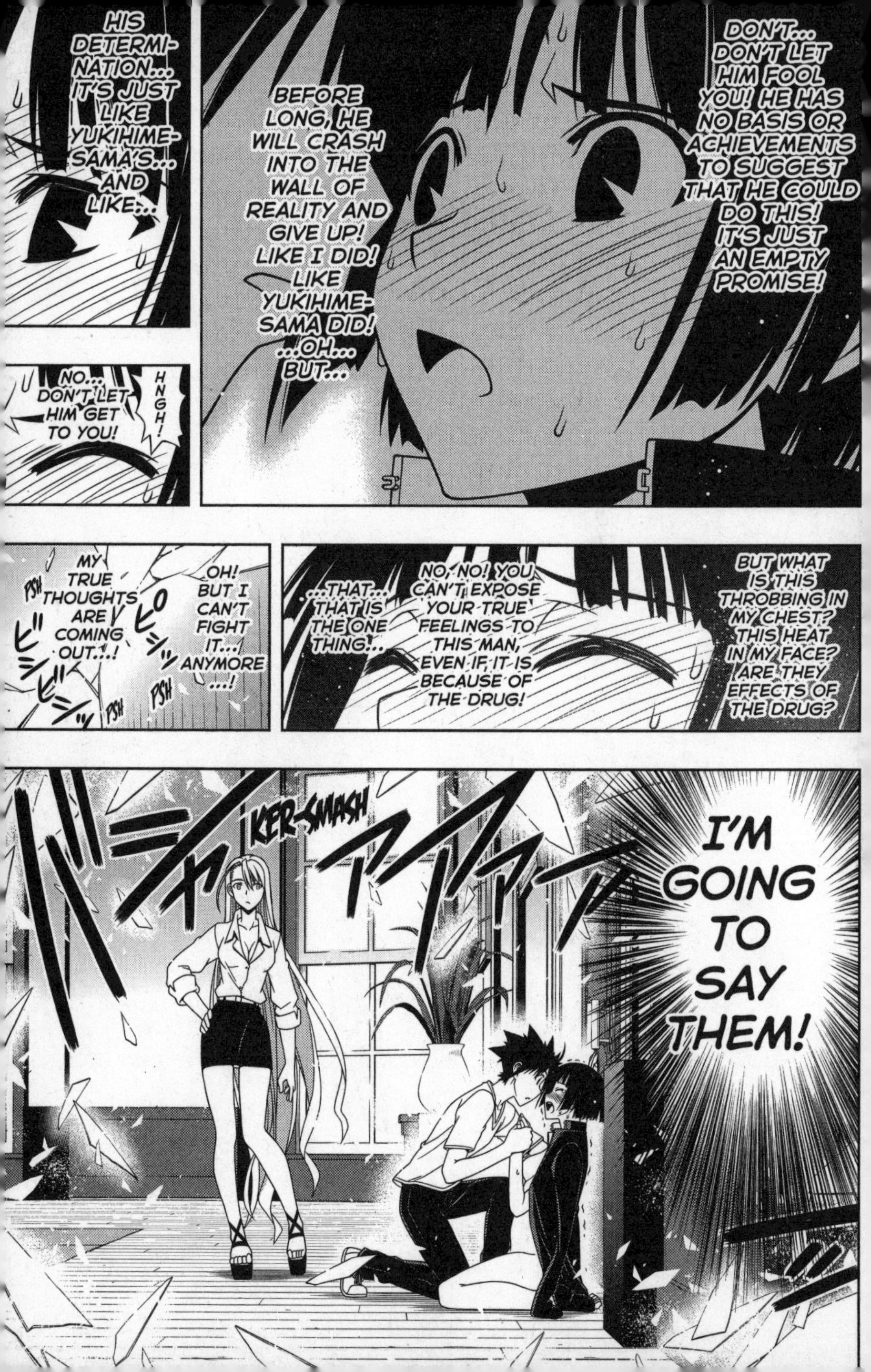
DON'T... DON'T LET HIM FOOL YOU! HE HAS NO BASIS OR ACHIEVEMENTS TO SUGGEST THAT HE COULD DO THIS! IT'S JUST AN EMPTY PROMISE!
BEFORE LONG, HE WILL CRASH INTO THE WALL OF REALITY AND GIVE UP! LIKE I DID! LIKE YUKIHIME-SAMA DID! ...OH... BUT...
HIS DETERMINATION... IT'S JUST LIKE YUKIHIME-SAMA'S... AND LIKE...
HNGH!
NO... DON'T LET HIM GET TO YOU!
BUT WHAT IS THIS THROBBING IN MY CHEST? THIS HEAT IN MY FACE? ARE THEY EFFECTS OF THE DRUG?
NO, NO! YOU CAN'T EXPOSE YOUR TRUE FEELINGS TO THIS MAN, EVEN IF IT IS BECAUSE OF THE DRUG!
...THAT... THAT IS THE ONE THING...
OH! BUT I CAN'T FIGHT IT... ANYMORE ...!
MY TRUE THOUGHTS ARE COMING OUT...!
PSH
PSH
PSH
I'M GOING TO SAY THEM!
KER-SMASH

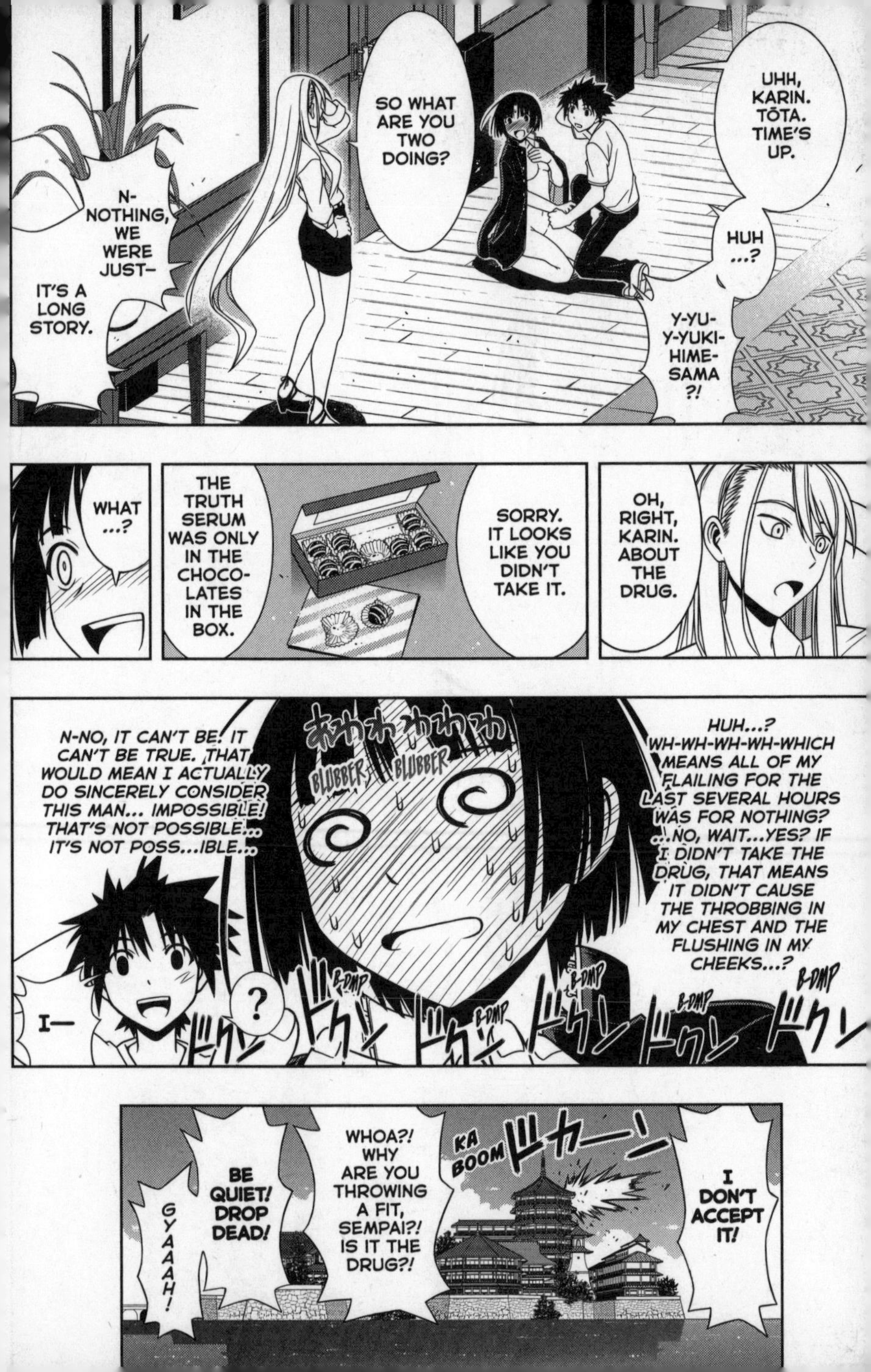
UHH, KARIN. TŌTA. TIME'S UP.
HUH...?
Y-YU-Y-YUKI-HIME-SAMA?!
SO WHAT ARE YOU TWO DOING?
N-NOTHING, WE WERE JUST–
IT'S A LONG STORY.
OH, RIGHT, KARIN. ABOUT THE DRUG.
SORRY. IT LOOKS LIKE YOU DIDN'T TAKE IT.
THE TRUTH SERUM WAS ONLY IN THE CHOCOLATES IN THE BOX.
WHAT...?
HUH...? WH-WH-WH-WH-WHICH MEANS ALL OF MY FLAILING FOR THE LAST SEVERAL HOURS WAS FOR NOTHING? ...NO, WAIT...YES? IF I DIDN'T TAKE THE DRUG, THAT MEANS IT DIDN'T CAUSE THE THROBBING IN MY CHEST AND THE FLUSHING IN MY CHEEKS...?
BLUBBER BLUBBER
N-NO, IT CAN'T BE. IT CAN'T BE TRUE. THAT WOULD MEAN I ACTUALLY DO SINCERELY CONSIDER THIS MAN... IMPOSSIBLE! THAT'S NOT POSSIBLE... IT'S NOT POSS...IBLE...
B-DMP B-DMP B-DMP B-DMP B-DMP
?
I—
I DON'T ACCEPT IT!
KA BOOM
WHOA?! WHY ARE YOU THROWING A FIT, SEMPAI?! IS IT THE DRUG?!
BE QUIET! DROP DEAD!
GYAAAAH!

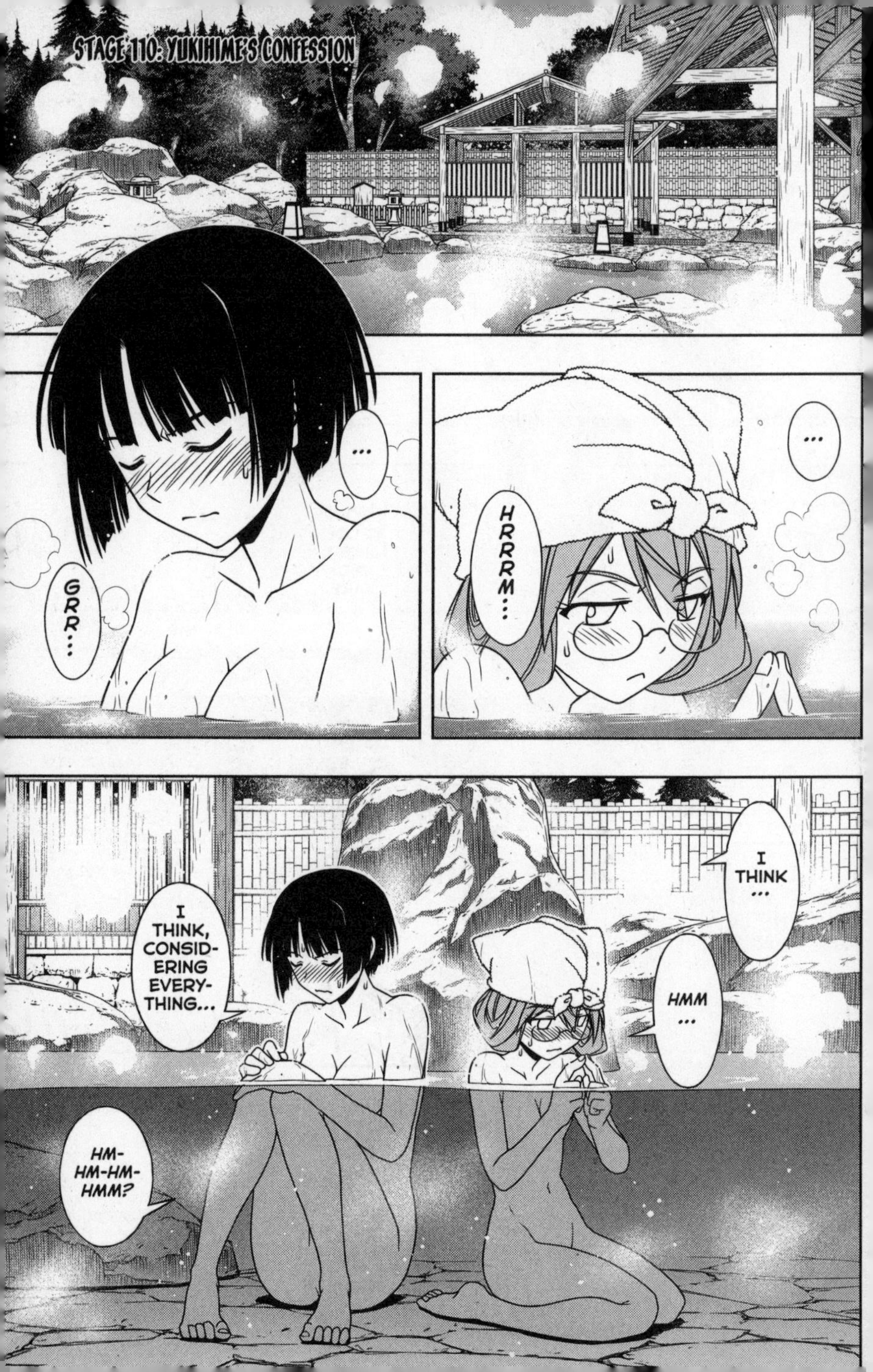
STAGE 110: YUKIHIME'S CONFESSION
...
HRRRM...
...
GRR...
I THINK...
HMM...
I THINK, CONSIDERING EVERYTHING...
HM-HM-HM-HMM?

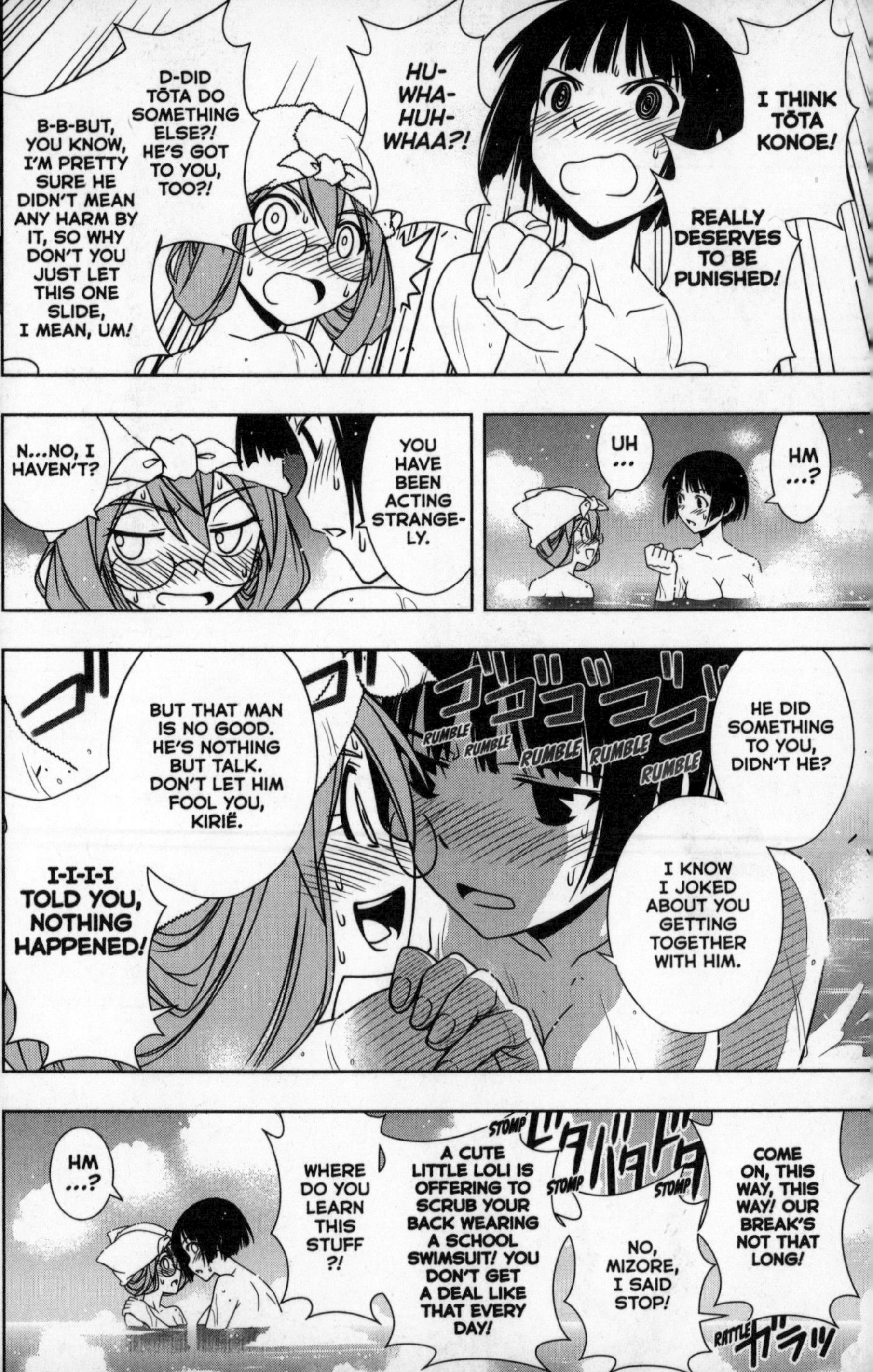
I THINK TŌTA KONOE!
REALLY DESERVES TO BE PUNISHED!
HU-WHA-HUH-WHAA?!
D-DID TŌTA DO SOMETHING ELSE?! HE'S GOT TO YOU, TOO?!
B-B-BUT, YOU KNOW, I'M PRETTY SURE HE DIDN'T MEAN ANY HARM BY IT, SO WHY DON'T YOU JUST LET THIS ONE SLIDE, I MEAN, UM!
HM...?
UH...
YOU HAVE BEEN ACTING STRANGE-LY.
N...NO, I HAVEN'T?
HE DID SOMETHING TO YOU, DIDN'T HE?
RUMBLE RUMBLE RUMBLE RUMBLE RUMBLE
I KNOW I JOKED ABOUT YOU GETTING TOGETHER WITH HIM.
BUT THAT MAN IS NO GOOD. HE'S NOTHING BUT TALK. DON'T LET HIM FOOL YOU, KIRIË.
I-I-I-I TOLD YOU, NOTHING HAPPENED!
COME ON, THIS WAY, THIS WAY! OUR BREAK'S NOT THAT LONG!
STOMP STOMP STOMP
NO, MIZORE, I SAID STOP!
RATTLE
A CUTE LITTLE LOLI IS OFFERING TO SCRUB YOUR BACK WEARING A SCHOOL SWIMSUIT! YOU DON'T GET A DEAL LIKE THAT EVERY DAY!
WHERE DO YOU LEARN THIS STUFF?!
HM...?

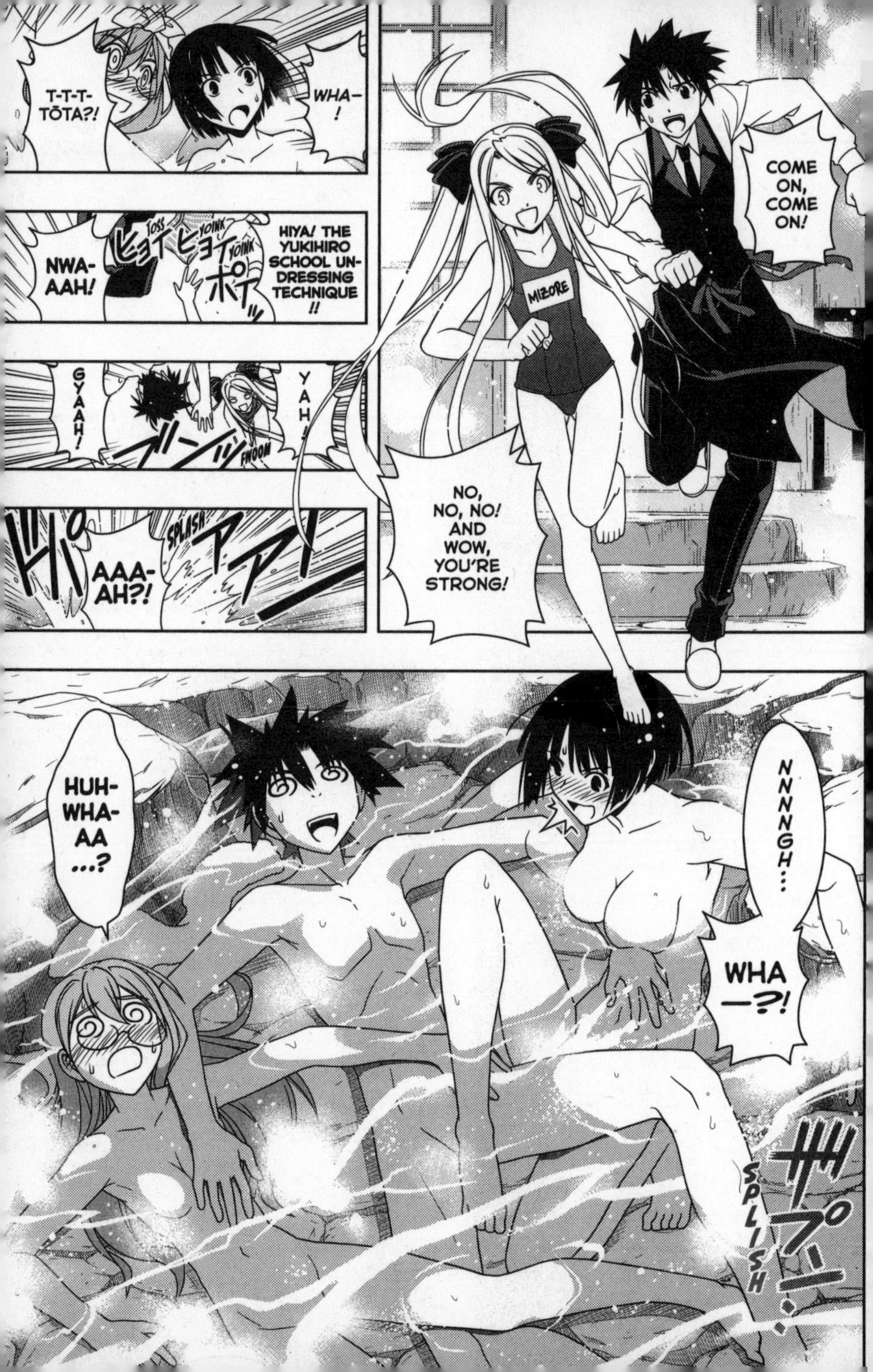
COME ON, COME ON!
NO, NO, NO! AND WOW, YOU'RE STRONG!
WHA-!
T-T-T-TŌTA?!
HIYA! THE YUKIHIRO SCHOOL UN-DRESSING TECHNIQUE!!
YOINK YOINK
TOSS
NWA-AAH!
YAH!
FWOOM
GYAAH!
SPLASH
AAA-AH?!
NNNNGH...
WHA—?!
HUH-WHAA-AA...?
SPLISH

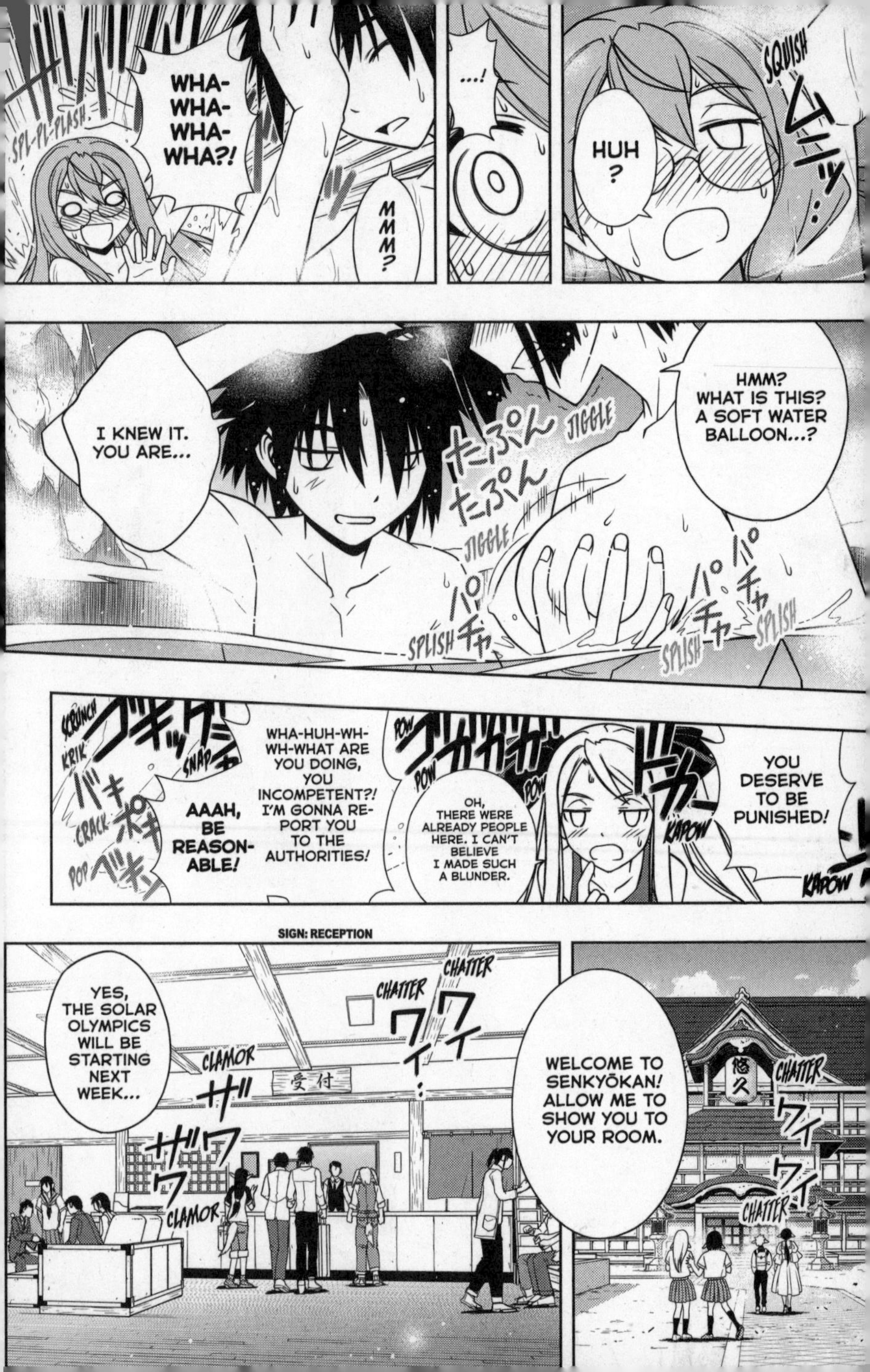
SQUISH
HUH?
...!
MMM?
WHA-WHA-WHA-WHA?!
SPL-PL-PLASH
HMM? WHAT IS THIS? A SOFT WATER BALLOON...?
JIGGLE
JIGGLE
SPLISH
SPLISH
SPLISH
I KNEW IT. YOU ARE...
KAPOW
YOU DESERVE TO BE PUNISHED!
KAPOW
OH, THERE WERE ALREADY PEOPLE HERE. I CAN'T BELIEVE I MADE SUCH A BLUNDER.
POW
POW
POW
WHA-HUH-WH-WH-WHAT ARE YOU DOING, YOU INCOMPETENT?! I'M GONNA REPORT YOU TO THE AUTHORITIES!
AAAH, BE REASONABLE!
SCRUNCH
SNAP
KRIK
CRACK
POP
SIGN: RECEPTION
CHATTER
WELCOME TO SENKYŌKAN! ALLOW ME TO SHOW YOU TO YOUR ROOM.
悠久
CHATTER
CHATTER
CHATTER
YES, THE SOLAR OLYMPICS WILL BE STARTING NEXT WEEK...
受付
CLAMOR
CLAMOR

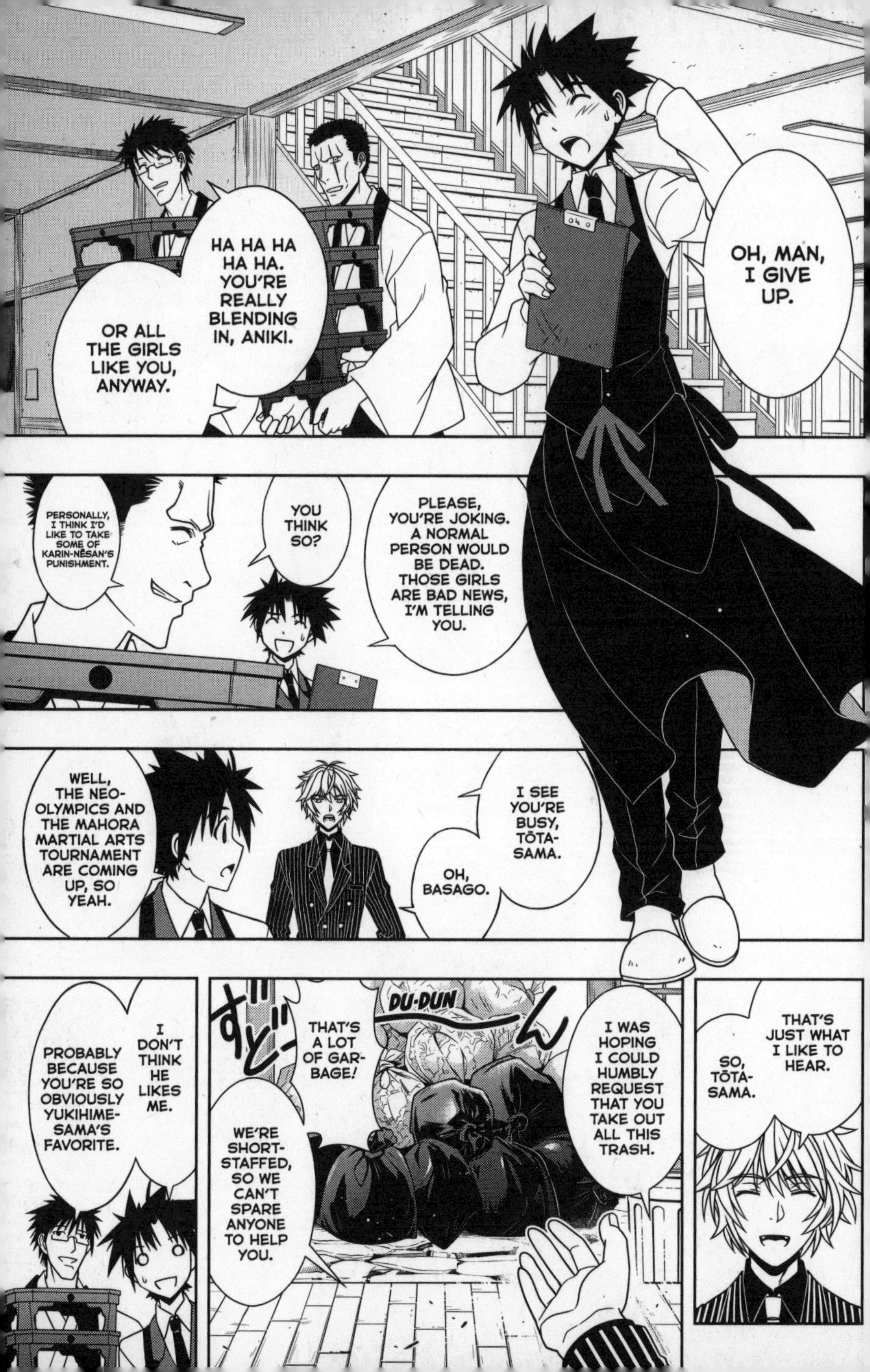
OH, MAN, I GIVE UP.
HA HA HA HA HA. YOU'RE REALLY BLENDING IN, ANIKI.
OR ALL THE GIRLS LIKE YOU, ANYWAY.
PLEASE, YOU'RE JOKING. A NORMAL PERSON WOULD BE DEAD. THOSE GIRLS ARE BAD NEWS, I'M TELLING YOU.
YOU THINK SO?
PERSONALLY, I THINK I'D LIKE TO TAKE SOME OF KARIN-NĒSAN'S PUNISHMENT.
I SEE YOU'RE BUSY, TŌTA-SAMA.
OH, BASAGO.
WELL, THE NEO-OLYMPICS AND THE MAHORA MARTIAL ARTS TOURNAMENT ARE COMING UP, SO YEAH.
THAT'S JUST WHAT I LIKE TO HEAR.
SO, TŌTA-SAMA.
I WAS HOPING I COULD HUMBLY REQUEST THAT YOU TAKE OUT ALL THIS TRASH.
DU-DUN
THAT'S A LOT OF GARBAGE!
WE'RE SHORT-STAFFED, SO WE CAN'T SPARE ANYONE TO HELP YOU.
I DON'T THINK HE LIKES ME.
PROBABLY BECAUSE YOU'RE SO OBVIOUSLY YUKIHIME-SAMA'S FAVORITE.

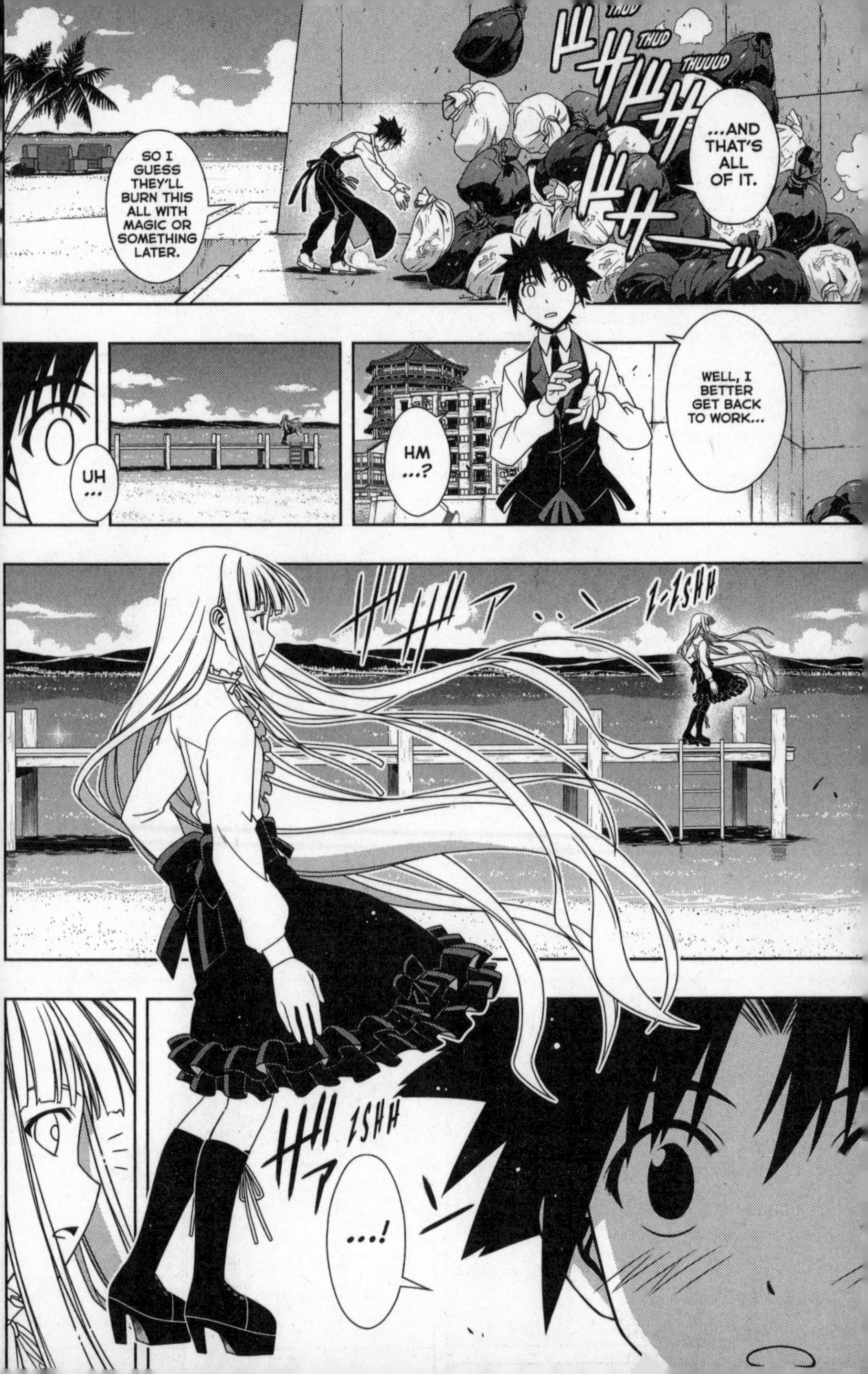
THUD
THUD
THUUUD
...AND THAT'S ALL OF IT.
SO I GUESS THEY'LL BURN THIS ALL WITH MAGIC OR SOMETHING LATER.
WELL, I BETTER GET BACK TO WORK...
HM ...?
UH ...
I-ISHH
ISHH
...!

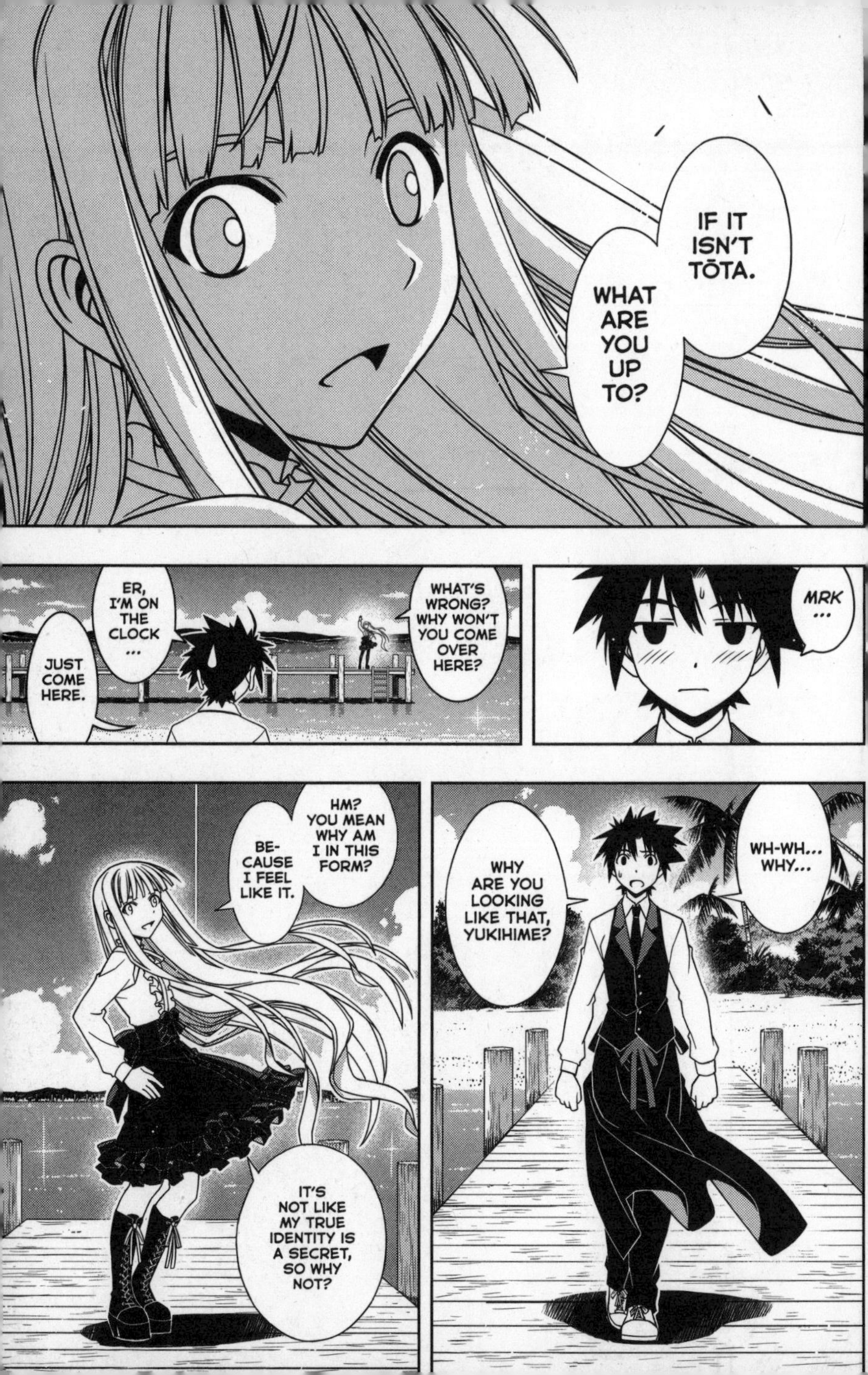
IF IT ISN'T TŌTA.
WHAT ARE YOU UP TO?
MRK ...
WHAT'S WRONG? WHY WON'T YOU COME OVER HERE?
ER, I'M ON THE CLOCK ...
JUST COME HERE.
WH-WH... WHY...
WHY ARE YOU LOOKING LIKE THAT, YUKIHIME?
HM? YOU MEAN WHY AM I IN THIS FORM?
BE-CAUSE I FEEL LIKE IT.
IT'S NOT LIKE MY TRUE IDENTITY IS A SECRET, SO WHY NOT?

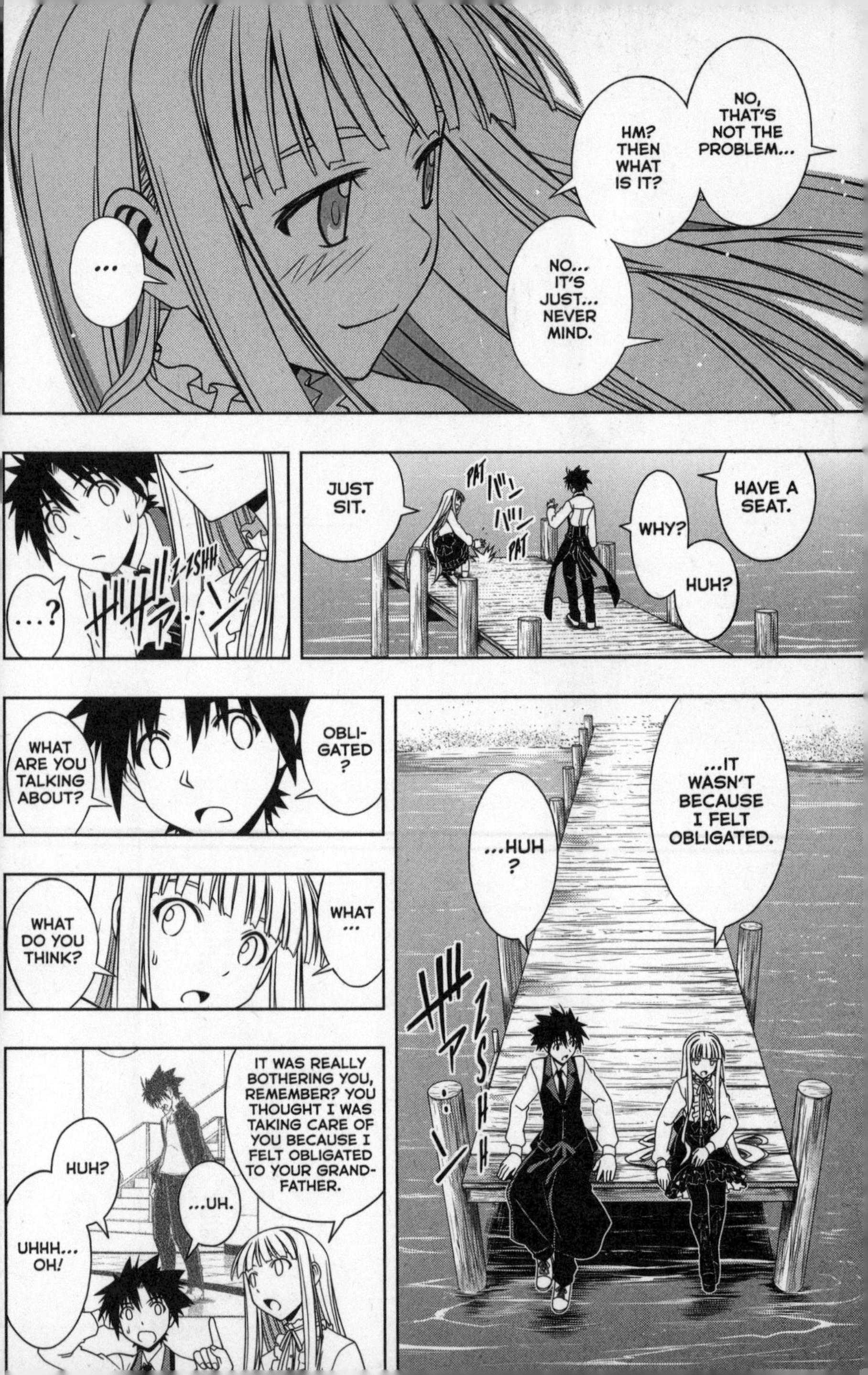
NO, THAT'S NOT THE PROBLEM...
HM? THEN WHAT IS IT?
NO... IT'S JUST... NEVER MIND.
...
HAVE A SEAT.
WHY?
HUH?
PAT
PAT
JUST SIT.
ZSHH
...?
...IT WASN'T BECAUSE I FELT OBLIGATED.
...HUH?
ZSHH
OBLIGATED?
WHAT ARE YOU TALKING ABOUT?
WHAT...
WHAT DO YOU THINK?
IT WAS REALLY BOTHERING YOU, REMEMBER? YOU THOUGHT I WAS TAKING CARE OF YOU BECAUSE I FELT OBLIGATED TO YOUR GRAND-FATHER.
...UH.
HUH?
UHHH... OH!

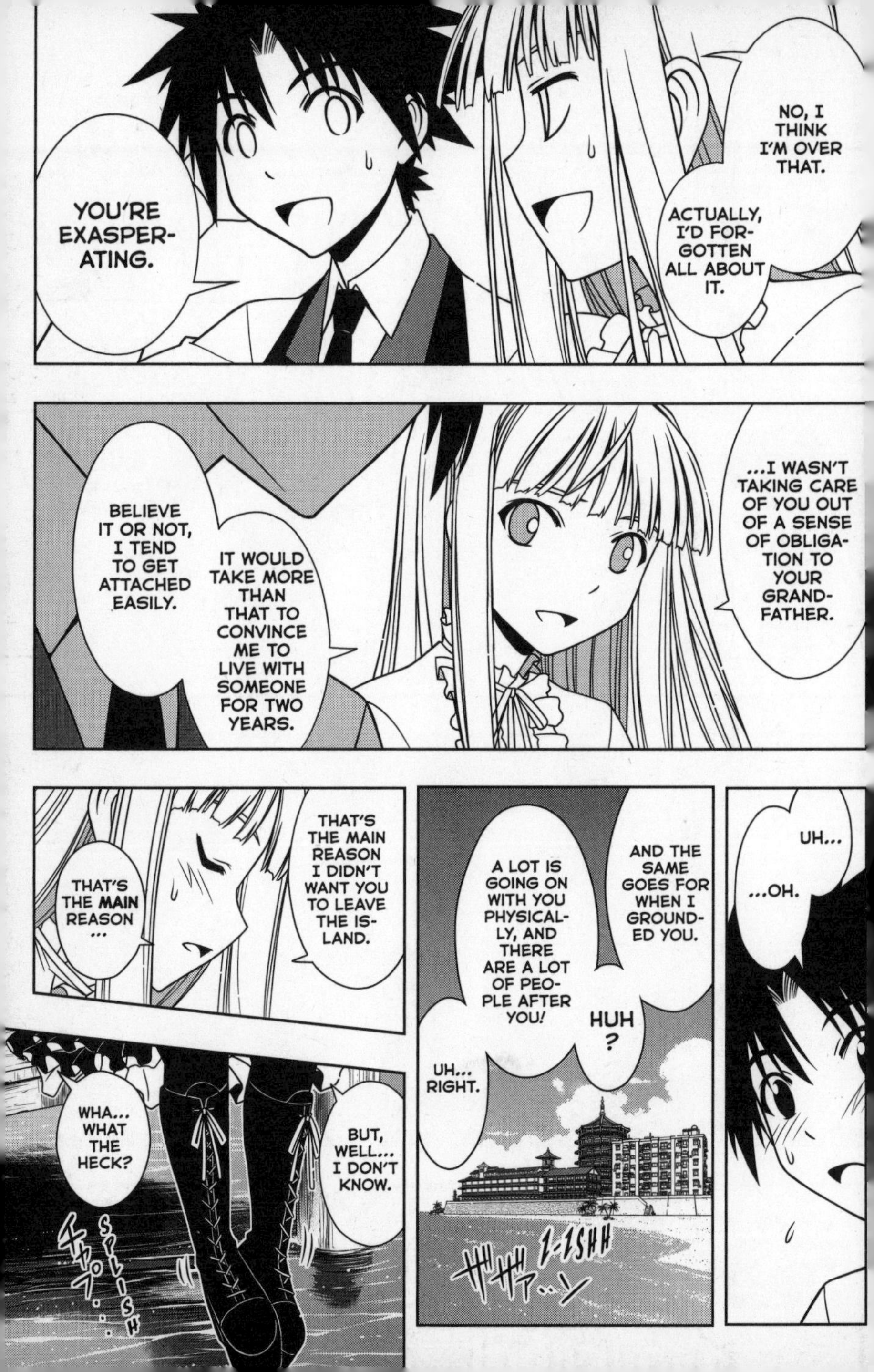
NO, I THINK I'M OVER THAT.
ACTUALLY, I'D FORGOTTEN ALL ABOUT IT.
YOU'RE EXASPERATING.
...I WASN'T TAKING CARE OF YOU OUT OF A SENSE OF OBLIGATION TO YOUR GRANDFATHER.
IT WOULD TAKE MORE THAN THAT TO CONVINCE ME TO LIVE WITH SOMEONE FOR TWO YEARS.
BELIEVE IT OR NOT, I TEND TO GET ATTACHED EASILY.
UH...
...OH.
AND THE SAME GOES FOR WHEN I GROUNDED YOU.
A LOT IS GOING ON WITH YOU PHYSICALLY, AND THERE ARE A LOT OF PEOPLE AFTER YOU!
HUH?
UH... RIGHT.
Z-ZSHH
THAT'S THE MAIN REASON I DIDN'T WANT YOU TO LEAVE THE ISLAND.
THAT'S THE **MAIN** REASON...
BUT, WELL... I DON'T KNOW.
WHA... WHAT THE HECK?
SPLISH

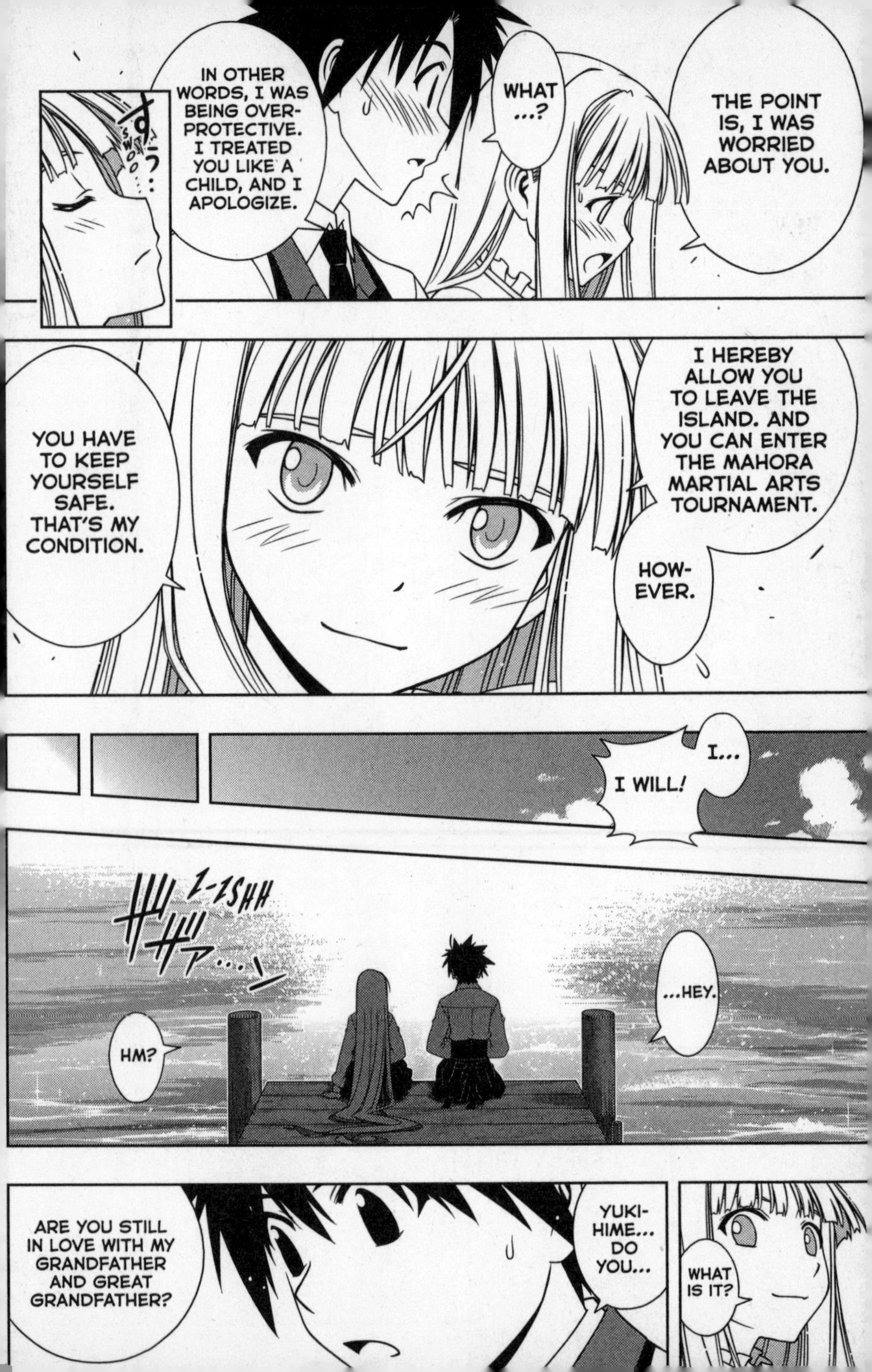
THE POINT IS, I WAS WORRIED ABOUT YOU.
WHAT ...?
IN OTHER WORDS, I WAS BEING OVER-PROTECTIVE. I TREATED YOU LIKE A CHILD, AND I APOLOGIZE.
SWOO...
I HEREBY ALLOW YOU TO LEAVE THE ISLAND. AND YOU CAN ENTER THE MAHORA MARTIAL ARTS TOURNAMENT.
HOW-EVER.
YOU HAVE TO KEEP YOURSELF SAFE. THAT'S MY CONDITION.
I...
I WILL!
Z-ZSHH
...HEY.
HM?
WHAT IS IT?
YUKI-HIME... DO YOU...
ARE YOU STILL IN LOVE WITH MY GRANDFATHER AND GREAT GRANDFATHER?

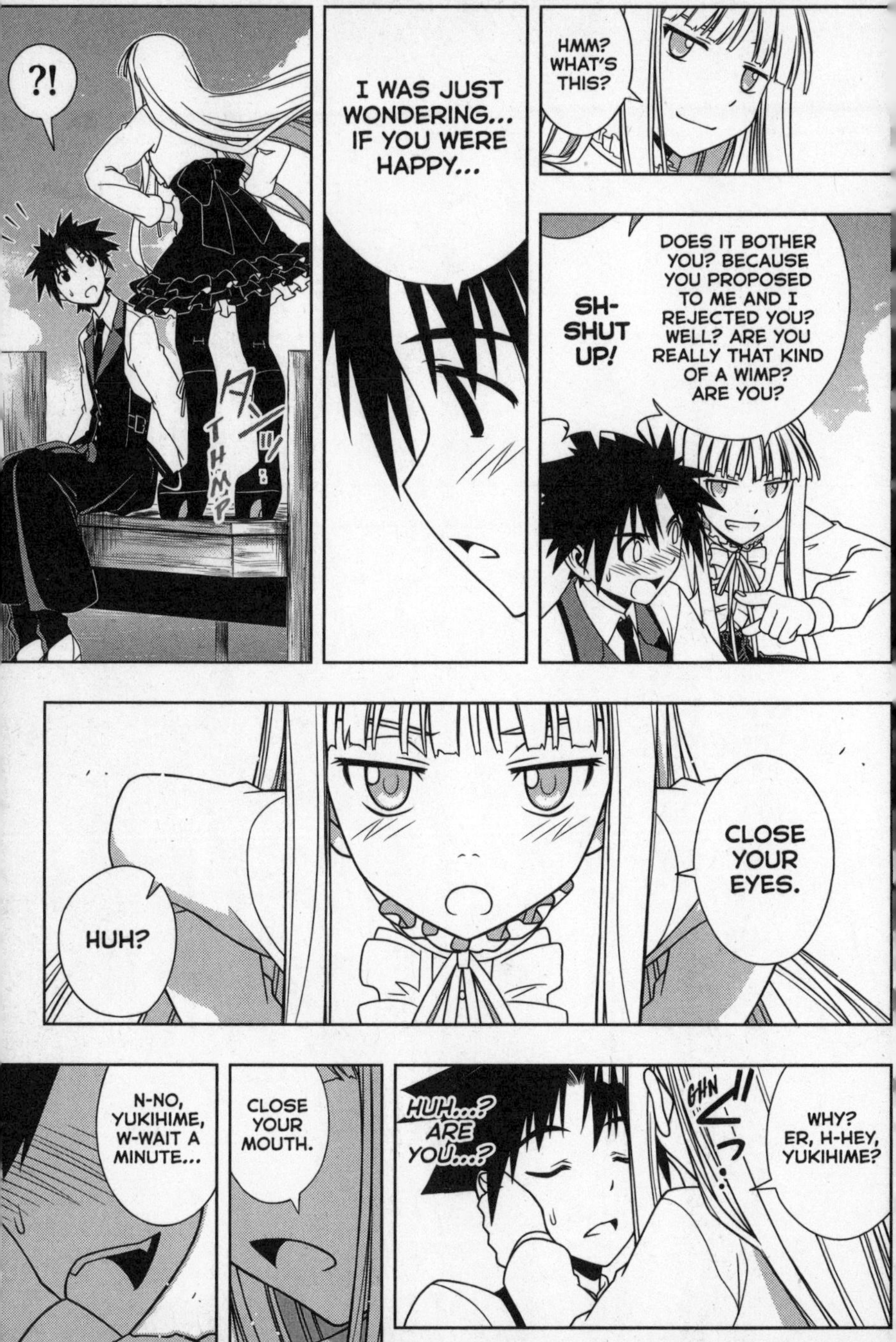
HMM? WHAT'S THIS?
DOES IT BOTHER YOU? BECAUSE YOU PROPOSED TO ME AND I REJECTED YOU? WELL? ARE YOU REALLY THAT KIND OF A WIMP? ARE YOU?
SH-SHUT UP!
I WAS JUST WONDERING... IF YOU WERE HAPPY...
?!
THMP
CLOSE YOUR EYES.
HUH?
WHY? ER, H-HEY, YUKIHIME?
GHN
HUH...? ARE YOU...?
CLOSE YOUR MOUTH.
N-NO, YUKIHIME, W-WAIT A MINUTE...

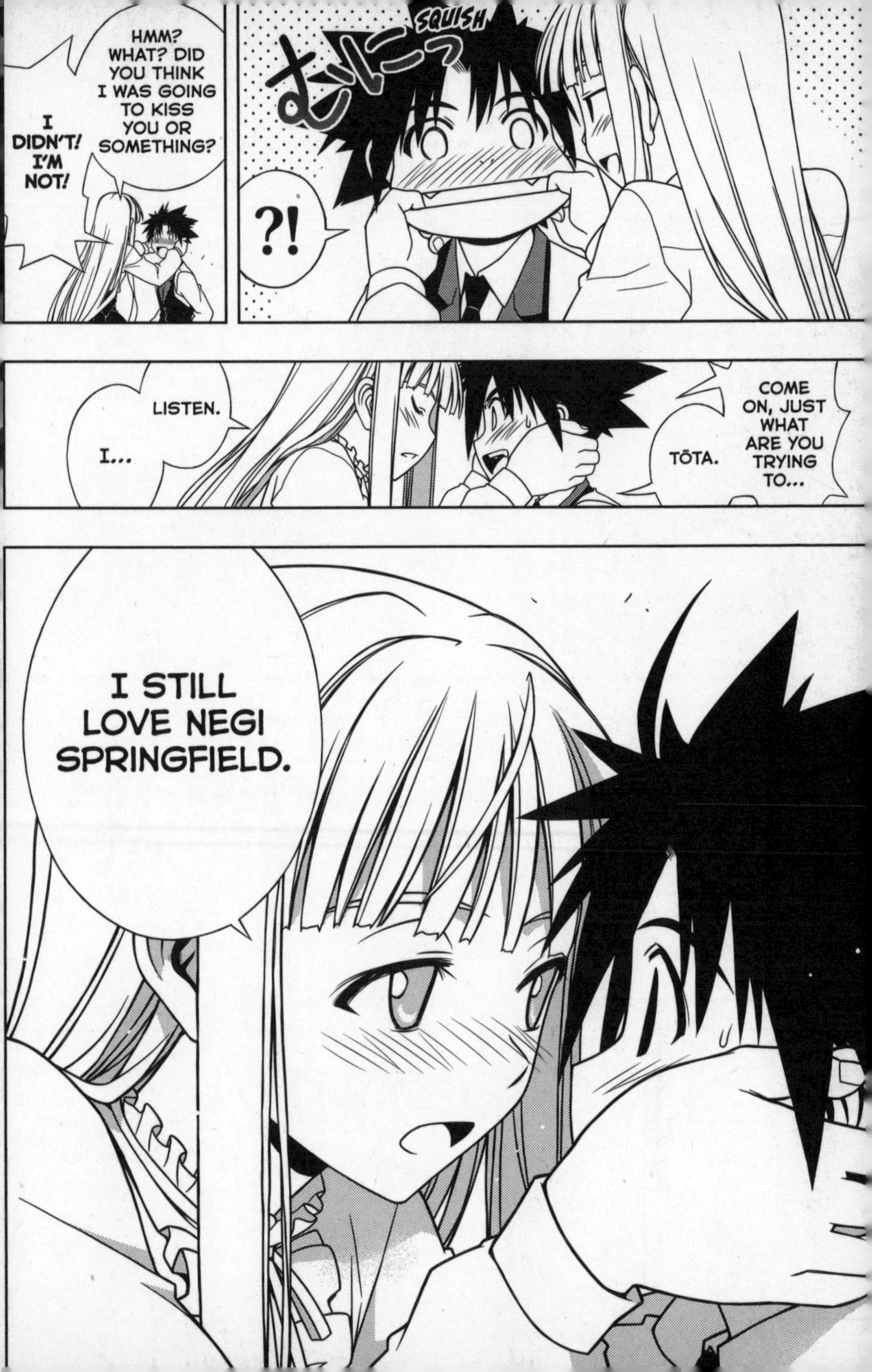
SQUISH
?!
HMM? WHAT? DID YOU THINK I WAS GOING TO KISS YOU OR SOMETHING?
I DIDN'T! I'M NOT!
COME ON, JUST WHAT ARE YOU TRYING TO...
TŌTA.
LISTEN.
I...
I STILL LOVE NEGI SPRINGFIELD.

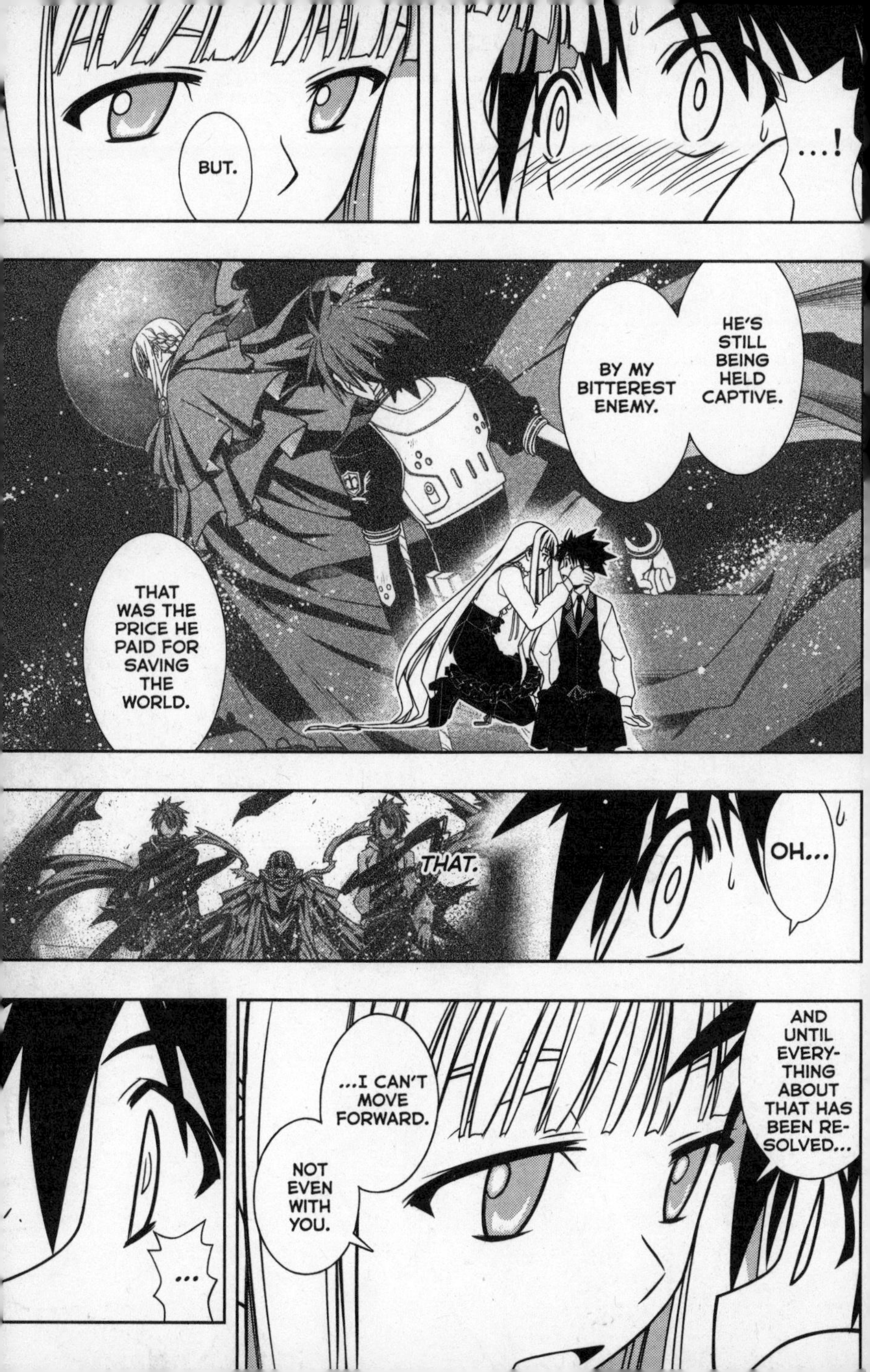
...!
BUT.
HE'S STILL BEING HELD CAPTIVE.
BY MY BITTEREST ENEMY.
THAT WAS THE PRICE HE PAID FOR SAVING THE WORLD.
OH...
THAT.
AND UNTIL EVERY-THING ABOUT THAT HAS BEEN RE-SOLVED...
...I CAN'T MOVE FORWARD.
NOT EVEN WITH YOU.
...

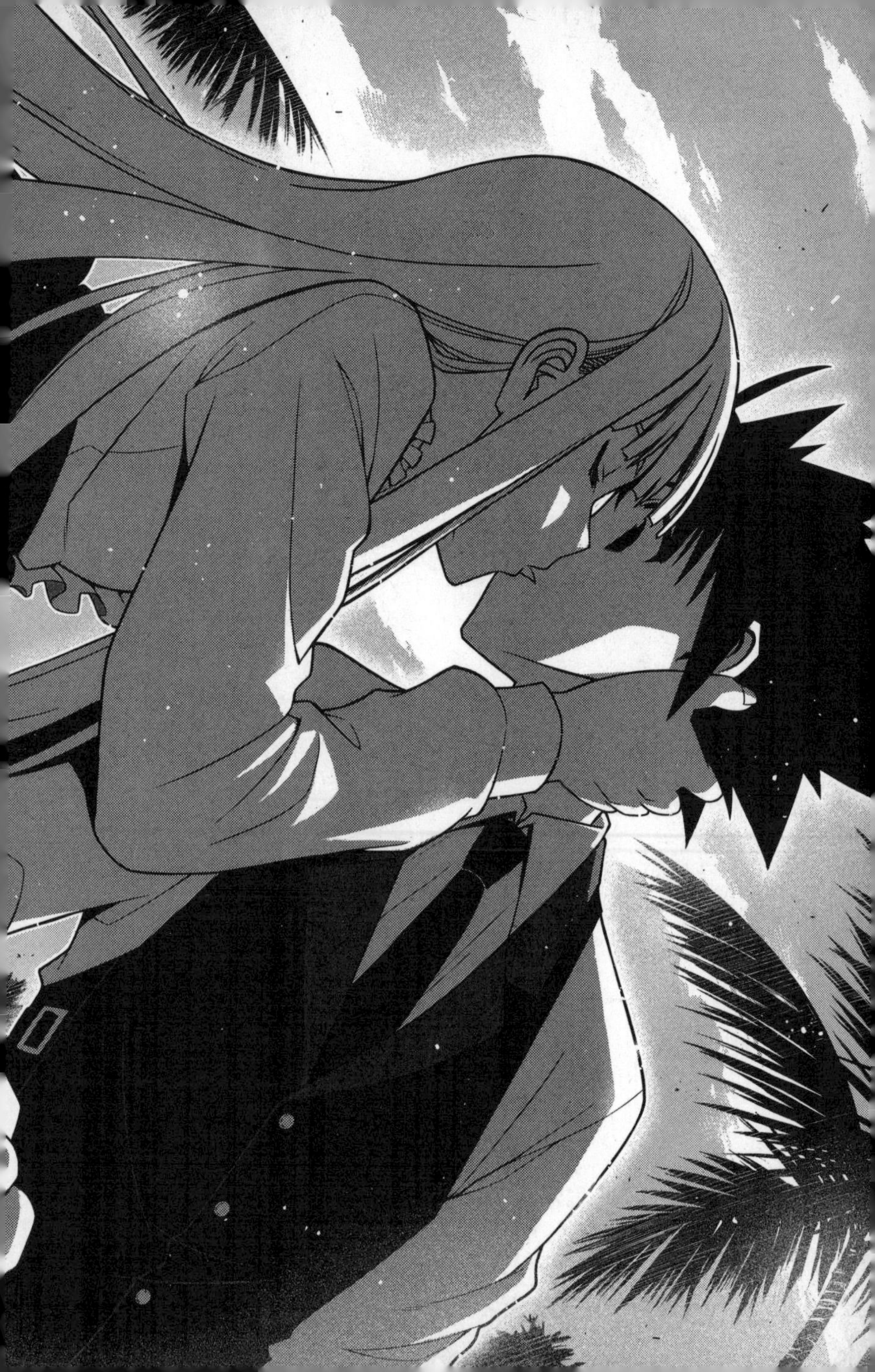

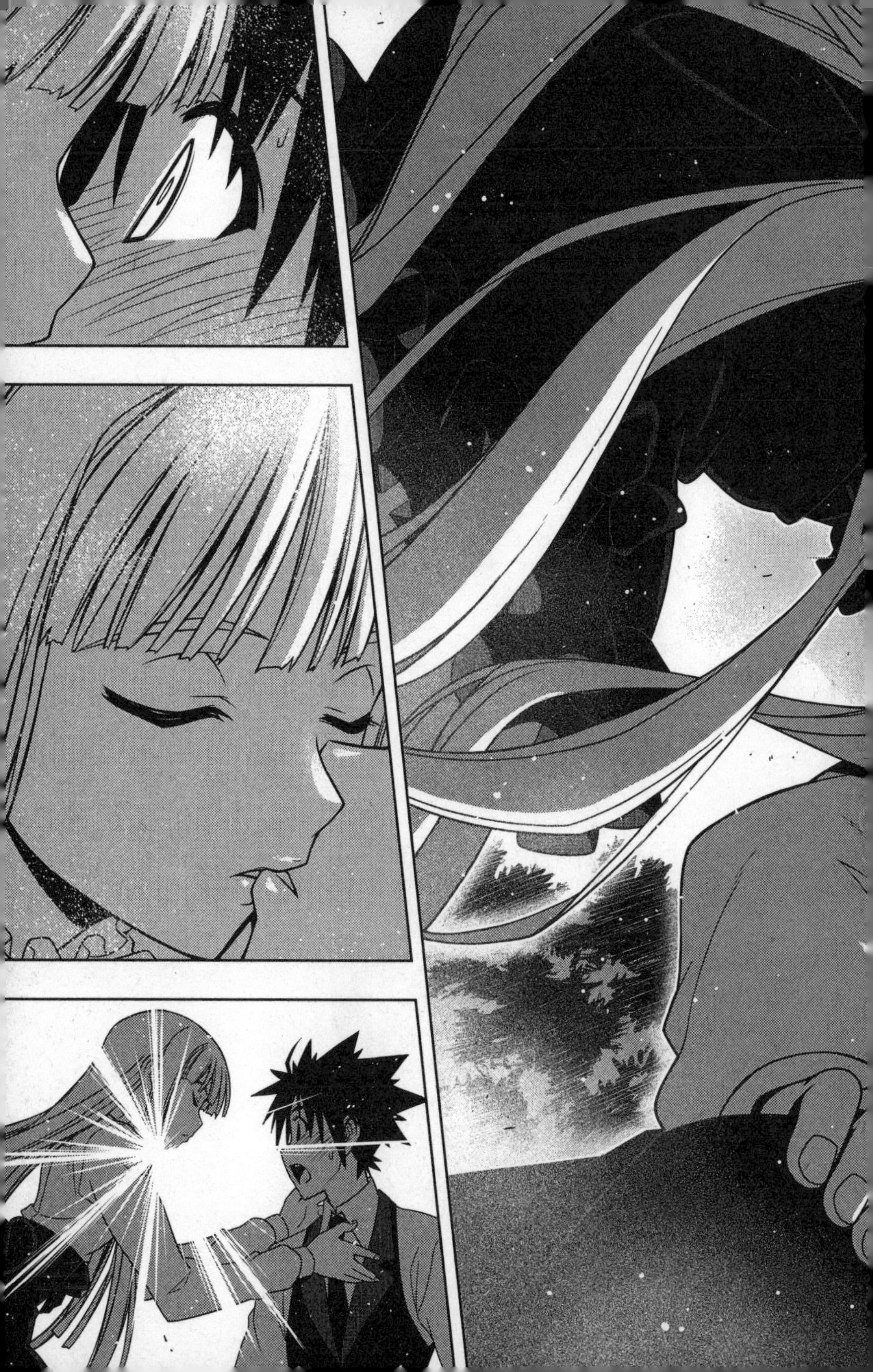

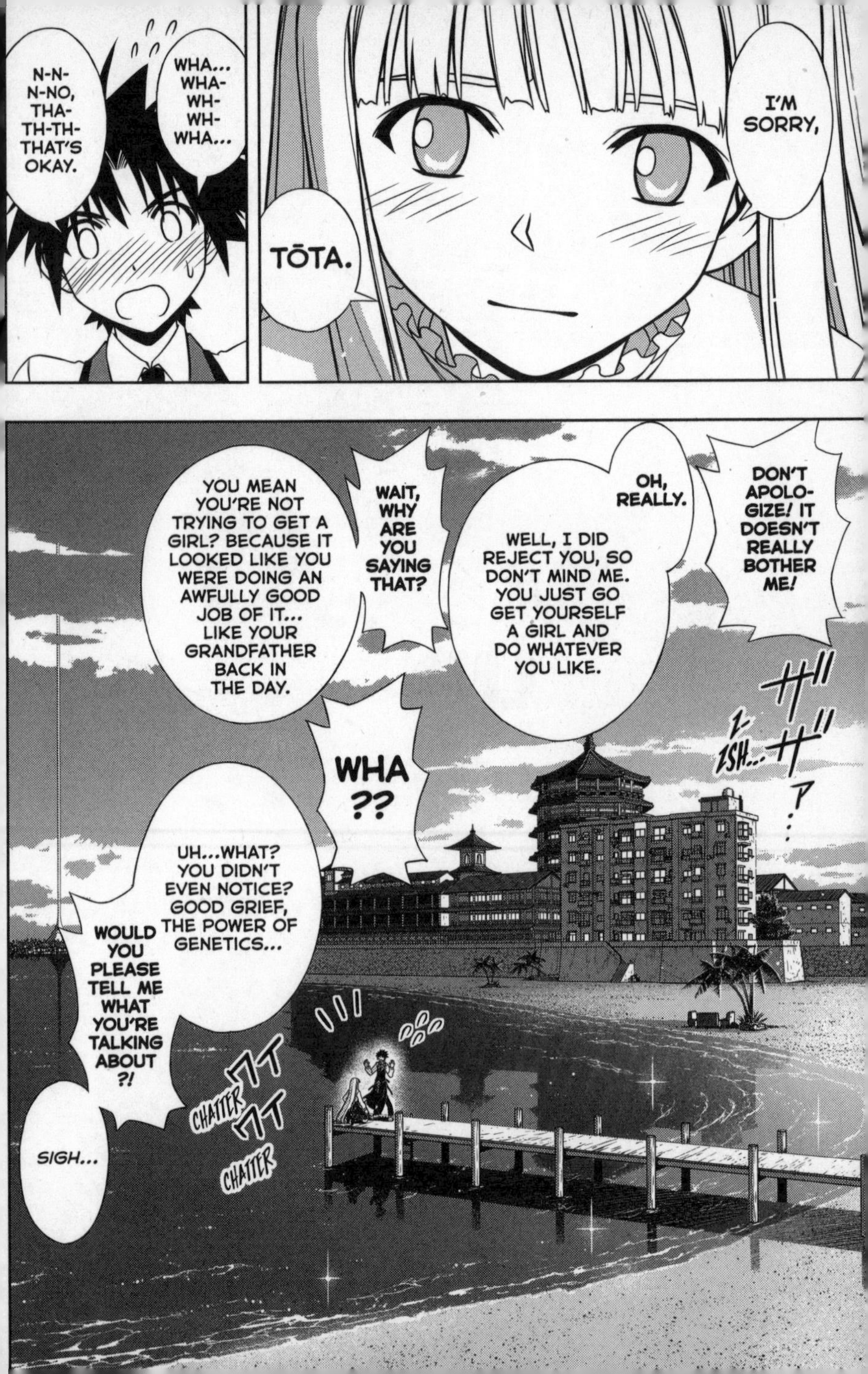
I'M SORRY,
TŌTA.
WHA... WHA- WH- WH- WHA...
N-N- N-NO, THA- TH-TH- THAT'S OKAY.
DON'T APOLOGIZE! IT DOESN'T REALLY BOTHER ME!
Z-ZSH...
OH, REALLY.
WELL, I DID REJECT YOU, SO DON'T MIND ME. YOU JUST GO GET YOURSELF A GIRL AND DO WHATEVER YOU LIKE.
WAIT, WHY ARE YOU SAYING THAT?
YOU MEAN YOU'RE NOT TRYING TO GET A GIRL? BECAUSE IT LOOKED LIKE YOU WERE DOING AN AWFULLY GOOD JOB OF IT... LIKE YOUR GRANDFATHER BACK IN THE DAY.
WHA ??
UH...WHAT? YOU DIDN'T EVEN NOTICE? GOOD GRIEF, THE POWER OF GENETICS...
WOULD YOU PLEASE TELL ME WHAT YOU'RE TALKING ABOUT ?!
CHATTER
CHATTER
SIGH...

UQ HOLDER!

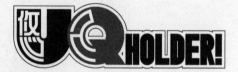

UQ HOLDER!

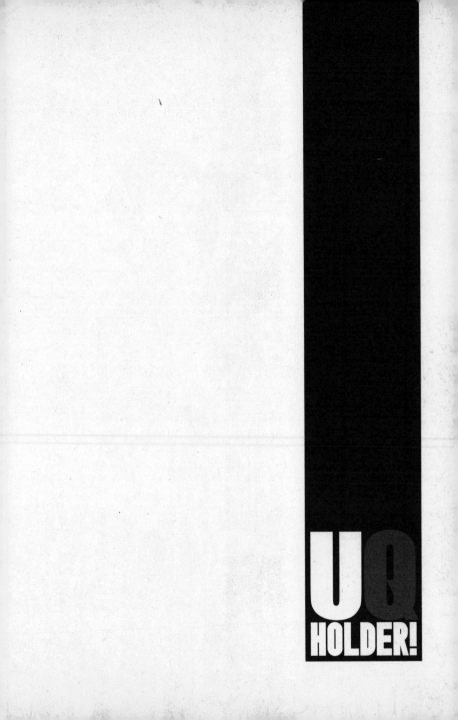

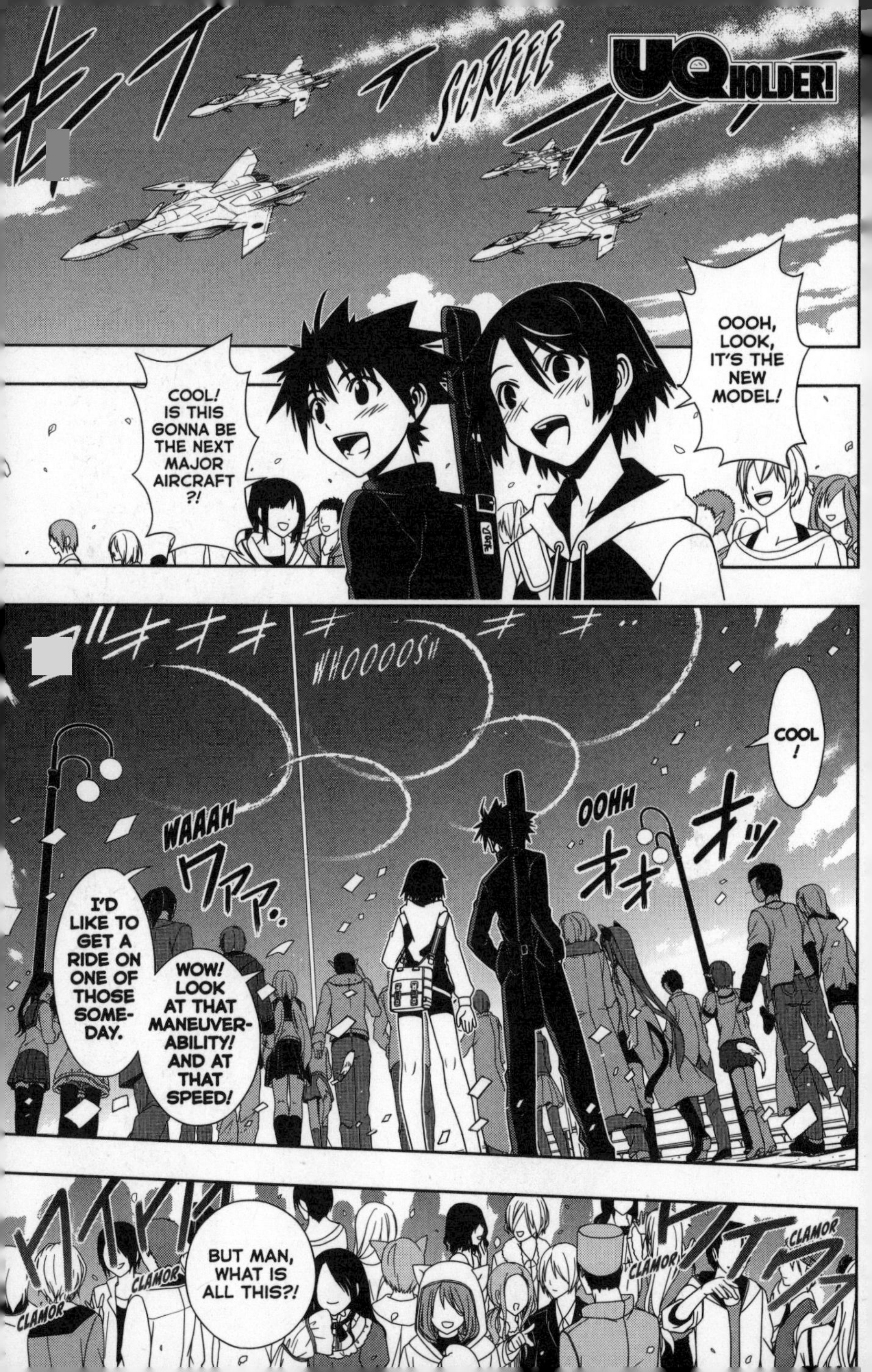
SCREEE
HOLDER!
OOOH, LOOK, IT'S THE NEW MODEL!
COOL! IS THIS GONNA BE THE NEXT MAJOR AIRCRAFT ?!
WHOOOOSH
COOL!
OOHH
WAAAH
WOW! LOOK AT THAT MANEUVERABILITY! AND AT THAT SPEED!
I'D LIKE TO GET A RIDE ON ONE OF THOSE SOMEDAY.
CLAMOR
CLAMOR
BUT MAN, WHAT IS ALL THIS?!
CLAMOR
CLAMOR

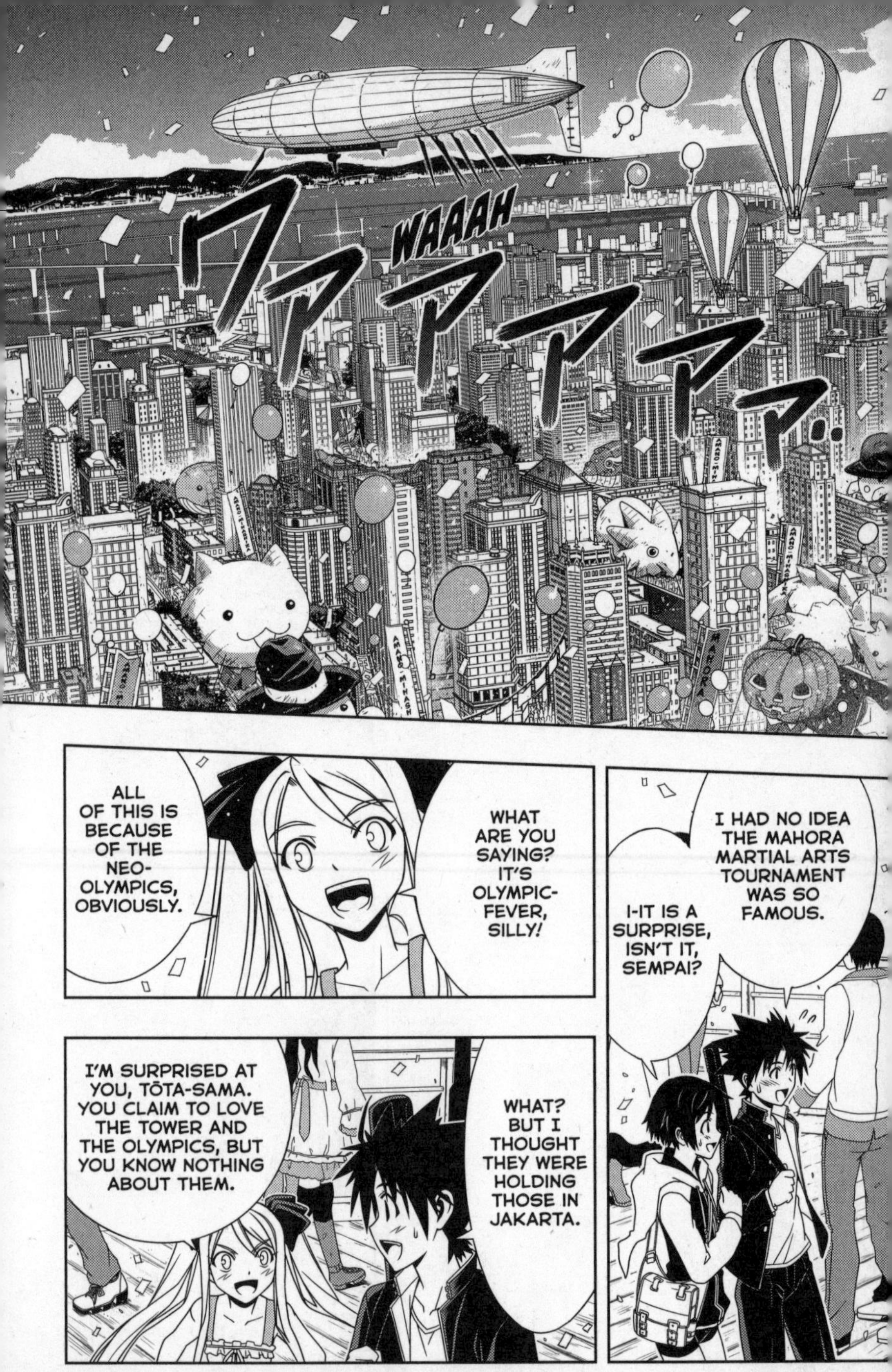
WAAAH
I HAD NO IDEA THE MAHORA MARTIAL ARTS TOURNAMENT WAS SO FAMOUS.
I-IT IS A SURPRISE, ISN'T IT, SEMPAI?
WHAT ARE YOU SAYING? IT'S OLYMPIC-FEVER, SILLY!
ALL OF THIS IS BECAUSE OF THE NEO-OLYMPICS, OBVIOUSLY.
WHAT? BUT I THOUGHT THEY WERE HOLDING THOSE IN JAKARTA.
I'M SURPRISED AT YOU, TŌTA-SAMA. YOU CLAIM TO LOVE THE TOWER AND THE OLYMPICS, BUT YOU KNOW NOTHING ABOUT THEM.

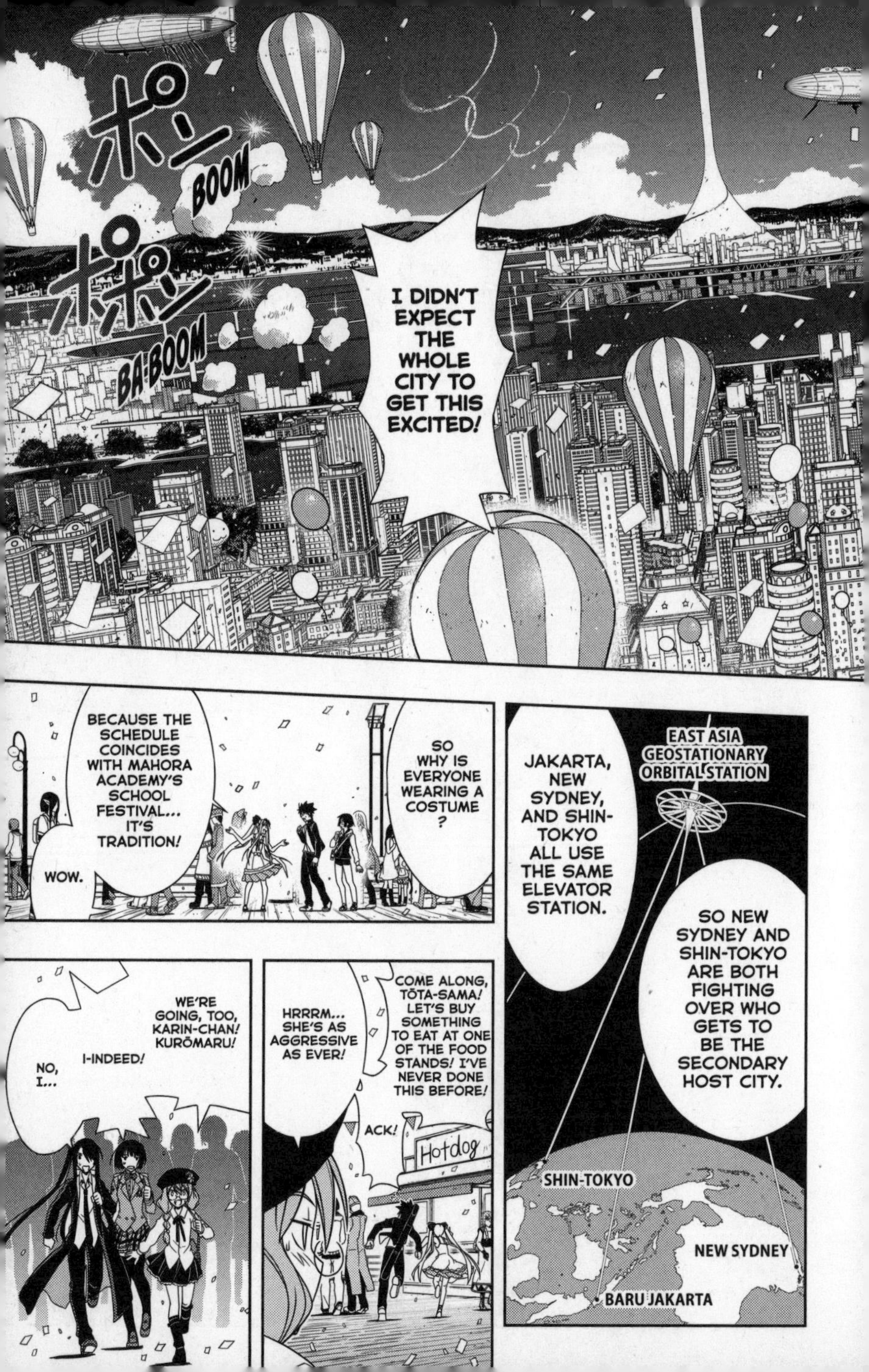
ポン
BOOM
ポポン
BA-BOOM
I DIDN'T EXPECT THE WHOLE CITY TO GET THIS EXCITED!
EAST ASIA GEOSTATIONARY ORBITAL STATION
JAKARTA, NEW SYDNEY, AND SHIN-TOKYO ALL USE THE SAME ELEVATOR STATION.
SO NEW SYDNEY AND SHIN-TOKYO ARE BOTH FIGHTING OVER WHO GETS TO BE THE SECONDARY HOST CITY.
SHIN-TOKYO
NEW SYDNEY
BARU JAKARTA
SO WHY IS EVERYONE WEARING A COSTUME?
BECAUSE THE SCHEDULE COINCIDES WITH MAHORA ACADEMY'S SCHOOL FESTIVAL... IT'S TRADITION!
WOW.
COME ALONG, TŌTA-SAMA! LET'S BUY SOMETHING TO EAT AT ONE OF THE FOOD STANDS! I'VE NEVER DONE THIS BEFORE!
HRRRM... SHE'S AS AGGRESSIVE AS EVER!
ACK!
Hotdog
WE'RE GOING, TOO, KARIN-CHAN! KURŌMARU!
I-INDEED!
NO, I...

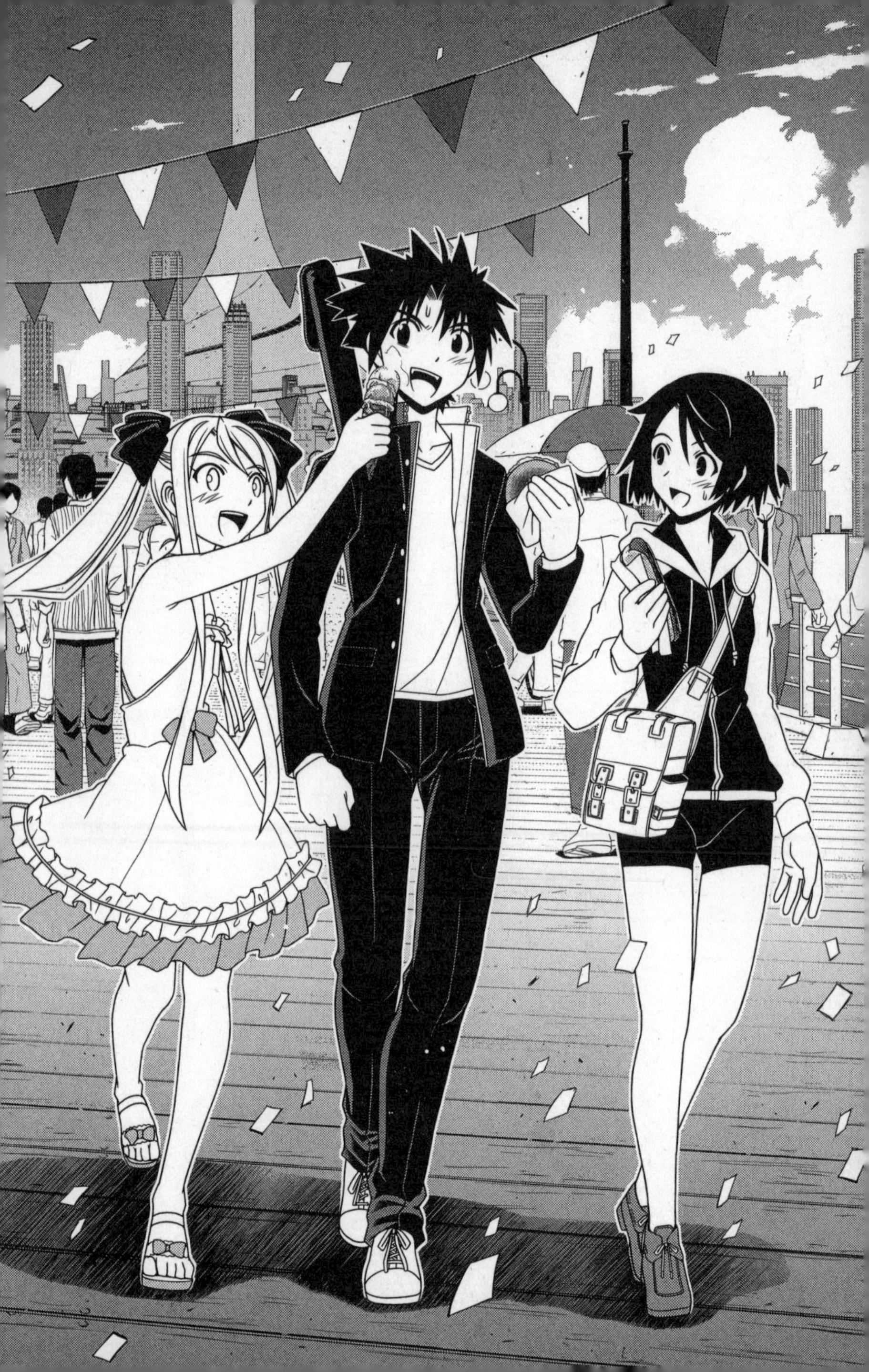

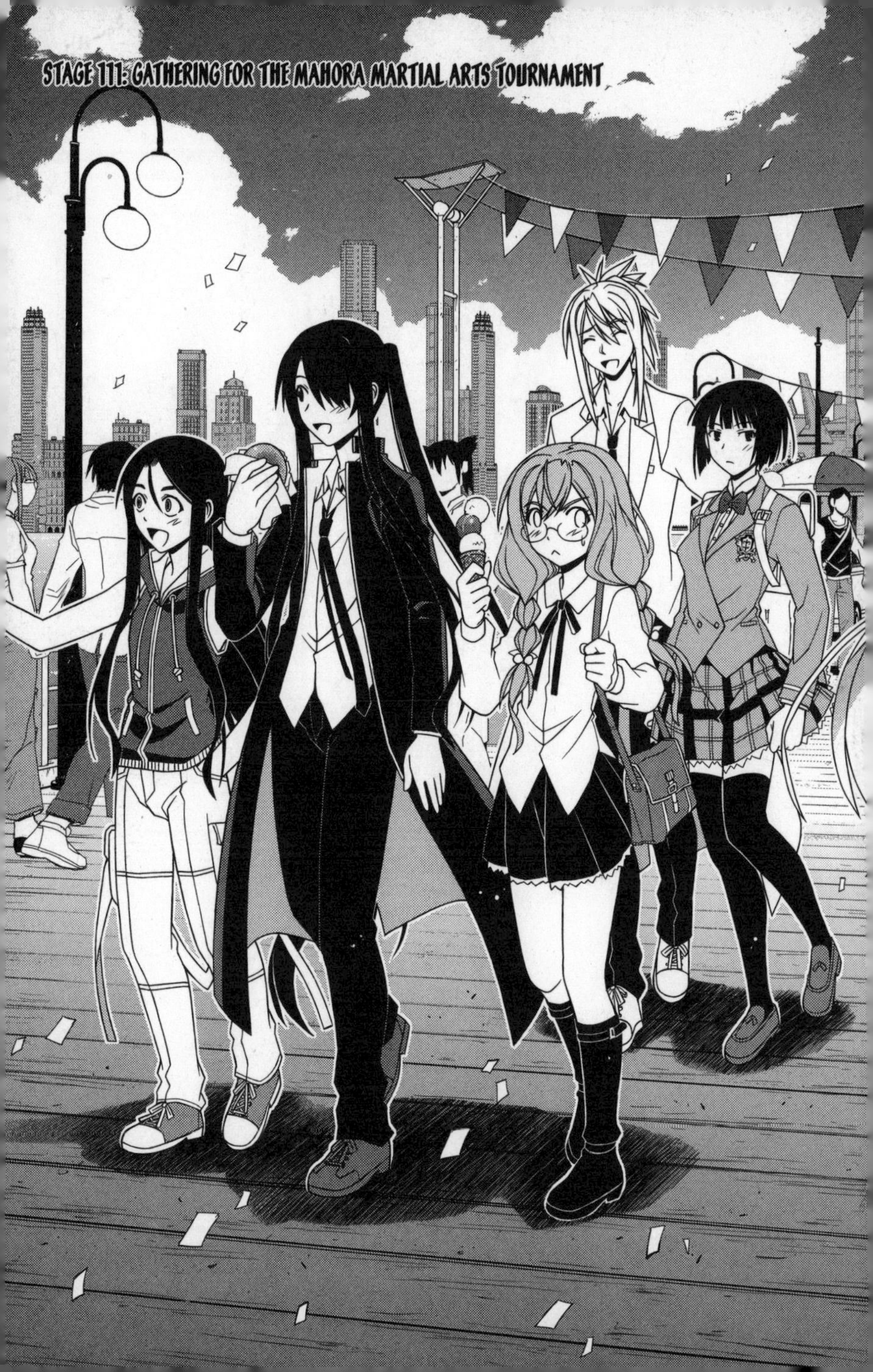
STAGE 111: GATHERING FOR THE MAHORA MARTIAL ARTS TOURNAMENT

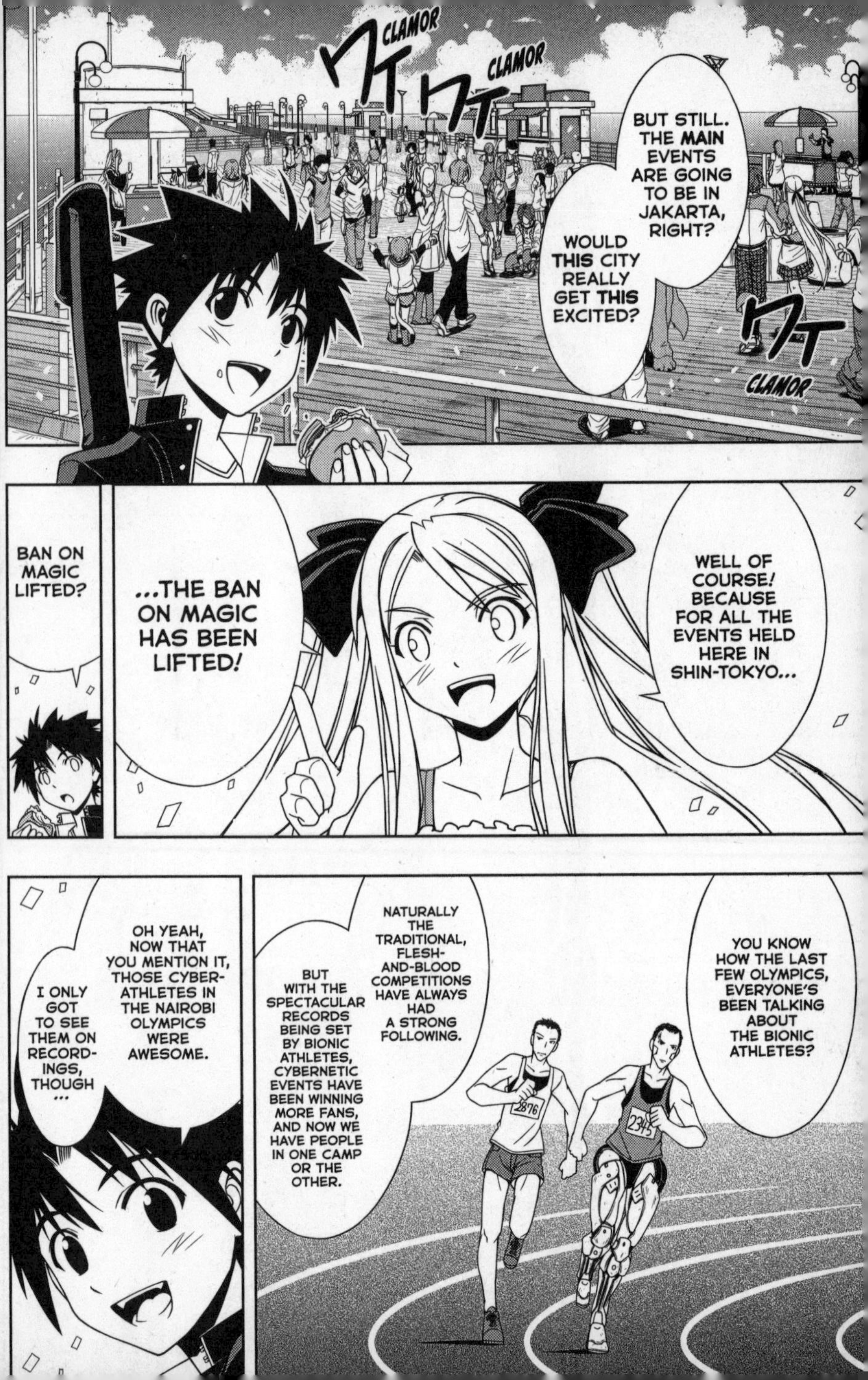
CLAMOR
CLAMOR
CLAMOR
BUT STILL. THE MAIN EVENTS ARE GOING TO BE IN JAKARTA, RIGHT?
WOULD THIS CITY REALLY GET THIS EXCITED?
WELL OF COURSE! BECAUSE FOR ALL THE EVENTS HELD HERE IN SHIN-TOKYO...
...THE BAN ON MAGIC HAS BEEN LIFTED!
BAN ON MAGIC LIFTED?
YOU KNOW HOW THE LAST FEW OLYMPICS, EVERYONE'S BEEN TALKING ABOUT THE BIONIC ATHLETES?
NATURALLY THE TRADITIONAL, FLESH-AND-BLOOD COMPETITIONS HAVE ALWAYS HAD A STRONG FOLLOWING.
BUT WITH THE SPECTACULAR RECORDS BEING SET BY BIONIC ATHLETES, CYBERNETIC EVENTS HAVE BEEN WINNING MORE FANS, AND NOW WE HAVE PEOPLE IN ONE CAMP OR THE OTHER.
2345
2876
OH YEAH, NOW THAT YOU MENTION IT, THOSE CYBER-ATHLETES IN THE NAIROBI OLYMPICS WERE AWESOME.
I ONLY GOT TO SEE THEM ON RECORD-INGS, THOUGH...

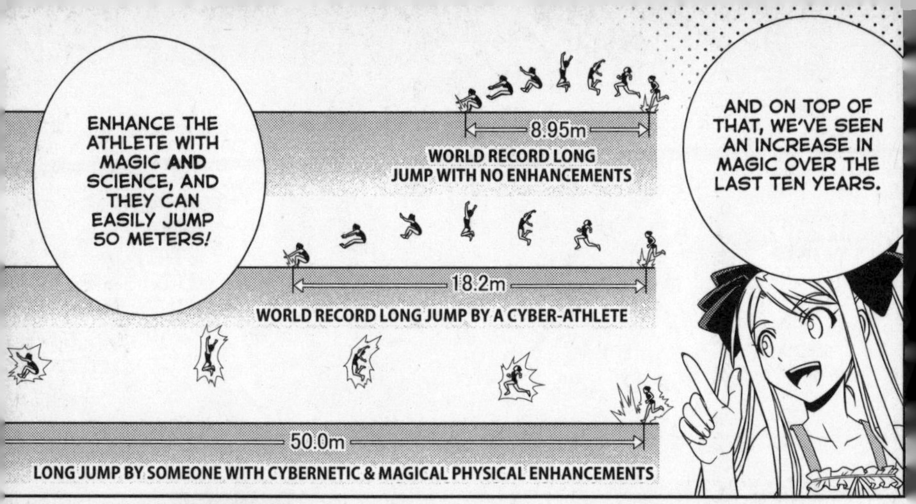
AND ON TOP OF THAT, WE'VE SEEN AN INCREASE IN MAGIC OVER THE LAST TEN YEARS.
ENHANCE THE ATHLETE WITH MAGIC AND SCIENCE, AND THEY CAN EASILY JUMP 50 METERS!
8.95m
WORLD RECORD LONG JUMP WITH NO ENHANCEMENTS
18.2m
WORLD RECORD LONG JUMP BY A CYBER-ATHLETE
50.0m
LONG JUMP BY SOMEONE WITH CYBERNETIC & MAGICAL PHYSICAL ENHANCEMENTS

Note: 8.95 m is 29.3 ft, 18.2 m is 59.7 ft, and 50 m is 164 ft.

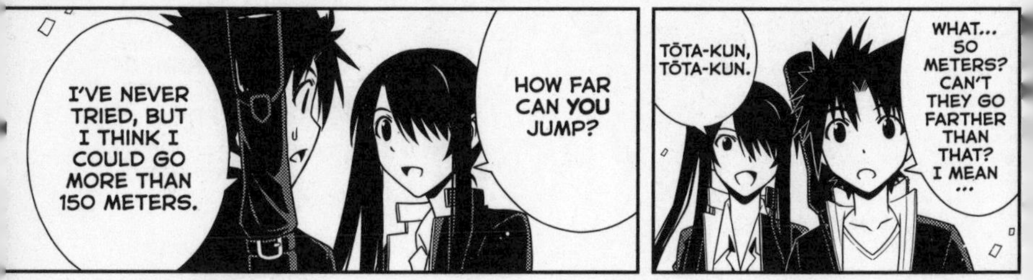
WHAT... 50 METERS? CAN'T THEY GO FARTHER THAN THAT? I MEAN ...
TŌTA-KUN, TŌTA-KUN.
HOW FAR CAN YOU JUMP?
I'VE NEVER TRIED, BUT I THINK I COULD GO MORE THAN 150 METERS.

Note: 150 m is 492 ft, and 1,500 m is 4,921.3 ft.

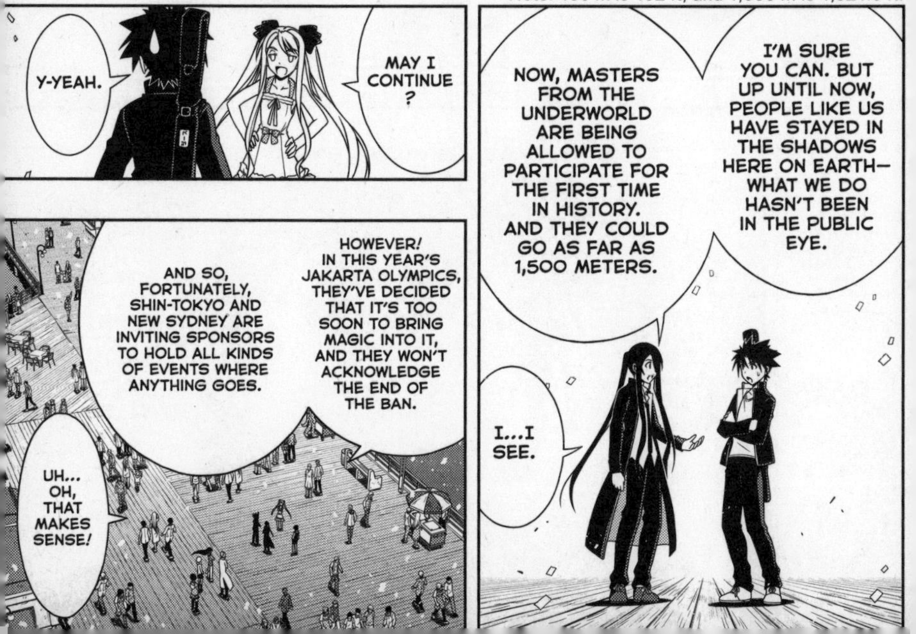
I'M SURE YOU CAN. BUT UP UNTIL NOW, PEOPLE LIKE US HAVE STAYED IN THE SHADOWS HERE ON EARTH—WHAT WE DO HASN'T BEEN IN THE PUBLIC EYE.
NOW, MASTERS FROM THE UNDERWORLD ARE BEING ALLOWED TO PARTICIPATE FOR THE FIRST TIME IN HISTORY. AND THEY COULD GO AS FAR AS 1,500 METERS.
I...I SEE.
MAY I CONTINUE ?
Y-YEAH.
HOWEVER! IN THIS YEAR'S JAKARTA OLYMPICS, THEY'VE DECIDED THAT IT'S TOO SOON TO BRING MAGIC INTO IT, AND THEY WON'T ACKNOWLEDGE THE END OF THE BAN.
AND SO, FORTUNATELY, SHIN-TOKYO AND NEW SYDNEY ARE INVITING SPONSORS TO HOLD ALL KINDS OF EVENTS WHERE ANYTHING GOES.
UH... OH, THAT MAKES SENSE!

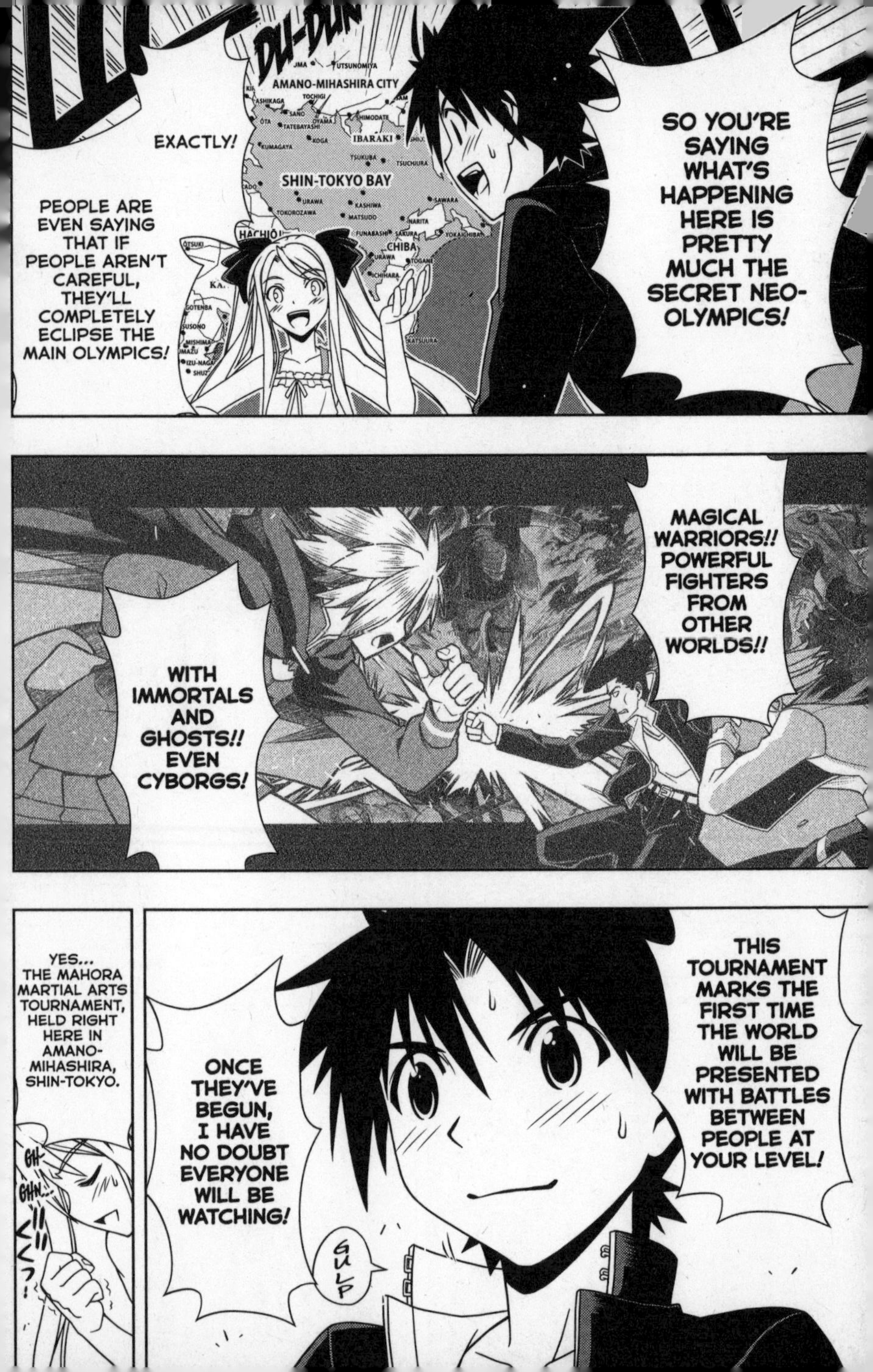
DU-DUN
JMA
UTSUNOMIYA
AMANO-MIHASHIRA CITY
ASHIKAGA
TOCHIGI
SANO
OYAMA
SHIMODATE
ŌTA
TATEBAYASHI
KOGA
IBARAKI
KUMAGAYA
TSUKUBA
TSUCHIURA
SHIN-TOKYO BAY
URAWA
KASHIWA
SAWARA
TOKOROZAWA
MATSUDO
NARITA
FUNABASHI
SAKURA
YOKAICHIBA
CHIBA
TOGANE
ICHIHARA
OTSUKI
GOTENBA
SUSONO
MISHIMA
KATSUURA
SO YOU'RE SAYING WHAT'S HAPPENING HERE IS PRETTY MUCH THE SECRET NEO-OLYMPICS!
EXACTLY!
PEOPLE ARE EVEN SAYING THAT IF PEOPLE AREN'T CAREFUL, THEY'LL COMPLETELY ECLIPSE THE MAIN OLYMPICS!
MAGICAL WARRIORS!! POWERFUL FIGHTERS FROM OTHER WORLDS!!
WITH IMMORTALS AND GHOSTS!! EVEN CYBORGS!
THIS TOURNAMENT MARKS THE FIRST TIME THE WORLD WILL BE PRESENTED WITH BATTLES BETWEEN PEOPLE AT YOUR LEVEL!
ONCE THEY'VE BEGUN, I HAVE NO DOUBT EVERYONE WILL BE WATCHING!
GULP
YES... THE MAHORA MARTIAL ARTS TOURNAMENT, HELD RIGHT HERE IN AMANO-MIHASHIRA, SHIN-TOKYO.
GH-GHN...

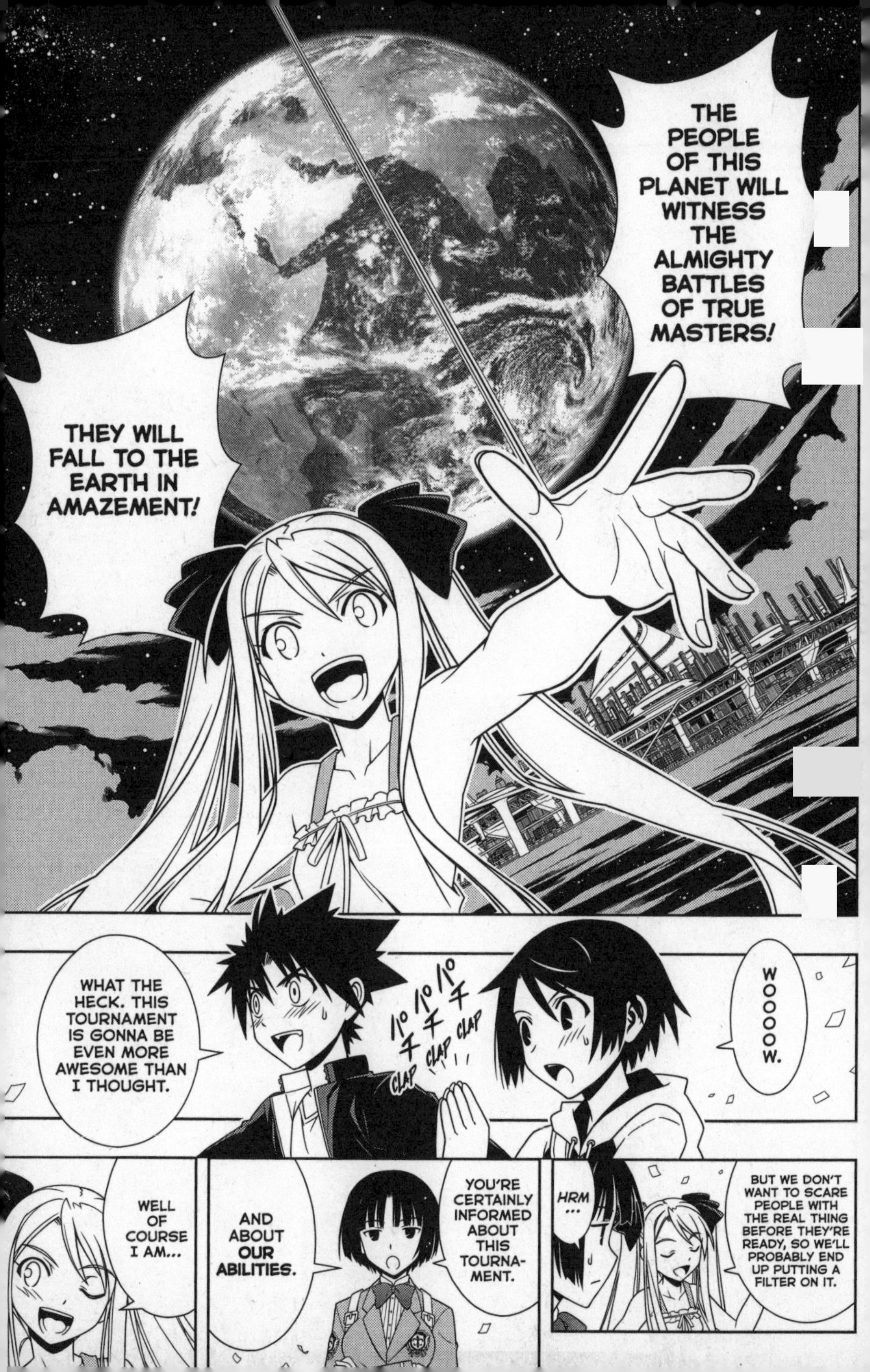
THE PEOPLE OF THIS PLANET WILL WITNESS THE ALMIGHTY BATTLES OF TRUE MASTERS!
THEY WILL FALL TO THE EARTH IN AMAZEMENT!
WOOOOOW.
パチパチパチ
CLAP CLAP CLAP CLAP
WHAT THE HECK. THIS TOURNAMENT IS GONNA BE EVEN MORE AWESOME THAN I THOUGHT.
BUT WE DON'T WANT TO SCARE PEOPLE WITH THE REAL THING BEFORE THEY'RE READY, SO WE'LL PROBABLY END UP PUTTING A FILTER ON IT.
HRM...
YOU'RE CERTAINLY INFORMED ABOUT THIS TOURNAMENT.
AND ABOUT OUR ABILITIES.
WELL OF COURSE I AM...

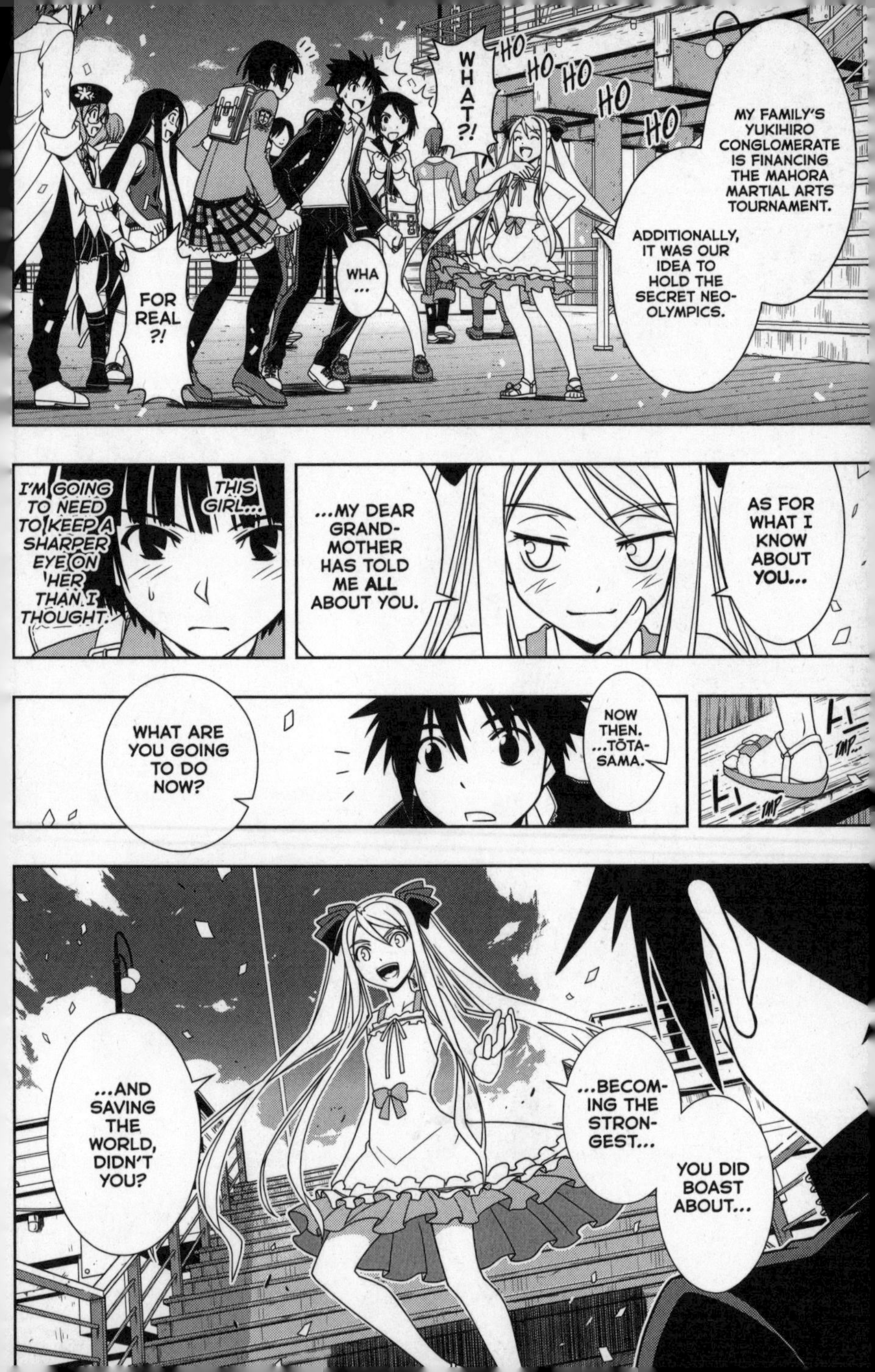
MY FAMILY'S YUKIHIRO CONGLOMERATE IS FINANCING THE MAHORA MARTIAL ARTS TOURNAMENT.
ADDITIONALLY, IT WAS OUR IDEA TO HOLD THE SECRET NEO-OLYMPICS.
HO HO HO HO HO
WHAT?!
WHA...
FOR REAL?!
AS FOR WHAT I KNOW ABOUT YOU...
...MY DEAR GRANDMOTHER HAS TOLD ME ALL ABOUT YOU.
THIS GIRL...
I'M GOING TO NEED TO KEEP A SHARPER EYE ON HER THAN I THOUGHT.
TMP... TMP
NOW THEN. ...TŌTA-SAMA.
WHAT ARE YOU GOING TO DO NOW?
YOU DID BOAST ABOUT...
...BECOMING THE STRONGEST...
...AND SAVING THE WORLD, DIDN'T YOU?

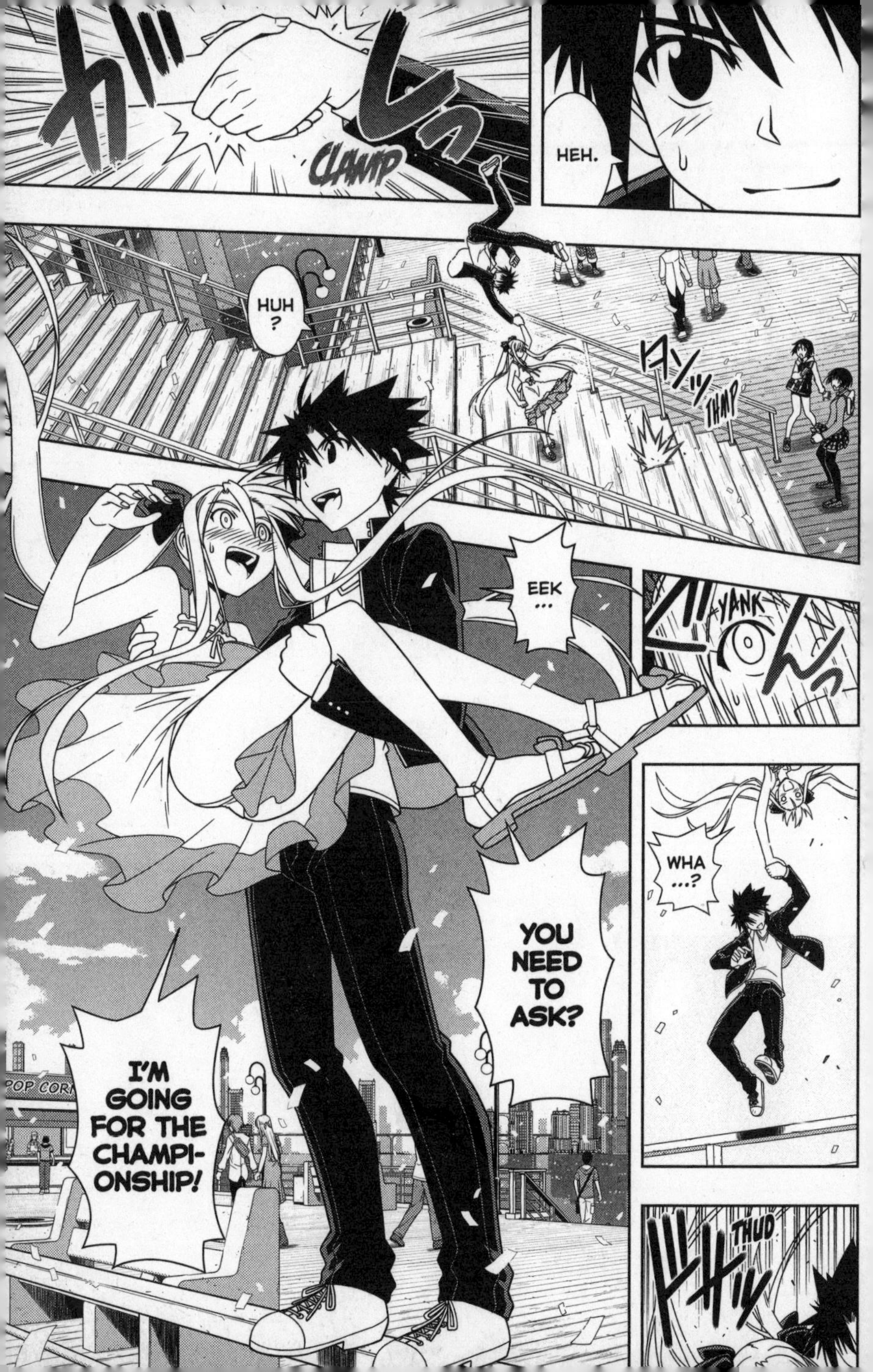
HEH.
CLAMP
HUH?
THMP
YANK
WHA...?
THUD
EEK...
YOU NEED TO ASK?
I'M GOING FOR THE CHAMPIONSHIP!
POP CORN

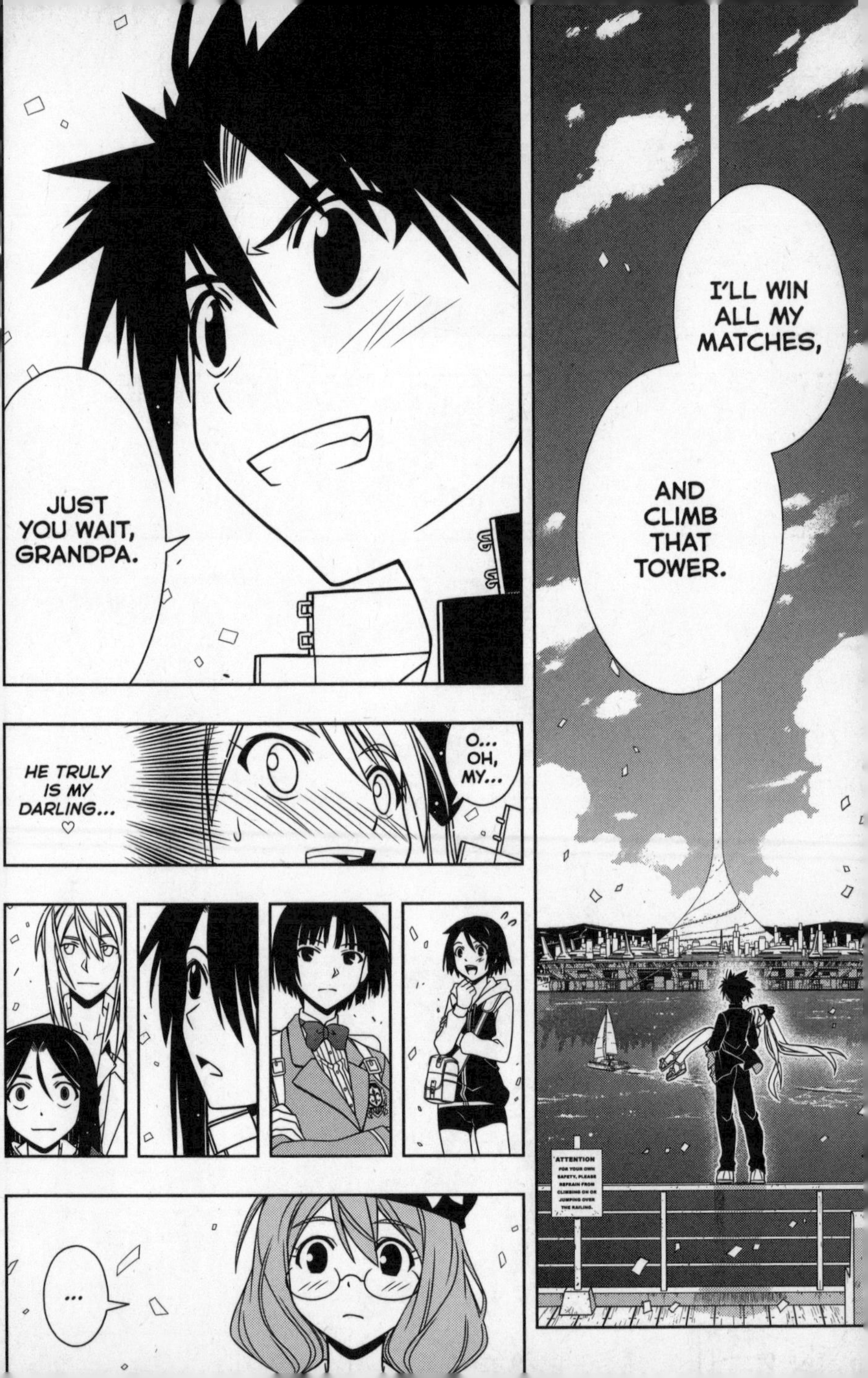
I'LL WIN ALL MY MATCHES,
AND CLIMB THAT TOWER.
ATTENTION
FOR YOUR OWN SAFETY, PLEASE REFRAIN FROM CLIMBING ON OR JUMPING OVER THE RAILING.
JUST YOU WAIT, GRANDPA.
O... OH, MY...
HE TRULY IS MY DARLING... ♡
...

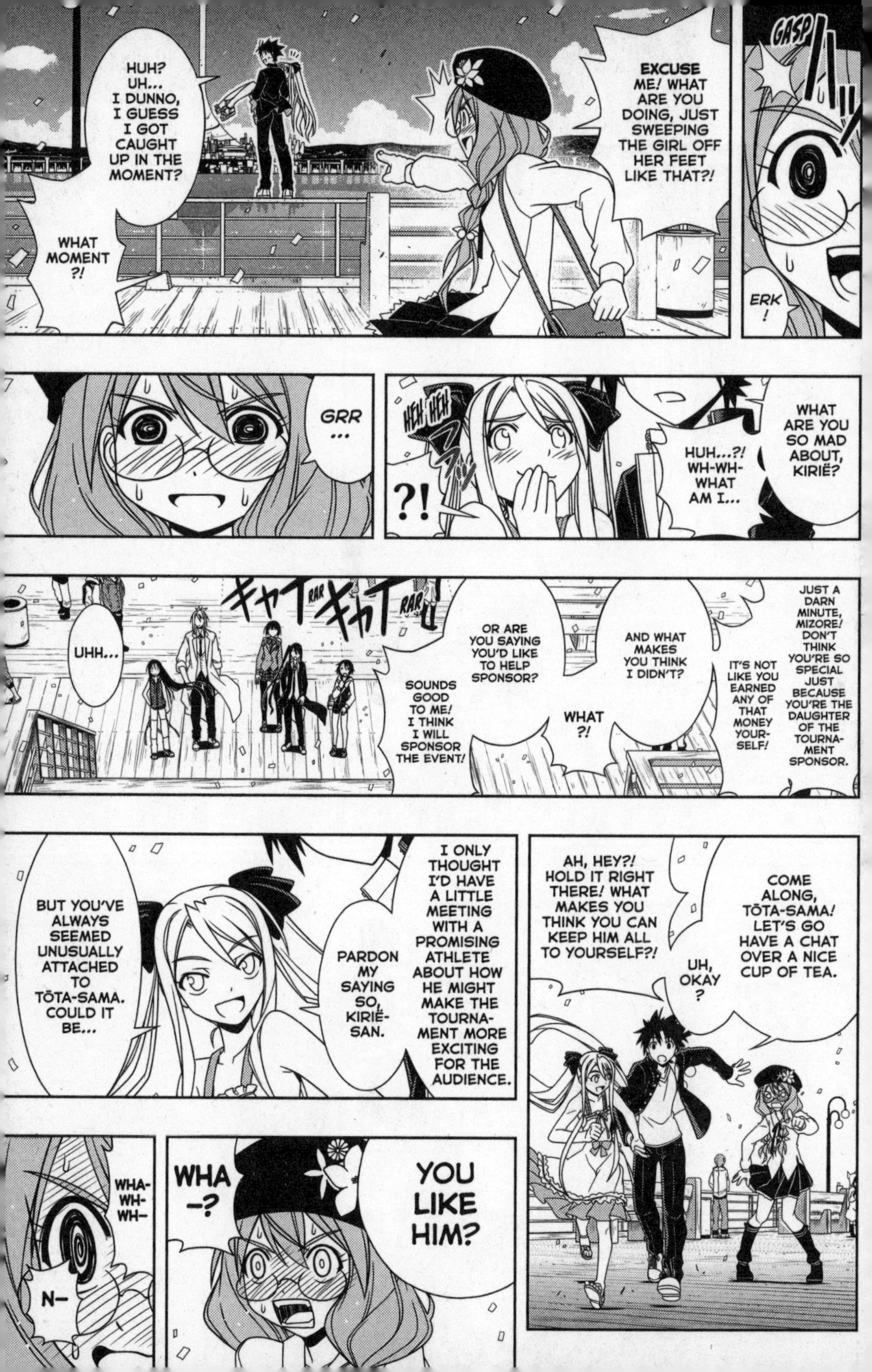
GASP
ERK!
EXCUSE ME! WHAT ARE YOU DOING, JUST SWEEPING THE GIRL OFF HER FEET LIKE THAT?!
HUH? UH... I DUNNO, I GUESS I GOT CAUGHT UP IN THE MOMENT?
WHAT MOMENT ?!
WHAT ARE YOU SO MAD ABOUT, KIRIË?
HUH...?! WH-WH-WHAT AM I...
HCH HCH
?!
GRR ...
JUST A DARN MINUTE, MIZORE! DON'T THINK YOU'RE SO SPECIAL JUST BECAUSE YOU'RE THE DAUGHTER OF THE TOURNA-MENT SPONSOR.
IT'S NOT LIKE YOU EARNED ANY OF THAT MONEY YOUR-SELF!
AND WHAT MAKES YOU THINK I DIDN'T?
WHAT ?!
OR ARE YOU SAYING YOU'D LIKE TO HELP SPONSOR?
SOUNDS GOOD TO ME! I THINK I WILL SPONSOR THE EVENT!
キャイ RAR キャイ RAR
UHH...
COME ALONG, TŌTA-SAMA! LET'S GO HAVE A CHAT OVER A NICE CUP OF TEA.
AH, HEY?! HOLD IT RIGHT THERE! WHAT MAKES YOU THINK YOU CAN KEEP HIM ALL TO YOURSELF?!
UH, OKAY ?
I ONLY THOUGHT I'D HAVE A LITTLE MEETING WITH A PROMISING ATHLETE ABOUT HOW HE MIGHT MAKE THE TOURNA-MENT MORE EXCITING FOR THE AUDIENCE.
PARDON MY SAYING SO, KIRIË-SAN.
BUT YOU'VE ALWAYS SEEMED UNUSUALLY ATTACHED TO TŌTA-SAMA. COULD IT BE...
YOU LIKE HIM?
WHA -?
WHA-WH-WH-
N-

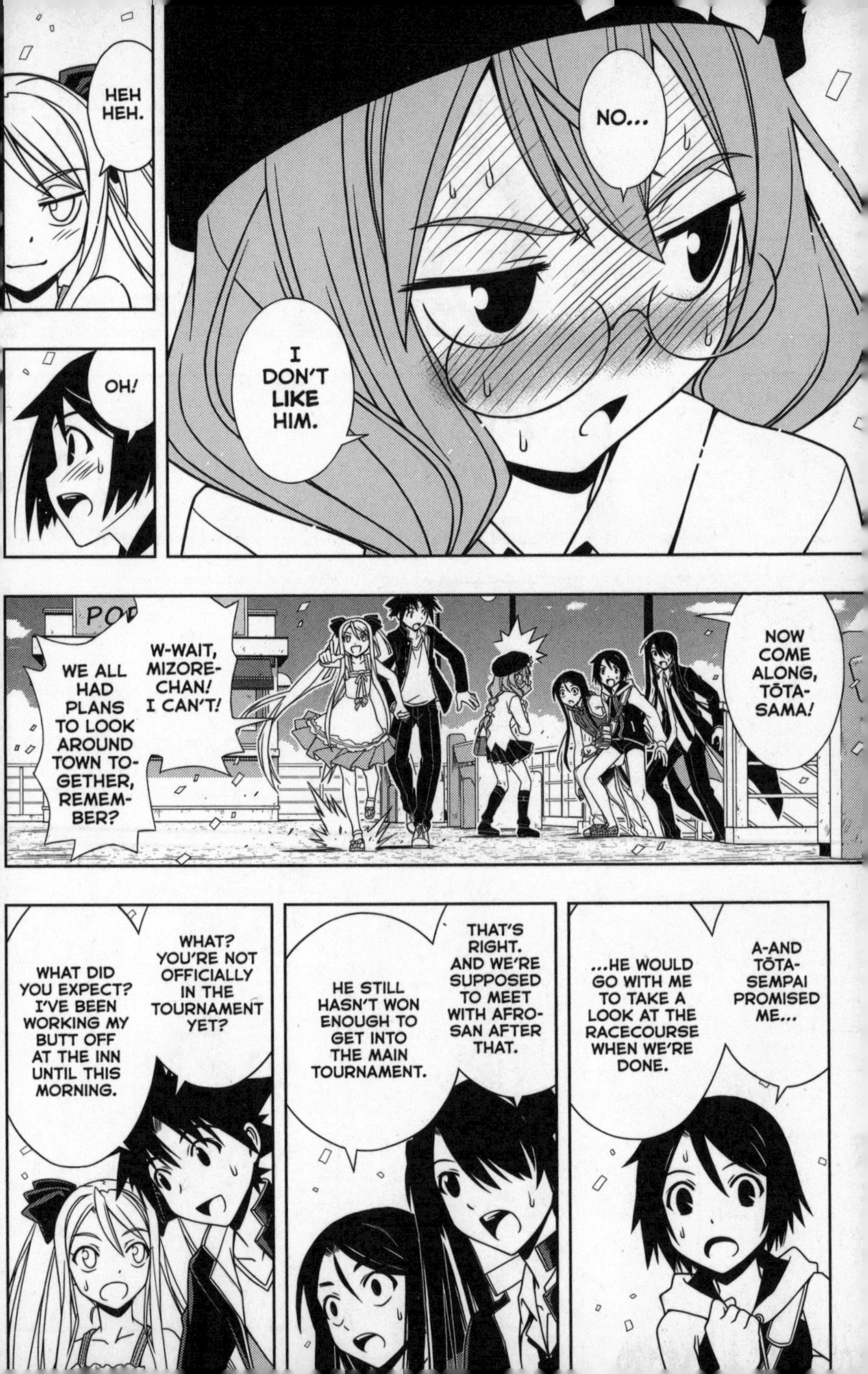
NO...
I DON'T LIKE HIM.
HEH HEH.
OH!
NOW COME ALONG, TŌTA-SAMA!
W-WAIT, MIZORE-CHAN! I CAN'T!
WE ALL HAD PLANS TO LOOK AROUND TOWN TO-GETHER, REMEMBER?
A-AND TŌTA-SEMPAI PROMISED ME...
...HE WOULD GO WITH ME TO TAKE A LOOK AT THE RACECOURSE WHEN WE'RE DONE.
THAT'S RIGHT. AND WE'RE SUPPOSED TO MEET WITH AFRO-SAN AFTER THAT.
HE STILL HASN'T WON ENOUGH TO GET INTO THE MAIN TOURNAMENT.
WHAT? YOU'RE NOT OFFICIALLY IN THE TOURNAMENT YET?
WHAT DID YOU EXPECT? I'VE BEEN WORKING MY BUTT OFF AT THE INN UNTIL THIS MORNING.

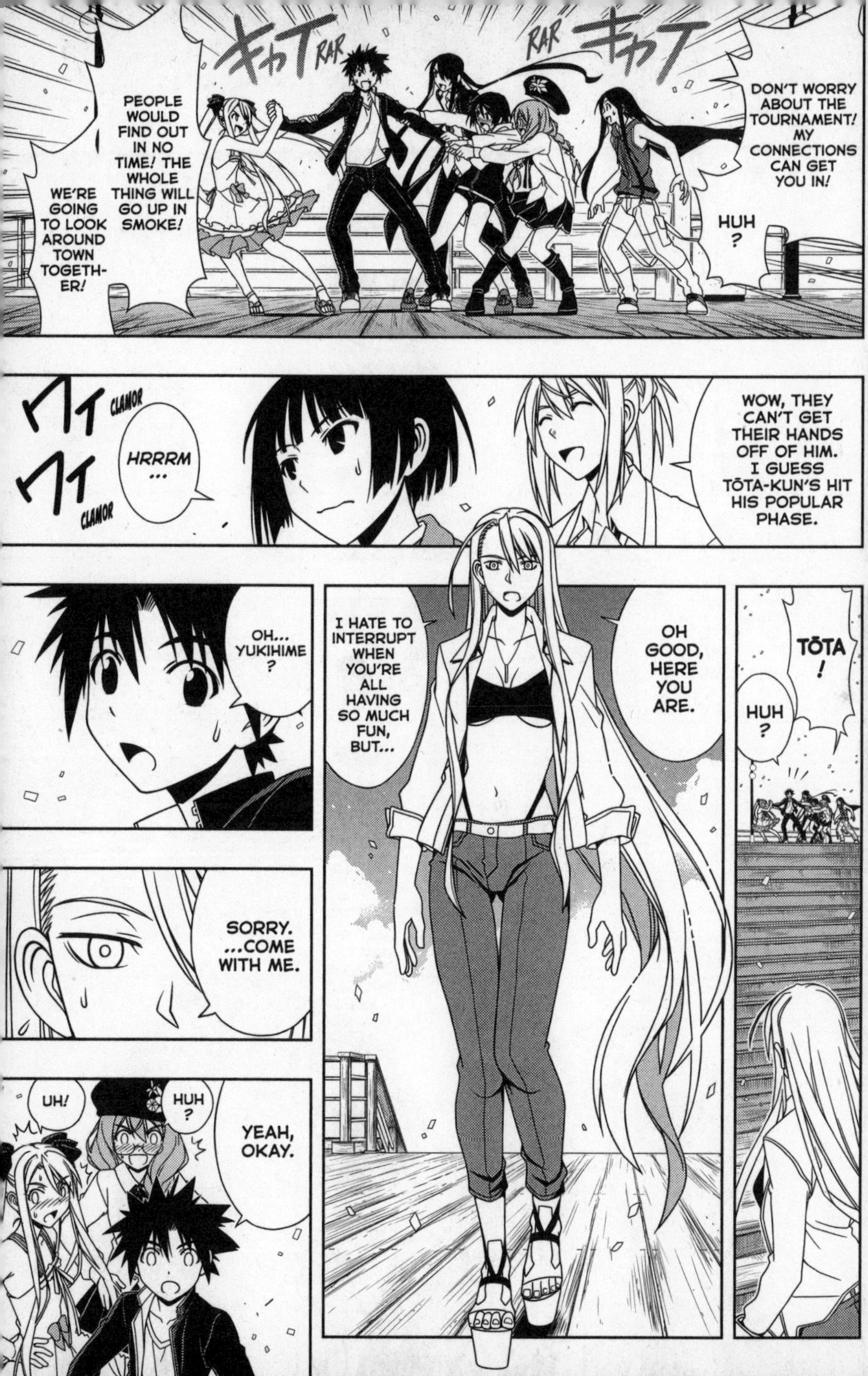
RAR キャア
キャア RAR
DON'T WORRY ABOUT THE TOURNAMENT! MY CONNECTIONS CAN GET YOU IN!
HUH?
PEOPLE WOULD FIND OUT IN NO TIME! THE WHOLE THING WILL GO UP IN SMOKE!
WE'RE GOING TO LOOK AROUND TOWN TOGETH-ER!
WOW, THEY CAN'T GET THEIR HANDS OFF OF HIM. I GUESS TŌTA-KUN'S HIT HIS POPULAR PHASE.
HRRRM...
ワイ CLAMOR
ワイ CLAMOR
TŌTA!
HUH?
OH GOOD, HERE YOU ARE.
I HATE TO INTERRUPT WHEN YOU'RE ALL HAVING SO MUCH FUN, BUT...
OH... YUKIHIME?
SORRY. ...COME WITH ME.
YEAH, OKAY.
HUH?
UH!

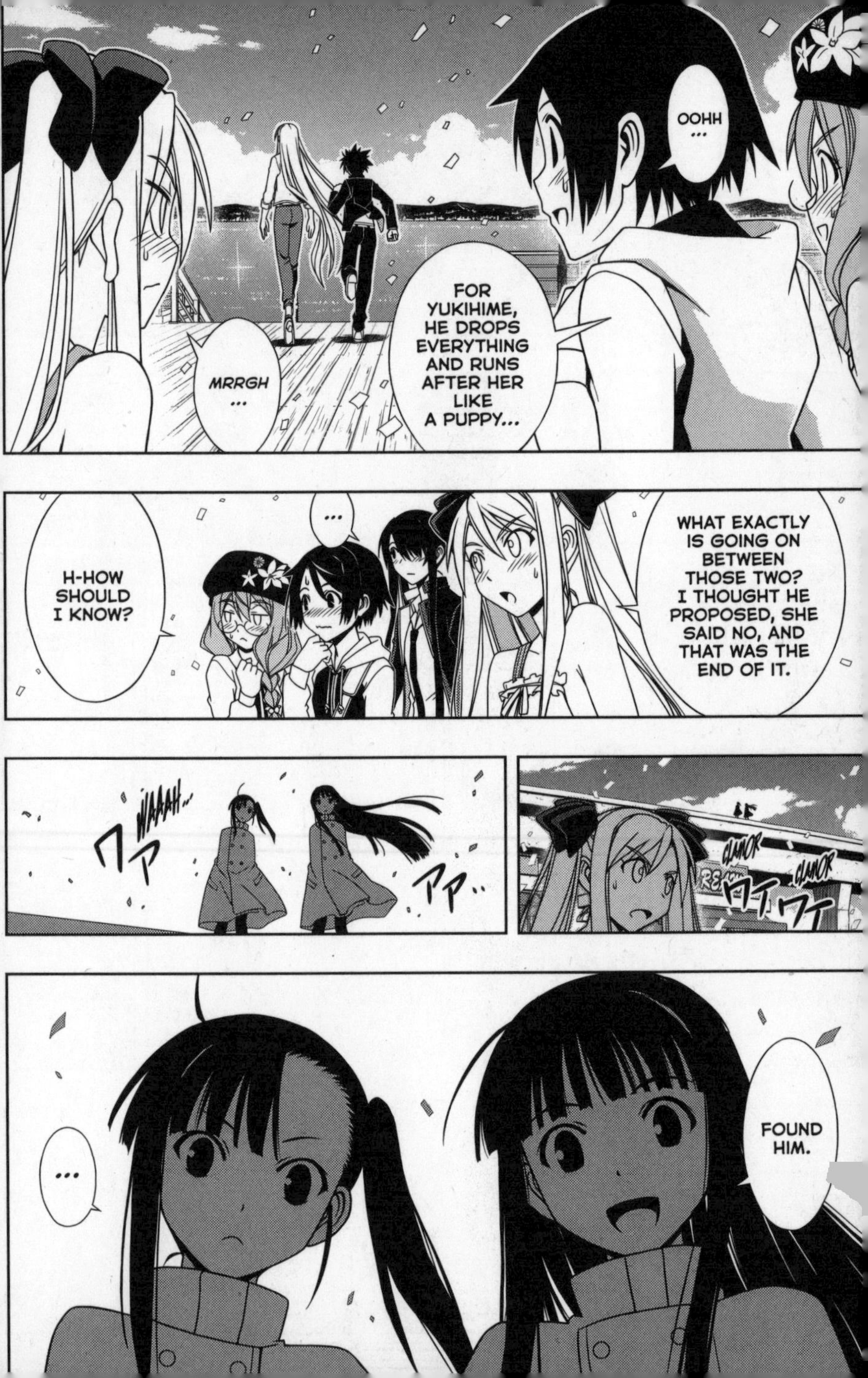
OOHH ...
FOR YUKIHIME, HE DROPS EVERYTHING AND RUNS AFTER HER LIKE A PUPPY...
MRRGH ...
WHAT EXACTLY IS GOING ON BETWEEN THOSE TWO? I THOUGHT HE PROPOSED, SHE SAID NO, AND THAT WAS THE END OF IT.
...
H-HOW SHOULD I KNOW?
CLAMOR
ワイ
CLAMOR
ワイ
WAAAH...
ワア
アア..
FOUND HIM.
...

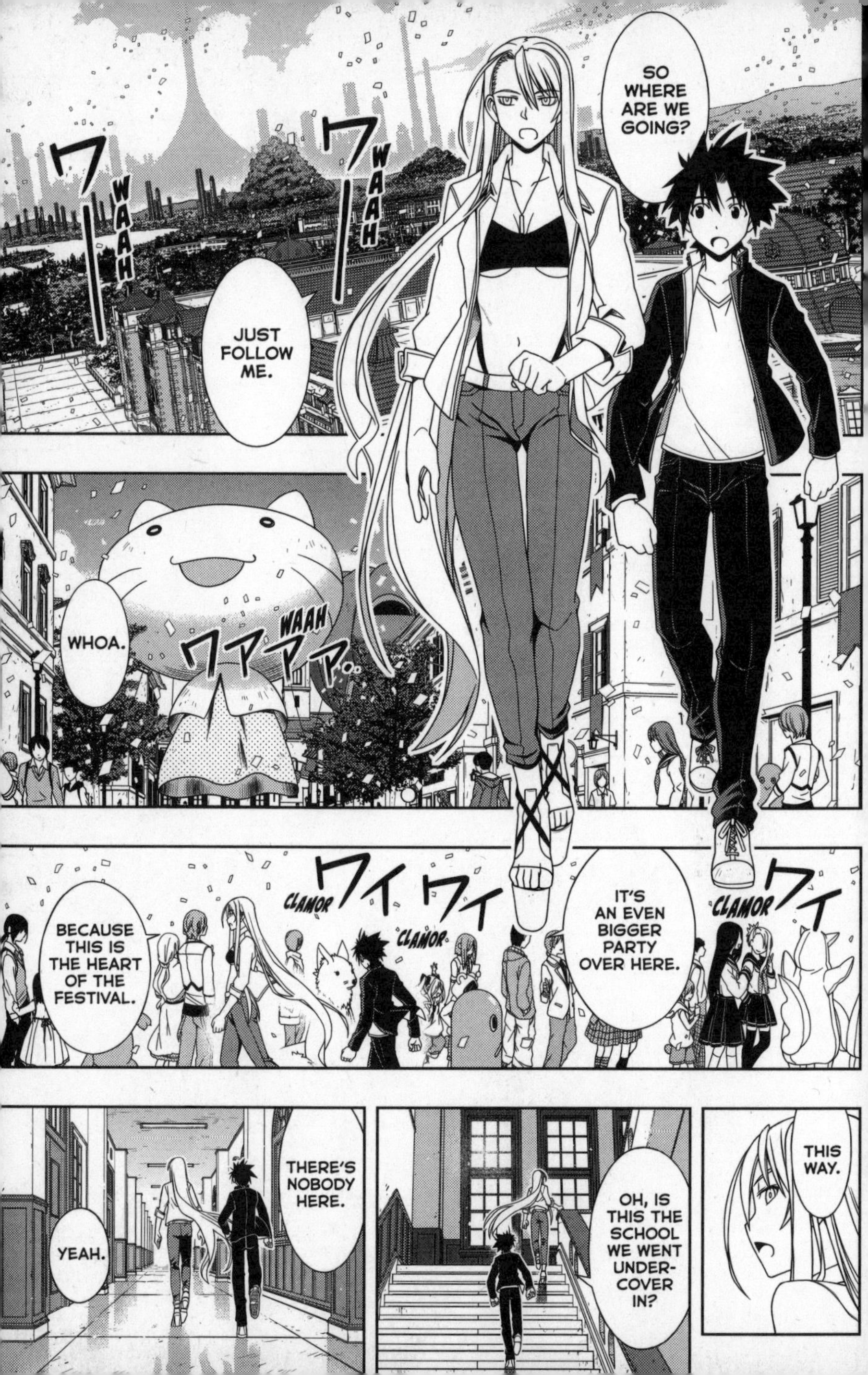
SO WHERE ARE WE GOING?
ワー
WAAH
JUST FOLLOW ME.
ワー
WAAH
WHOA.
ワアアァ
WAAH
CLAMOR
ワイ
IT'S AN EVEN BIGGER PARTY OVER HERE.
ワイワイ
CLAMOR
CLAMOR
BECAUSE THIS IS THE HEART OF THE FESTIVAL.
THIS WAY.
OH, IS THIS THE SCHOOL WE WENT UNDER-COVER IN?
THERE'S NOBODY HERE.
YEAH.

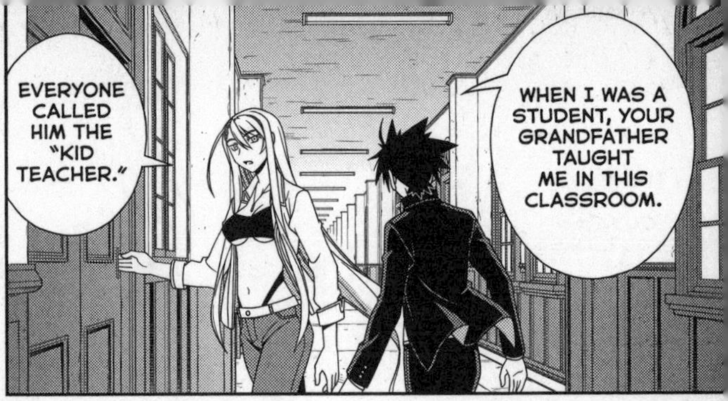
WHEN I WAS A STUDENT, YOUR GRANDFATHER TAUGHT ME IN THIS CLASSROOM.
EVERYONE CALLED HIM THE "KID TEACHER."
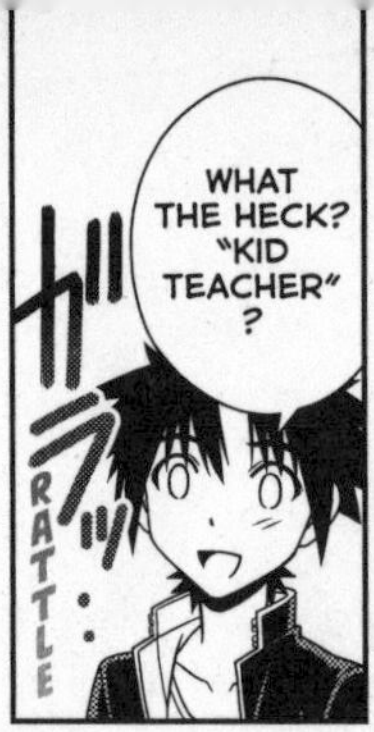
RATTLE
WHAT THE HECK? "KID TEACHER" ?
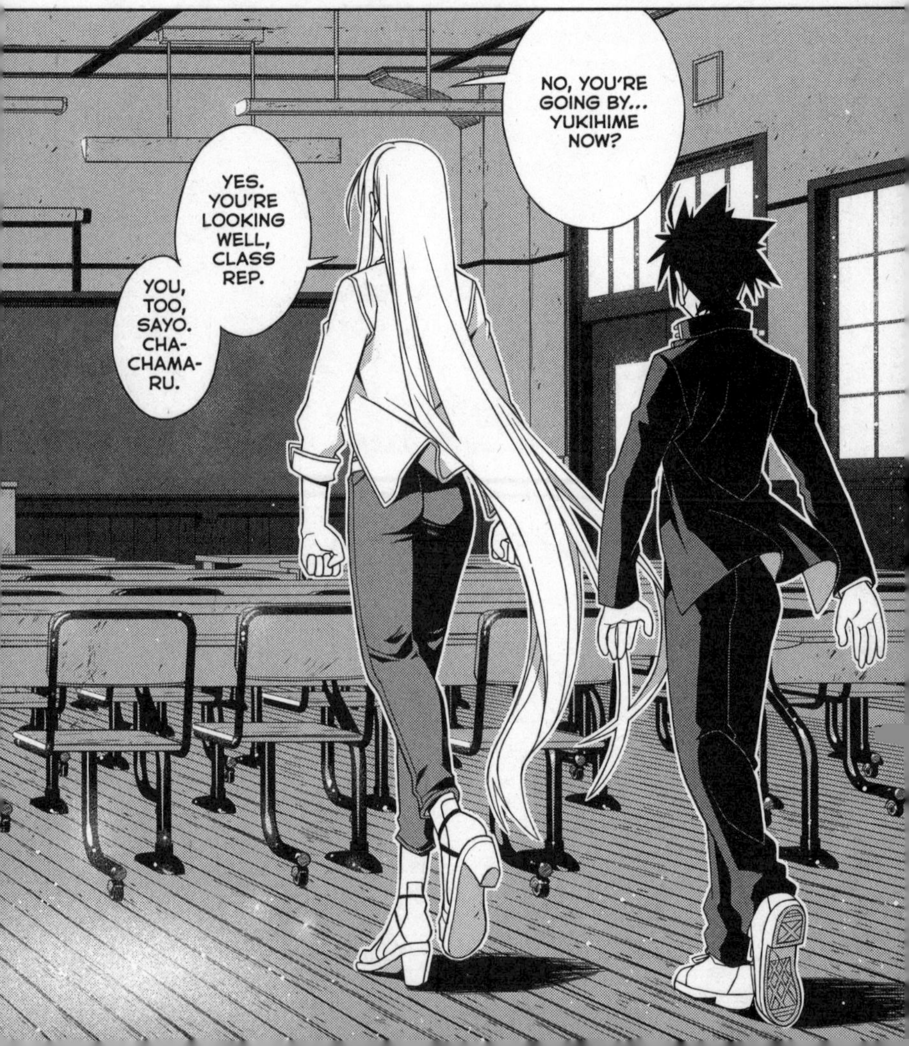
NO, YOU'RE GOING BY... YUKIHIME NOW?
YES. YOU'RE LOOKING WELL, CLASS REP.
YOU, TOO, SAYO. CHA-CHAMA-RU.

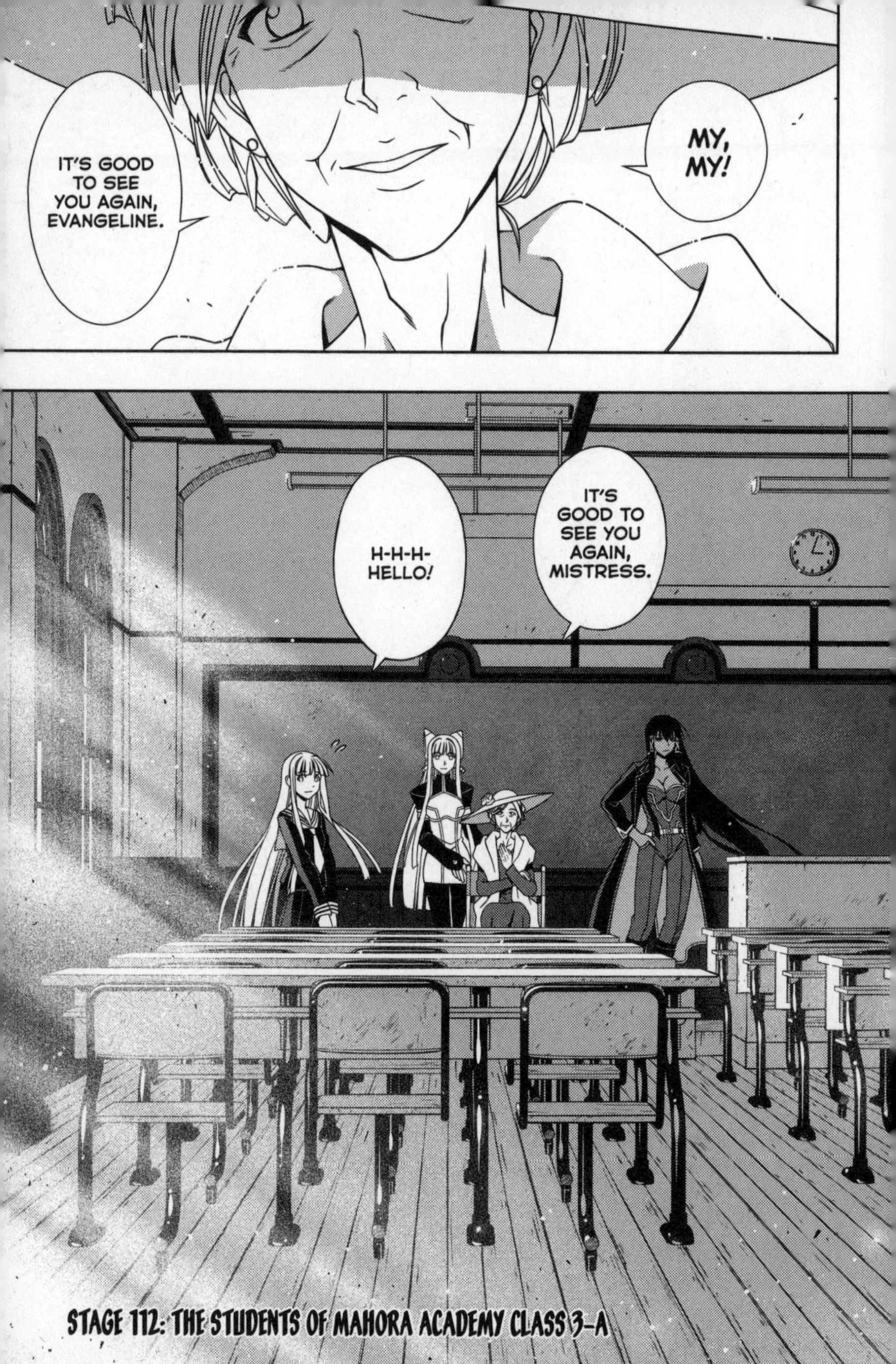
MY, MY!
IT'S GOOD TO SEE YOU AGAIN, EVANGELINE.
IT'S GOOD TO SEE YOU AGAIN, MISTRESS.
H-H-H-HELLO!
STAGE 112: THE STUDENTS OF MAHORA ACADEMY CLASS 3-A

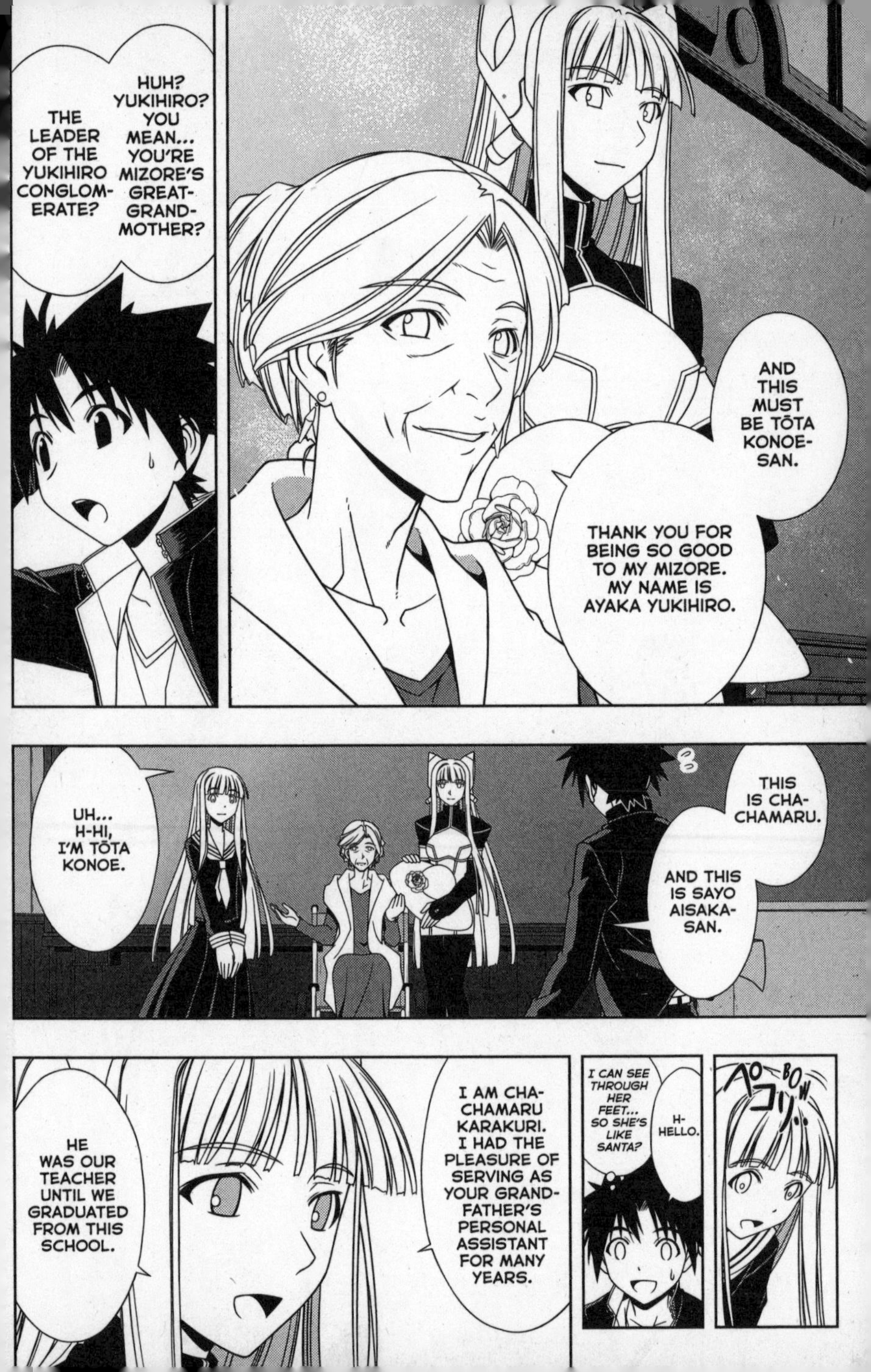
AND THIS MUST BE TŌTA KONOE-SAN.
THANK YOU FOR BEING SO GOOD TO MY MIZORE. MY NAME IS AYAKA YUKIHIRO.
HUH? YUKIHIRO? YOU MEAN... YOU'RE MIZORE'S GREAT-GRANDMOTHER?
THE LEADER OF THE YUKIHIRO CONGLOMERATE?
THIS IS CHACHAMARU.
AND THIS IS SAYO AISAKA-SAN.
UH... H-HI, I'M TŌTA KONOE.
BOW
H-HELLO.
I CAN SEE THROUGH HER FEET... SO SHE'S LIKE SANTA?
I AM CHACHAMARU KARAKURI. I HAD THE PLEASURE OF SERVING AS YOUR GRANDFATHER'S PERSONAL ASSISTANT FOR MANY YEARS.
HE WAS OUR TEACHER UNTIL WE GRADUATED FROM THIS SCHOOL.

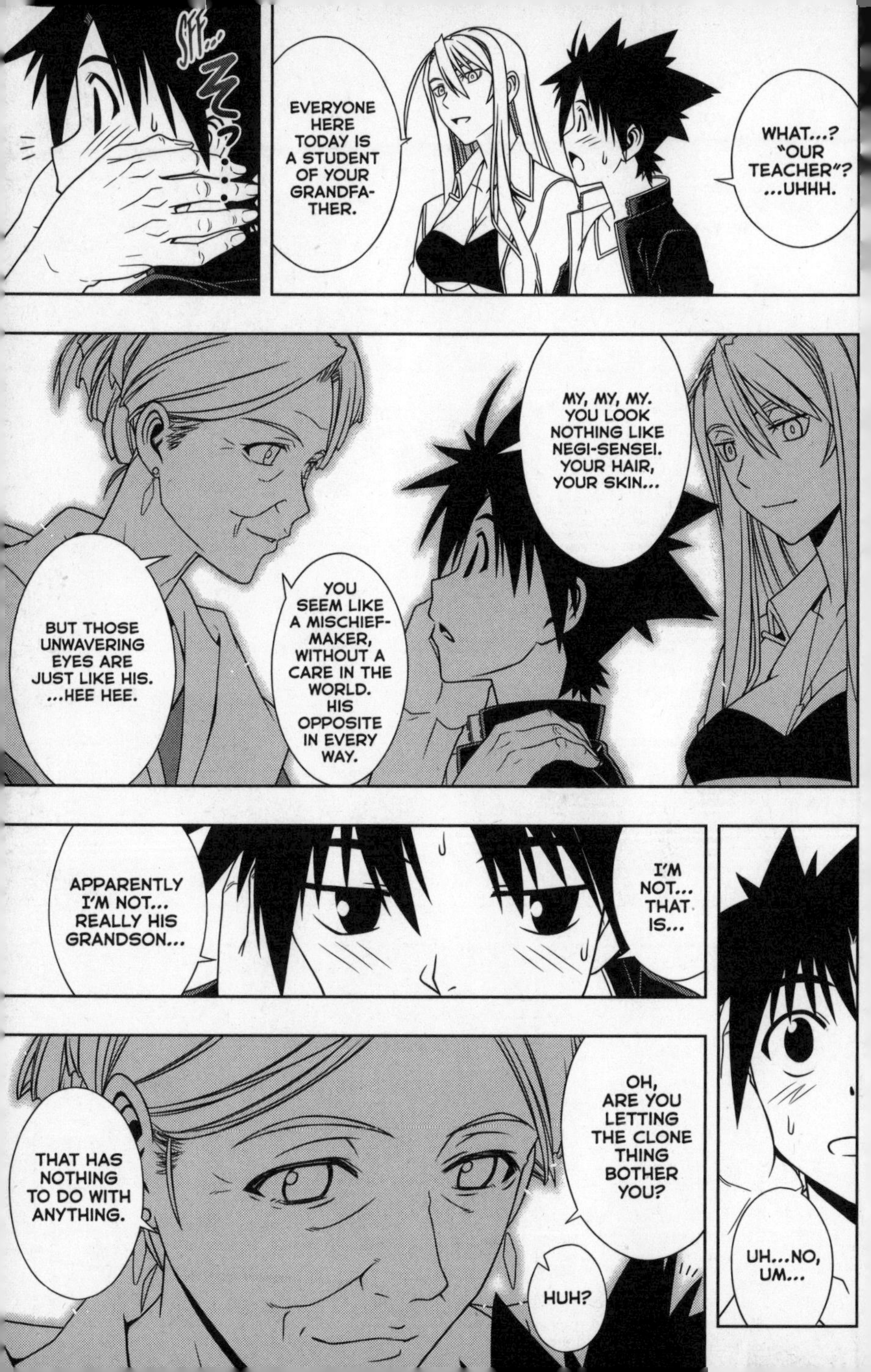
WHAT...? "OUR TEACHER"? ...UHHH.
EVERYONE HERE TODAY IS A STUDENT OF YOUR GRANDFATHER.
MY, MY, MY. YOU LOOK NOTHING LIKE NEGI-SENSEI. YOUR HAIR, YOUR SKIN...
YOU SEEM LIKE A MISCHIEF-MAKER, WITHOUT A CARE IN THE WORLD. HIS OPPOSITE IN EVERY WAY.
BUT THOSE UNWAVERING EYES ARE JUST LIKE HIS. ...HEE HEE.
UH...NO, UM...
I'M NOT... THAT IS...
APPARENTLY I'M NOT... REALLY HIS GRANDSON...
OH, ARE YOU LETTING THE CLONE THING BOTHER YOU?
HUH?
THAT HAS NOTHING TO DO WITH ANYTHING.

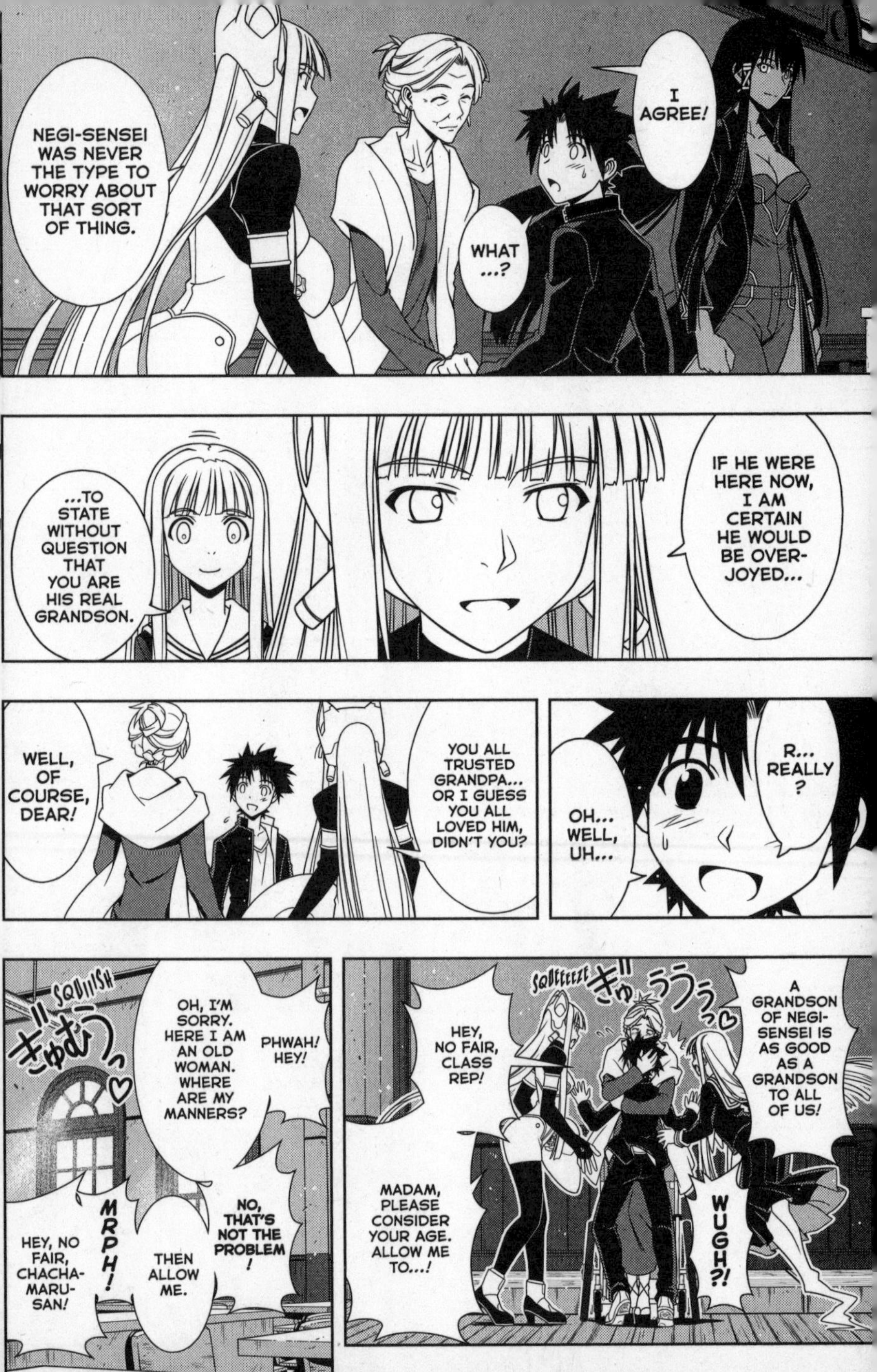
I AGREE!
WHAT...?
NEGI-SENSEI WAS NEVER THE TYPE TO WORRY ABOUT THAT SORT OF THING.
IF HE WERE HERE NOW, I AM CERTAIN HE WOULD BE OVER-JOYED...
...TO STATE WITHOUT QUESTION THAT YOU ARE HIS REAL GRANDSON.
R... REALLY?
OH... WELL, UH...
YOU ALL TRUSTED GRANDPA... OR I GUESS YOU ALL LOVED HIM, DIDN'T YOU?
WELL, OF COURSE, DEAR!
A GRANDSON OF NEGI-SENSEI IS AS GOOD AS A GRANDSON TO ALL OF US!
SQUEEEEZE
ぎゅううう
HEY, NO FAIR, CLASS REP!
WUGH?!
MADAM, PLEASE CONSIDER YOUR AGE. ALLOW ME TO...!
PHWAH! HEY!
OH, I'M SORRY. HERE I AM AN OLD WOMAN. WHERE ARE MY MANNERS?
SQUIIISH
ぎゅむうっ
NO, THAT'S NOT THE PROBLEM!
THEN ALLOW ME.
MRPH!
HEY, NO FAIR, CHACHAMARU-SAN!

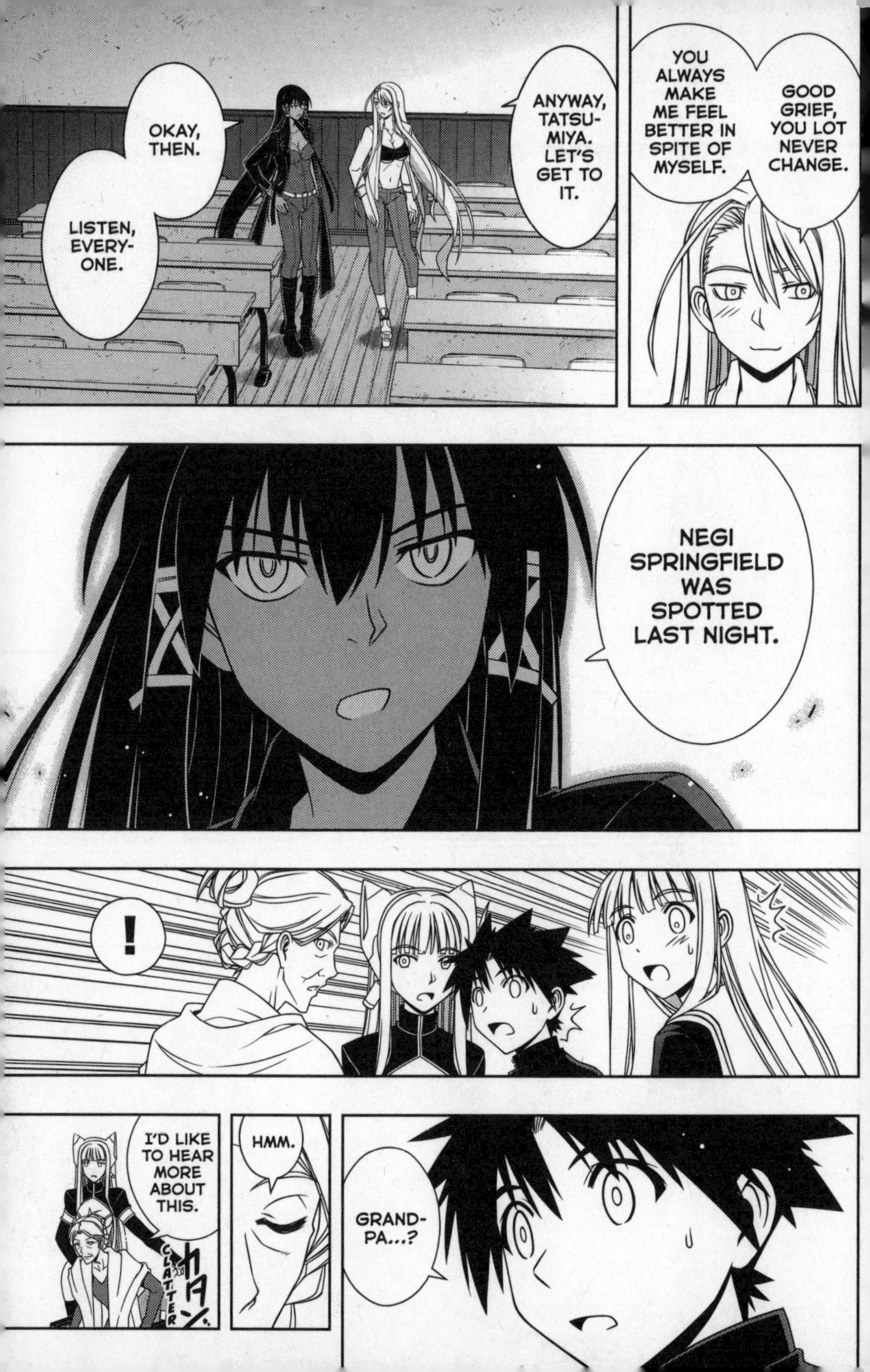
GOOD GRIEF, YOU LOT NEVER CHANGE.
YOU ALWAYS MAKE ME FEEL BETTER IN SPITE OF MYSELF.
ANYWAY, TATSU-MIYA. LET'S GET TO IT.
OKAY, THEN.
LISTEN, EVERY-ONE.
NEGI SPRINGFIELD WAS SPOTTED LAST NIGHT.
!
GRAND-PA...?
HMM.
I'D LIKE TO HEAR MORE ABOUT THIS.
CLATTER
カタン

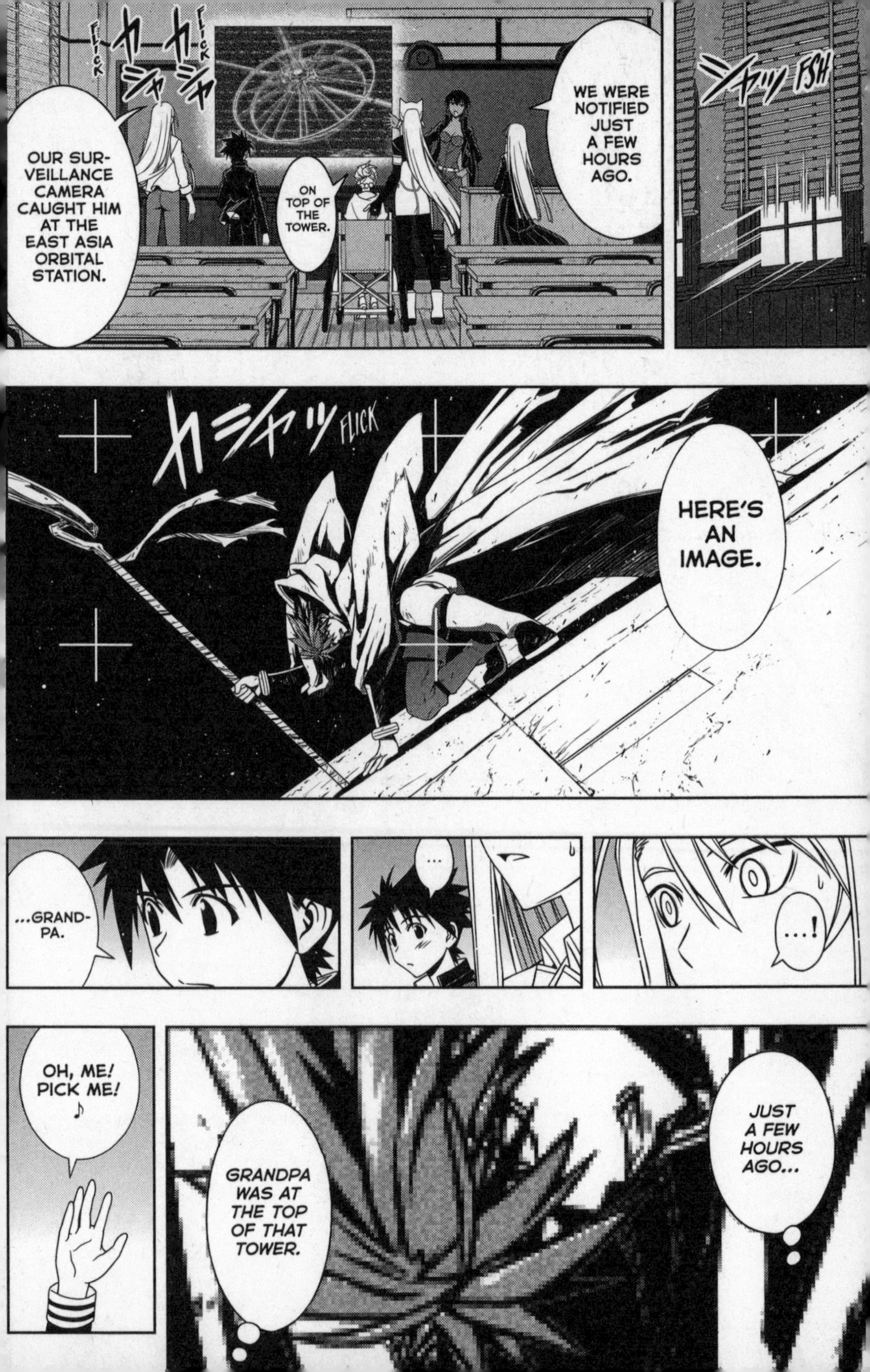
シャッ FSH
WE WERE NOTIFIED JUST A FEW HOURS AGO.
カシャ FLICK
カシャ FLICK
ON TOP OF THE TOWER.
OUR SUR-VEILLANCE CAMERA CAUGHT HIM AT THE EAST ASIA ORBITAL STATION.
HERE'S AN IMAGE.
カシャッ FLICK
...!
...
...GRAND-PA.
JUST A FEW HOURS AGO...
GRANDPA WAS AT THE TOP OF THAT TOWER.
OH, ME! PICK ME! ♪

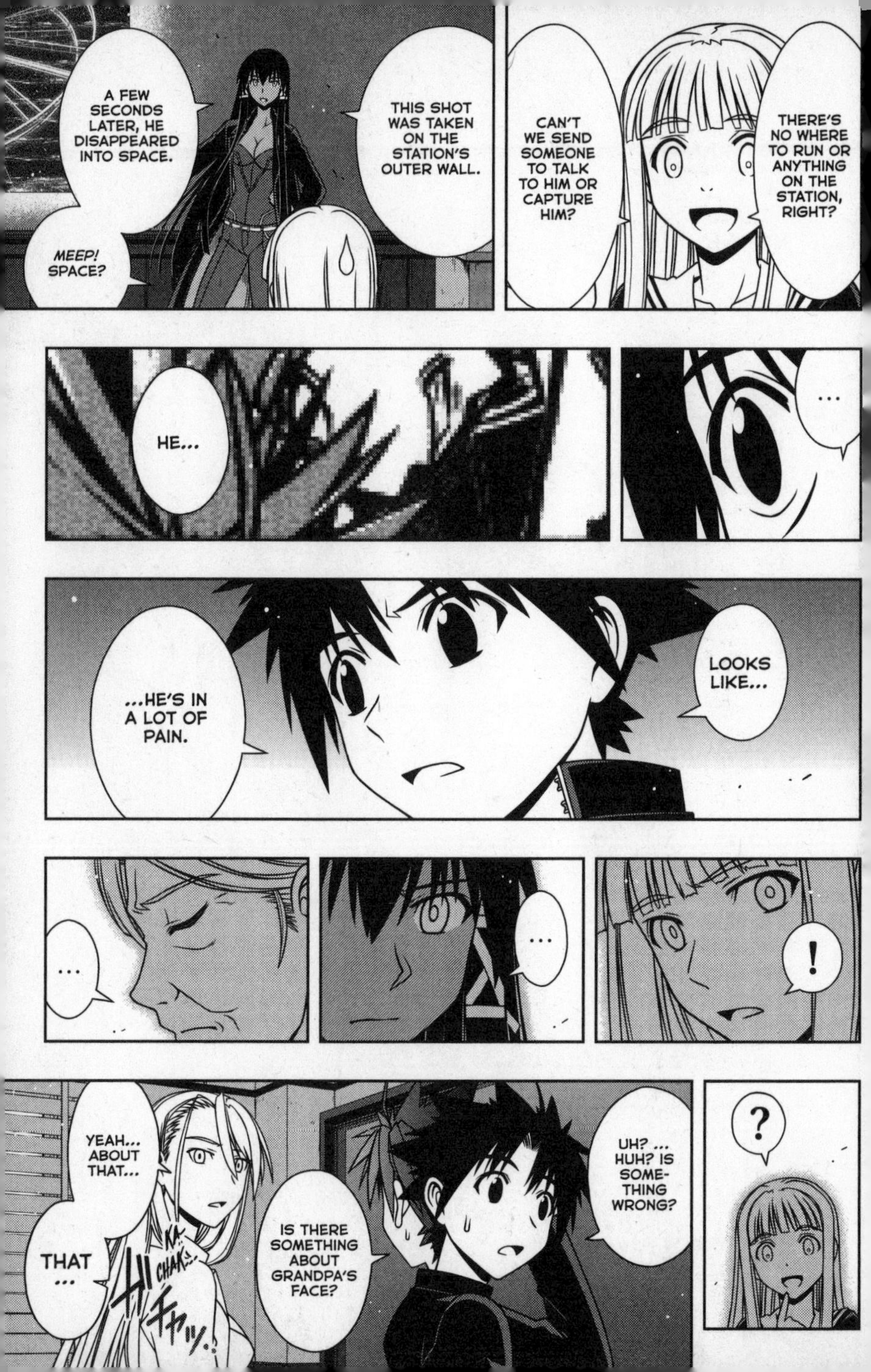

THERE'S NO WHERE TO RUN OR ANYTHING ON THE STATION, RIGHT?
CAN'T WE SEND SOMEONE TO TALK TO HIM OR CAPTURE HIM?
THIS SHOT WAS TAKEN ON THE STATION'S OUTER WALL.
A FEW SECONDS LATER, HE DISAPPEARED INTO SPACE.
MEEP! SPACE?
...
HE...
LOOKS LIKE...
...HE'S IN A LOT OF PAIN.
!
...
...
?
UH? ... HUH? IS SOME-THING WRONG?
YEAH... ABOUT THAT...
IS THERE SOMETHING ABOUT GRANDPA'S FACE?
THAT ...
KA-CHAK

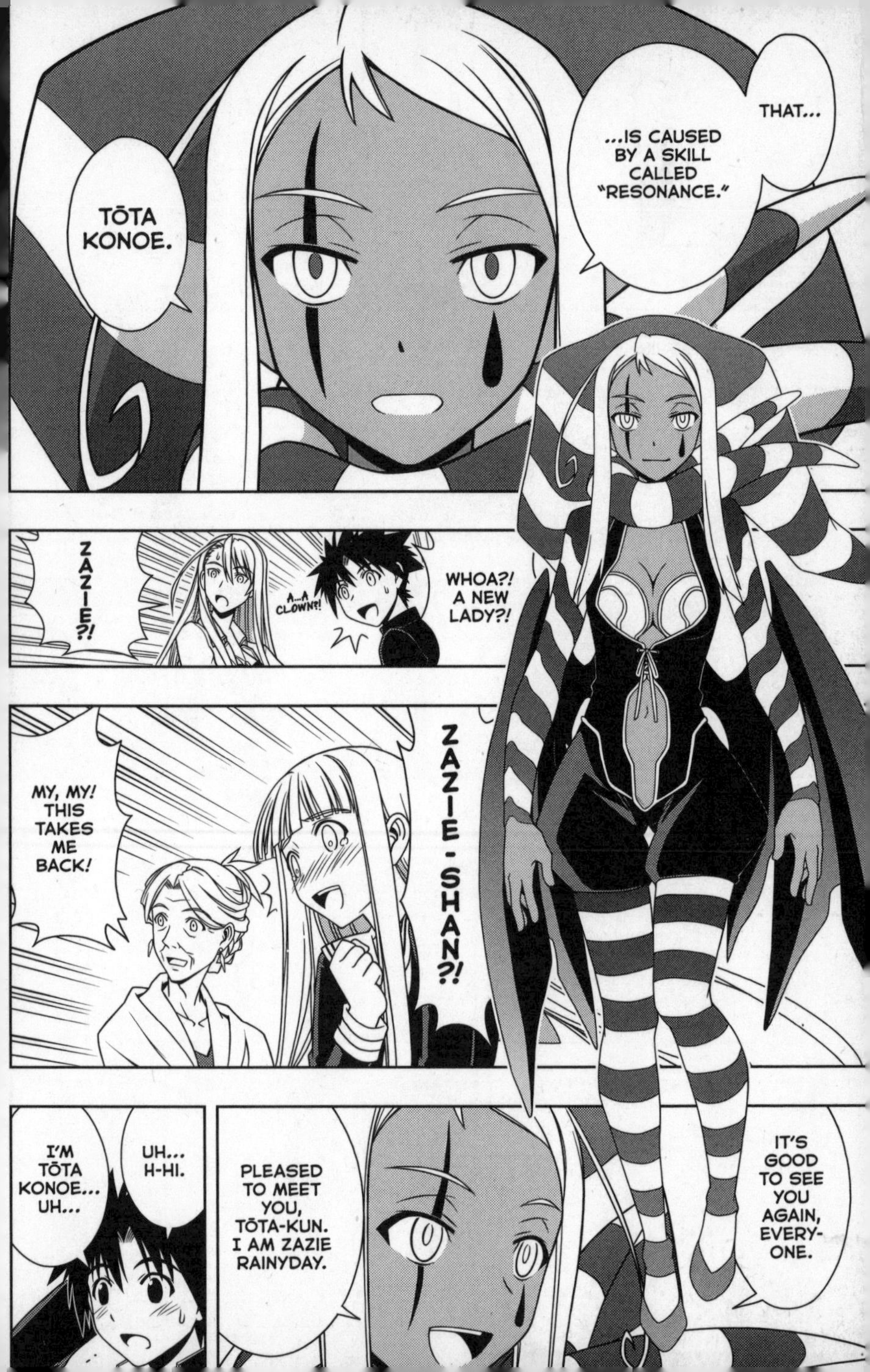
THAT...
...IS CAUSED BY A SKILL CALLED "RESONANCE."
TŌTA KONOE.
WHOA?! A NEW LADY?!
A...A CLOWN?!
ZAZIE?!
ZAZIE-SHAN?!
MY, MY! THIS TAKES ME BACK!
IT'S GOOD TO SEE YOU AGAIN, EVERY-ONE.
PLEASED TO MEET YOU, TŌTA-KUN. I AM ZAZIE RAINYDAY.
UH... H-HI.
I'M TŌTA KONOE... UH...

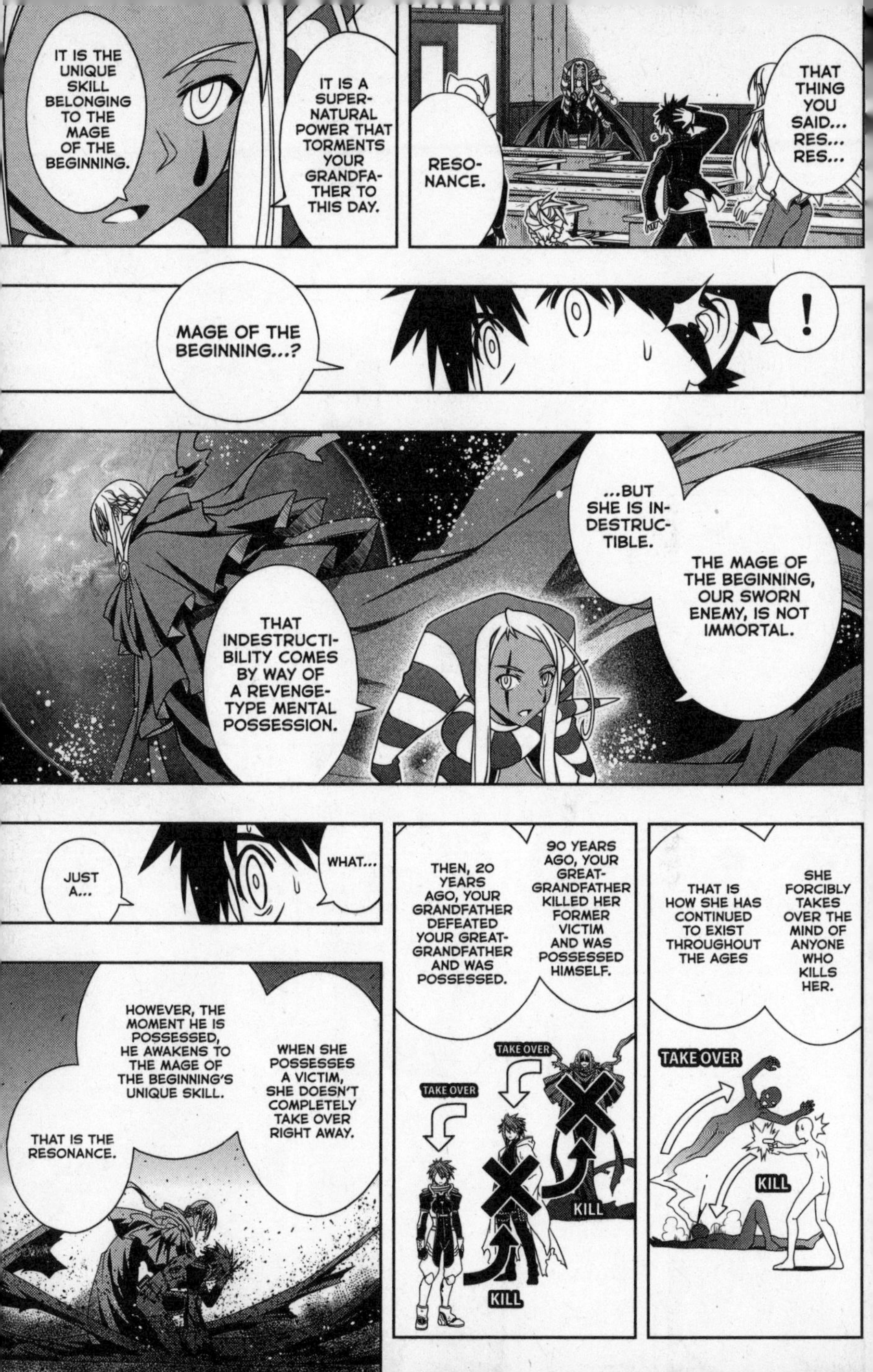
THAT THING YOU SAID... RES... RES...
RESO-NANCE.
IT IS A SUPER-NATURAL POWER THAT TORMENTS YOUR GRANDFA-THER TO THIS DAY.
IT IS THE UNIQUE SKILL BELONGING TO THE MAGE OF THE BEGINNING.
!
MAGE OF THE BEGINNING...?
THE MAGE OF THE BEGINNING, OUR SWORN ENEMY, IS NOT IMMORTAL.
...BUT SHE IS IN-DESTRUC-TIBLE.
THAT INDESTRUCTI-BILITY COMES BY WAY OF A REVENGE-TYPE MENTAL POSSESSION.
SHE FORCIBLY TAKES OVER THE MIND OF ANYONE WHO KILLS HER.
THAT IS HOW SHE HAS CONTINUED TO EXIST THROUGHOUT THE AGES
TAKE OVER
KILL
90 YEARS AGO, YOUR GREAT-GRANDFATHER KILLED HER FORMER VICTIM AND WAS POSSESSED HIMSELF.
THEN, 20 YEARS AGO, YOUR GRANDFATHER DEFEATED YOUR GREAT-GRANDFATHER AND WAS POSSESSED.
TAKE OVER
TAKE OVER
KILL
KILL
WHAT...
JUST A...
WHEN SHE POSSESSES A VICTIM, SHE DOESN'T COMPLETELY TAKE OVER RIGHT AWAY.
HOWEVER, THE MOMENT HE IS POSSESSED, HE AWAKENS TO THE MAGE OF THE BEGINNING'S UNIQUE SKILL.
THAT IS THE RESONANCE.

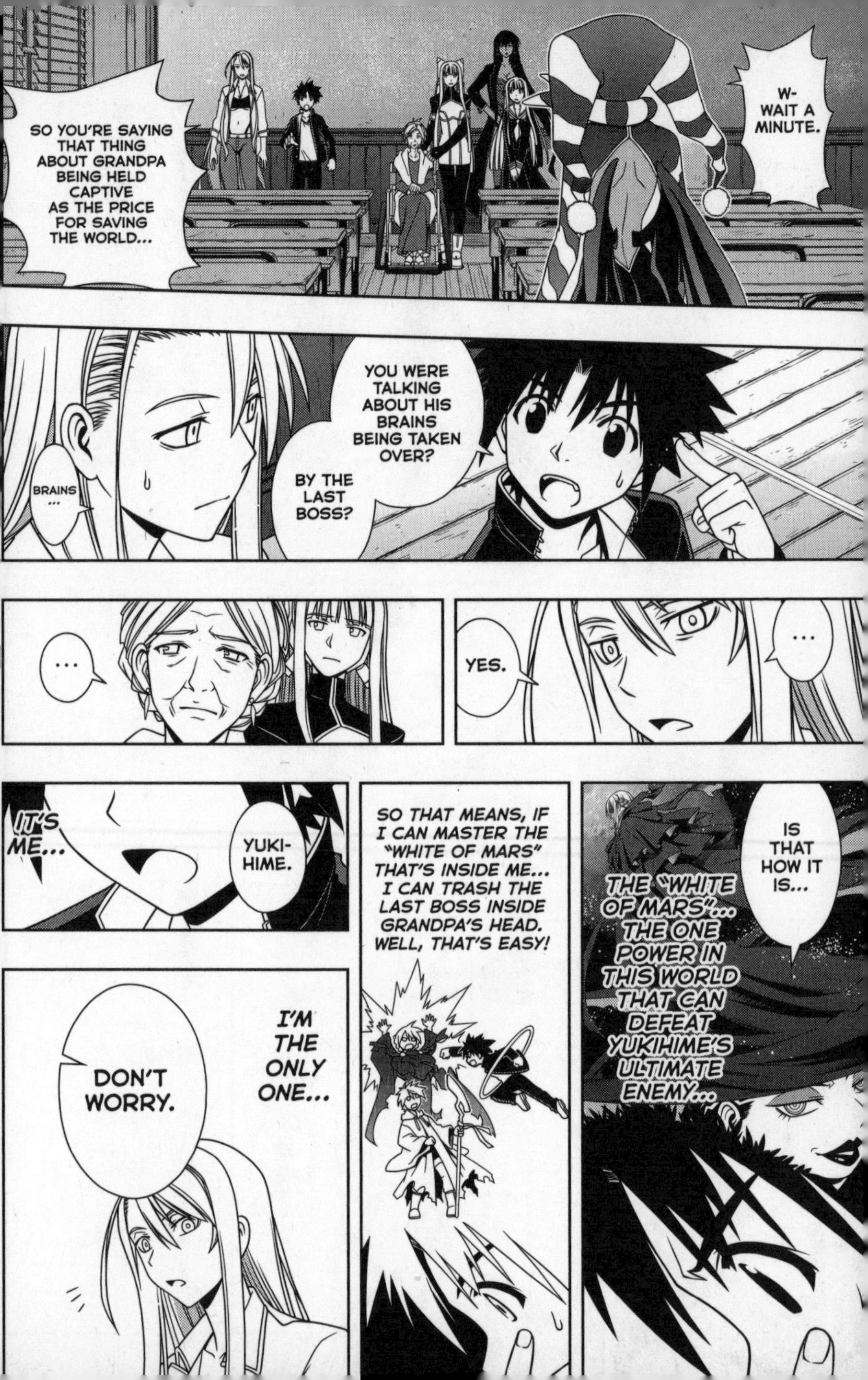
W- WAIT A MINUTE.
SO YOU'RE SAYING THAT THING ABOUT GRANDPA BEING HELD CAPTIVE AS THE PRICE FOR SAVING THE WORLD...
YOU WERE TALKING ABOUT HIS BRAINS BEING TAKEN OVER?
BY THE LAST BOSS?
BRAINS ...
...
YES.
...
IS THAT HOW IT IS...
THE "WHITE OF MARS"... THE ONE POWER IN THIS WORLD THAT CAN DEFEAT YUKIHIME'S ULTIMATE ENEMY...
SO THAT MEANS, IF I CAN MASTER THE "WHITE OF MARS" THAT'S INSIDE ME... I CAN TRASH THE LAST BOSS INSIDE GRANDPA'S HEAD. WELL, THAT'S EASY!
IT'S ME...
YUKI-HIME.
I'M THE ONLY ONE...
DON'T WORRY.

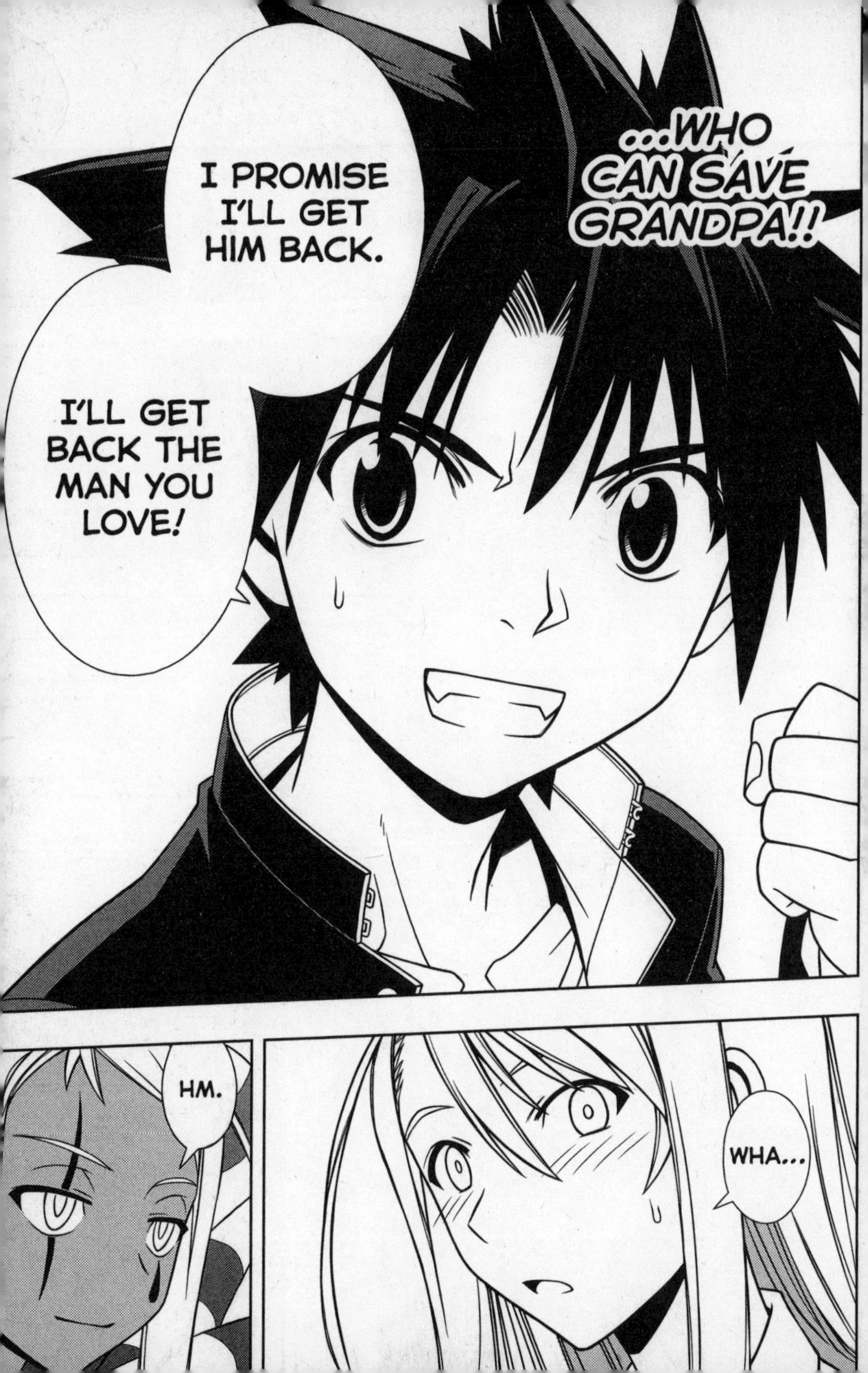
...WHO CAN SAVE GRANDPA!!
I PROMISE I'LL GET HIM BACK.
I'LL GET BACK THE MAN YOU LOVE!
WHA...
HM.

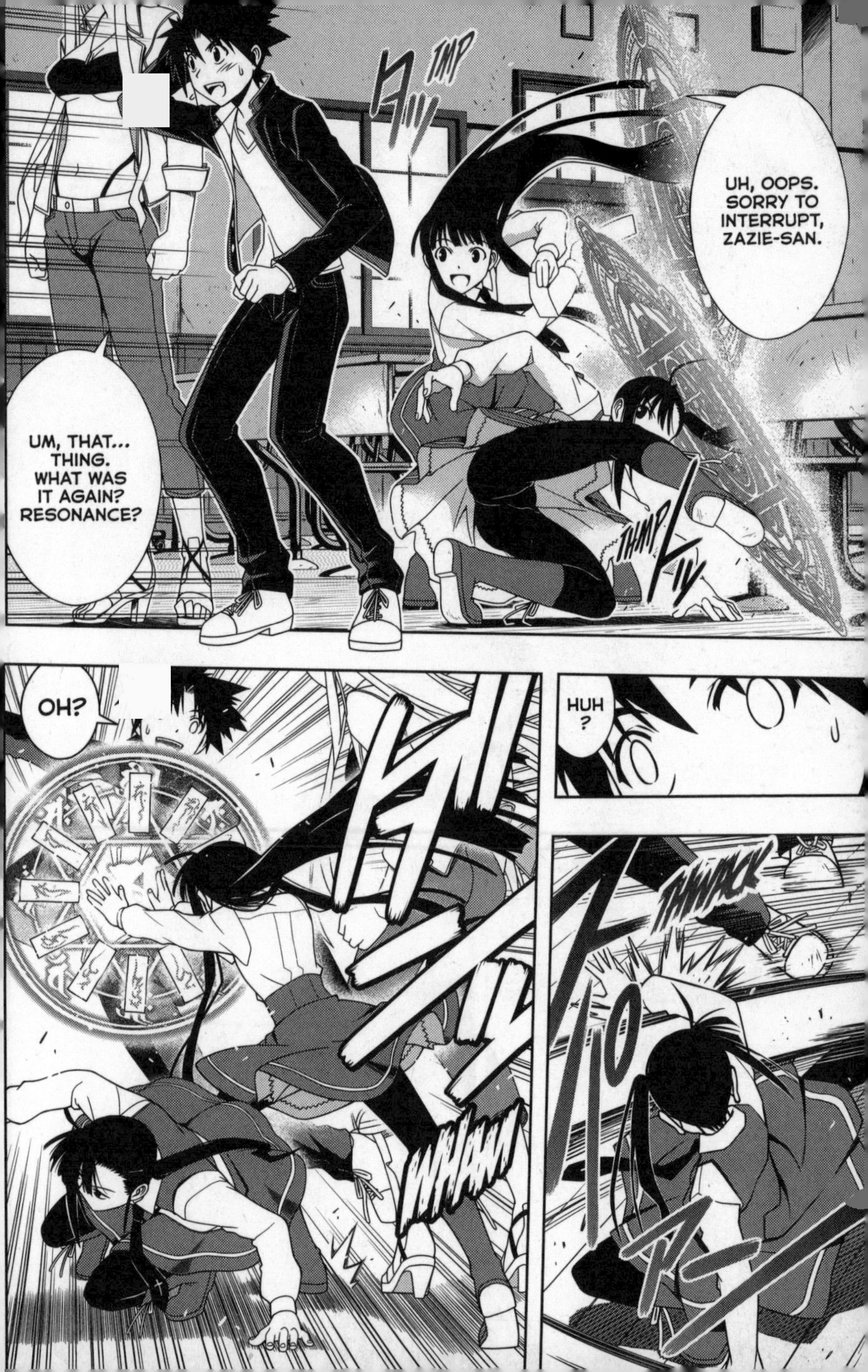
TMP
UH, OOPS. SORRY TO INTERRUPT, ZAZIE-SAN.
THMP
UM, THAT... THING. WHAT WAS IT AGAIN? RESONANCE?
HUH ?
THWACK
OH?

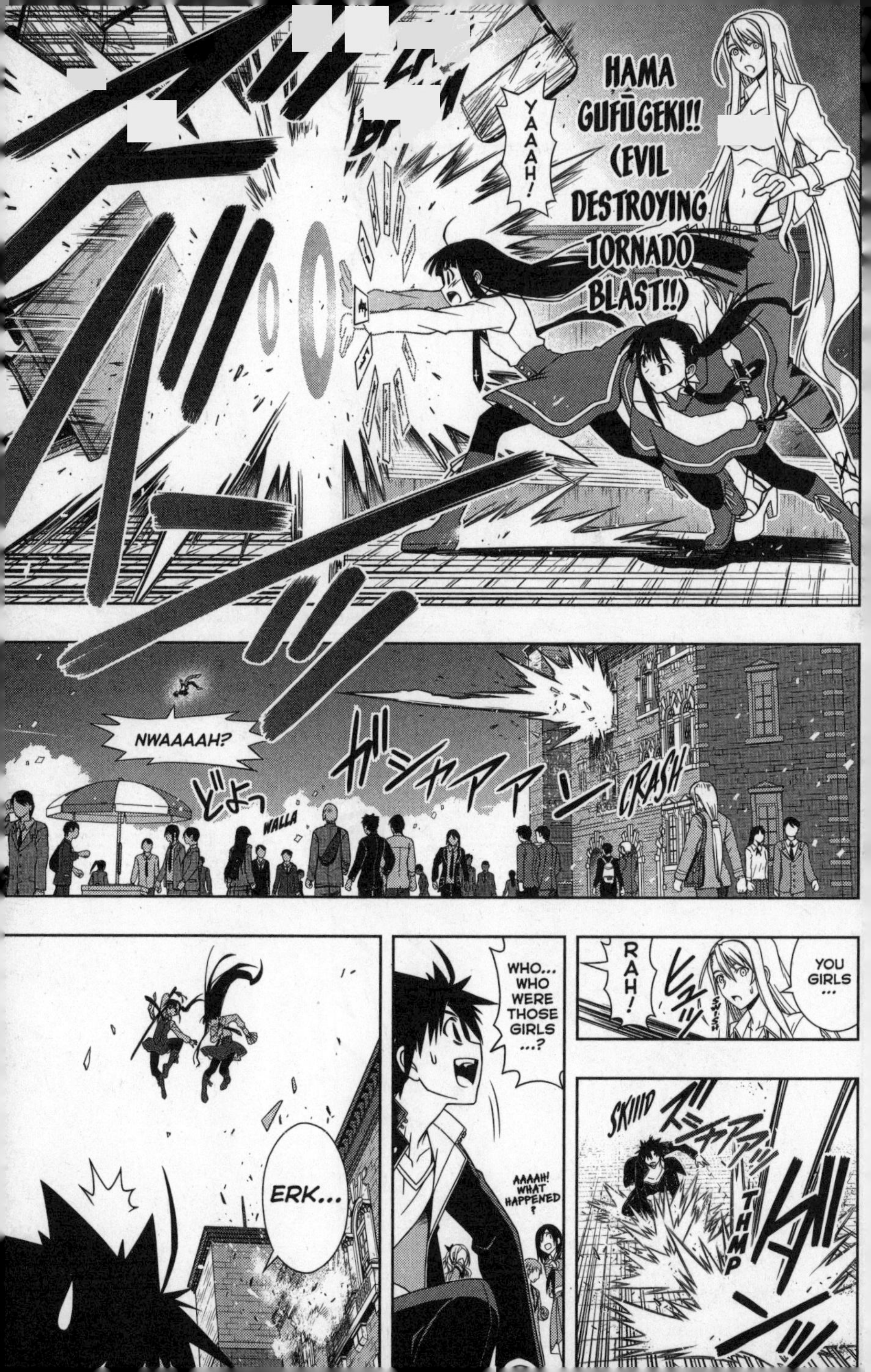
HAMA GUFŪ GEKI!! (EVIL DESTROYING TORNADO BLAST!!)
YAAAH!
CRASH
NWAAAAH?
WALLA
どよっ
YOU GIRLS...
SWISH
RAH!
SKIIID
ズシャアッ
THMP
WHO... WHO WERE THOSE GIRLS...?
AAAAH! WHAT HAPPENED?
ERK...

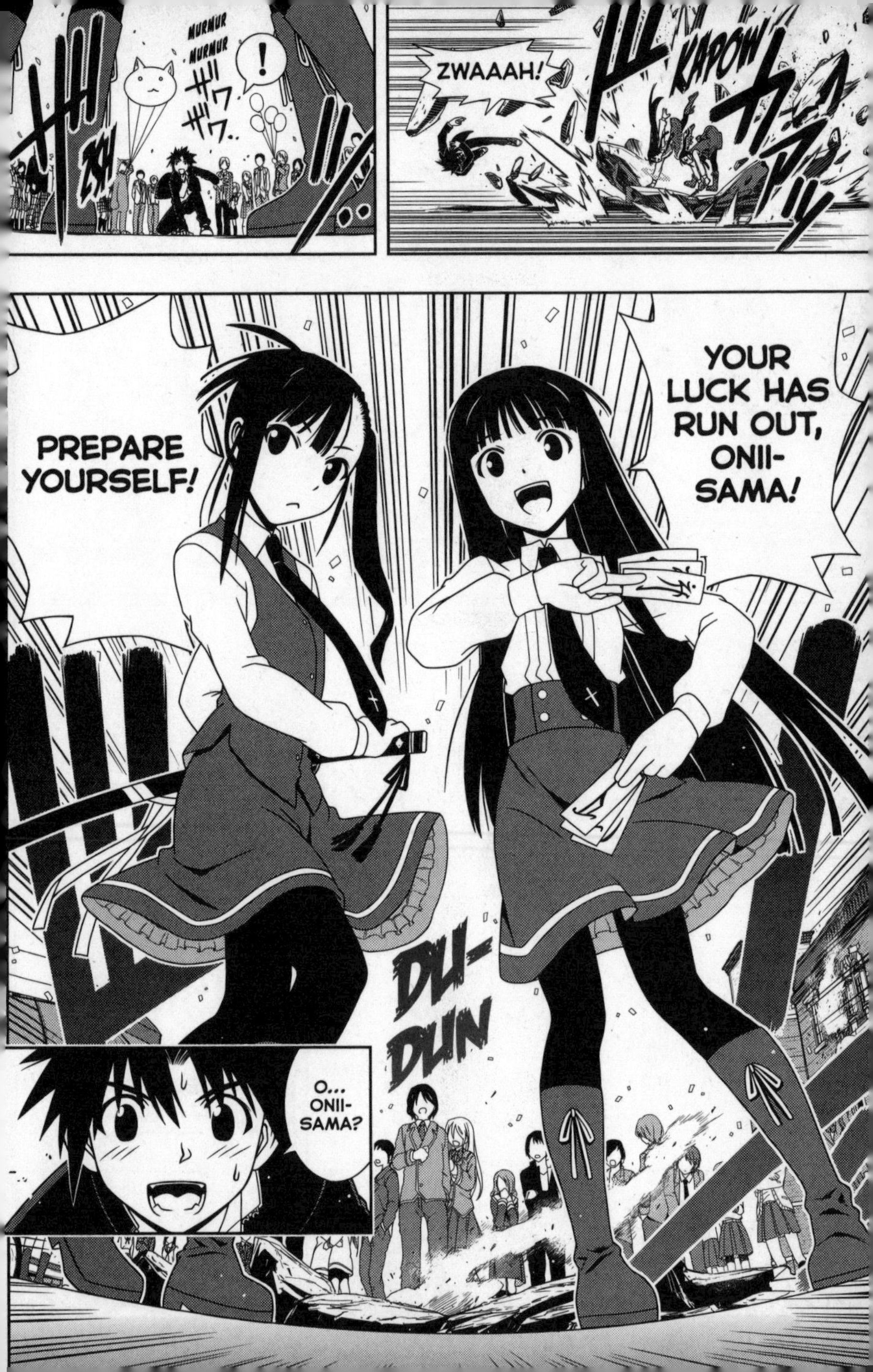

ZWAAAH!
KAPOW
MURMUR MURMUR
ザワザワ..
!
ZSH
YOUR LUCK HAS RUN OUT, ONII-SAMA!
PREPARE YOURSELF!
DU-DUN
O... ONII-SAMA?

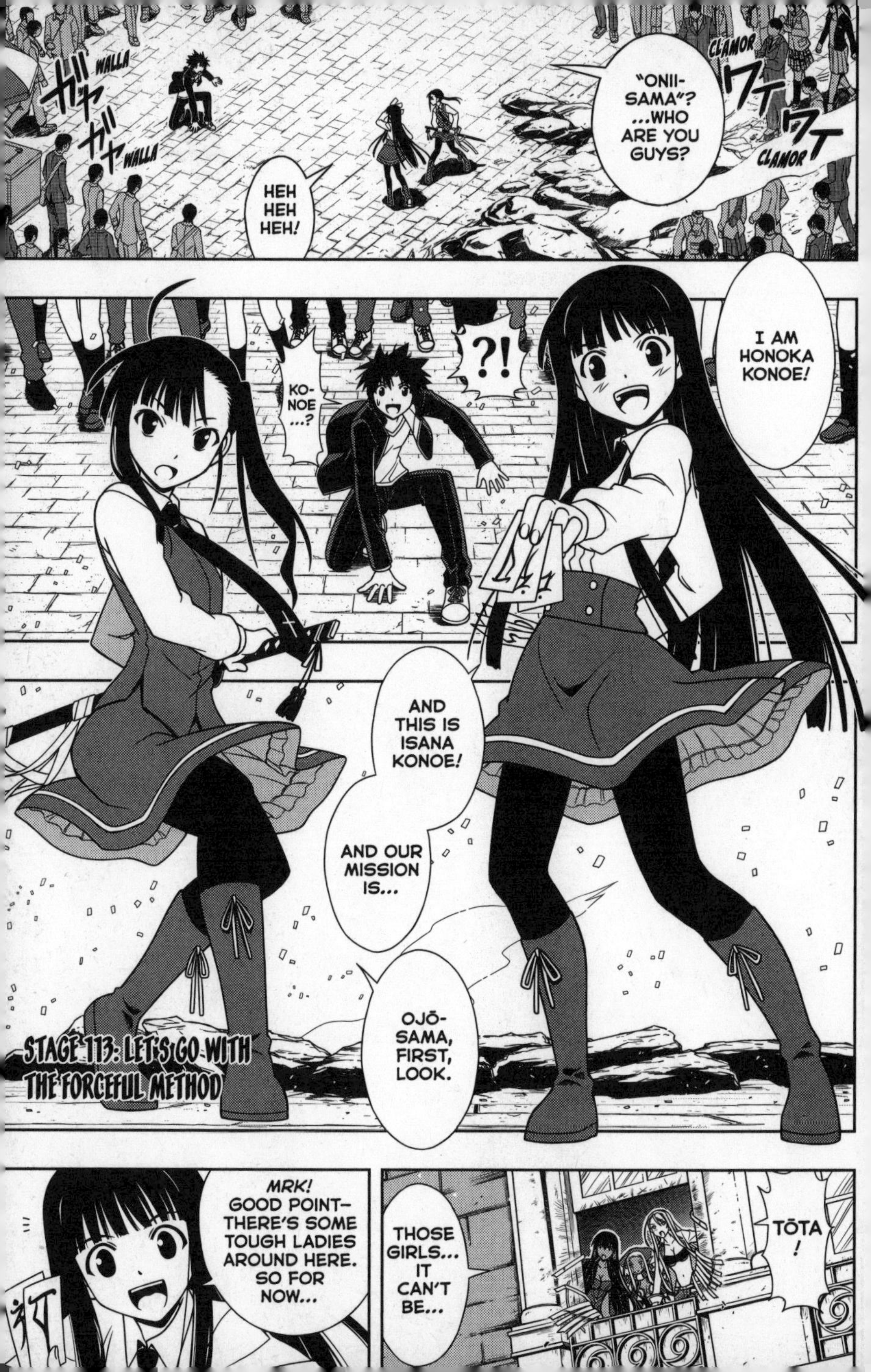
CLAMOR CLAMOR
"ONII-SAMA"? ...WHO ARE YOU GUYS?
HEH HEH HEH!
WALLA WALLA
I AM HONOKA KONOE!
?!
KO-NOE ...?
AND THIS IS ISANA KONOE!
AND OUR MISSION IS...
OJŌ-SAMA, FIRST, LOOK.
STAGE 113: LET'S GO WITH THE FORCEFUL METHOD
TŌTA!
THOSE GIRLS... IT CAN'T BE...
MRK! GOOD POINT—THERE'S SOME TOUGH LADIES AROUND HERE. SO FOR NOW...

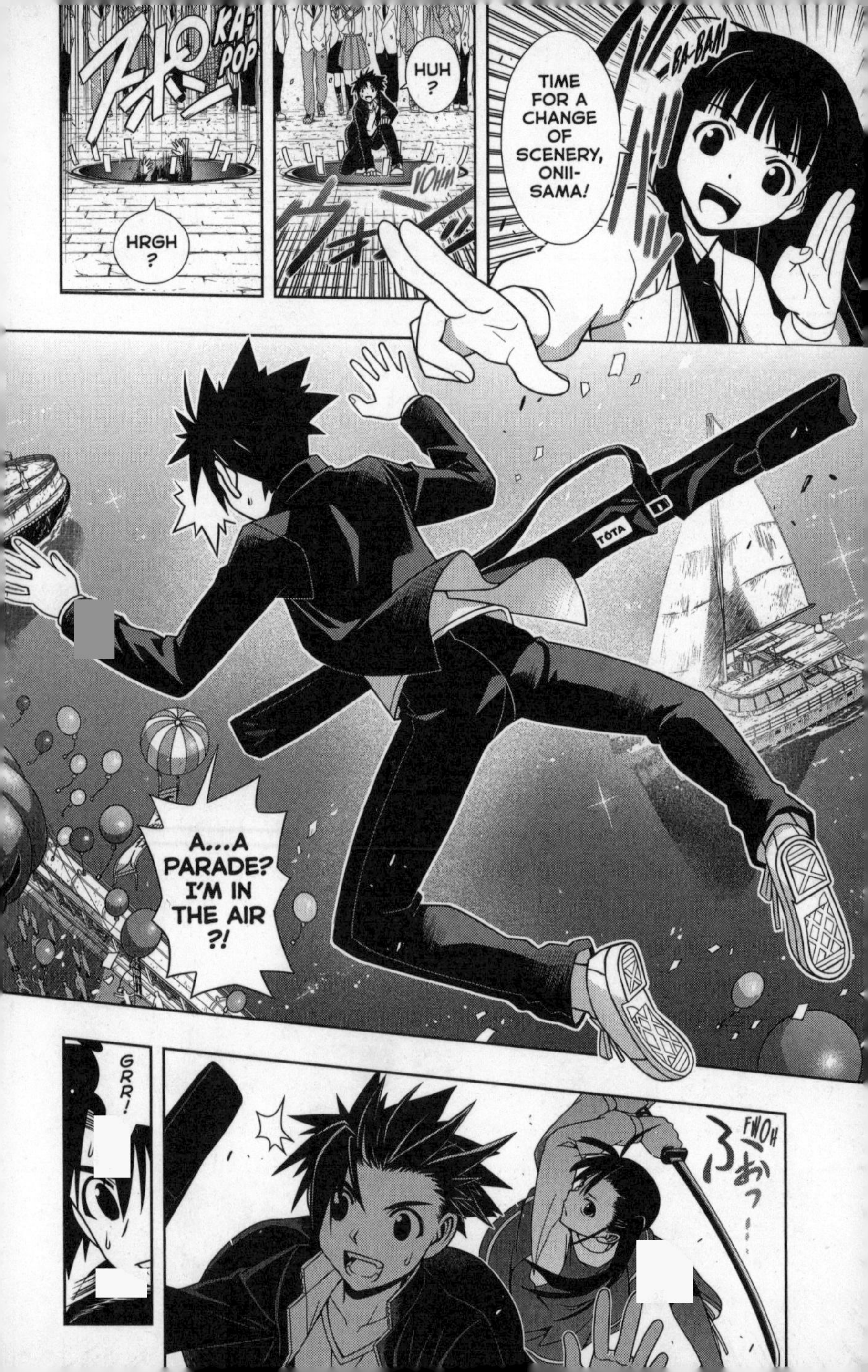
BA-BAM
TIME FOR A CHANGE OF SCENERY, ONII-SAMA!
HUH?
VOHM
KA-POP
HRGH?
TŌTA
A...A PARADE? I'M IN THE AIR?!
FWOH
ふぉっ
GRR!

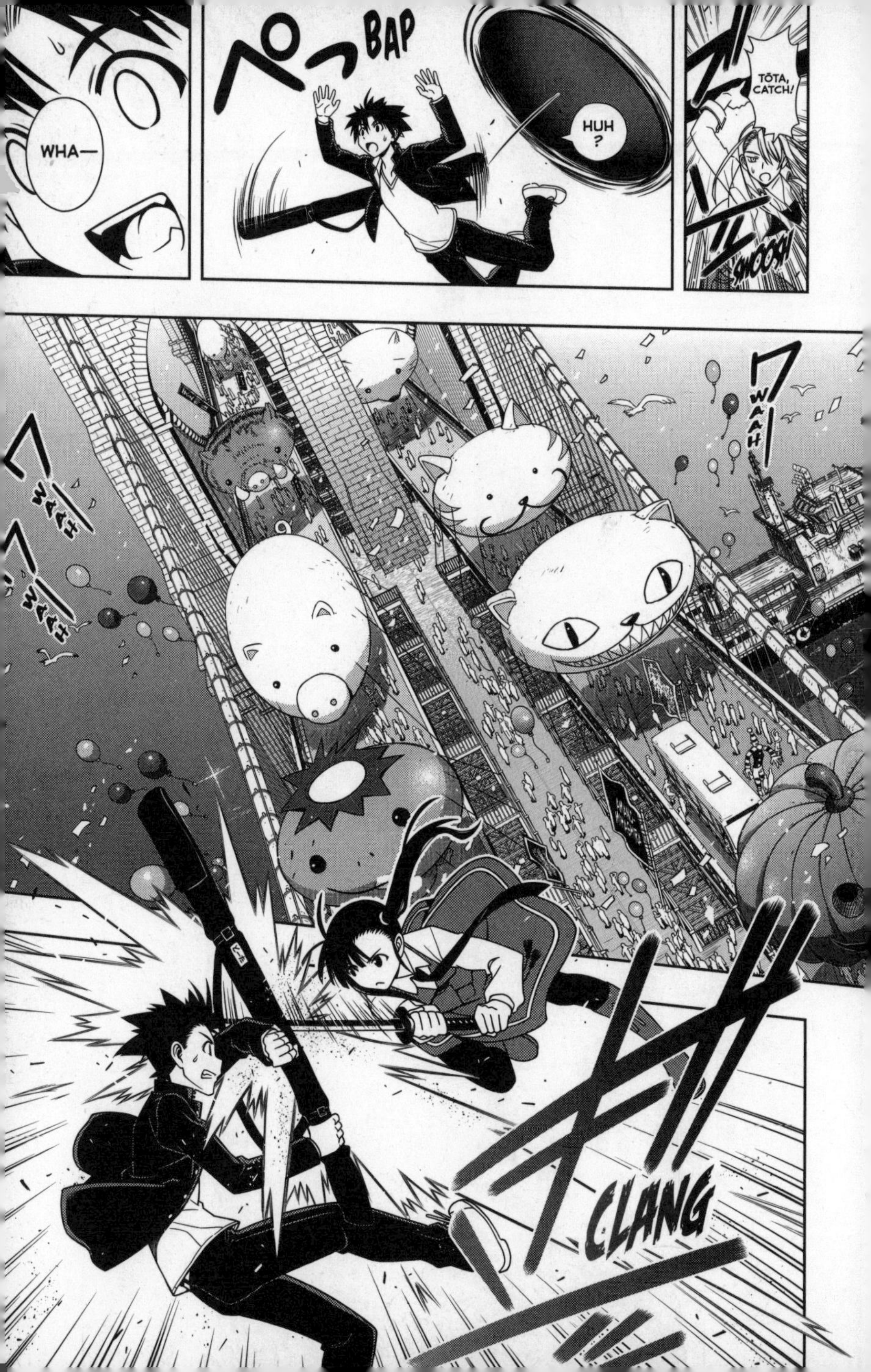
TŌTA, CATCH!
WHOOSH
HUH ?
ぺっ
BAP
WHA—
WAAH
WAAH
WAAH
CLANG

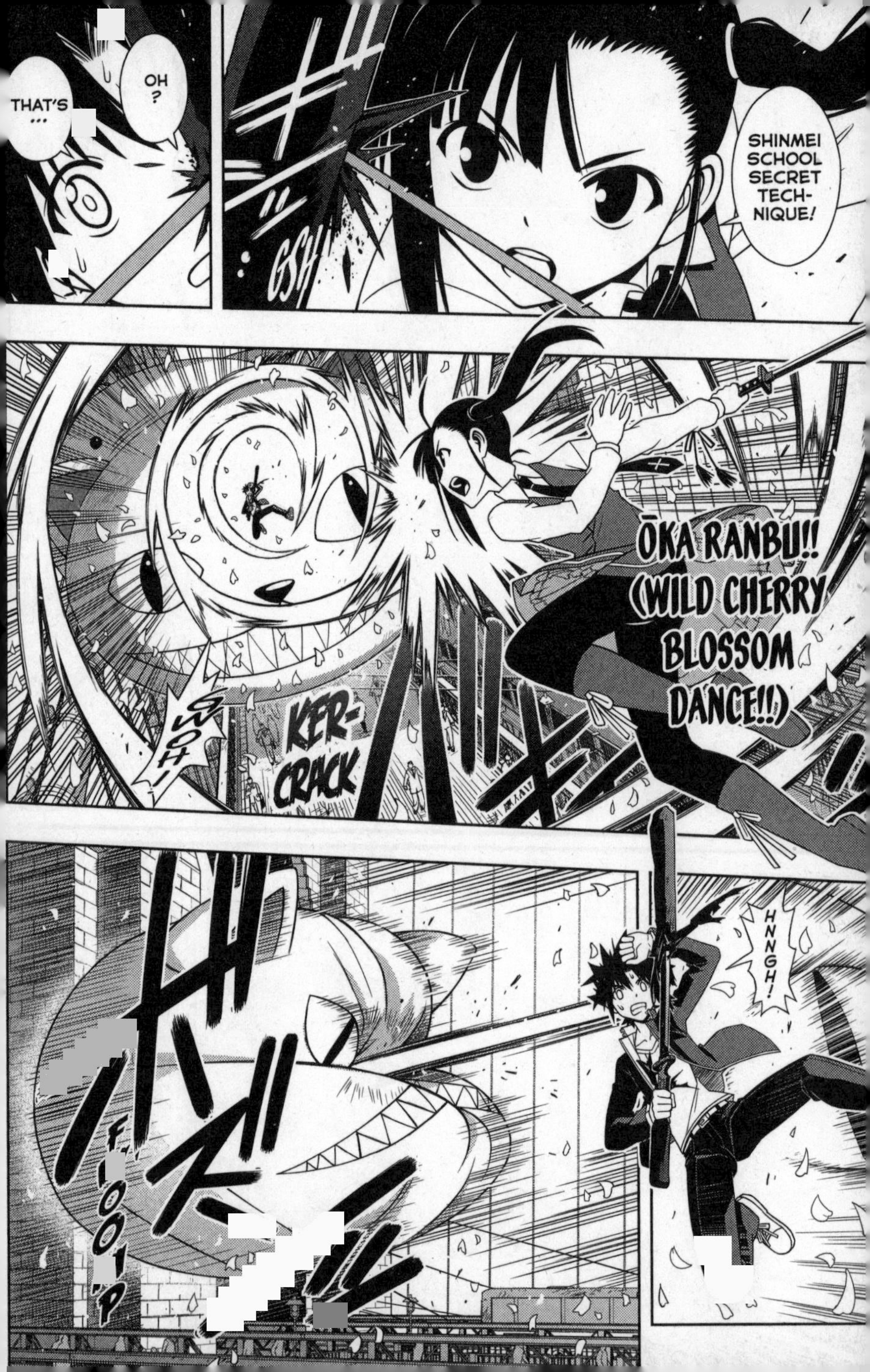
SHINMEI SCHOOL SECRET TECH-NIQUE!
GSH
OH ?
THAT'S ...
ŌKA RANBU!! (WILD CHERRY BLOSSOM DANCE!!)
KER-CRACK
GWOH!
HNNGH!

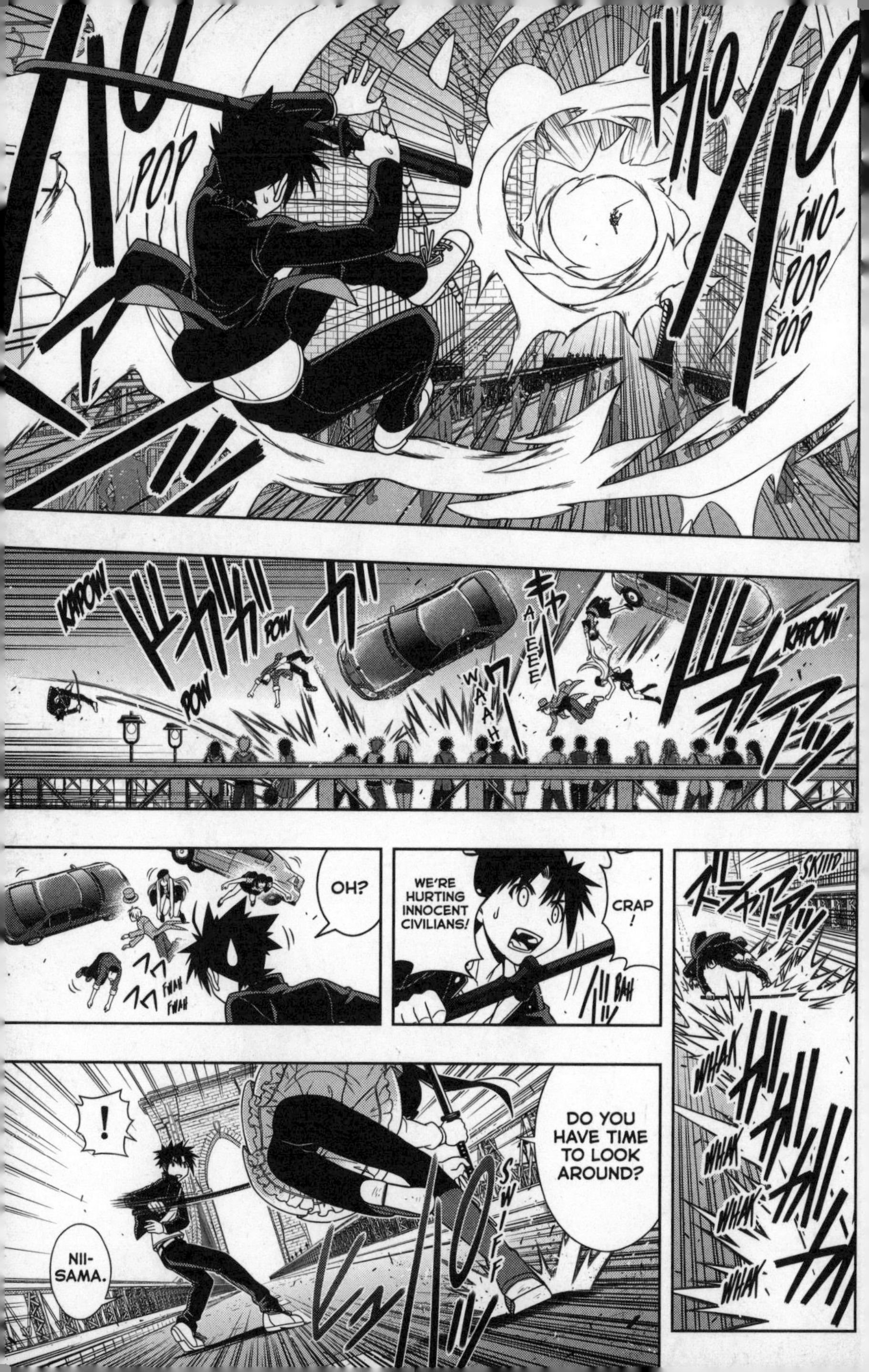
FWO-POP POP POP
POP
KAPOW
AIEEE
WAAAH
POW
POW
KAPOW
SKIID
WHAK
WHAK
WHAK
WHAK
WHAK
CRAP!
WE'RE HURTING INNOCENT CIVILIANS!
BAH
OH?
FWAH FWAH
DO YOU HAVE TIME TO LOOK AROUND?
SWIFF
!
NII-SAMA.

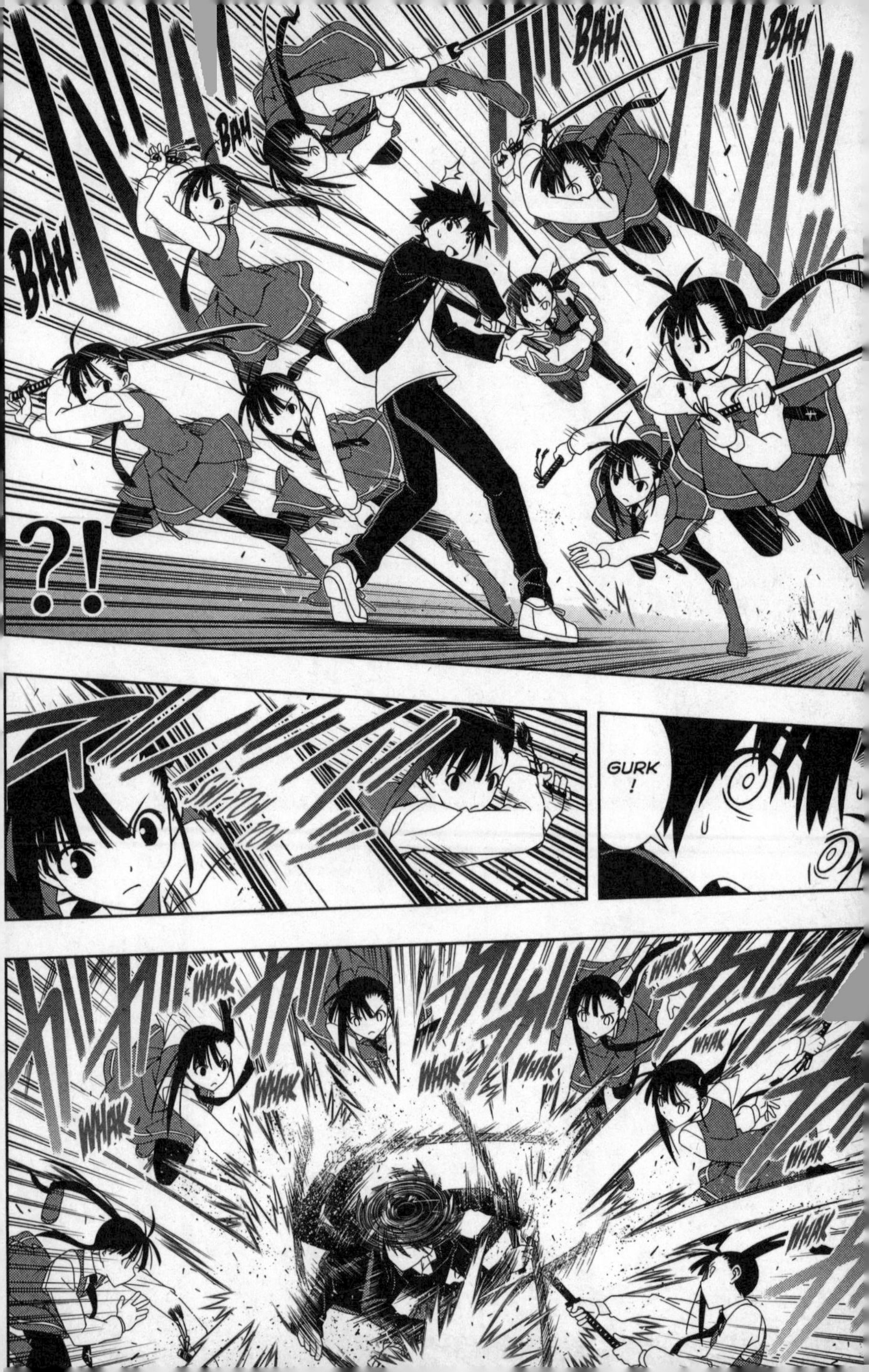
BAH
BAH
BAH
BAH
?!
GURK !
WHAK
WHAK
WHAK
WHAK
WHAK
WHAK
WHAK
WHAK
WHAK

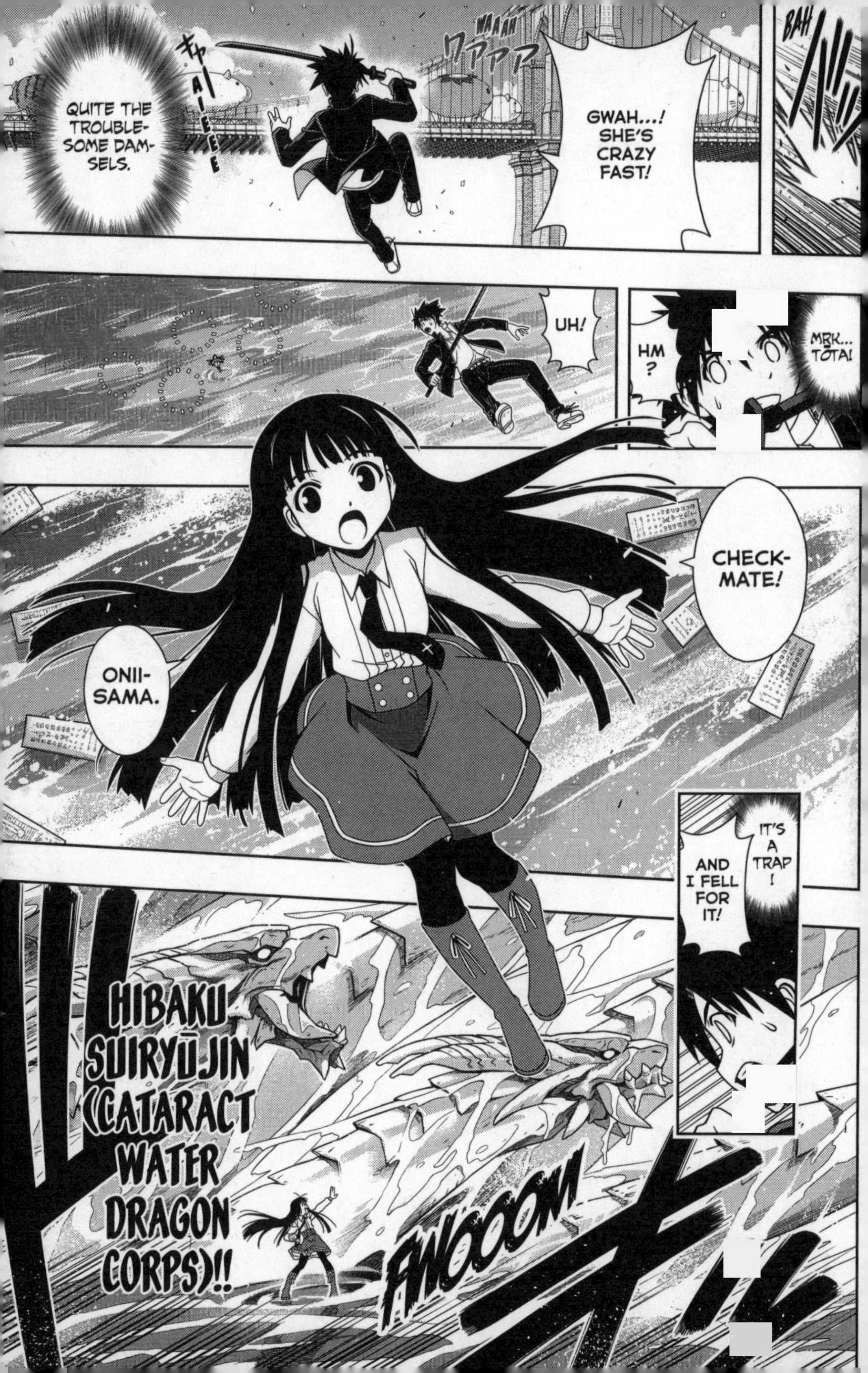
BAH
WAAAH
GWAH...! SHE'S CRAZY FAST!
AIEEEE
QUITE THE TROUBLE-SOME DAM-SELS.
MRK... TŌTA!
HM ?
UH!
CHECK-MATE!
ONII-SAMA.
IT'S A TRAP!
AND I FELL FOR IT!
HIBAKU SUIRYŪJIN (CATARACT WATER DRAGON CORPS)!!
FWOOOM

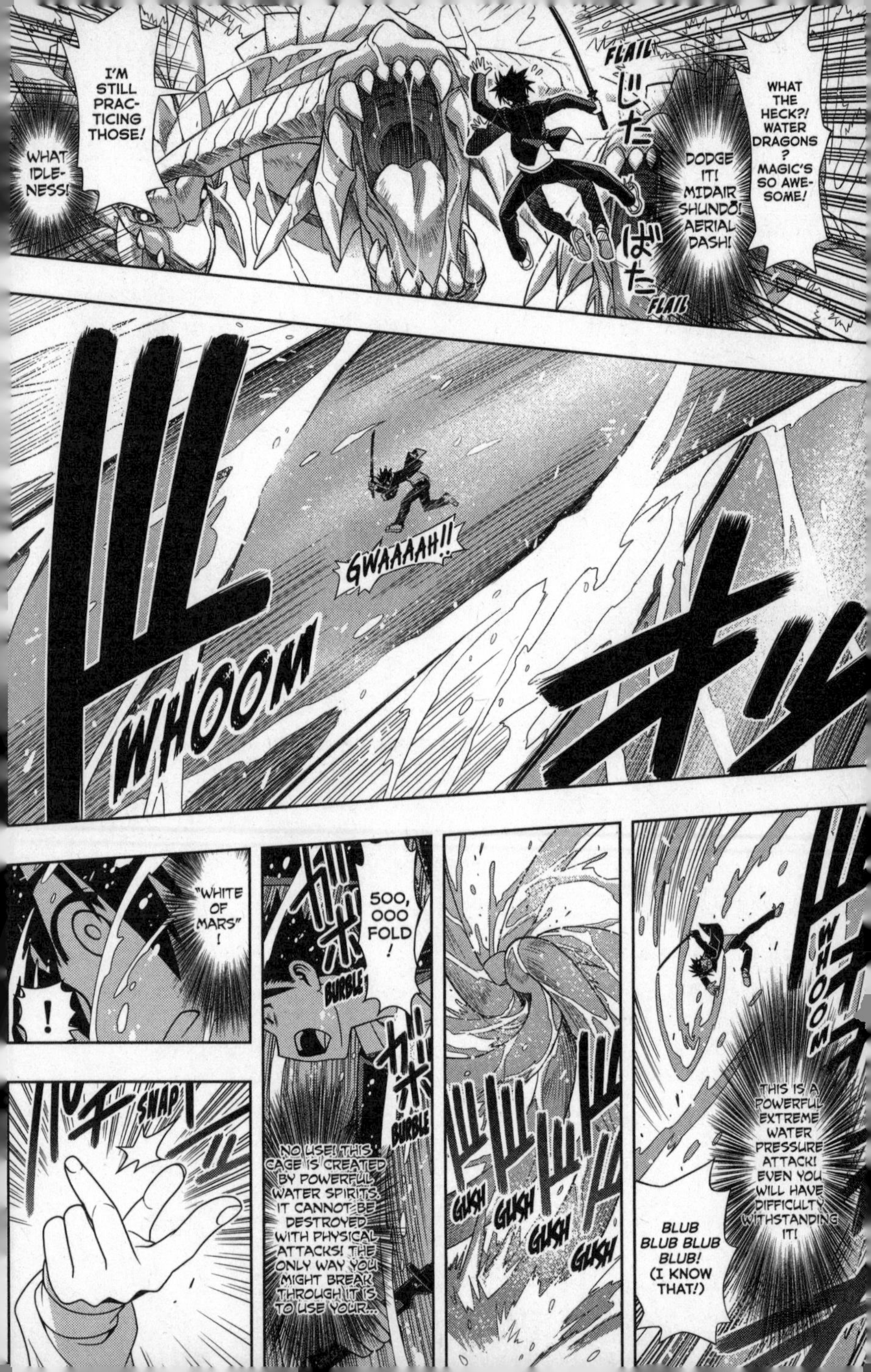
WHAT THE HECK?! WATER DRAGONS? MAGIC'S SO AWE-SOME!
FLAIL
じた
DODGE IT! MIDAIR SHUNDŌ! AERIAL DASH!
ばた
FLAIL
I'M STILL PRAC-TICING THOSE!
WHAT IDLE-NESS!
WHOOM
GWAAAAH!!
WHOOM
THIS IS A POWERFUL EXTREME WATER PRESSURE ATTACK! EVEN YOU WILL HAVE DIFFICULTY WITHSTANDING IT!
BLUB BLUB BLUB BLUB! (I KNOW THAT!)
GUSH
GUSH
GUSH
GUSH
500, 000 FOLD!
BURBLE
BURBLE
NO USE! THIS CAGE IS CREATED BY POWERFUL WATER SPIRITS. IT CANNOT BE DESTROYED WITH PHYSICAL ATTACKS! THE ONLY WAY YOU MIGHT BREAK THROUGH IT IS TO USE YOUR...
"WHITE OF MARS"!
!
SNAP

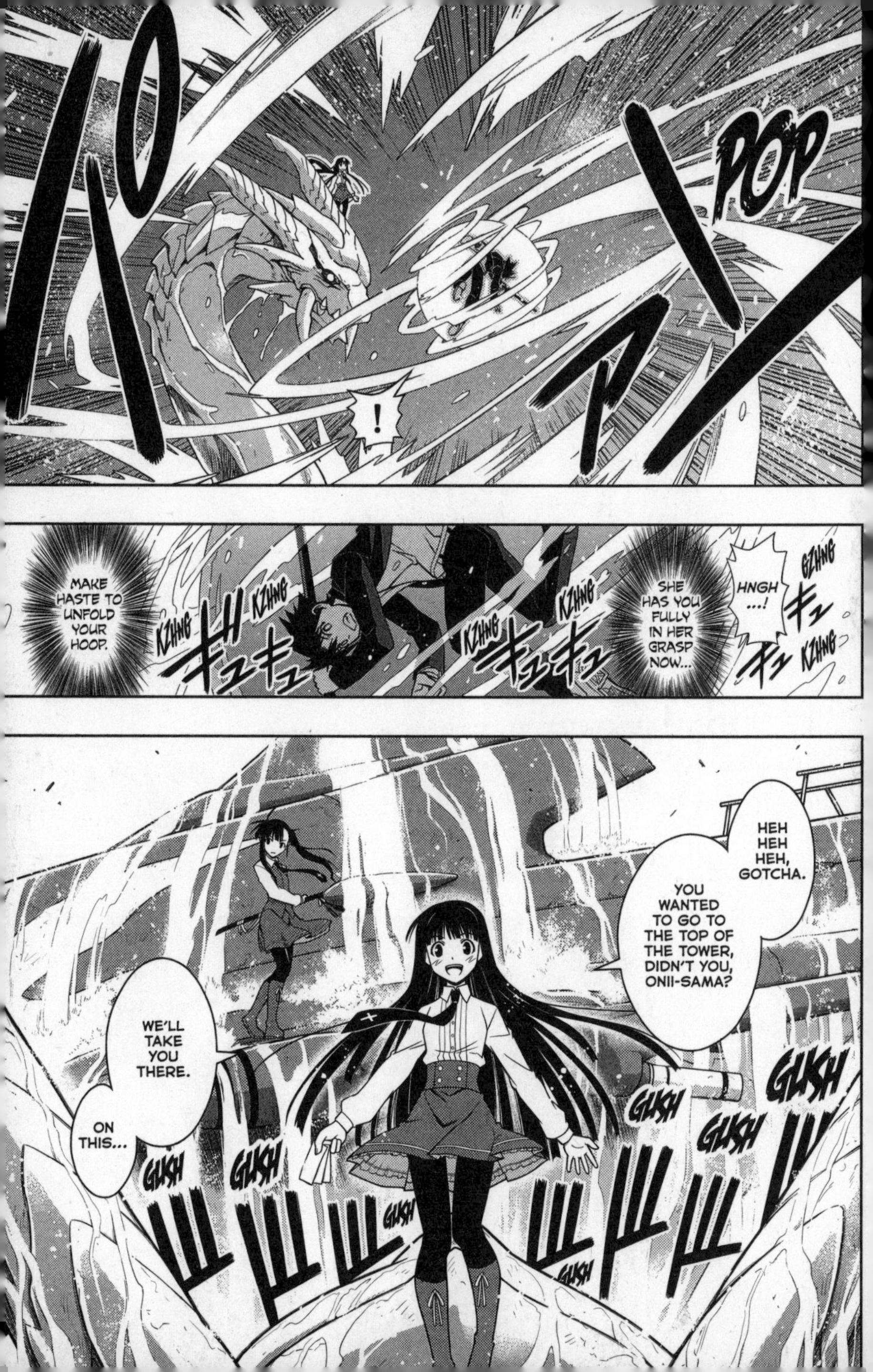
POP
!
GZHNG
KZHNG
HNGH ...!
SHE HAS YOU FULLY IN HER GRASP NOW...
KZHNG
KZHNG
KZHNG
KZHNG
MAKE HASTE TO UNFOLD YOUR HOOP.
HEH HEH HEH, GOTCHA.
YOU WANTED TO GO TO THE TOP OF THE TOWER, DIDN'T YOU, ONII-SAMA?
GUSH
GUSH
GUSH
GUSH
WE'LL TAKE YOU THERE.
ON THIS...
GUSH
GUSH
GUSH

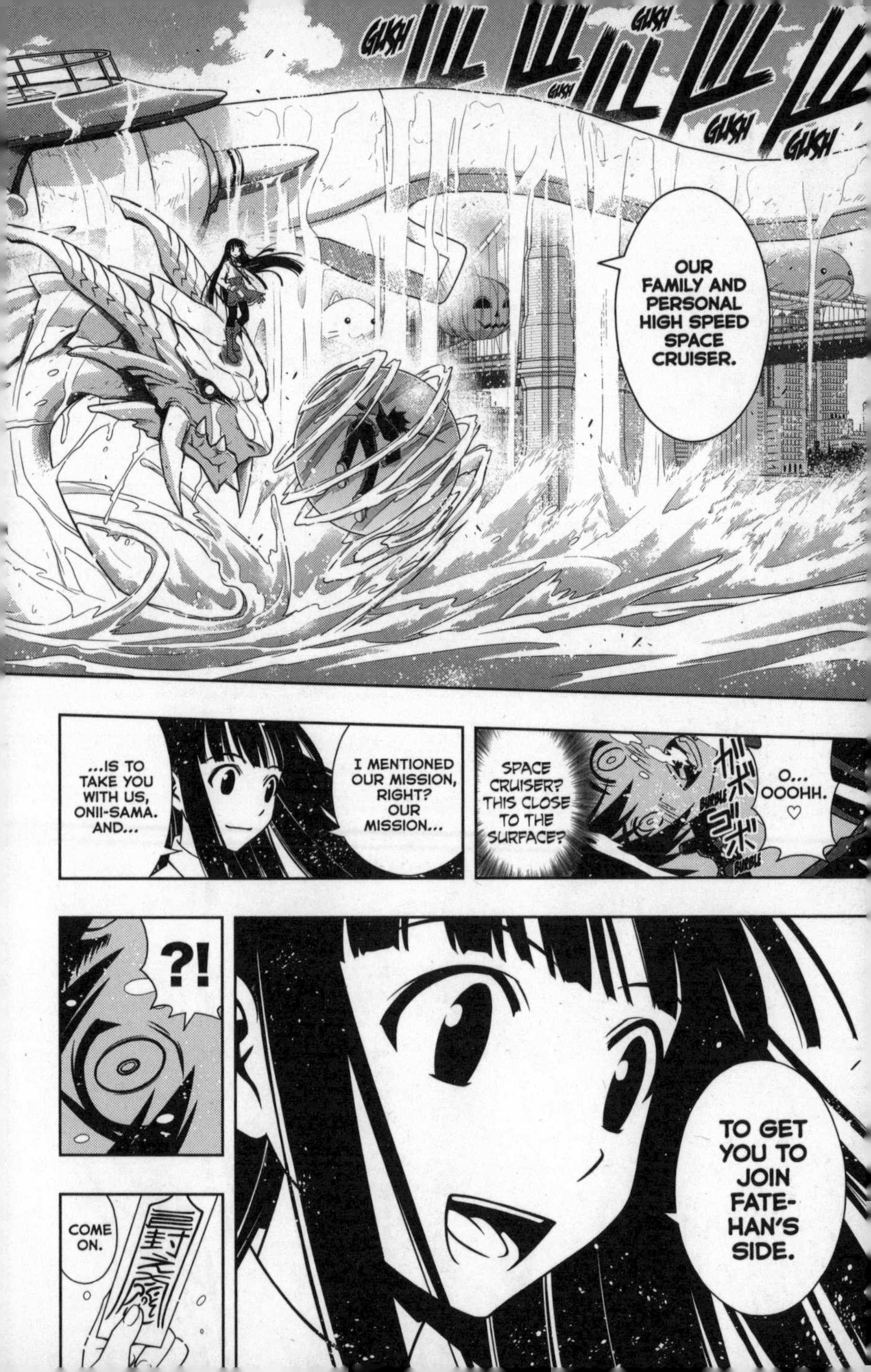
GUSH
GUSH
GUSH
GUSH
GUSH
OUR FAMILY AND PERSONAL HIGH SPEED SPACE CRUISER.
SPACE CRUISER? THIS CLOSE TO THE SURFACE?
BURBLE
BURBLE
O... OOOHH. ♡
I MENTIONED OUR MISSION, RIGHT? OUR MISSION...
...IS TO TAKE YOU WITH US, ONII-SAMA. AND...
TO GET YOU TO JOIN FATE-HAN'S SIDE.
?!
COME ON.

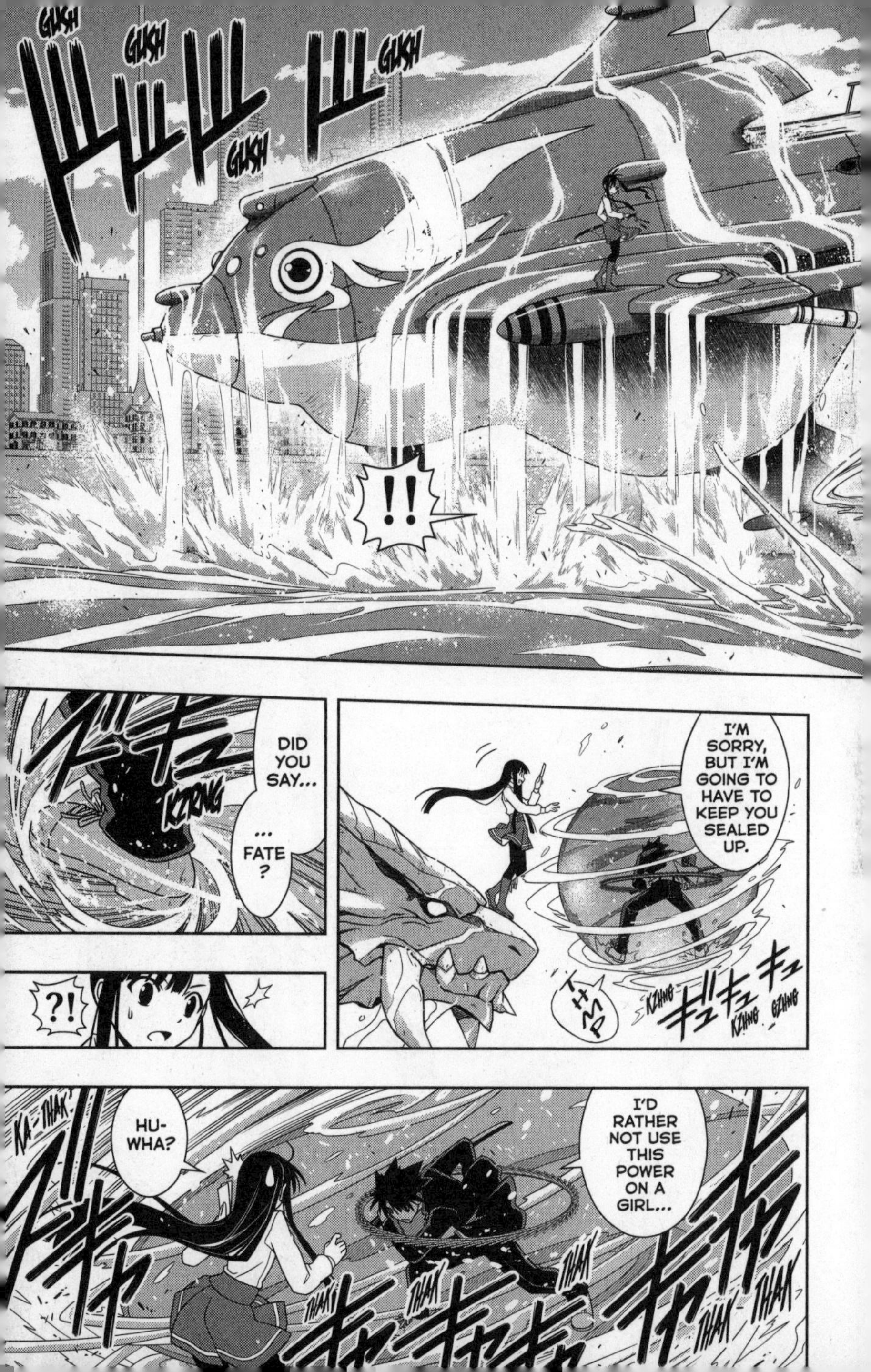
GUSH
GUSH
GUSH
GUSH
!!
I'M SORRY, BUT I'M GOING TO HAVE TO KEEP YOU SEALED UP.
KZHNG
KZHNG
GZHNG
DID YOU SAY...
... FATE?
KZRNG
?!
I'D RATHER NOT USE THIS POWER ON A GIRL...
HU-WHA?
KA-THAK
THAK
THAK
THAK
THAK
THAK
THAK

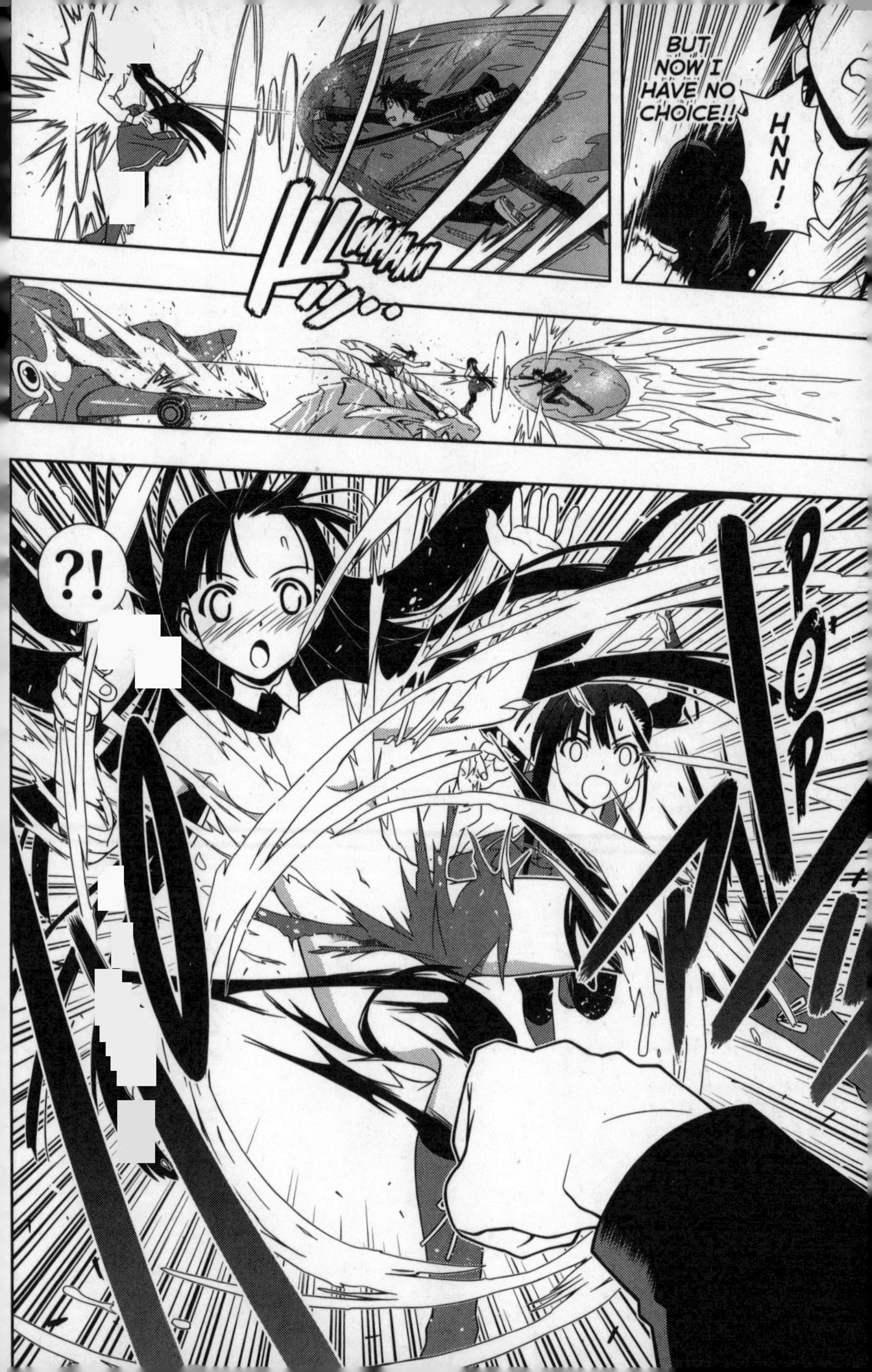
BUT NOW I HAVE NO CHOICE!!
HNN!
?!
POP

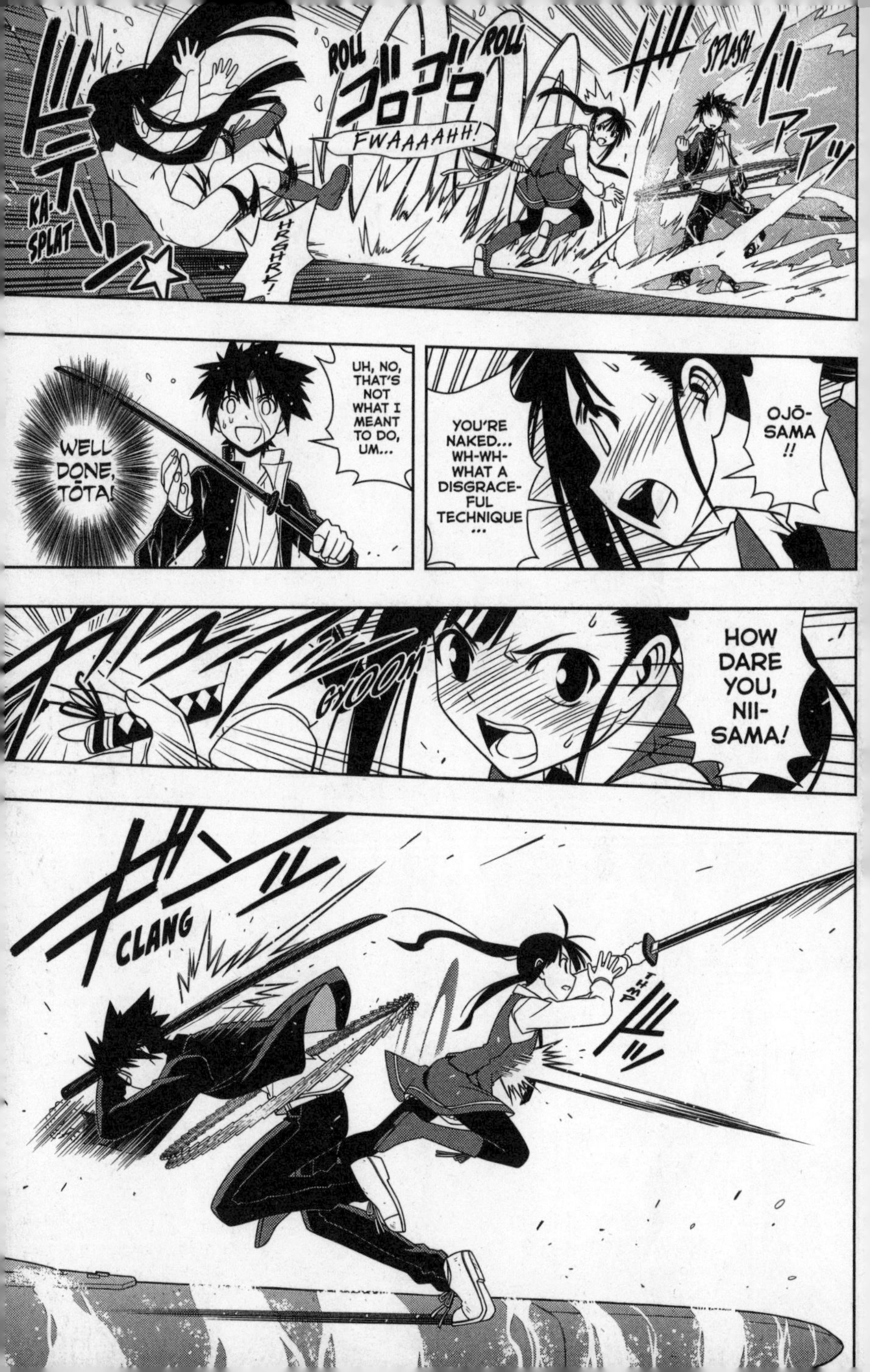
SPLASH
ROLL
ROLL
FWAAAAHH!
KA-SPLAT
HRGHRK!
OJŌ-SAMA!!
YOU'RE NAKED... WH-WH-WHAT A DISGRACEFUL TECHNIQUE...
UH, NO, THAT'S NOT WHAT I MEANT TO DO, UM...
WELL DONE, TŌTA!
HOW DARE YOU, NII-SAMA!
GYOOM
THMP
CLANG

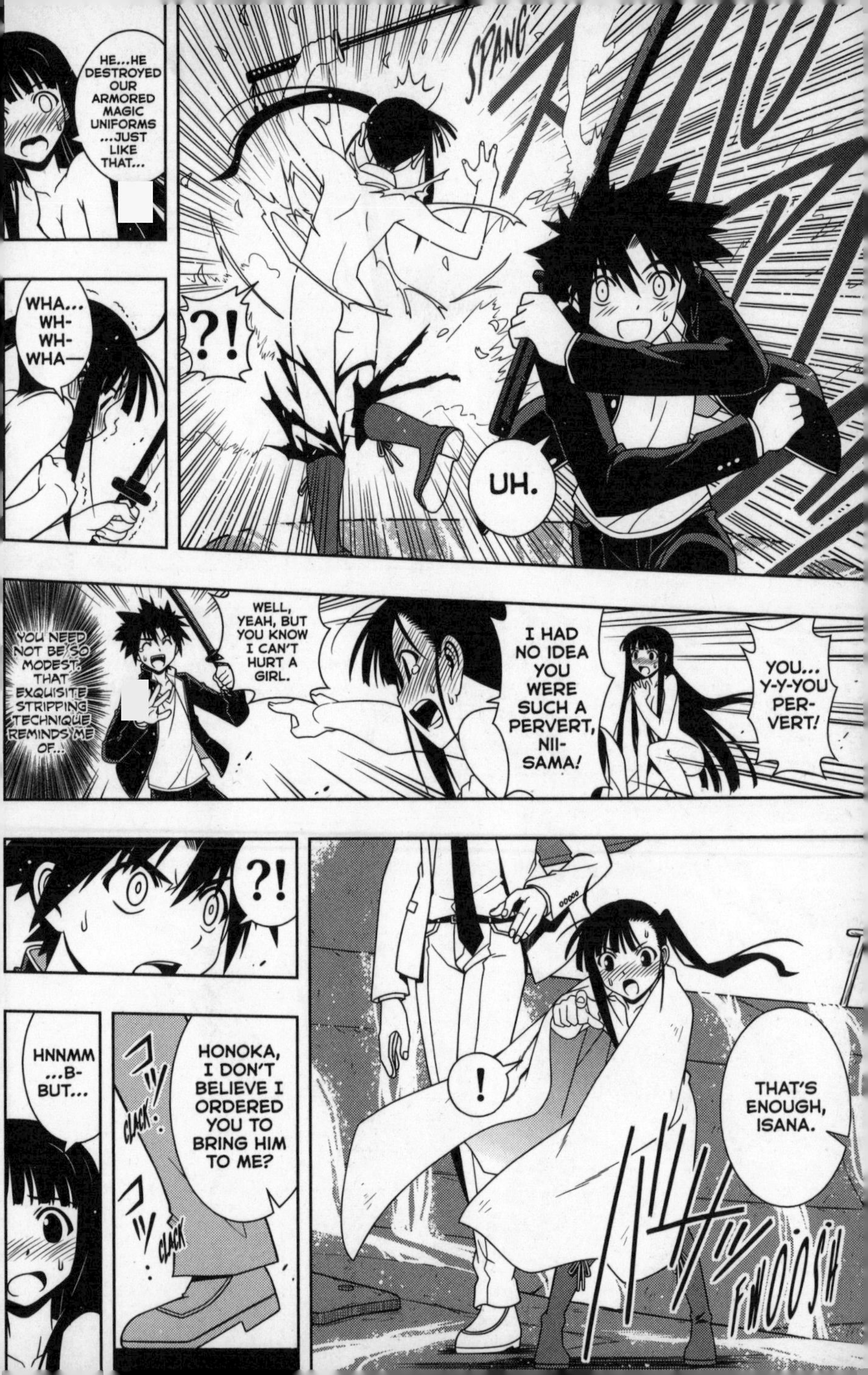
SPANG
?!
UH.
HE...HE DESTROYED OUR ARMORED MAGIC UNIFORMS ...JUST LIKE THAT...
WHA... WH- WH- WHA—
YOU... Y-Y-YOU PER-VERT!
I HAD NO IDEA YOU WERE SUCH A PERVERT, NII-SAMA!
WELL, YEAH, BUT YOU KNOW I CAN'T HURT A GIRL.
YOU NEED NOT BE SO MODEST. THAT EXQUISITE STRIPPING TECHNIQUE REMINDS ME OF...
THAT'S ENOUGH, ISANA.
!
FWOOSH
?!
HONOKA, I DON'T BELIEVE I ORDERED YOU TO BRING HIM TO ME?
CLACK
CLACK
HNNMM ...B-BUT...

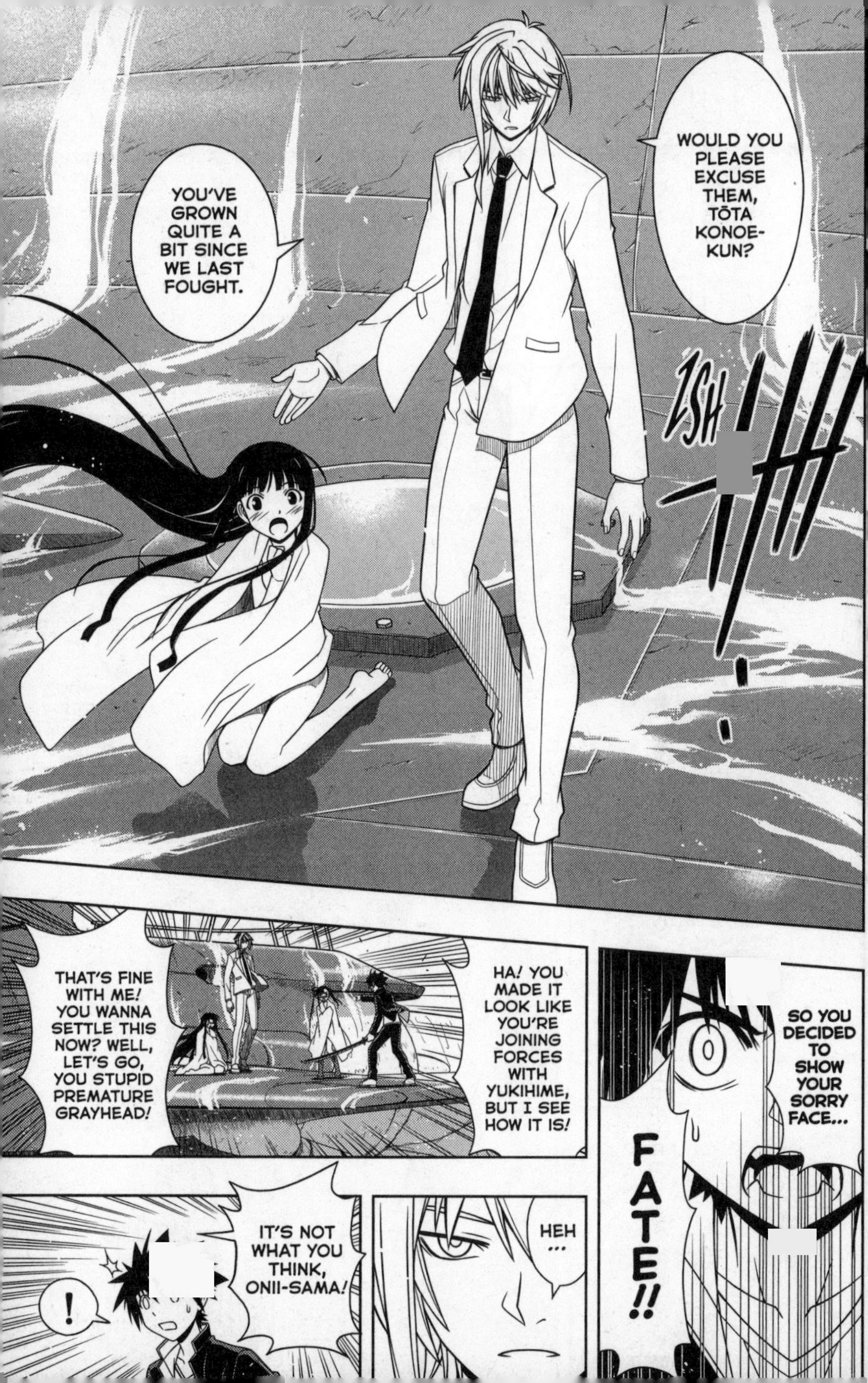
WOULD YOU PLEASE EXCUSE THEM, TŌTA KONOE-KUN?
YOU'VE GROWN QUITE A BIT SINCE WE LAST FOUGHT.
ZSH
SO YOU DECIDED TO SHOW YOUR SORRY FACE...
FATE!!
HA! YOU MADE IT LOOK LIKE YOU'RE JOINING FORCES WITH YUKIHIME, BUT I SEE HOW IT IS!
THAT'S FINE WITH ME! YOU WANNA SETTLE THIS NOW? WELL, LET'S GO, YOU STUPID PREMATURE GRAYHEAD!
HEH...
IT'S NOT WHAT YOU THINK, ONII-SAMA!
!

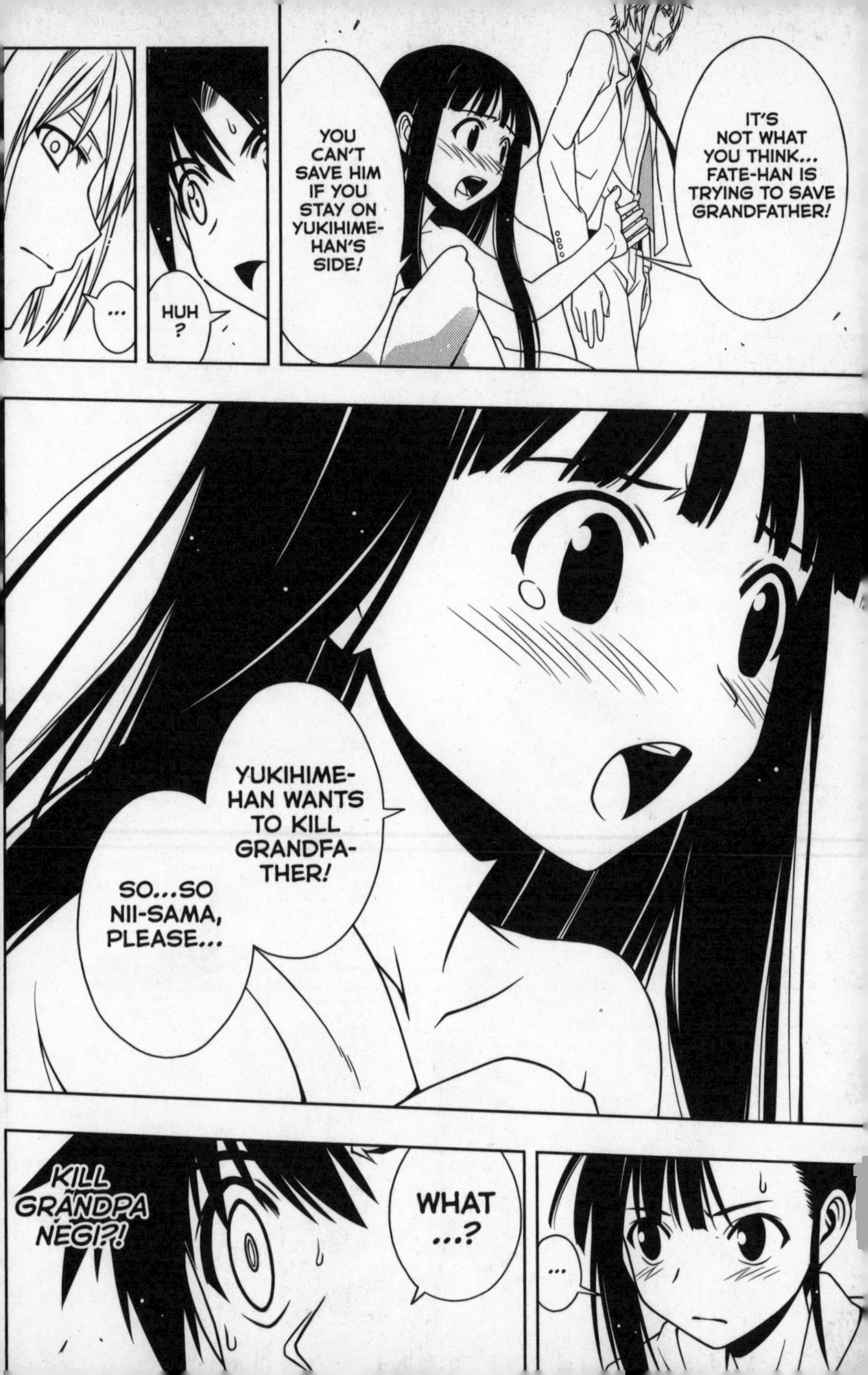
IT'S NOT WHAT YOU THINK... FATE-HAN IS TRYING TO SAVE GRANDFATHER!
YOU CAN'T SAVE HIM IF YOU STAY ON YUKIHIME-HAN'S SIDE!
HUH?
...
YUKIHIME-HAN WANTS TO KILL GRANDFATHER!
SO...SO NII-SAMA, PLEASE...
...
WHAT ...?
KILL GRANDPA NEGI?!

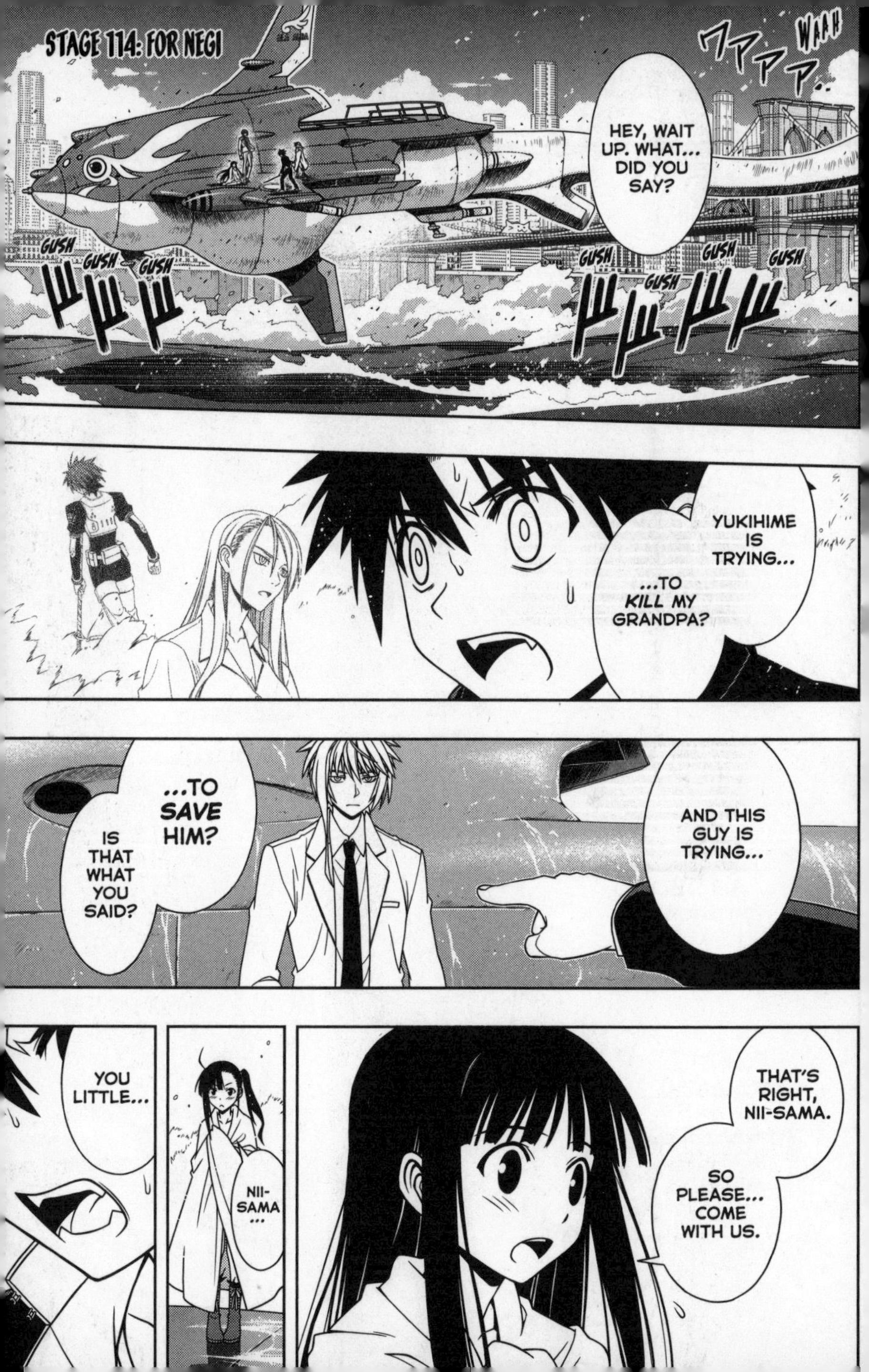
STAGE 114: FOR NEGI
ワアア..
WAAH
HEY, WAIT UP. WHAT... DID YOU SAY?
GUSH
GUSH
GUSH
GUSH
GUSH
GUSH
GUSH
YUKIHIME IS TRYING...
...TO KILL MY GRANDPA?
AND THIS GUY IS TRYING...
...TO SAVE HIM?
IS THAT WHAT YOU SAID?
THAT'S RIGHT, NII-SAMA.
SO PLEASE... COME WITH US.
NII-SAMA...
YOU LITTLE...

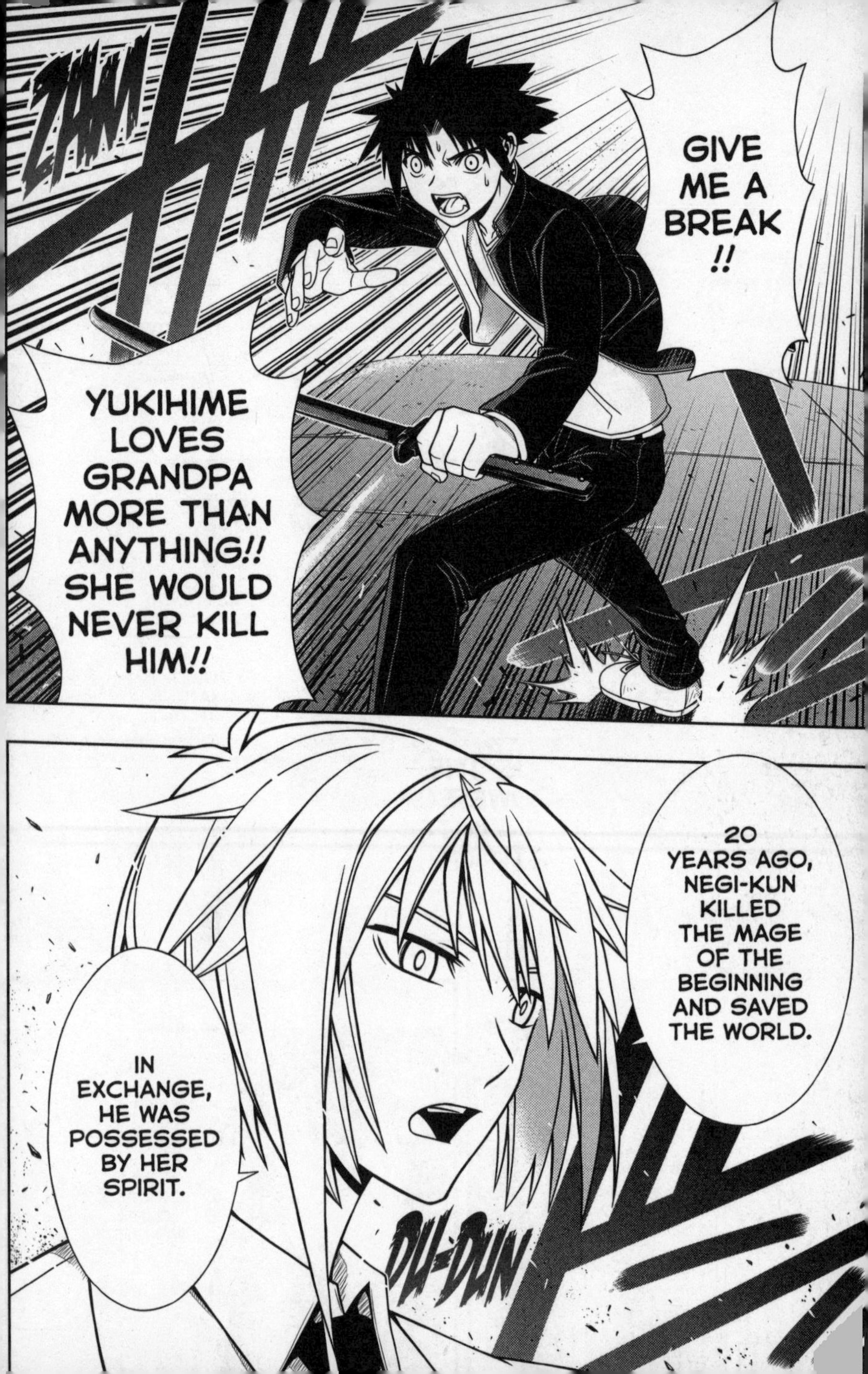
GIVE ME A BREAK!!
ZHAA
YUKIHIME LOVES GRANDPA MORE THAN ANYTHING!! SHE WOULD NEVER KILL HIM!!
20 YEARS AGO, NEGI-KUN KILLED THE MAGE OF THE BEGINNING AND SAVED THE WORLD.
IN EXCHANGE, HE WAS POSSESSED BY HER SPIRIT.
DU-DUN

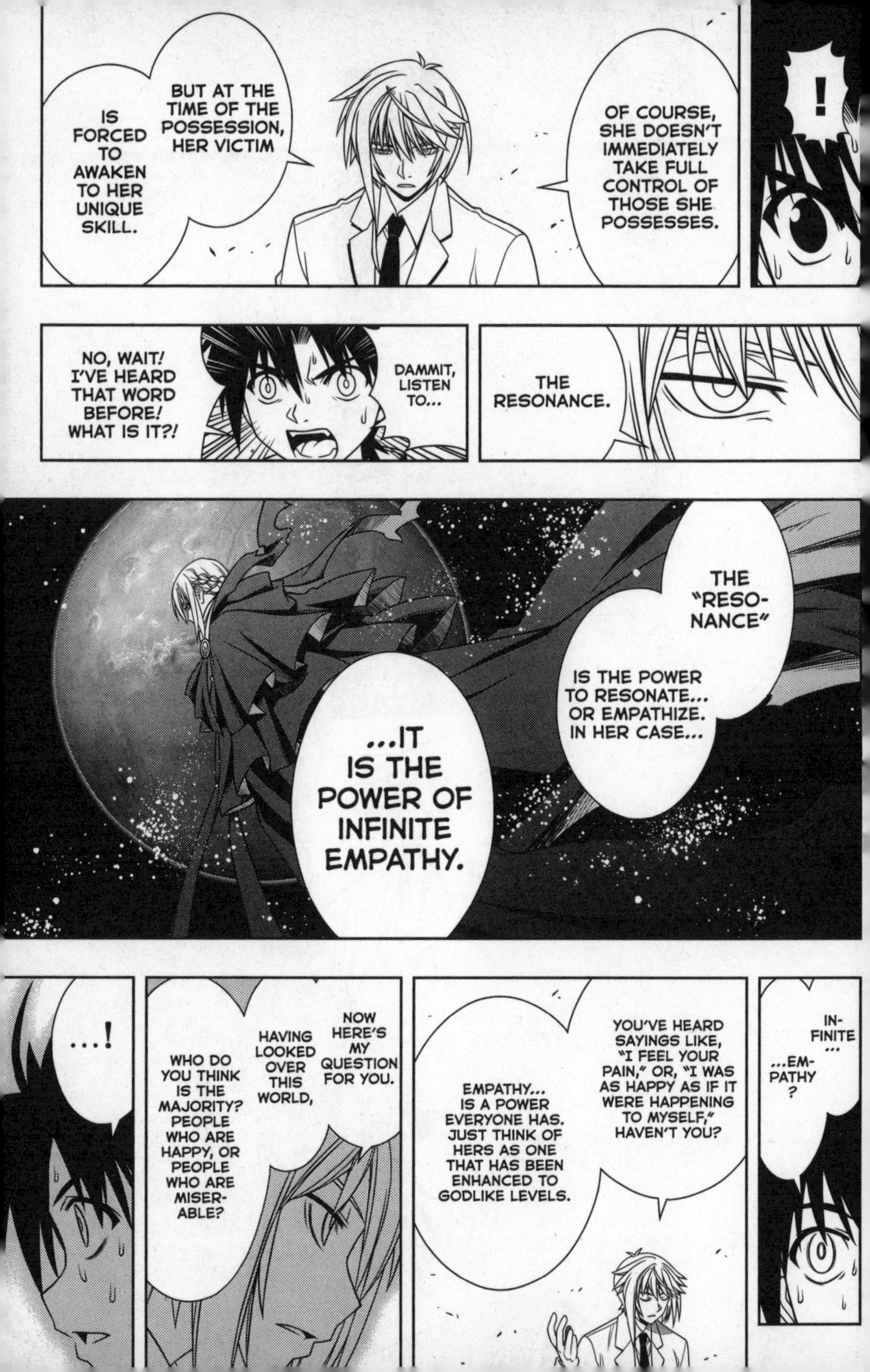
!
OF COURSE, SHE DOESN'T IMMEDIATELY TAKE FULL CONTROL OF THOSE SHE POSSESSES.
BUT AT THE TIME OF THE POSSESSION, HER VICTIM
IS FORCED TO AWAKEN TO HER UNIQUE SKILL.
THE RESONANCE.
DAMMIT, LISTEN TO...
NO, WAIT! I'VE HEARD THAT WORD BEFORE! WHAT IS IT?!
THE "RESO-NANCE"
IS THE POWER TO RESONATE... OR EMPATHIZE. IN HER CASE...
...IT IS THE POWER OF INFINITE EMPATHY.
IN-FINITE...
...EM-PATHY?
YOU'VE HEARD SAYINGS LIKE, "I FEEL YOUR PAIN," OR, "I WAS AS HAPPY AS IF IT WERE HAPPENING TO MYSELF," HAVEN'T YOU?
EMPATHY... IS A POWER EVERYONE HAS. JUST THINK OF HERS AS ONE THAT HAS BEEN ENHANCED TO GODLIKE LEVELS.
NOW HERE'S MY QUESTION FOR YOU.
HAVING LOOKED OVER THIS WORLD,
WHO DO YOU THINK IS THE MAJORITY? PEOPLE WHO ARE HAPPY, OR PEOPLE WHO ARE MISER-ABLE?
...!

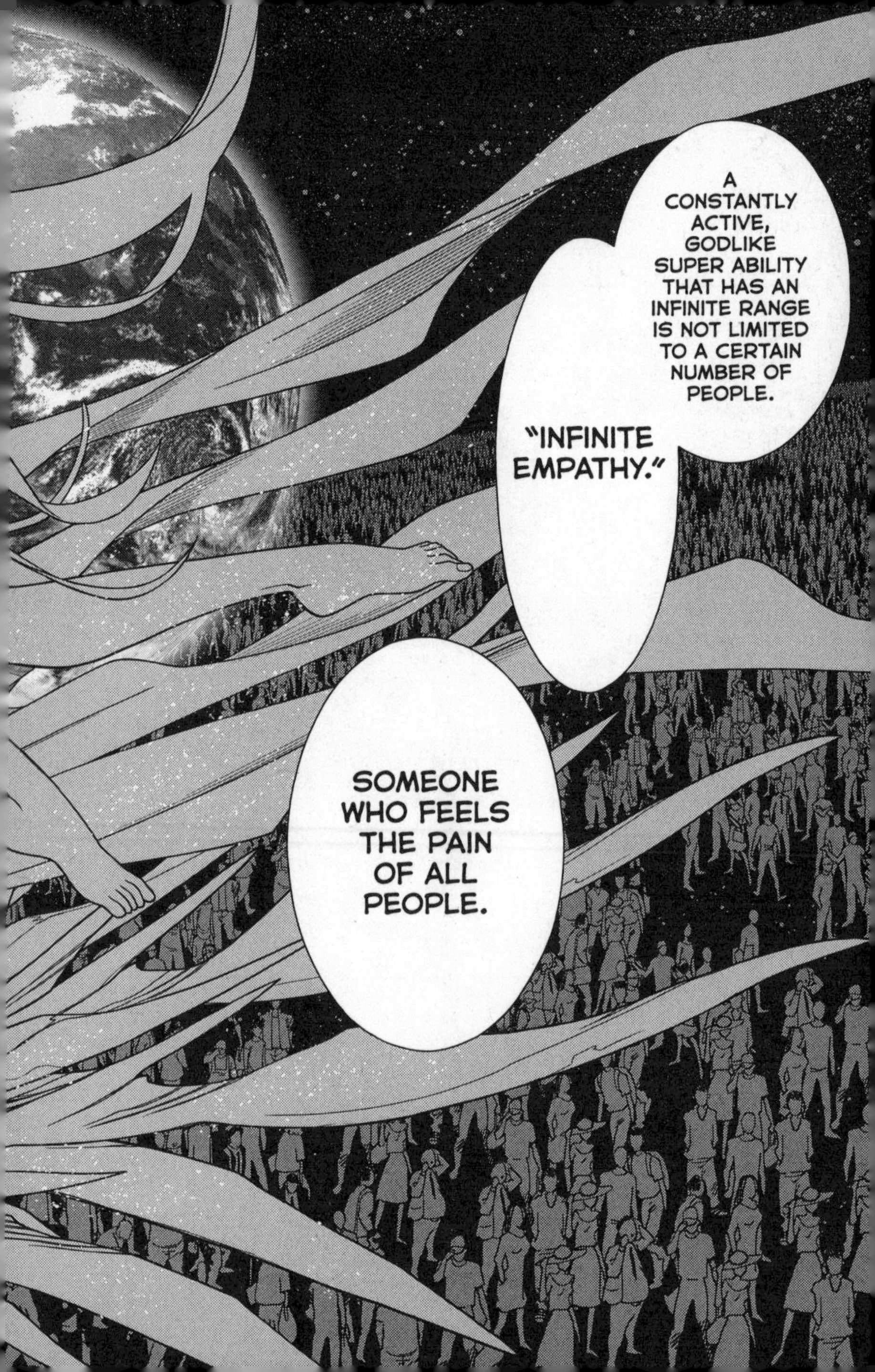
A CONSTANTLY ACTIVE, GODLIKE SUPER ABILITY THAT HAS AN INFINITE RANGE IS NOT LIMITED TO A CERTAIN NUMBER OF PEOPLE.
"INFINITE EMPATHY."
SOMEONE WHO FEELS THE PAIN OF ALL PEOPLE.

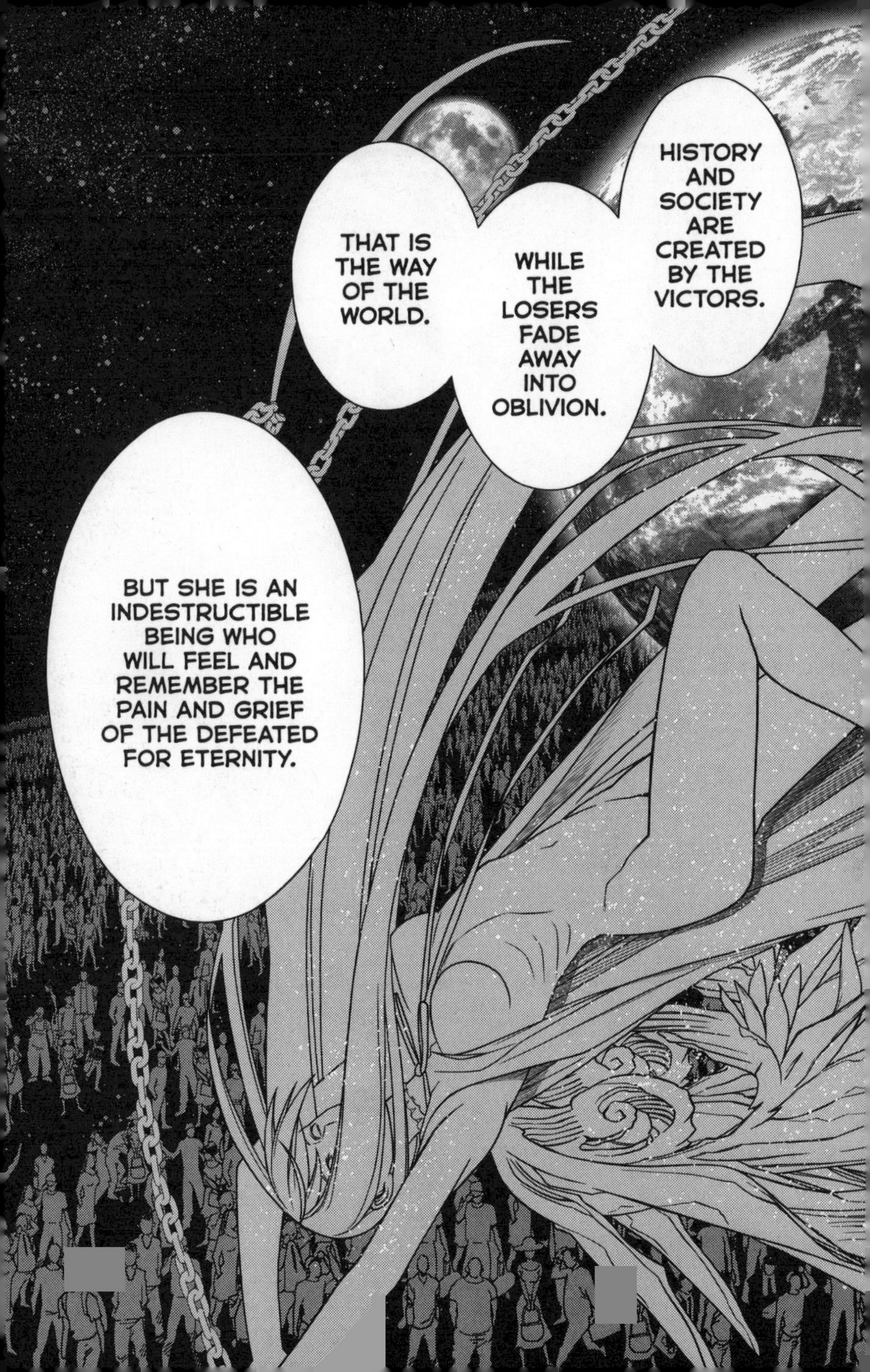
HISTORY AND SOCIETY ARE CREATED BY THE VICTORS.
WHILE THE LOSERS FADE AWAY INTO OBLIVION.
THAT IS THE WAY OF THE WORLD.
BUT SHE IS AN INDESTRUCTIBLE BEING WHO WILL FEEL AND REMEMBER THE PAIN AND GRIEF OF THE DEFEATED FOR ETERNITY.

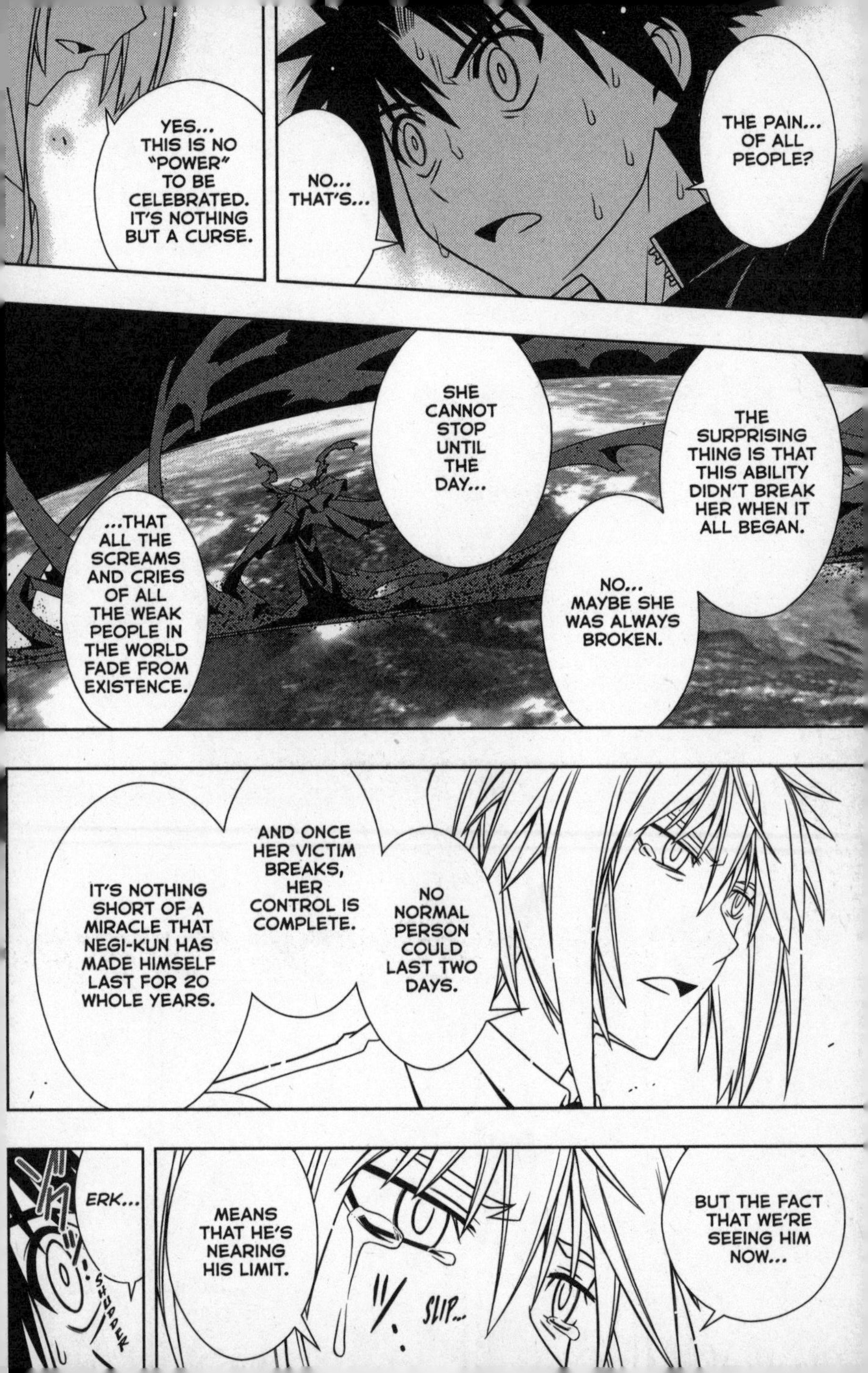
THE PAIN... OF ALL PEOPLE?
NO... THAT'S...
YES... THIS IS NO "POWER" TO BE CELEBRATED. IT'S NOTHING BUT A CURSE.
THE SURPRISING THING IS THAT THIS ABILITY DIDN'T BREAK HER WHEN IT ALL BEGAN.
NO... MAYBE SHE WAS ALWAYS BROKEN.
SHE CANNOT STOP UNTIL THE DAY...
...THAT ALL THE SCREAMS AND CRIES OF ALL THE WEAK PEOPLE IN THE WORLD FADE FROM EXISTENCE.
NO NORMAL PERSON COULD LAST TWO DAYS.
AND ONCE HER VICTIM BREAKS, HER CONTROL IS COMPLETE.
IT'S NOTHING SHORT OF A MIRACLE THAT NEGI-KUN HAS MADE HIMSELF LAST FOR 20 WHOLE YEARS.
BUT THE FACT THAT WE'RE SEEING HIM NOW...
MEANS THAT HE'S NEARING HIS LIMIT.
SLIP...
ERK...
SHUDDER

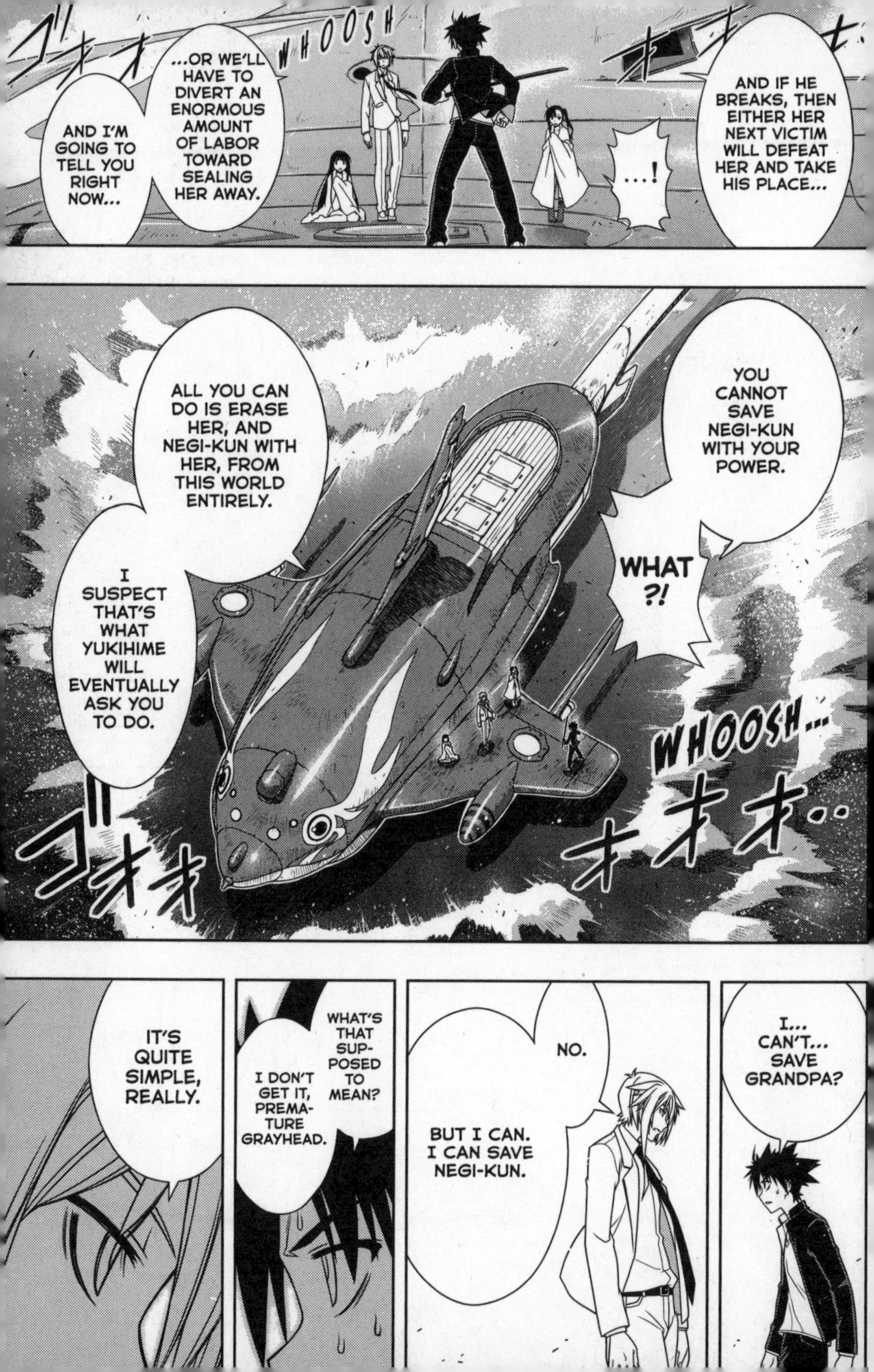
WHOOSH
AND IF HE BREAKS, THEN EITHER HER NEXT VICTIM WILL DEFEAT HER AND TAKE HIS PLACE...
...!
...OR WE'LL HAVE TO DIVERT AN ENORMOUS AMOUNT OF LABOR TOWARD SEALING HER AWAY.
AND I'M GOING TO TELL YOU RIGHT NOW...
YOU CANNOT SAVE NEGI-KUN WITH YOUR POWER.
WHAT?!
ALL YOU CAN DO IS ERASE HER, AND NEGI-KUN WITH HER, FROM THIS WORLD ENTIRELY.
I SUSPECT THAT'S WHAT YUKIHIME WILL EVENTUALLY ASK YOU TO DO.
WHOOSH...
ゴオオオオオ..
I... CAN'T... SAVE GRANDPA?
NO.
BUT I CAN. I CAN SAVE NEGI-KUN.
WHAT'S THAT SUP-POSED TO MEAN?
I DON'T GET IT, PREMA-TURE GRAYHEAD.
IT'S QUITE SIMPLE, REALLY.

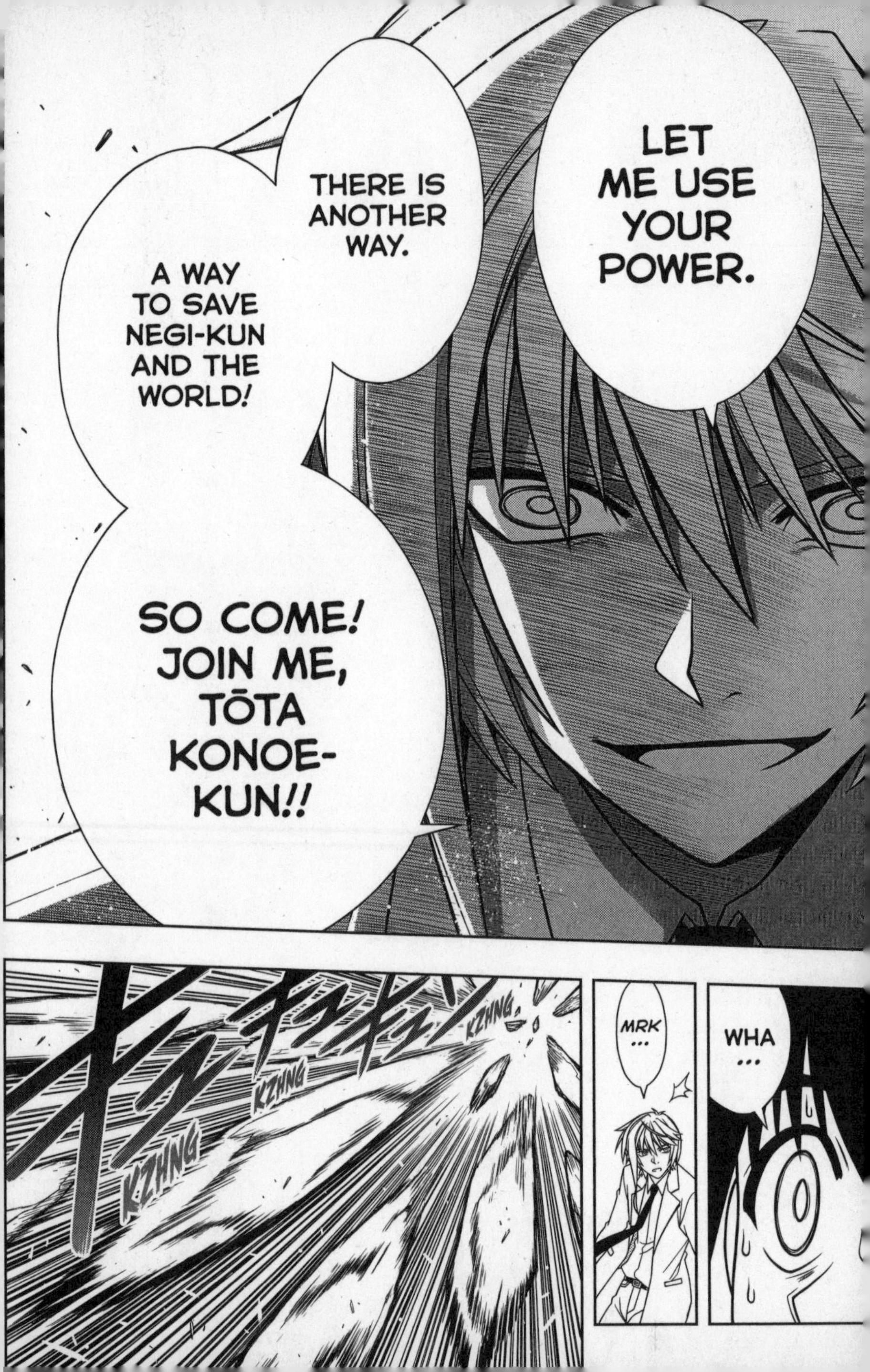
LET ME USE YOUR POWER.
THERE IS ANOTHER WAY.
A WAY TO SAVE NEGI-KUN AND THE WORLD!
SO COME! JOIN ME, TŌTA KONOE-KUN!!
WHA ...
MRK ...
KZHNG
KZHNG
KZHNG
KZHNG

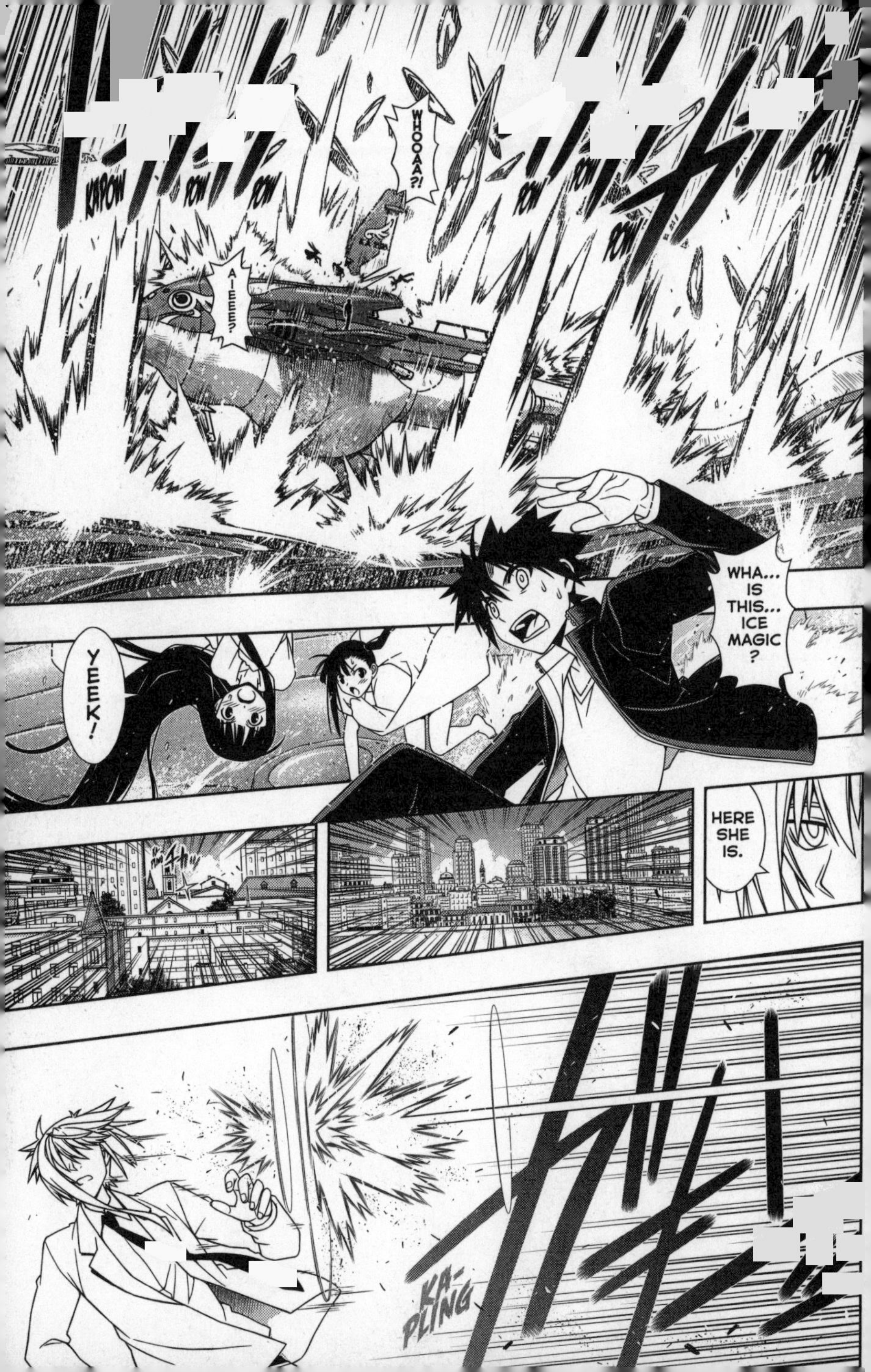
POW
POW
POW
WHOOAA?!
POW
POW
POW
KAPOW
AIEEE?
WHA... IS THIS... ICE MAGIC?
YEEK!
HERE SHE IS.
KA-PLING

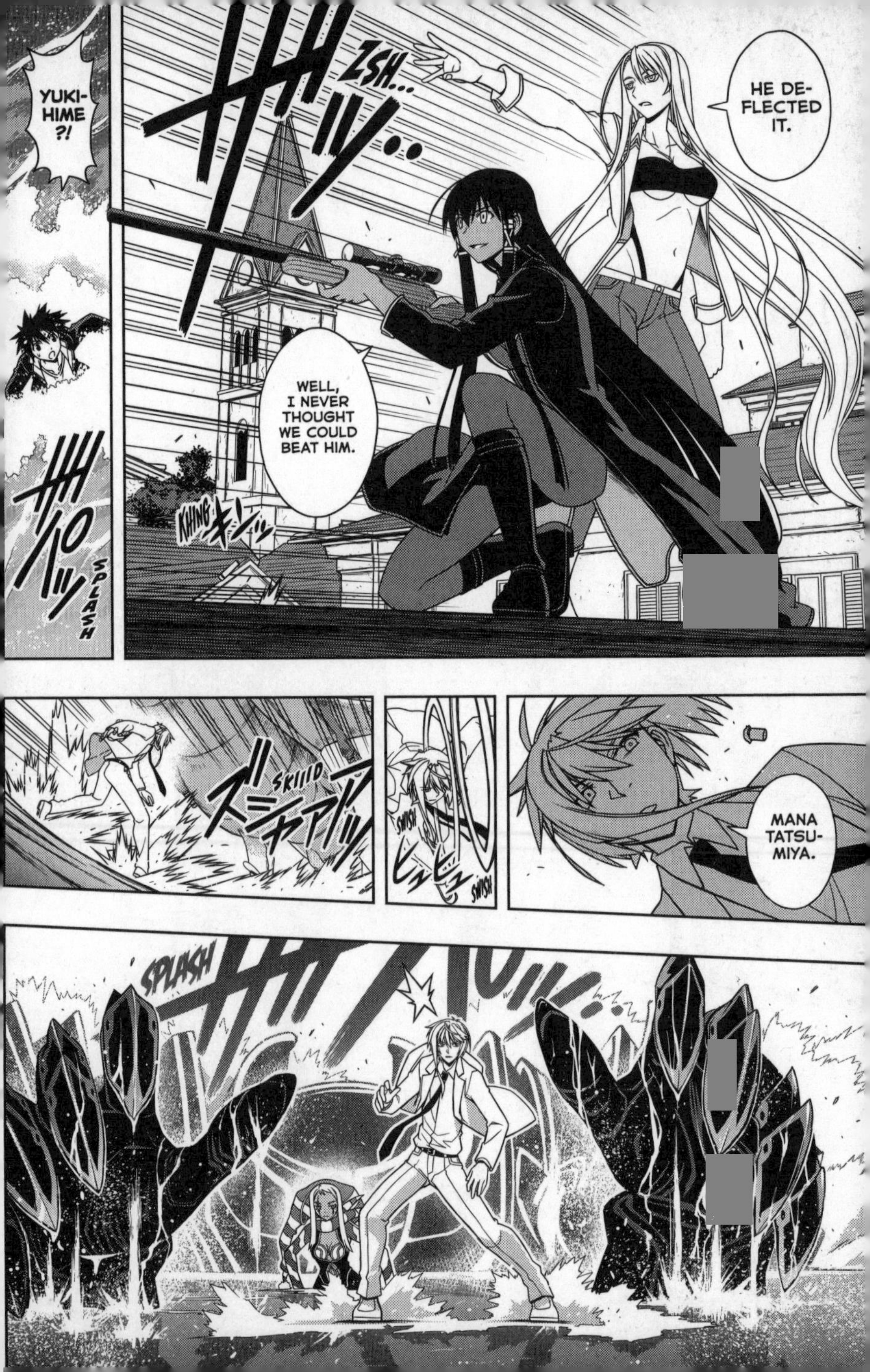
ZSH...
HE DE-FLECTED IT.
WELL, I NEVER THOUGHT WE COULD BEAT HIM.
KHING
YUKI-HIME ?!
SPLASH
MANA TATSU-MIYA.
SWISH
SWISH
SKIIID
SPLASH

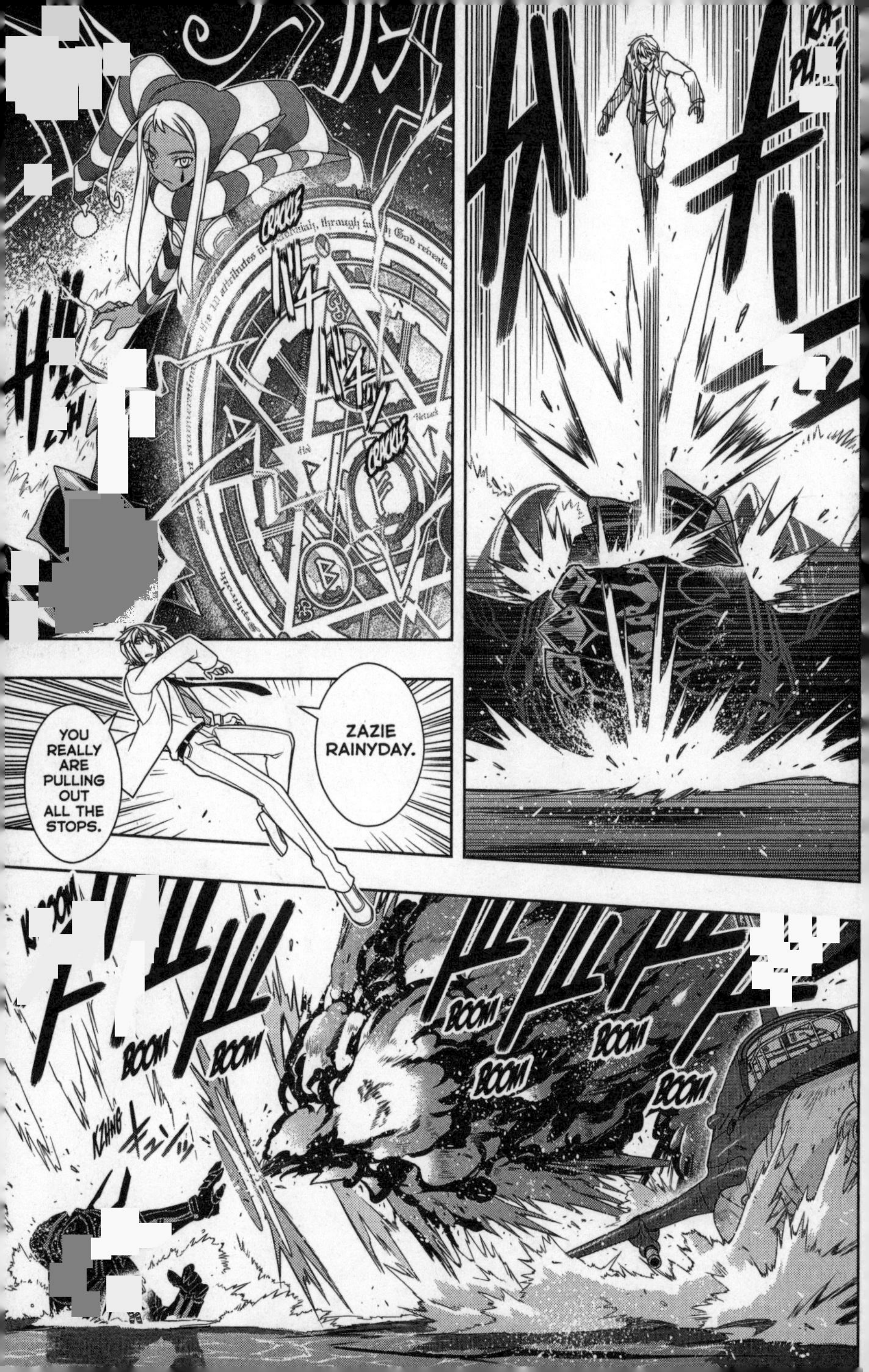
CRACKLE
CRACKLE
ZAZIE RAINYDAY.
YOU REALLY ARE PULLING OUT ALL THE STOPS.
BOOM
BOOM
BOOM
BOOM
BOOM
BOOM
BOOM
KZHING

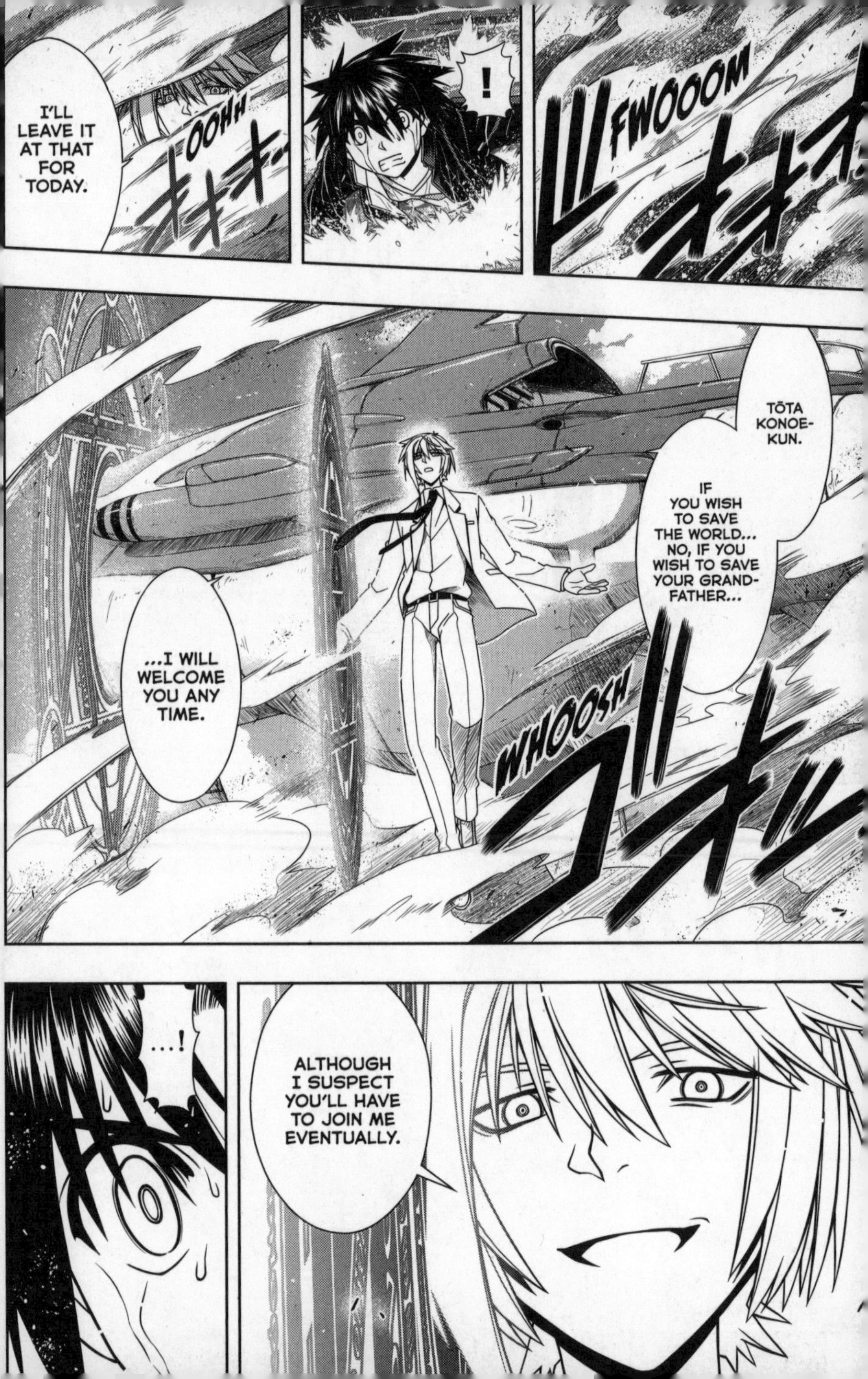
FWOOOM
!
OOHH
I'LL LEAVE IT AT THAT FOR TODAY.
TŌTA KONOE-KUN.
IF YOU WISH TO SAVE THE WORLD... NO, IF YOU WISH TO SAVE YOUR GRAND-FATHER...
WHOOSH
...I WILL WELCOME YOU ANY TIME.
ALTHOUGH I SUSPECT YOU'LL HAVE TO JOIN ME EVENTUALLY.
...!

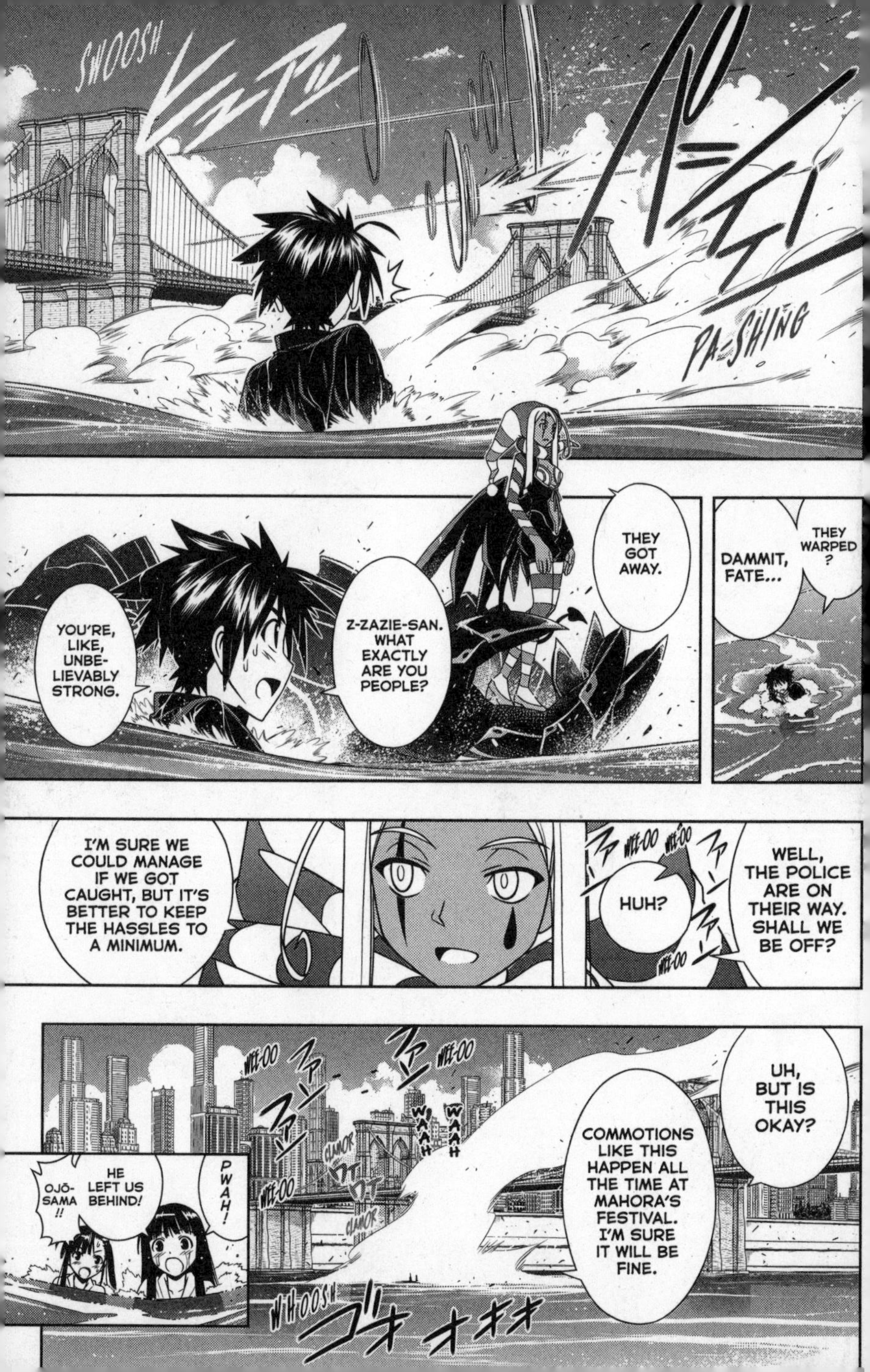
SWOOSH
PA-SHING
THEY WARPED?
DAMMIT, FATE...
THEY GOT AWAY.
Z-ZAZIE-SAN. WHAT EXACTLY ARE YOU PEOPLE?
YOU'RE, LIKE, UNBELIEVABLY STRONG.
WELL, THE POLICE ARE ON THEIR WAY. SHALL WE BE OFF?
WEE-OO
WEE-OO
HUH?
WEE-OO
I'M SURE WE COULD MANAGE IF WE GOT CAUGHT, BUT IT'S BETTER TO KEEP THE HASSLES TO A MINIMUM.
UH, BUT IS THIS OKAY?
COMMOTIONS LIKE THIS HAPPEN ALL THE TIME AT MAHORA'S FESTIVAL. I'M SURE IT WILL BE FINE.
WEE-OO
WAAAH
WAAAH
WEE-OO
CLAMOR
CLAMOR
WEE-OO
WHOOSH
PWAH!
HE LEFT US BEHIND!
OJŌ-SAMA!!

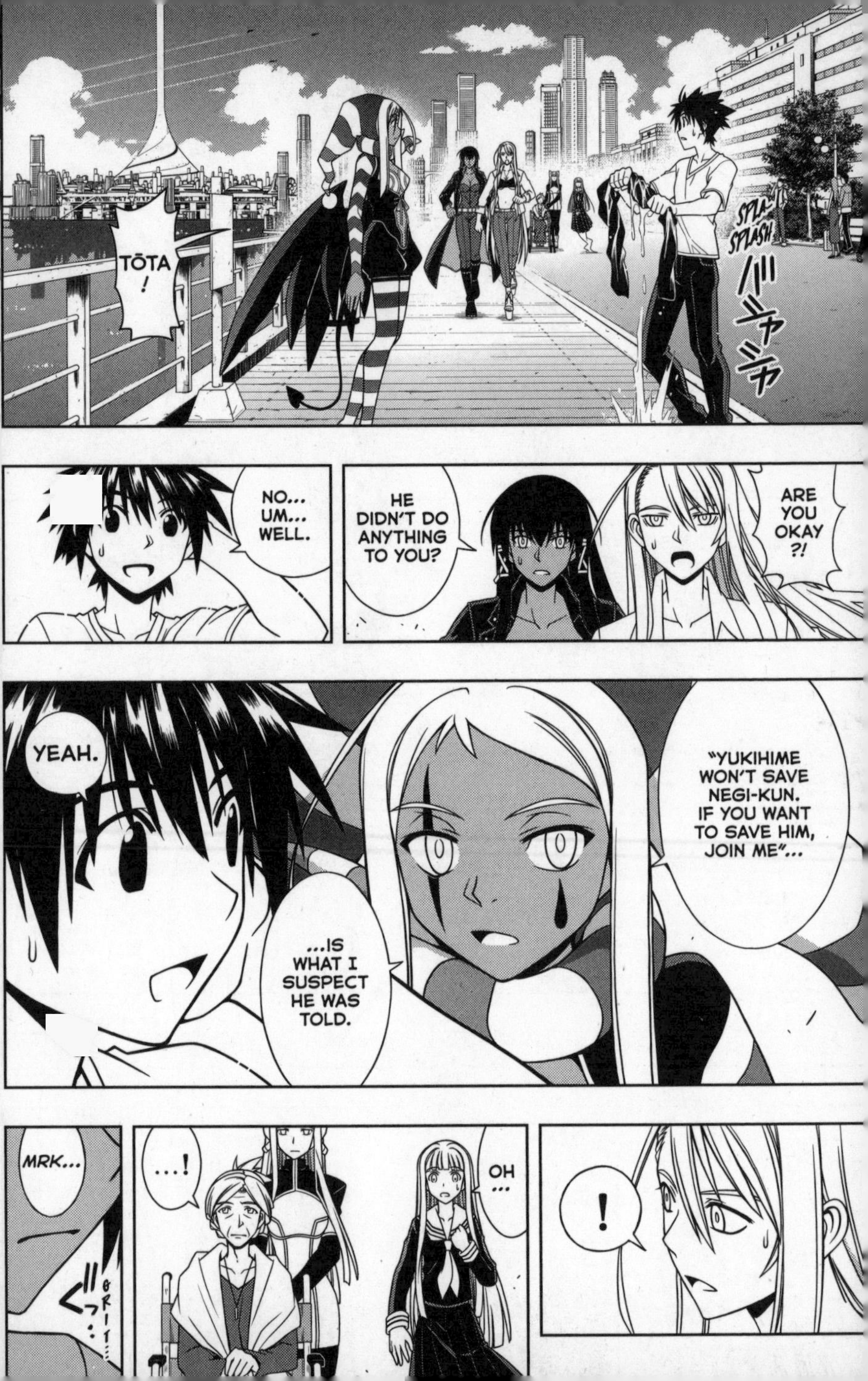
TŌTA!
SPLA- SPLASH
ARE YOU OKAY?!
HE DIDN'T DO ANYTHING TO YOU?
NO... UM... WELL.
"YUKIHIME WON'T SAVE NEGI-KUN. IF YOU WANT TO SAVE HIM, JOIN ME"...
...IS WHAT I SUSPECT HE WAS TOLD.
YEAH.
!
OH...
...!
MRK...
GRIT...

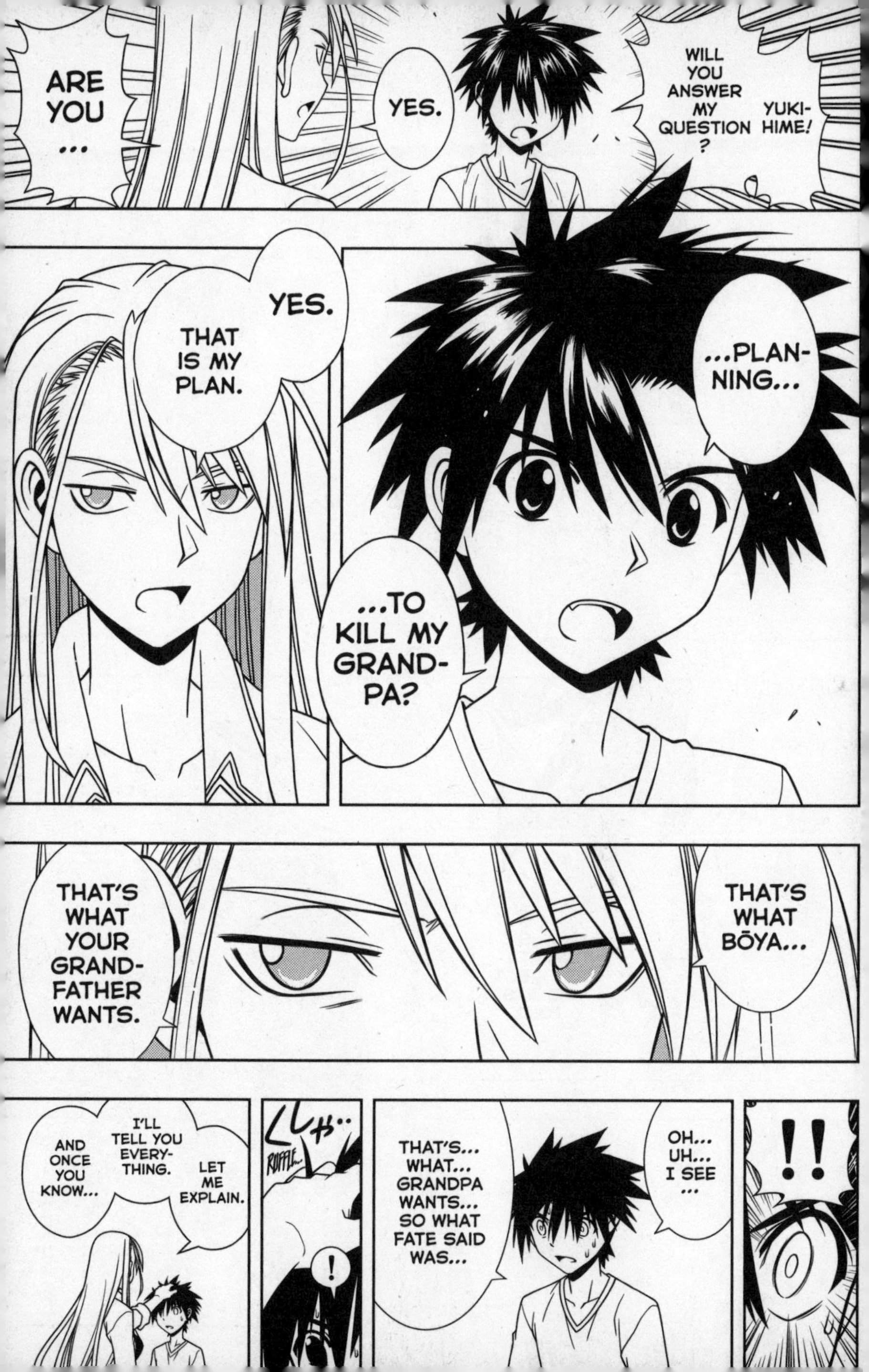
YUKI-HIME!
WILL YOU ANSWER MY QUESTION?
YES.
ARE YOU ...
...PLANNING...
...TO KILL MY GRANDPA?
YES.
THAT IS MY PLAN.
THAT'S WHAT BŌYA...
THAT'S WHAT YOUR GRANDFATHER WANTS.
!!
OH... UH... I SEE...
THAT'S... WHAT... GRANDPA WANTS... SO WHAT FATE SAID WAS...
くしゃ‥
RUFFLE...
!
LET ME EXPLAIN.
I'LL TELL YOU EVERYTHING.
AND ONCE YOU KNOW...

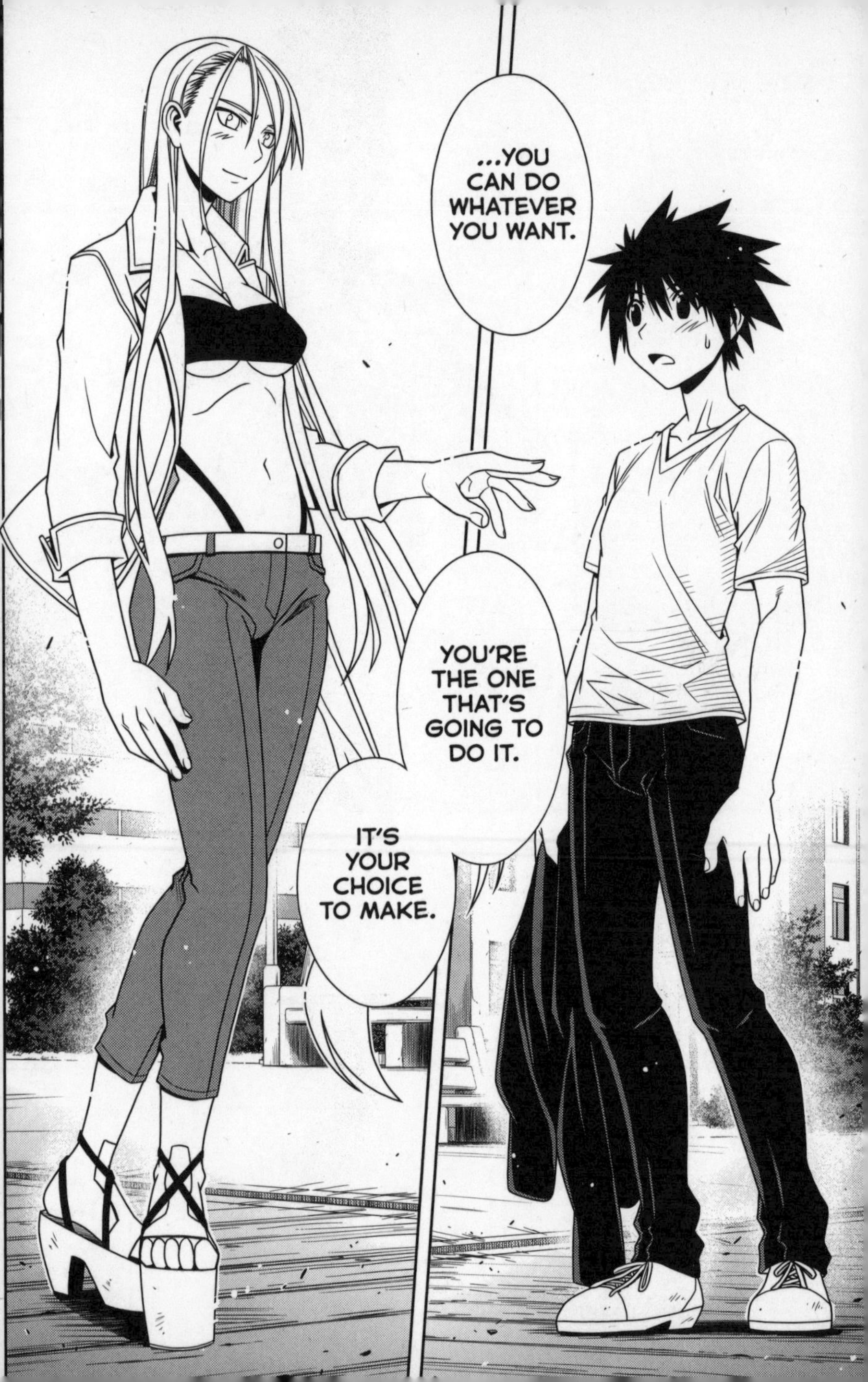
...YOU CAN DO WHATEVER YOU WANT.
YOU'RE THE ONE THAT'S GOING TO DO IT.
IT'S YOUR CHOICE TO MAKE.

UQ HOLDER!

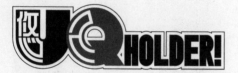

UQ
HOLDER!

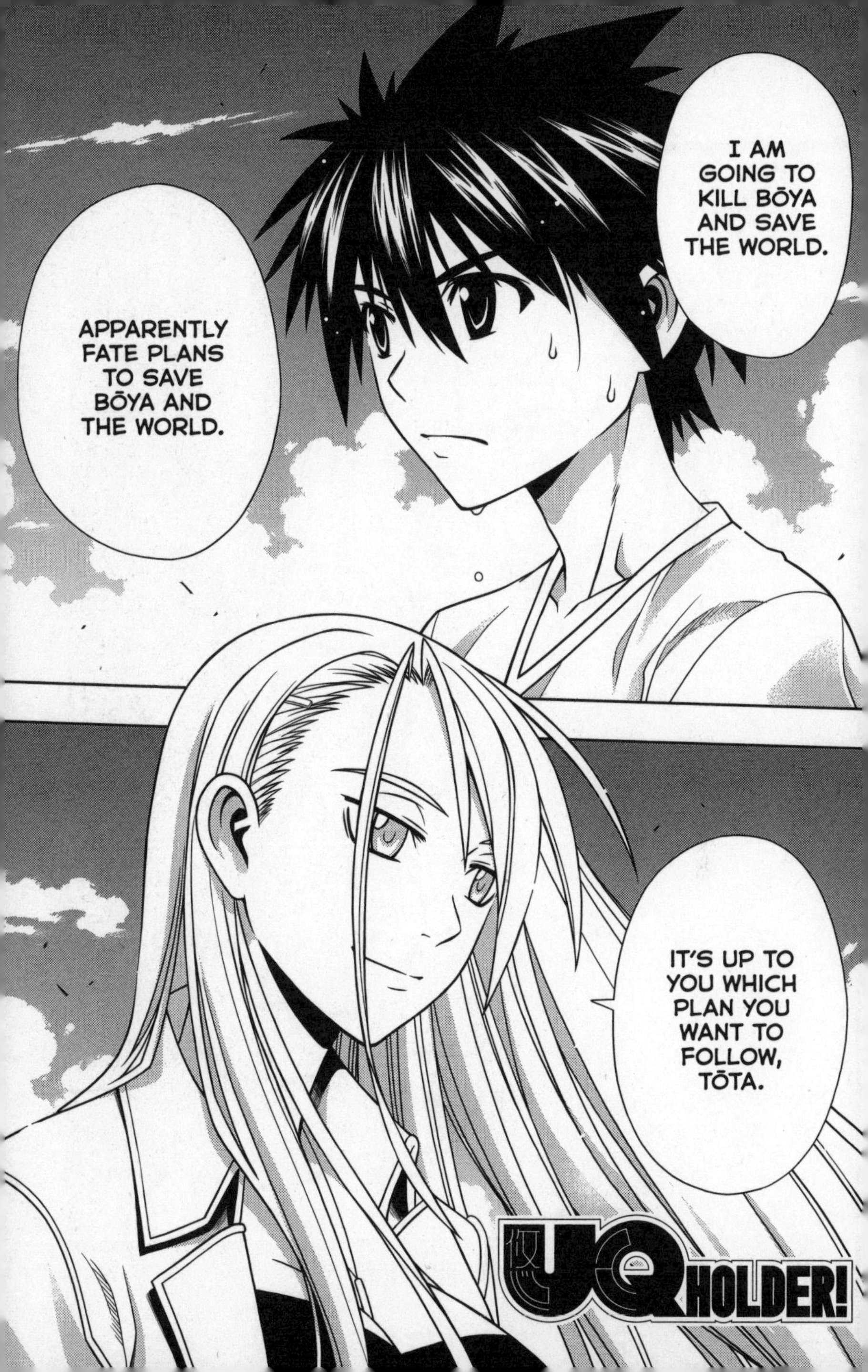
I AM GOING TO KILL BŌYA AND SAVE THE WORLD.
APPARENTLY FATE PLANS TO SAVE BŌYA AND THE WORLD.
IT'S UP TO YOU WHICH PLAN YOU WANT TO FOLLOW, TŌTA.
UQ HOLDER!

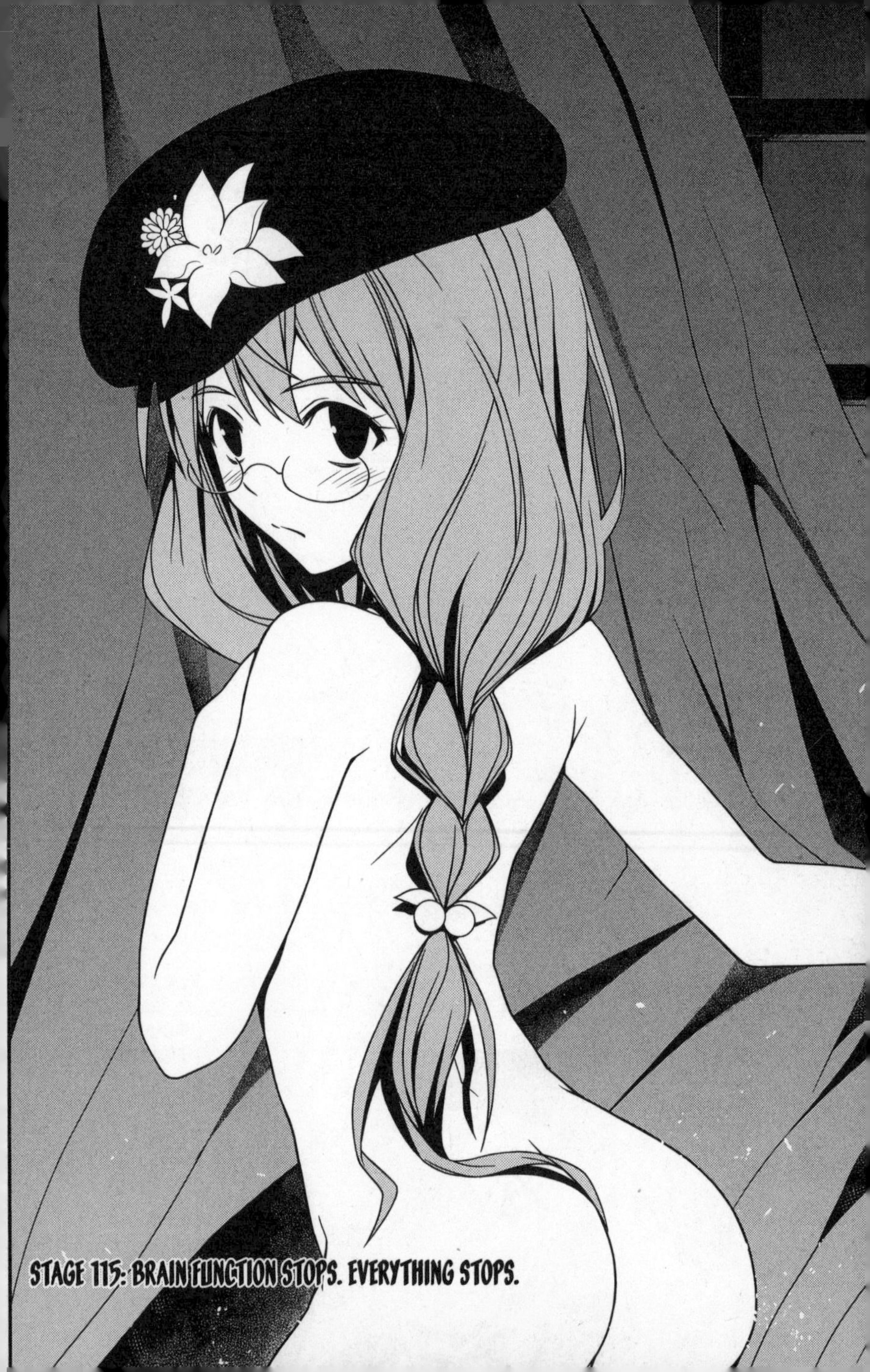
STAGE 115: BRAIN FUNCTION STOPS. EVERYTHING STOPS.

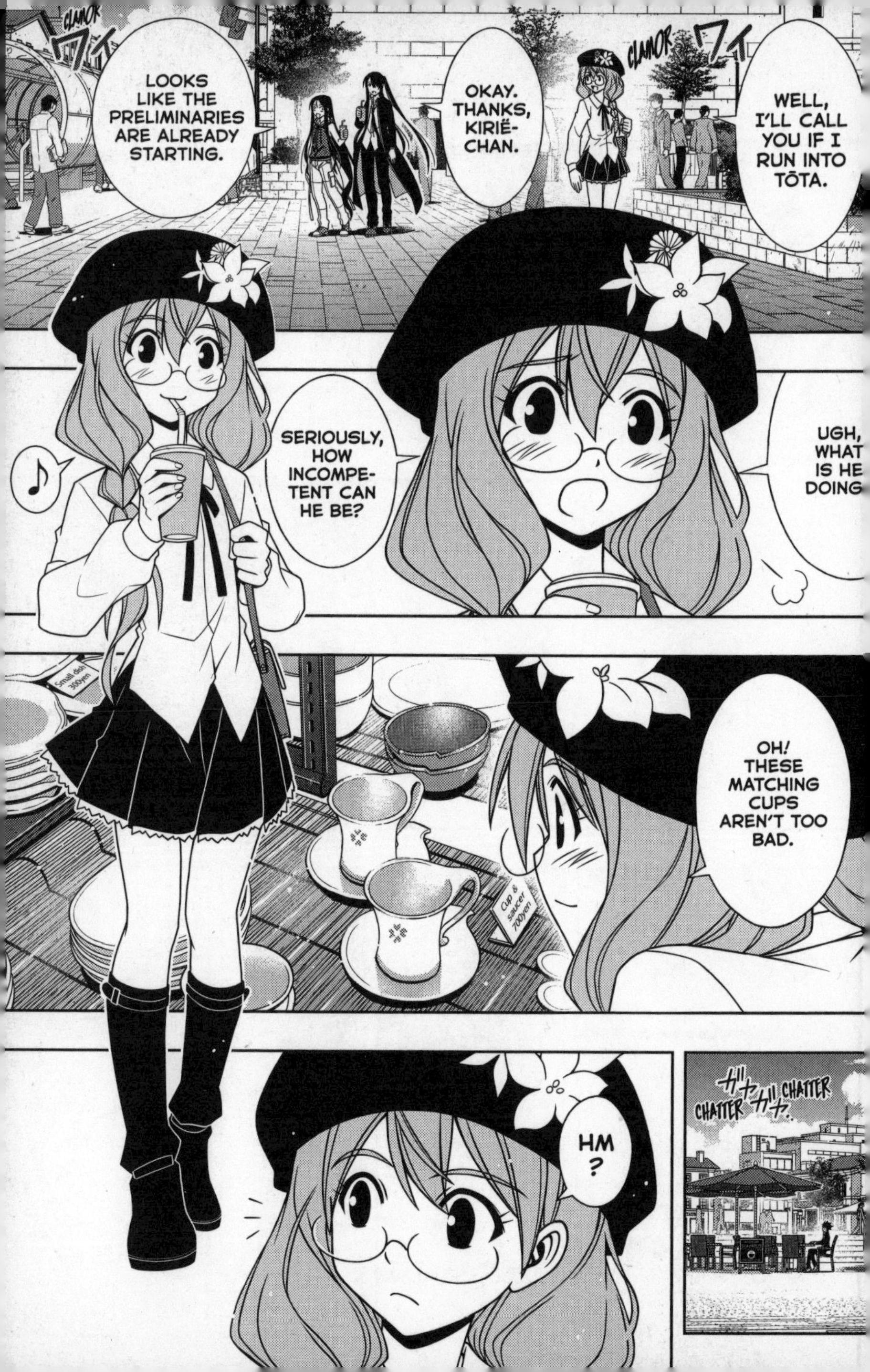
CLAMOR ワイ
WELL, I'LL CALL YOU IF I RUN INTO TŌTA.
OKAY. THANKS, KIRIÉ-CHAN.
LOOKS LIKE THE PRELIMINARIES ARE ALREADY STARTING.
CLAMOR ワイ
UGH, WHAT IS HE DOING
SERIOUSLY, HOW INCOMPE-TENT CAN HE BE?
OH! THESE MATCHING CUPS AREN'T TOO BAD.
Cup & saucer 700yen
Small dish 300yen
♪
CHATTER ガヤ ガヤ CHATTER
HM ?

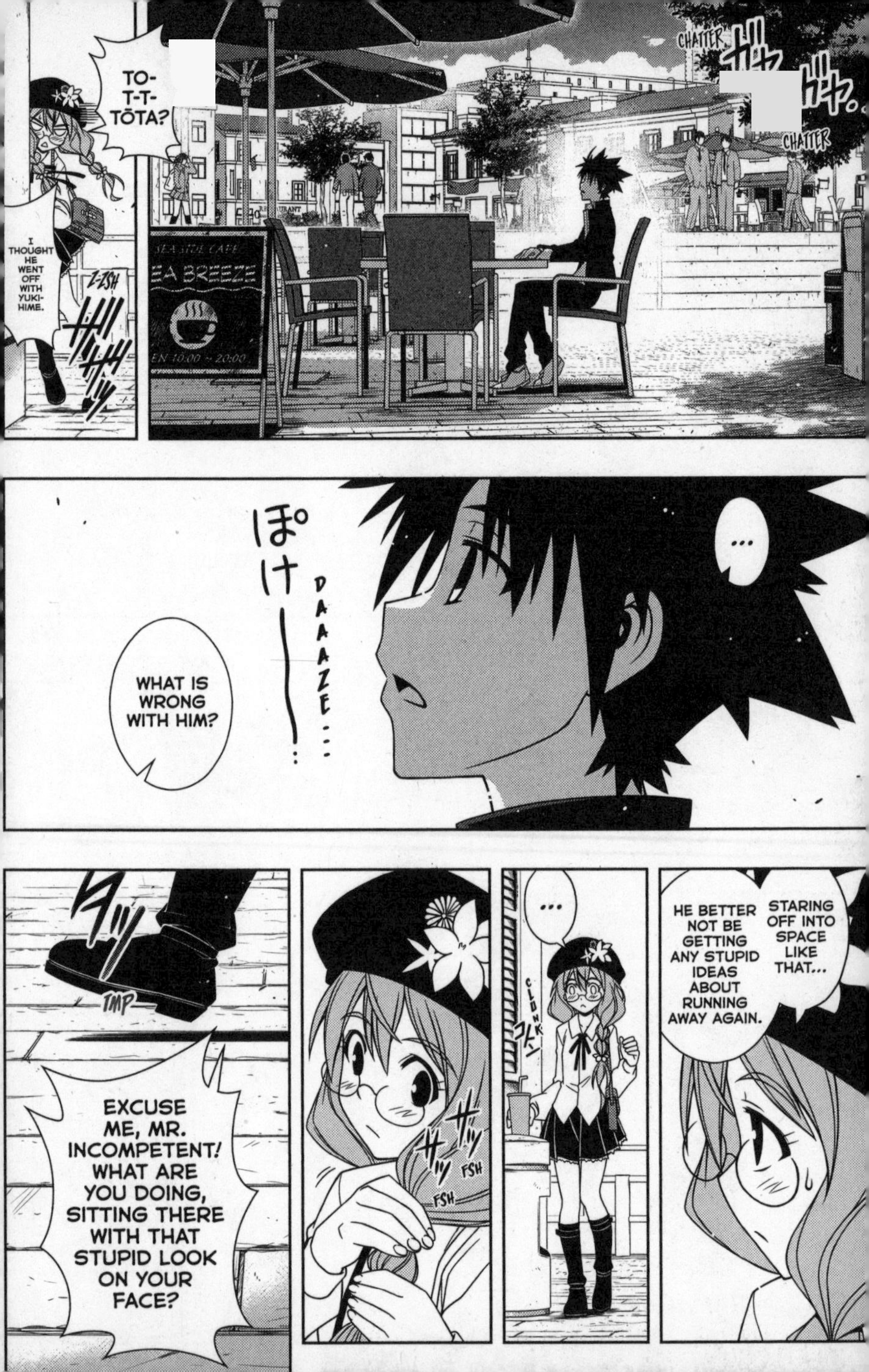
CHATTER
CHATTER
TO- T-T- TŌTA?
I THOUGHT HE WENT OFF WITH YUKI-HIME.
Z-ZSH
...
ぽけー
DAAAAZE...
WHAT IS WRONG WITH HIM?
STARING OFF INTO SPACE LIKE THAT...
HE BETTER NOT BE GETTING ANY STUPID IDEAS ABOUT RUNNING AWAY AGAIN.
...
CLONK
FSH
FSH
TMP
EXCUSE ME, MR. INCOMPETENT! WHAT ARE YOU DOING, SITTING THERE WITH THAT STUPID LOOK ON YOUR FACE?

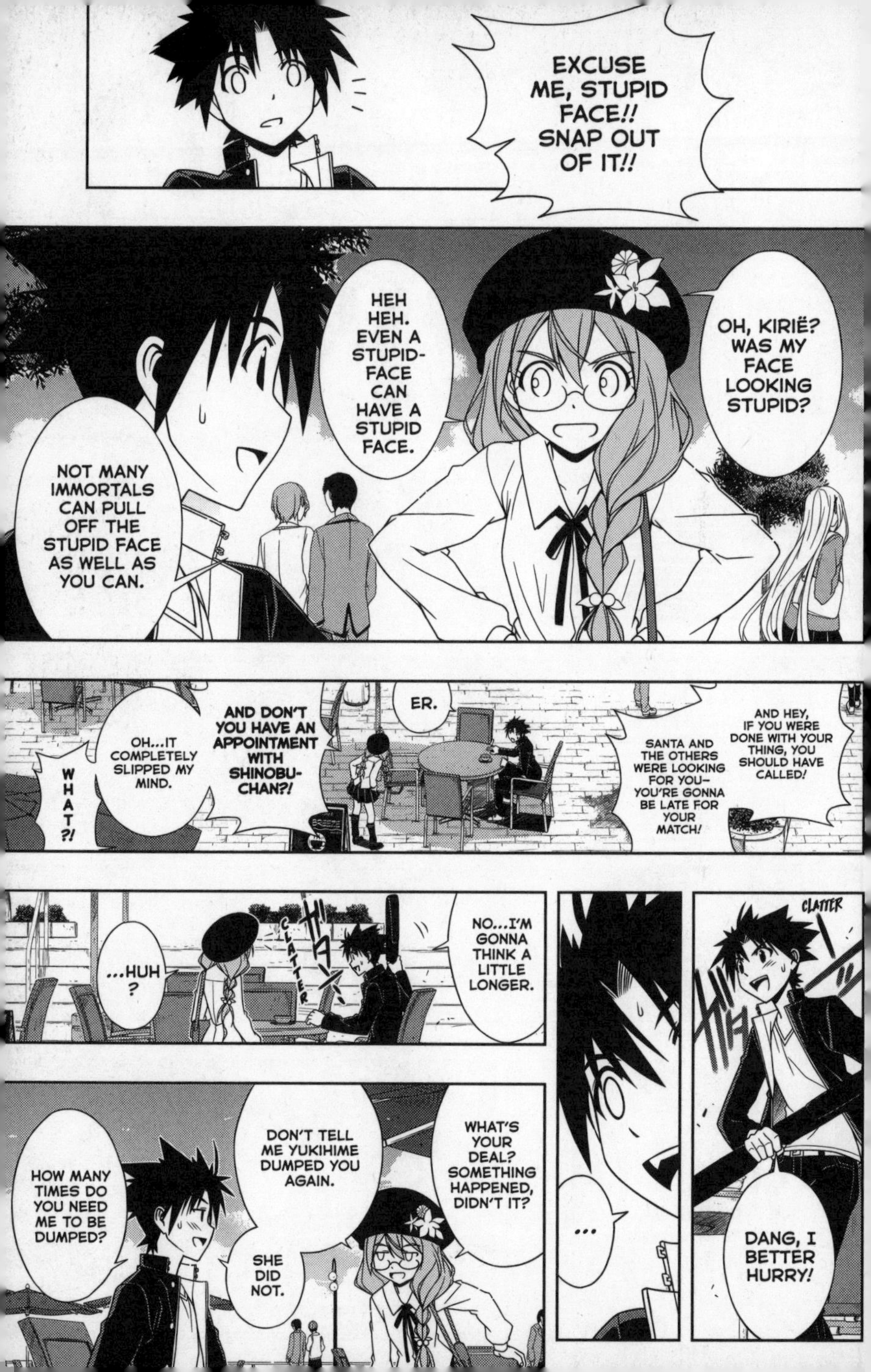
EXCUSE ME, STUPID FACE!! SNAP OUT OF IT!!
OH, KIRIË? WAS MY FACE LOOKING STUPID?
HEH HEH. EVEN A STUPID-FACE CAN HAVE A STUPID FACE.
NOT MANY IMMORTALS CAN PULL OFF THE STUPID FACE AS WELL AS YOU CAN.
AND HEY, IF YOU WERE DONE WITH YOUR THING, YOU SHOULD HAVE CALLED!
SANTA AND THE OTHERS WERE LOOKING FOR YOU– YOU'RE GONNA BE LATE FOR YOUR MATCH!
ER.
AND DON'T YOU HAVE AN APPOINTMENT WITH SHINOBU-CHAN?!
OH...IT COMPLETELY SLIPPED MY MIND.
WHAT?!
CLATTER
DANG, I BETTER HURRY!
...
NO...I'M GONNA THINK A LITTLE LONGER.
CLATTER
...HUH?
WHAT'S YOUR DEAL? SOMETHING HAPPENED, DIDN'T IT?
DON'T TELL ME YUKIHIME DUMPED YOU AGAIN.
HOW MANY TIMES DO YOU NEED ME TO BE DUMPED?
SHE DID NOT.

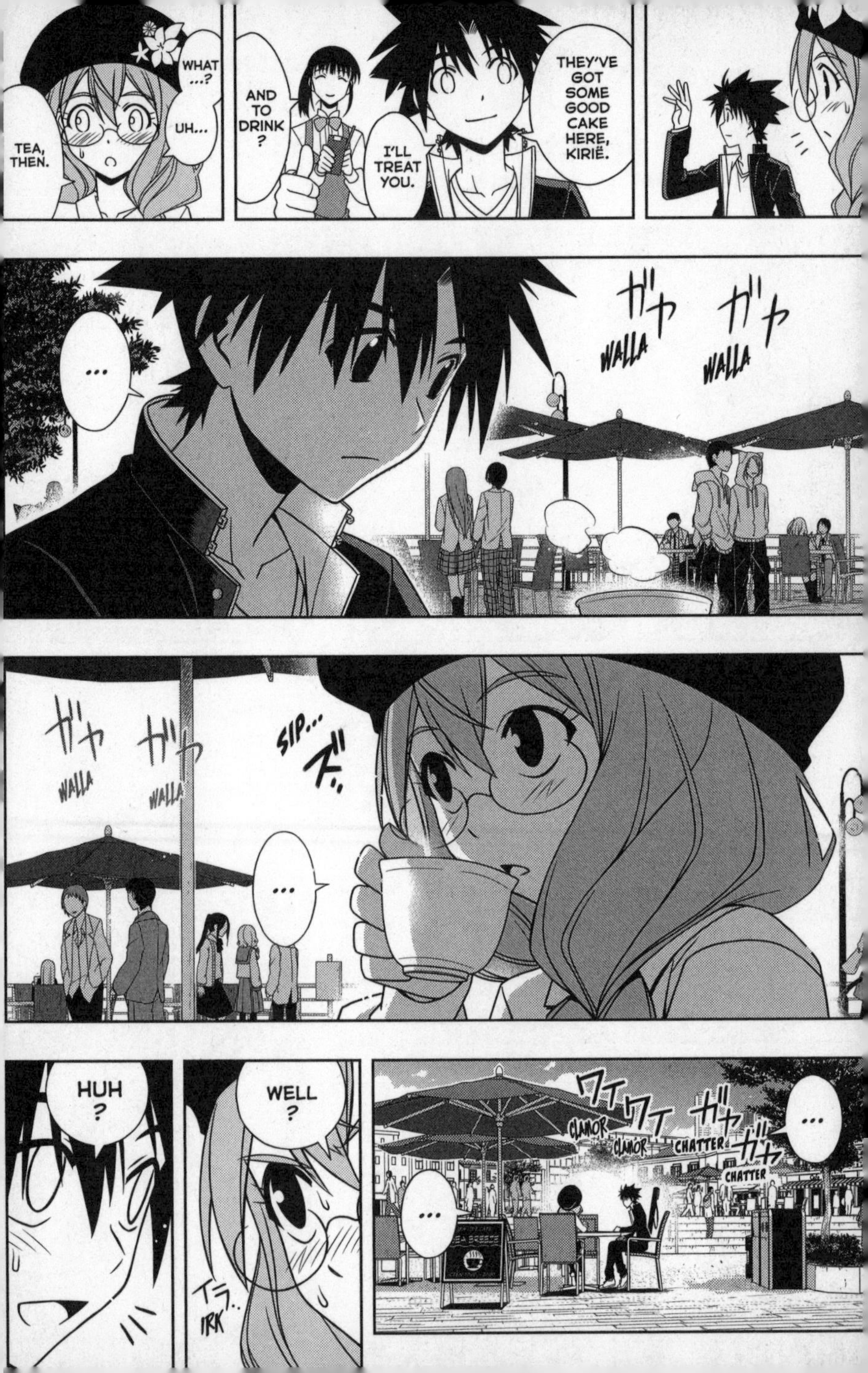
THEY'VE GOT SOME GOOD CAKE HERE, KIRIË.
I'LL TREAT YOU.
AND TO DRINK?
WHAT ...?
UH...
TEA, THEN.
ガヤ
WALLA
ガヤ
WALLA
...
SIP...
ズ..
...
ガヤ
WALLA
ガヤ
WALLA
...
ガヤ
CHATTER
ガヤ
CHATTER
ワイ
CLAMOR
ワイ
CLAMOR
...
WELL?
イラ..
IRK
HUH?

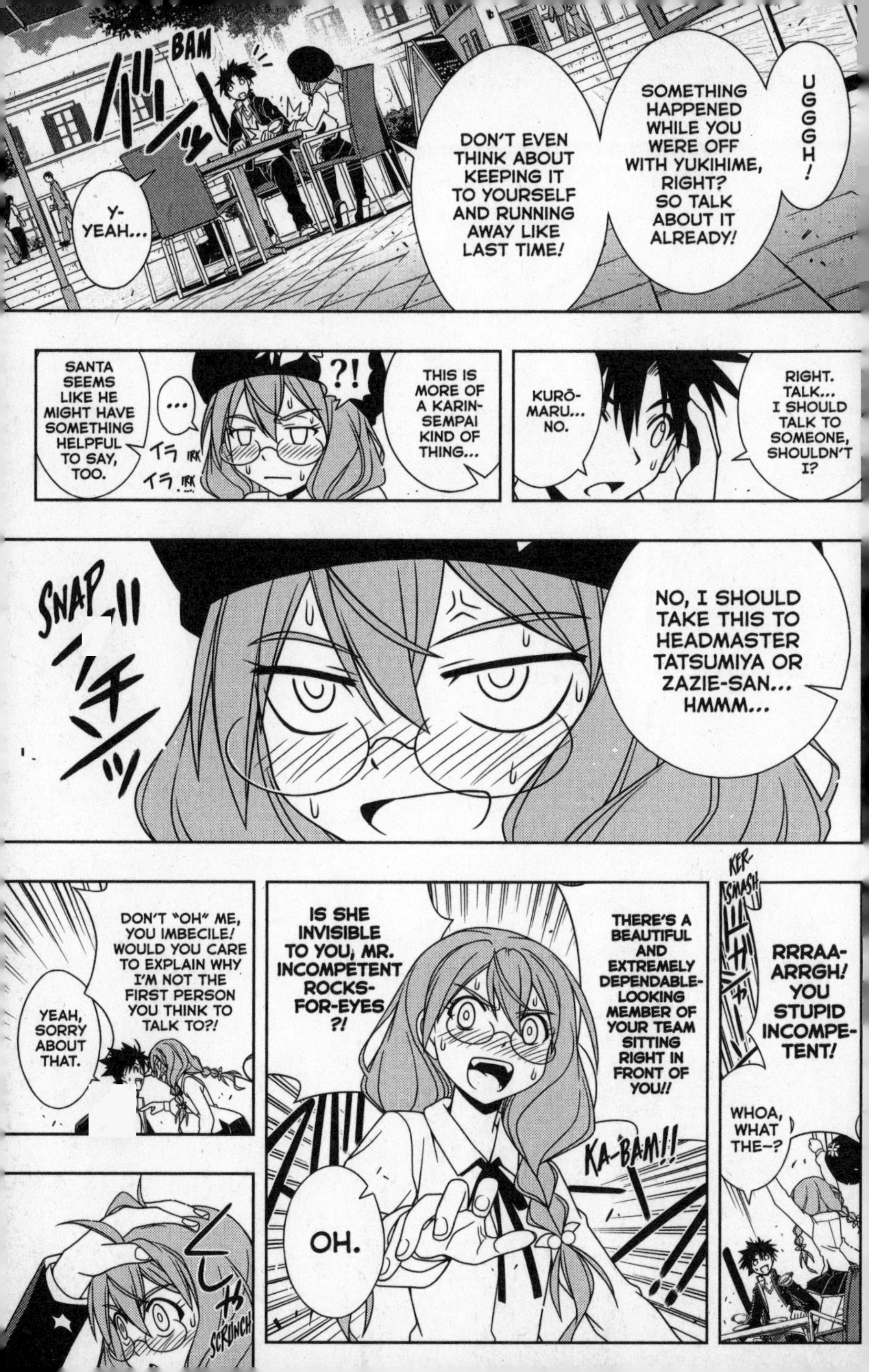
UGGGH!
SOMETHING HAPPENED WHILE YOU WERE OFF WITH YUKIHIME, RIGHT? SO TALK ABOUT IT ALREADY!
DON'T EVEN THINK ABOUT KEEPING IT TO YOURSELF AND RUNNING AWAY LIKE LAST TIME!
BAM
Y-YEAH...
RIGHT. TALK... I SHOULD TALK TO SOMEONE, SHOULDN'T I?
KURŌ-MARU... NO.
THIS IS MORE OF A KARIN-SEMPAI KIND OF THING...
?!
...
SANTA SEEMS LIKE HE MIGHT HAVE SOMETHING HELPFUL TO SAY, TOO.
イラ IRK
イラ IRK
NO, I SHOULD TAKE THIS TO HEADMASTER TATSUMIYA OR ZAZIE-SAN... HMMM...
SNAP
KER-SMASH
RRRAA-ARRGH! YOU STUPID INCOMPETENT!
WHOA, WHAT THE-?
THERE'S A BEAUTIFUL AND EXTREMELY DEPENDABLE-LOOKING MEMBER OF YOUR TEAM SITTING RIGHT IN FRONT OF YOU!!
IS SHE INVISIBLE TO YOU, MR. INCOMPETENT ROCKS-FOR-EYES?!
KA-BAM!!
OH.
DON'T "OH" ME, YOU IMBECILE! WOULD YOU CARE TO EXPLAIN WHY I'M NOT THE FIRST PERSON YOU THINK TO TALK TO?!
YEAH, SORRY ABOUT THAT.
SCRUNCH

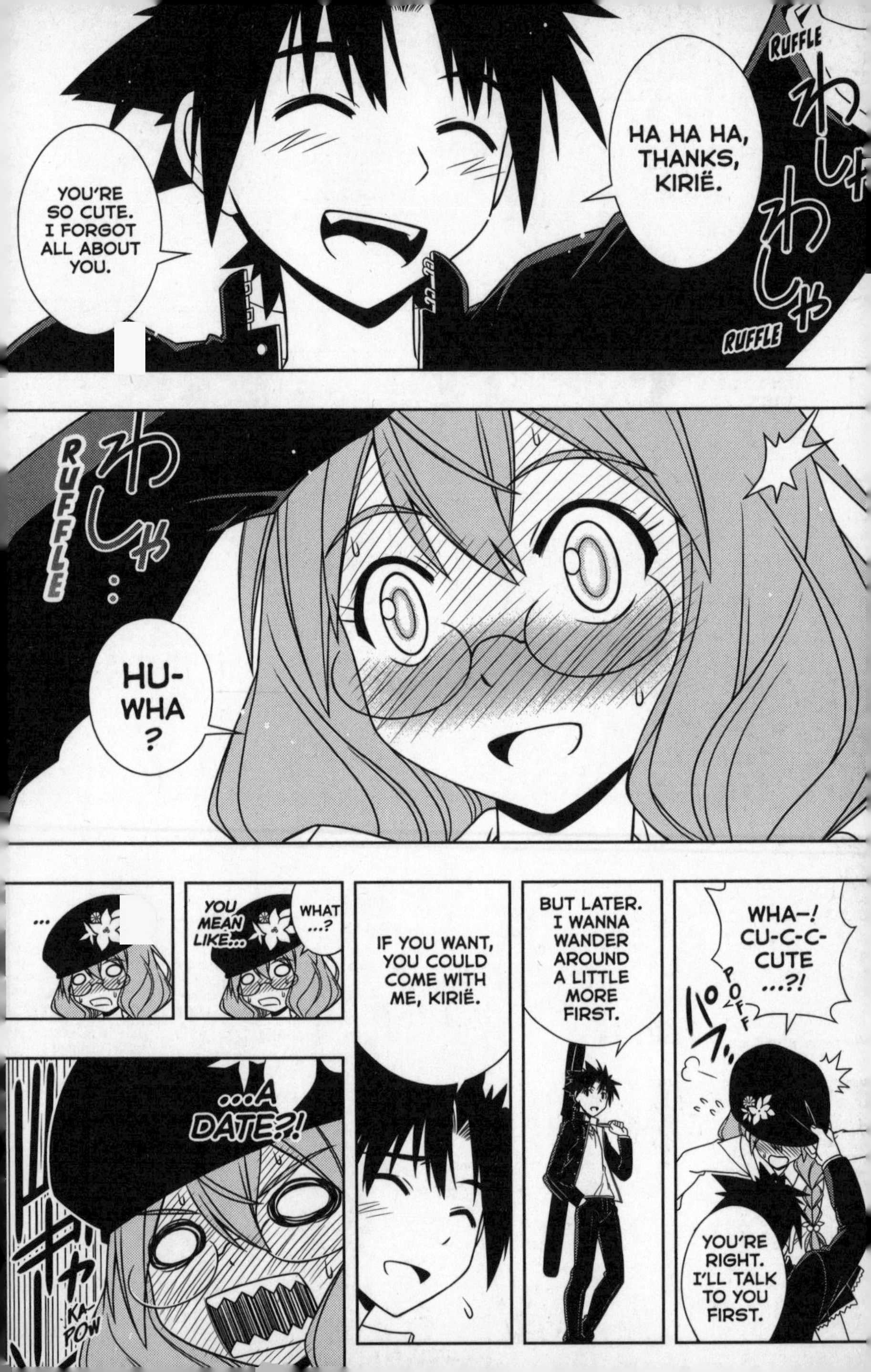RUFFLE
わしゃわしゃ
RUFFLE
HA HA HA, THANKS, KIRIË.
YOU'RE SO CUTE. I FORGOT ALL ABOUT YOU.
RUFFLE
わしゃ
HU-WHA?
WHA–! CU-C-C-CUTE ...?!
POFF
YOU'RE RIGHT. I'LL TALK TO YOU FIRST.
BUT LATER. I WANNA WANDER AROUND A LITTLE MORE FIRST.
IF YOU WANT, YOU COULD COME WITH ME, KIRIË.
WHAT ...?
YOU MEAN LIKE...
...
...A DATE?!
KA-POW

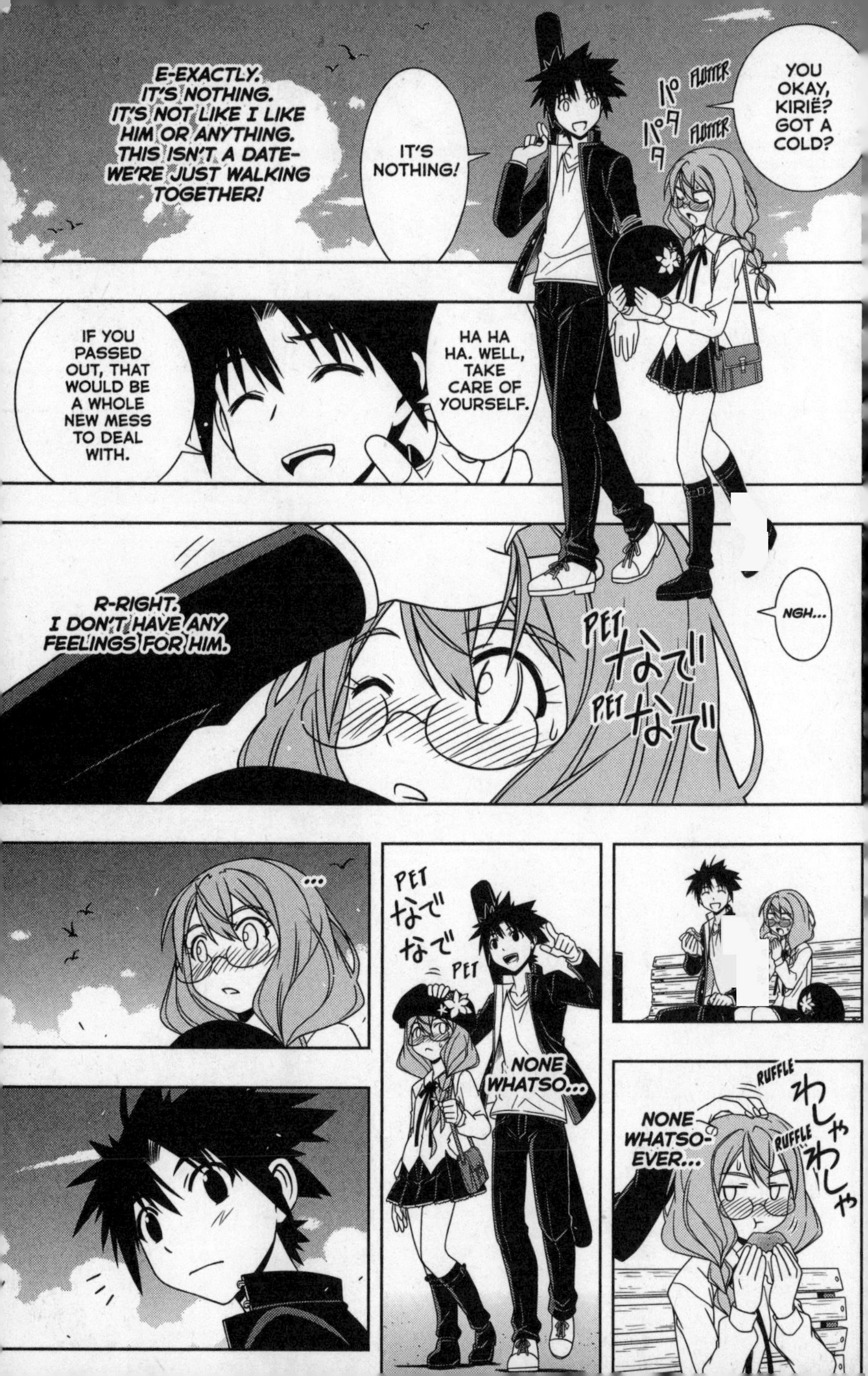
YOU OKAY, KIRIË? GOT A COLD?
パタパタ FLUTTER FLUTTER
IT'S NOTHING!
E-EXACTLY. IT'S NOTHING. IT'S NOT LIKE I LIKE HIM OR ANYTHING. THIS ISN'T A DATE-WE'RE JUST WALKING TOGETHER!
HA HA HA. WELL, TAKE CARE OF YOURSELF.
IF YOU PASSED OUT, THAT WOULD BE A WHOLE NEW MESS TO DEAL WITH.
NGH...
なで PET なで PET
R-RIGHT. I DON'T HAVE ANY FEELINGS FOR HIM.
わしゃわしゃ RUFFLE RUFFLE
NONE WHATSO-EVER...
PET なでなで PET
NONE WHATSO...
...

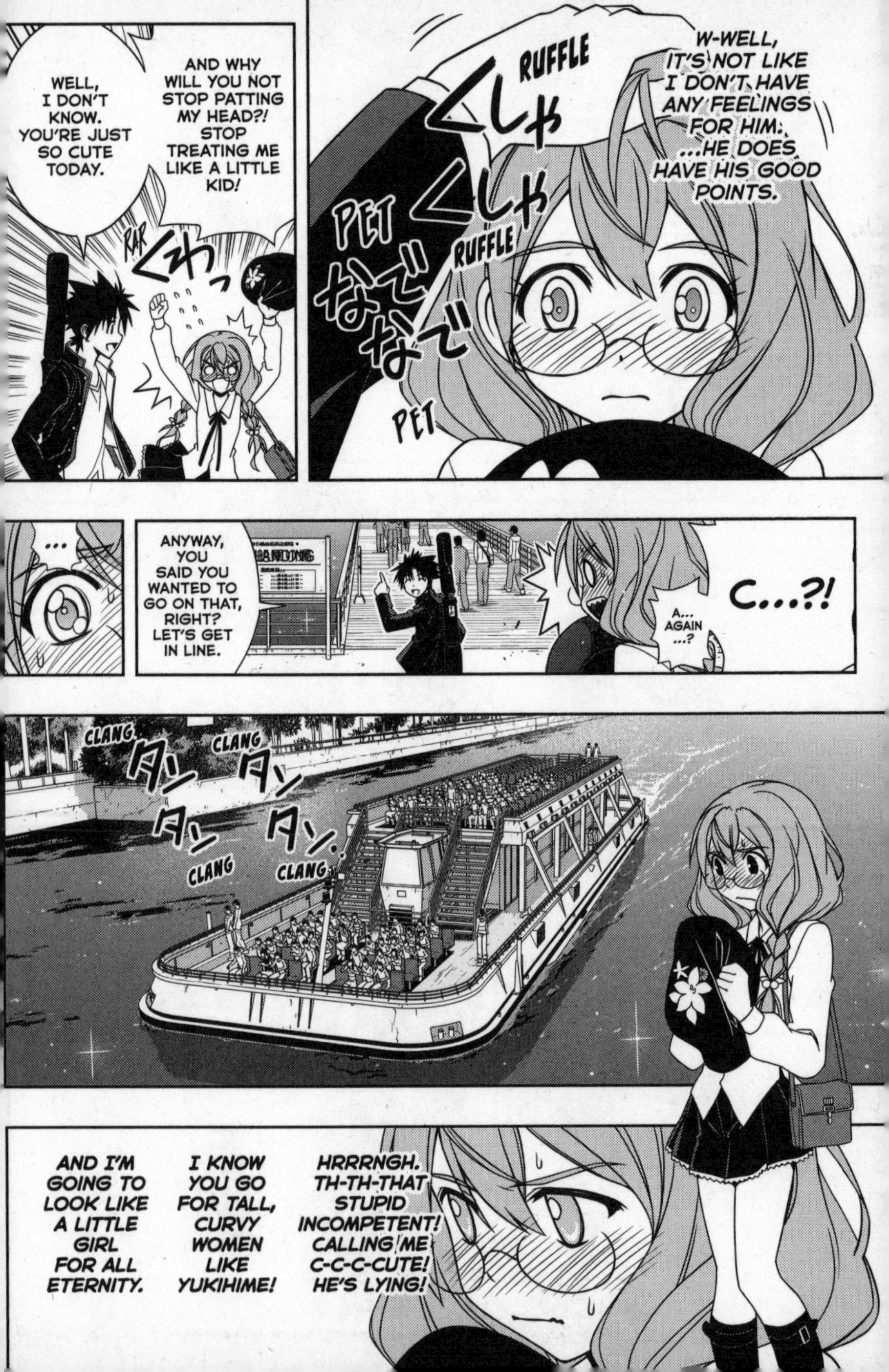
W-WELL, IT'S NOT LIKE I DON'T HAVE ANY FEELINGS FOR HIM. ...HE DOES HAVE HIS GOOD POINTS.
RUFFLE
くしゃ
くしゃ
RUFFLE
PET
なでなで
PET
AND WHY WILL YOU NOT STOP PATTING MY HEAD?! STOP TREATING ME LIKE A LITTLE KID!
WELL, I DON'T KNOW. YOU'RE JUST SO CUTE TODAY.
RAR
くわっ
C...?!
A... AGAIN ...?
ANYWAY, YOU SAID YOU WANTED TO GO ON THAT, RIGHT? LET'S GET IN LINE.
...
CLANG
タン
CLANG
タン
タン
タン
CLANG
CLANG
HRRRNGH. TH-TH-THAT STUPID INCOMPETENT! CALLING ME C-C-C-CUTE! HE'S LYING!
I KNOW YOU GO FOR TALL, CURVY WOMEN LIKE YUKIHIME!
AND I'M GOING TO LOOK LIKE A LITTLE GIRL FOR ALL ETERNITY.

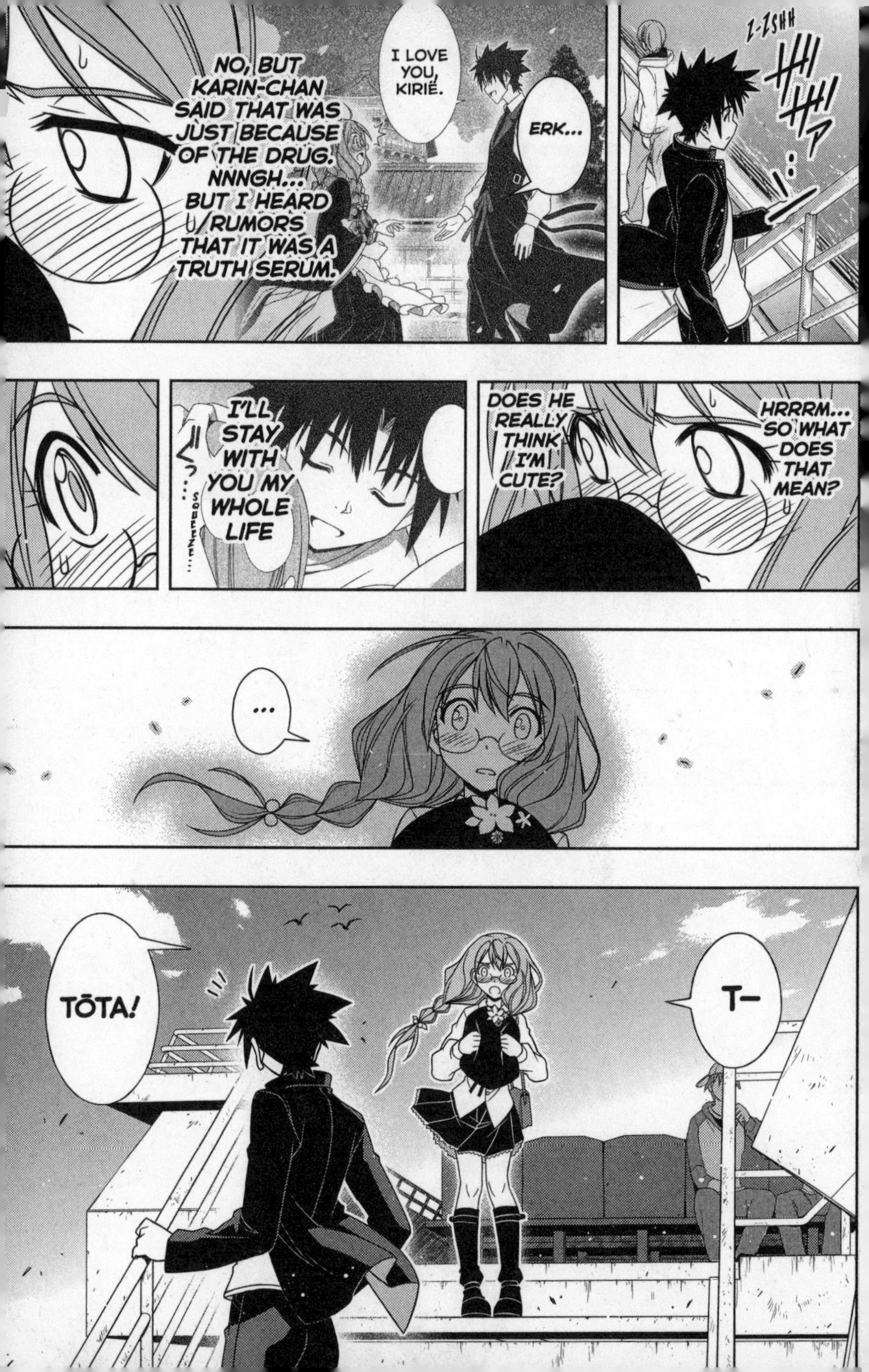
Z-ZSHH
I LOVE YOU, KIRIE.
ERK...
NO, BUT KARIN-CHAN SAID THAT WAS JUST BECAUSE OF THE DRUG. NNNGH... BUT I HEARD RUMORS THAT IT WAS A TRUTH SERUM.
HRRRM... SO WHAT DOES THAT MEAN?
DOES HE REALLY THINK I'M CUTE?
I'LL STAY WITH YOU MY WHOLE LIFE
SQUEEZE...
...
T–
TŌTA!

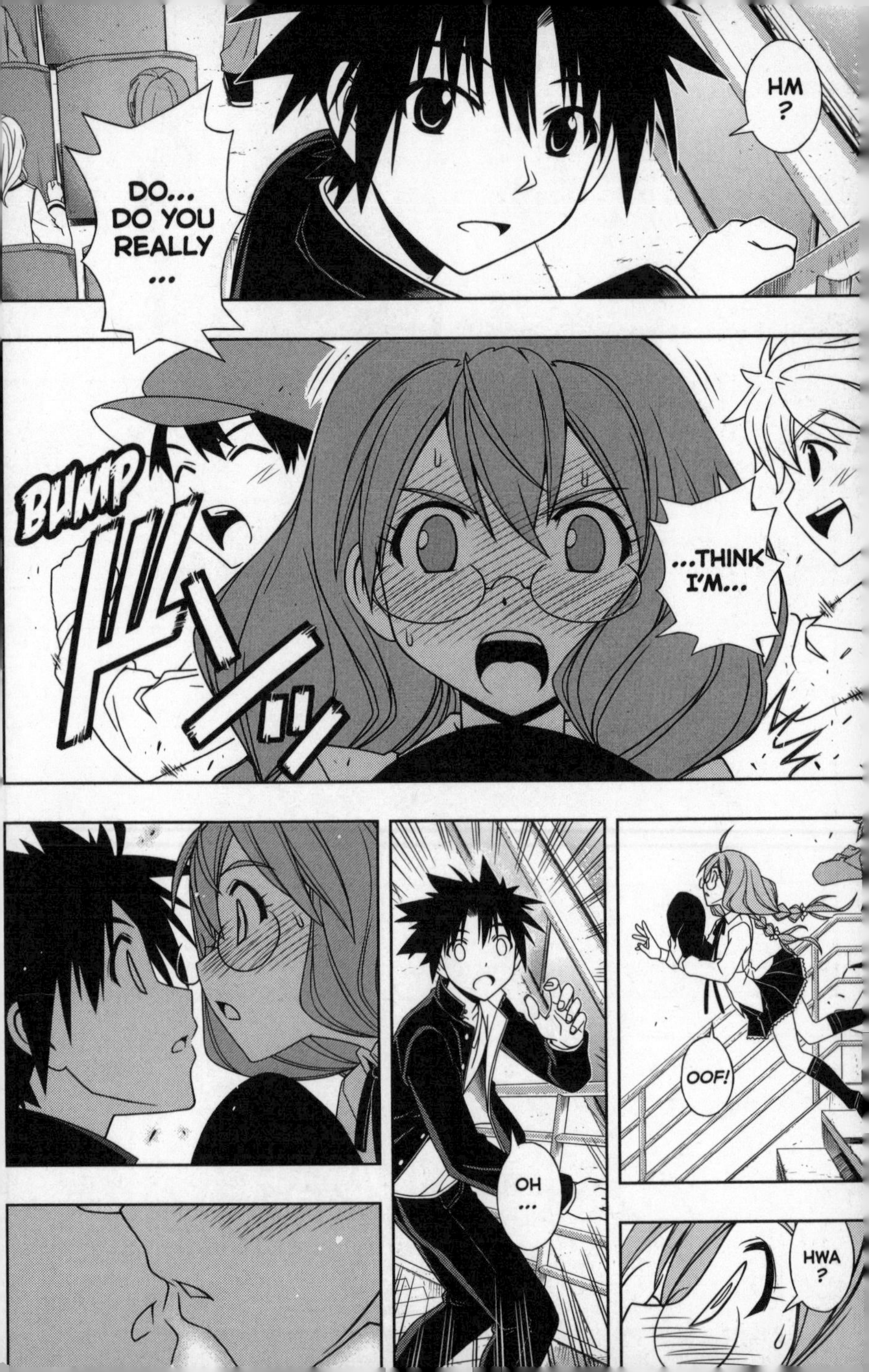
HM ?
DO... DO YOU REALLY ...
...THINK I'M...
BUMP
OOF!
HWA ?
OH ...

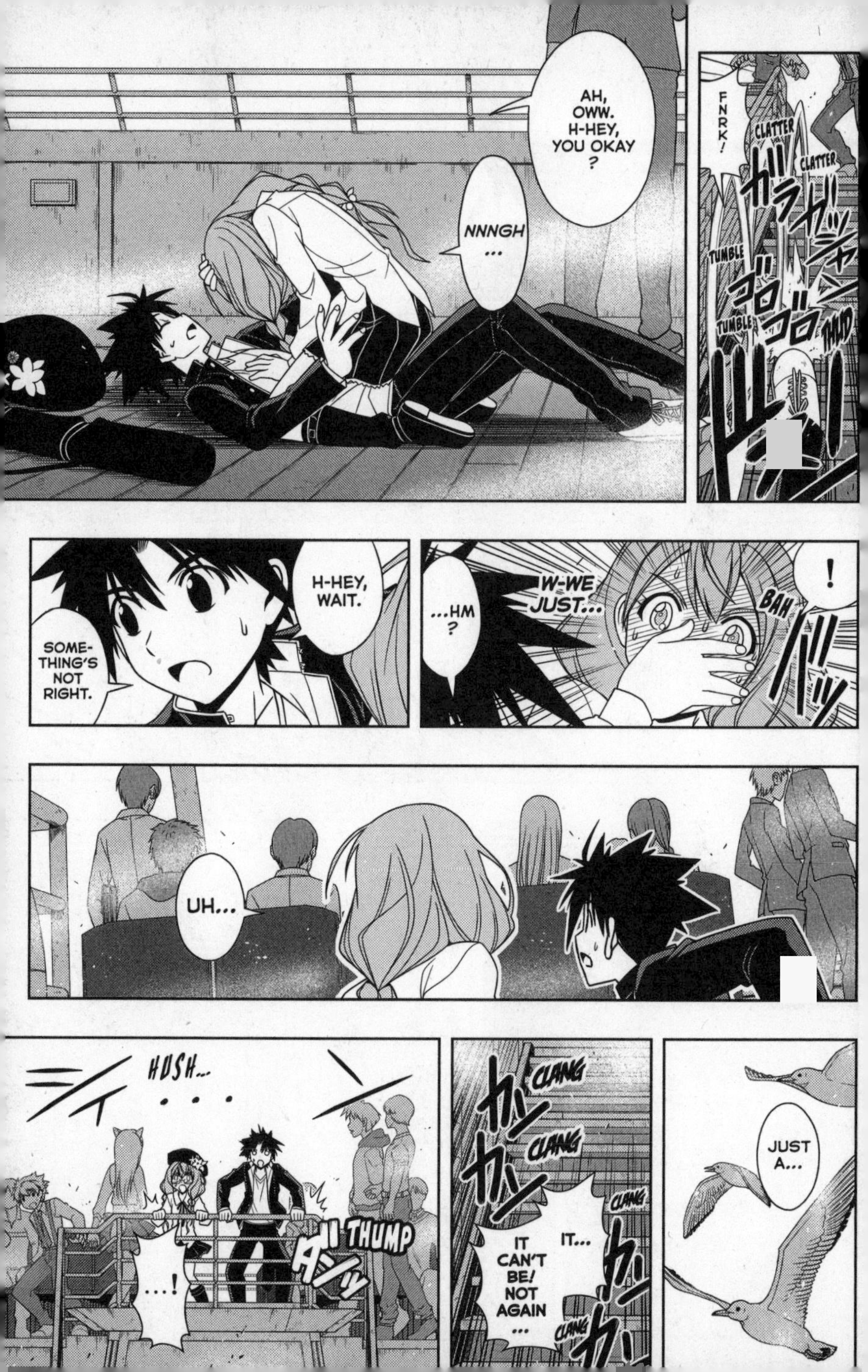
FNRK!
CLATTER
CLATTER
TUMBLE
TUMBLE
THUD
AH, OWW. H-HEY, YOU OKAY?
NNNGH...
!
BAH
W-WE JUST...
...HM?
H-HEY, WAIT.
SOME-THING'S NOT RIGHT.
UH...
JUST A...
CLANG
CLANG
CLANG
IT...
IT CAN'T BE! NOT AGAIN...
CLANG
HUSH...
...
THUMP
...!

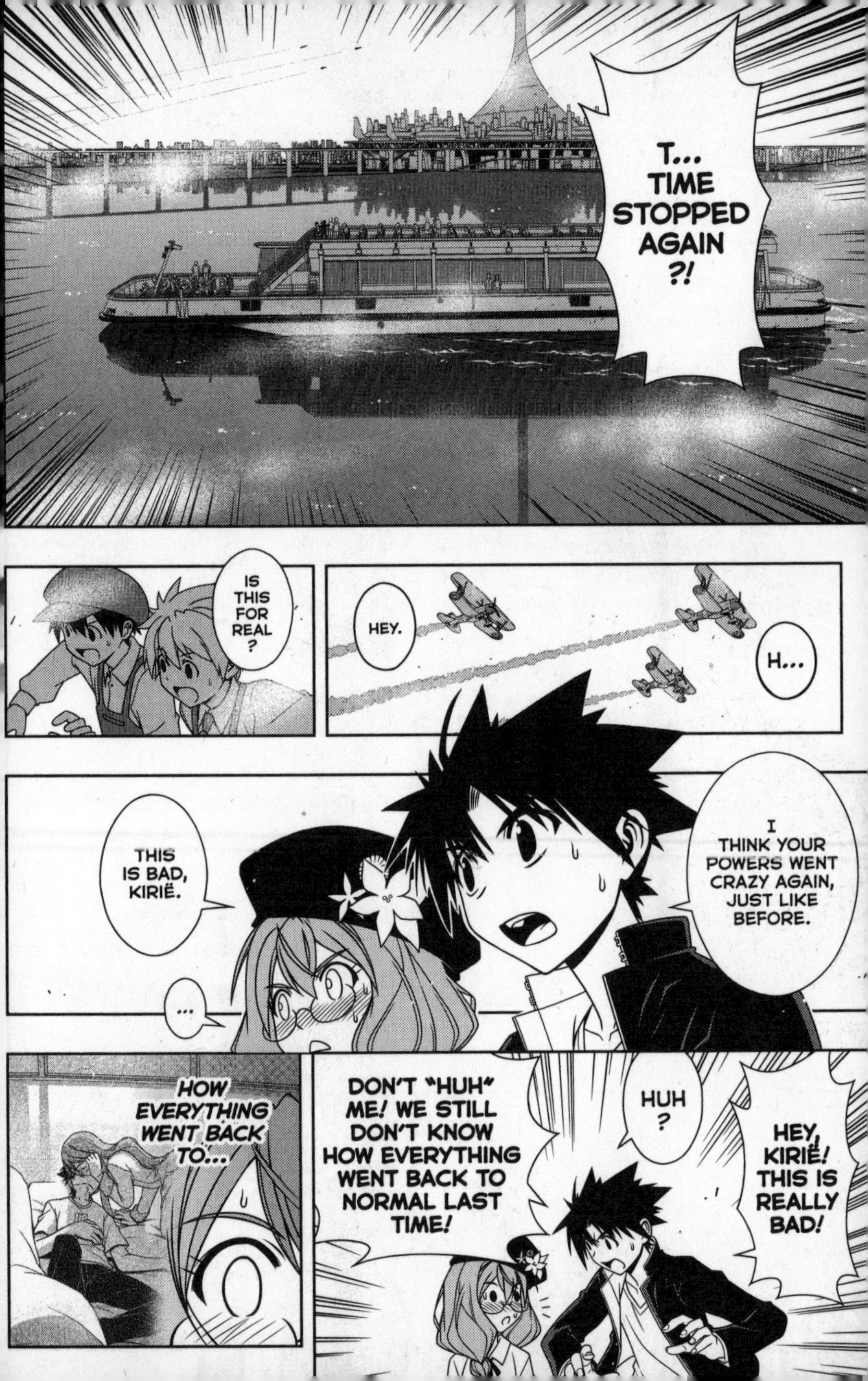
T... TIME STOPPED AGAIN?!
H...
HEY.
IS THIS FOR REAL?
I THINK YOUR POWERS WENT CRAZY AGAIN, JUST LIKE BEFORE.
THIS IS BAD, KIRIË.
...
HEY, KIRIË! THIS IS REALLY BAD!
HUH?
DON'T "HUH" ME! WE STILL DON'T KNOW HOW EVERYTHING WENT BACK TO NORMAL LAST TIME!
HOW EVERYTHING WENT BACK TO...

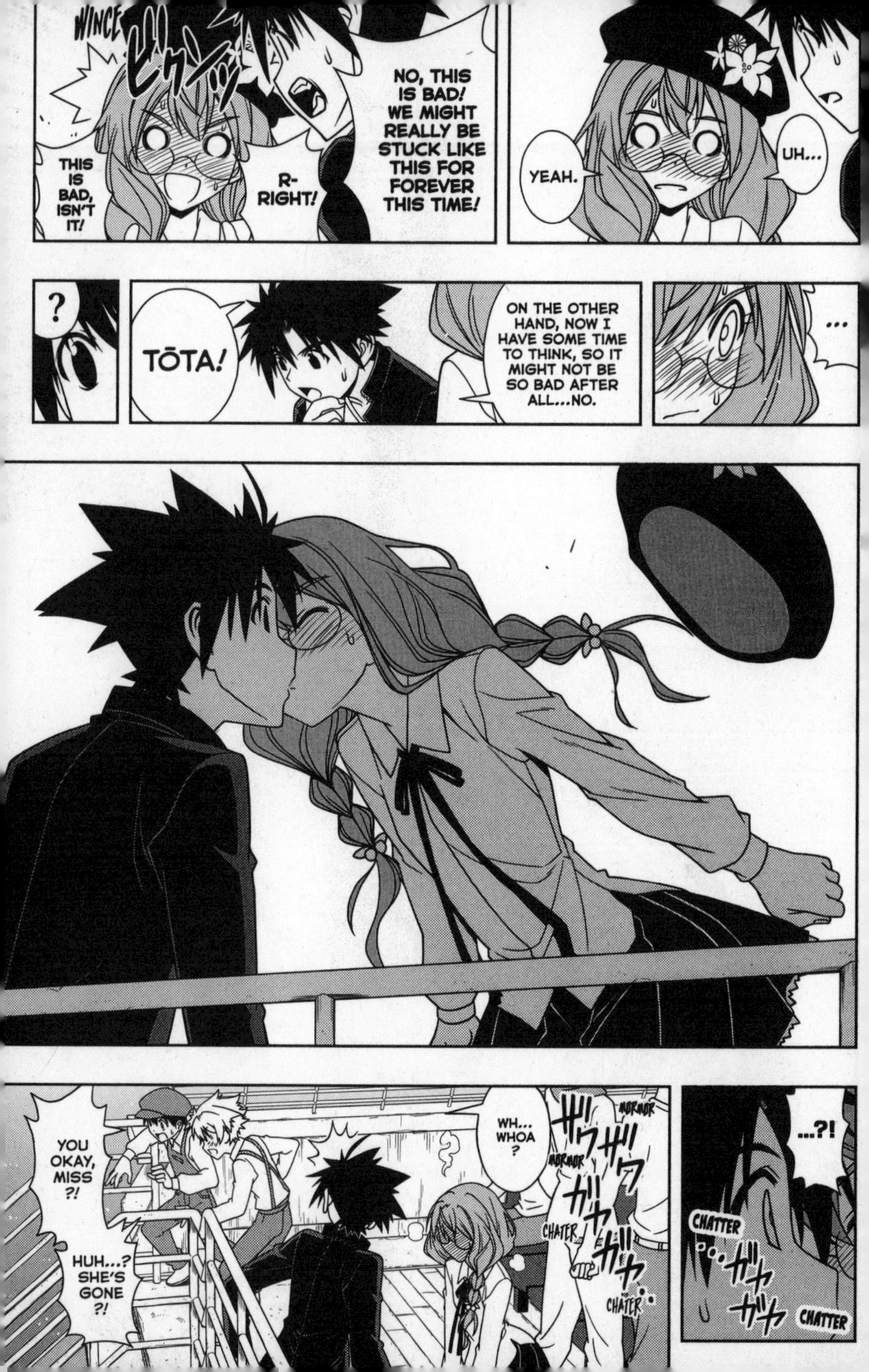
UH...
YEAH.
NO, THIS IS BAD! WE MIGHT REALLY BE STUCK LIKE THIS FOR FOREVER THIS TIME!
WINCE
R-RIGHT!
THIS IS BAD, ISN'T IT!
...
ON THE OTHER HAND, NOW I HAVE SOME TIME TO THINK, SO IT MIGHT NOT BE SO BAD AFTER ALL...NO.
TŌTA!
?
...?!
CHATTER
CHATTER
MURMUR
WH... WHOA?
MURMUR
CHATER
CHATER
YOU OKAY, MISS?!
HUH...? SHE'S GONE?!

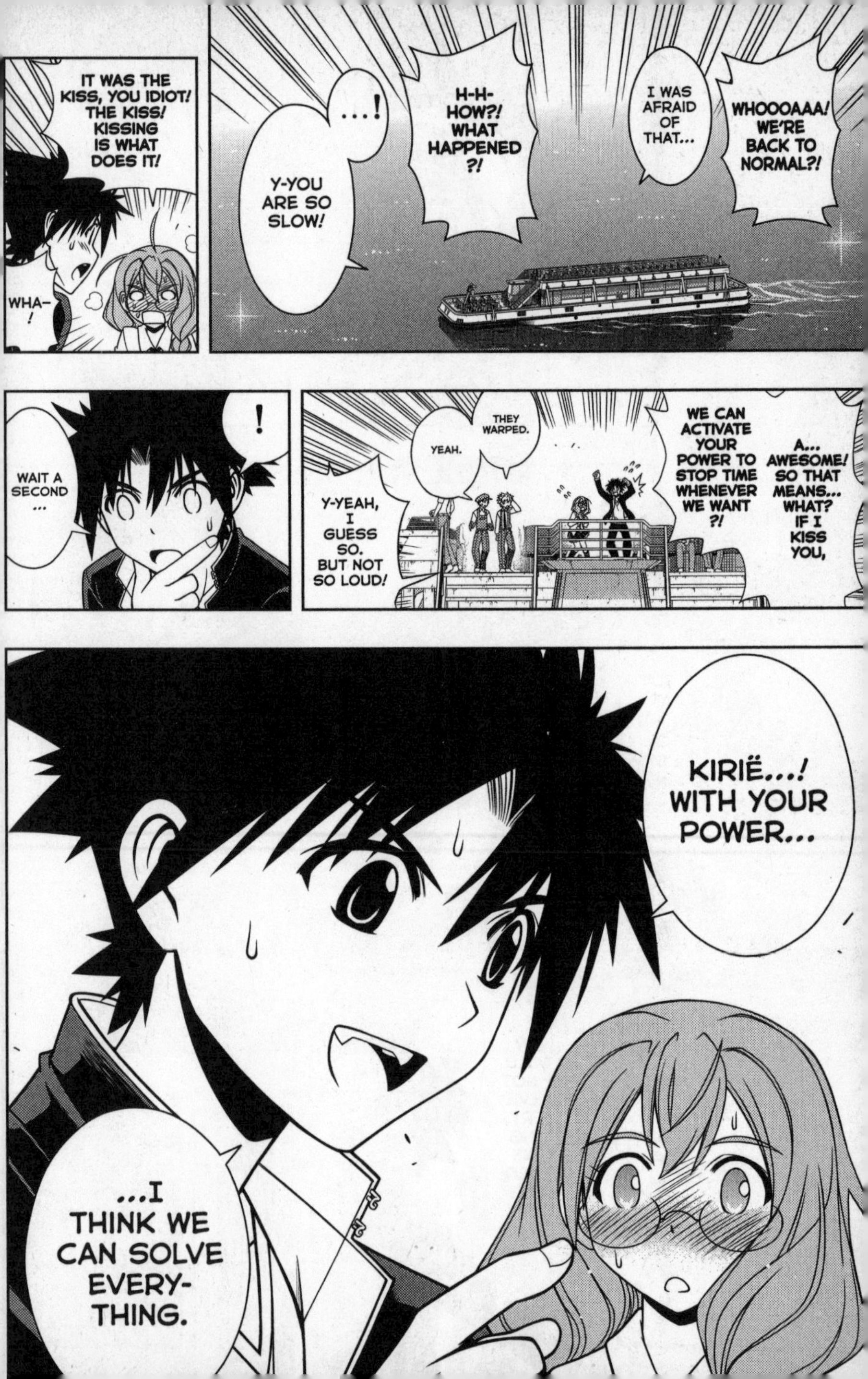
WHOOOAAA! WE'RE BACK TO NORMAL?!
I WAS AFRAID OF THAT...
H-H-HOW?! WHAT HAPPENED ?!
...!
Y-YOU ARE SO SLOW!
IT WAS THE KISS, YOU IDIOT! THE KISS! KISSING IS WHAT DOES IT!
WHA- !
A... AWESOME! SO THAT MEANS... WHAT? IF I KISS YOU,
WE CAN ACTIVATE YOUR POWER TO STOP TIME WHENEVER WE WANT ?!
THEY WARPED.
YEAH.
Y-YEAH, I GUESS SO. BUT NOT SO LOUD!
!
WAIT A SECOND ...
KIRIË...! WITH YOUR POWER...
...I THINK WE CAN SOLVE EVERY-THING.

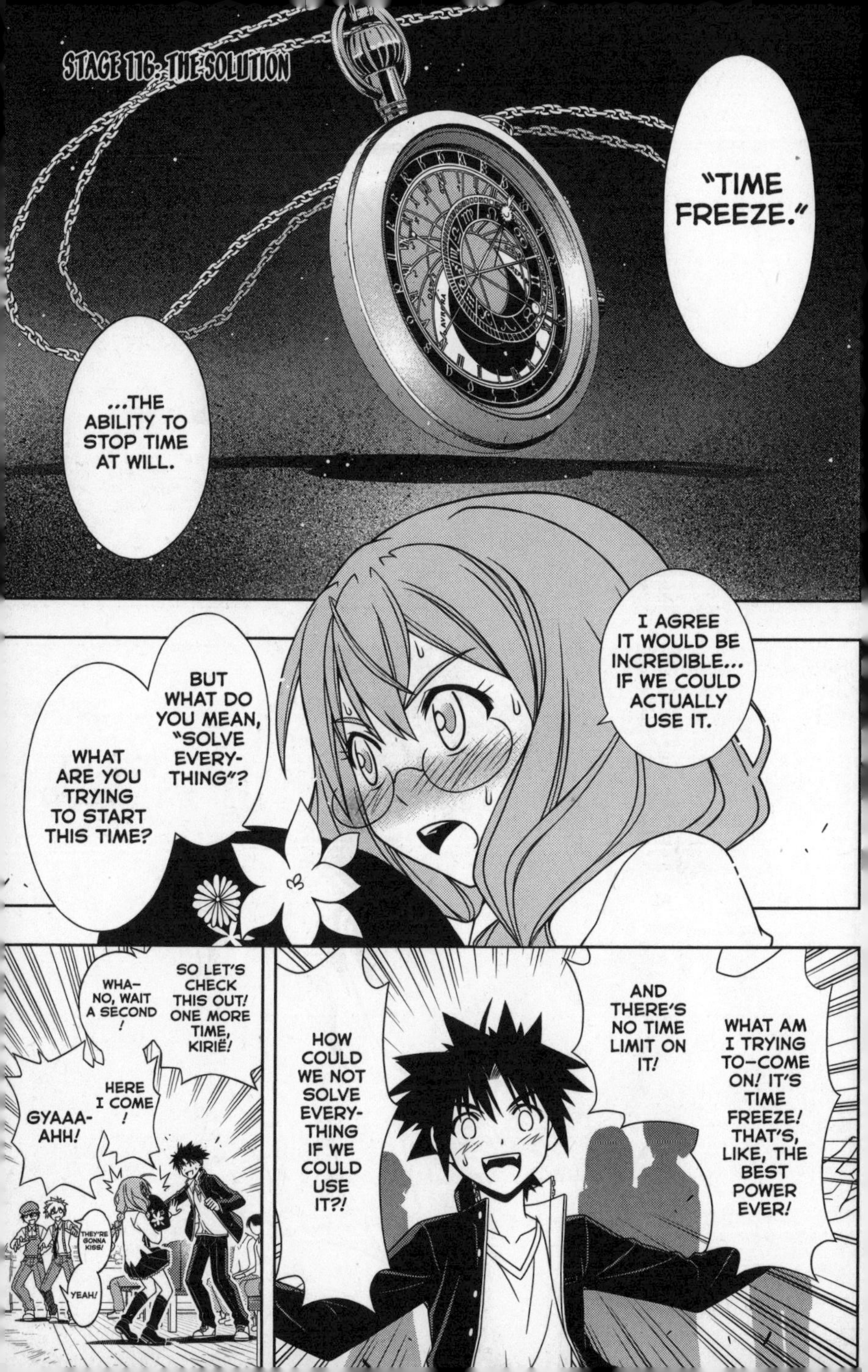
STAGE 116: THE SOLUTION
"TIME FREEZE."
...THE ABILITY TO STOP TIME AT WILL.
I AGREE IT WOULD BE INCREDIBLE... IF WE COULD ACTUALLY USE IT.
BUT WHAT DO YOU MEAN, "SOLVE EVERY-THING"?
WHAT ARE YOU TRYING TO START THIS TIME?
WHAT AM I TRYING TO—COME ON! IT'S TIME FREEZE! THAT'S, LIKE, THE BEST POWER EVER!
AND THERE'S NO TIME LIMIT ON IT!
HOW COULD WE NOT SOLVE EVERY-THING IF WE COULD USE IT?!
SO LET'S CHECK THIS OUT! ONE MORE TIME, KIRIË!
WHA—NO, WAIT A SECOND!
HERE I COME!
GYAAA-AHH!
THEY'RE GONNA KISS!
YEAH!

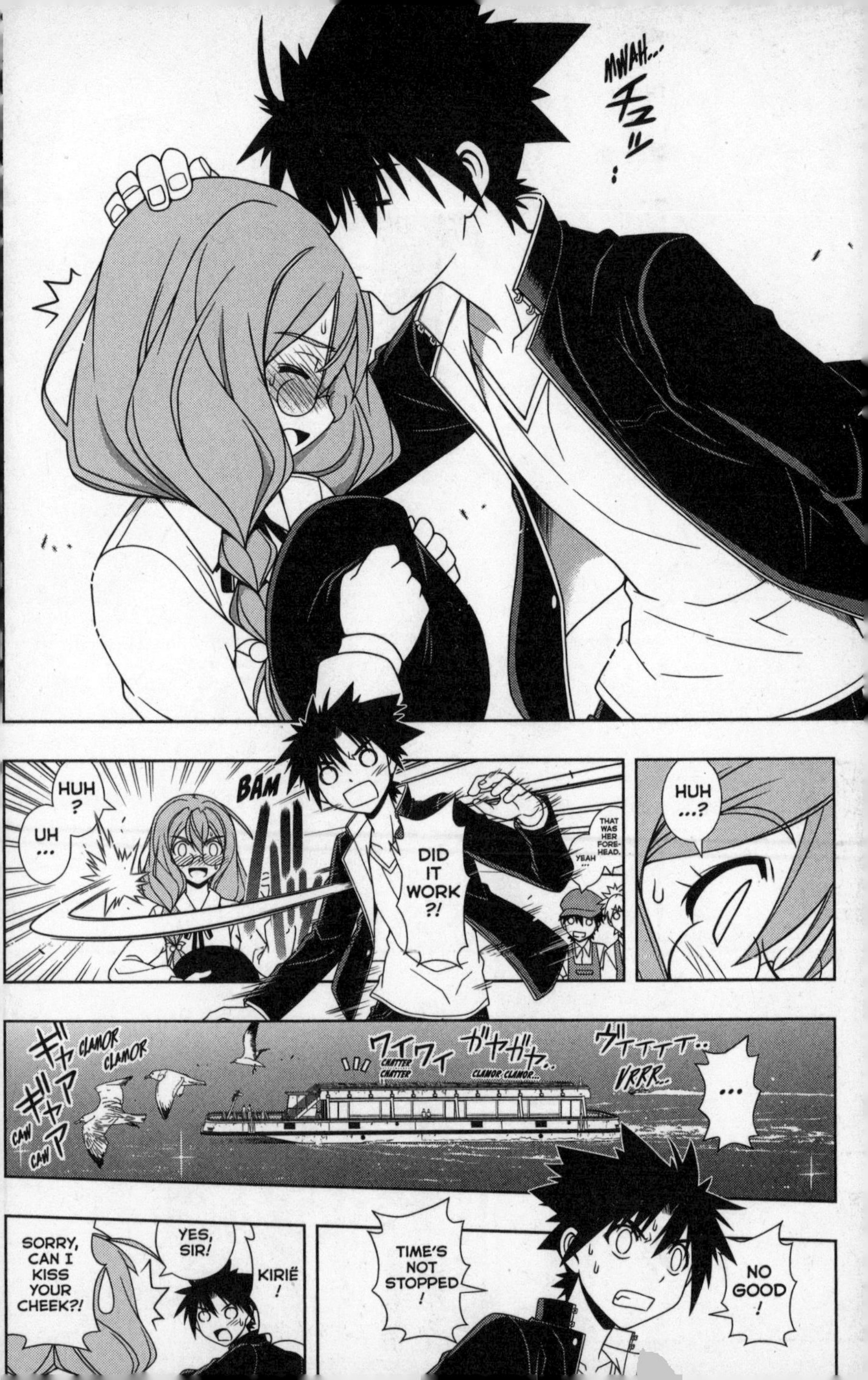
MWAH...
チュッ
BAM
DID IT WORK ?!
HUH ?
UH ...
THAT WAS HER FOREHEAD.
YEAH ...
HUH ...?
ヴィィィィ…
VRRR...
...
ガヤガヤ…
CLAMOR CLAMOR...
ワイワイ
CHATTER CHATTER
ギャアギャア
CLAMOR CLAMOR
CAW CAW
NO GOOD !
TIME'S NOT STOPPED !
KIRIË !
SORRY, CAN I KISS YOUR CHEEK?!
YES, SIR!

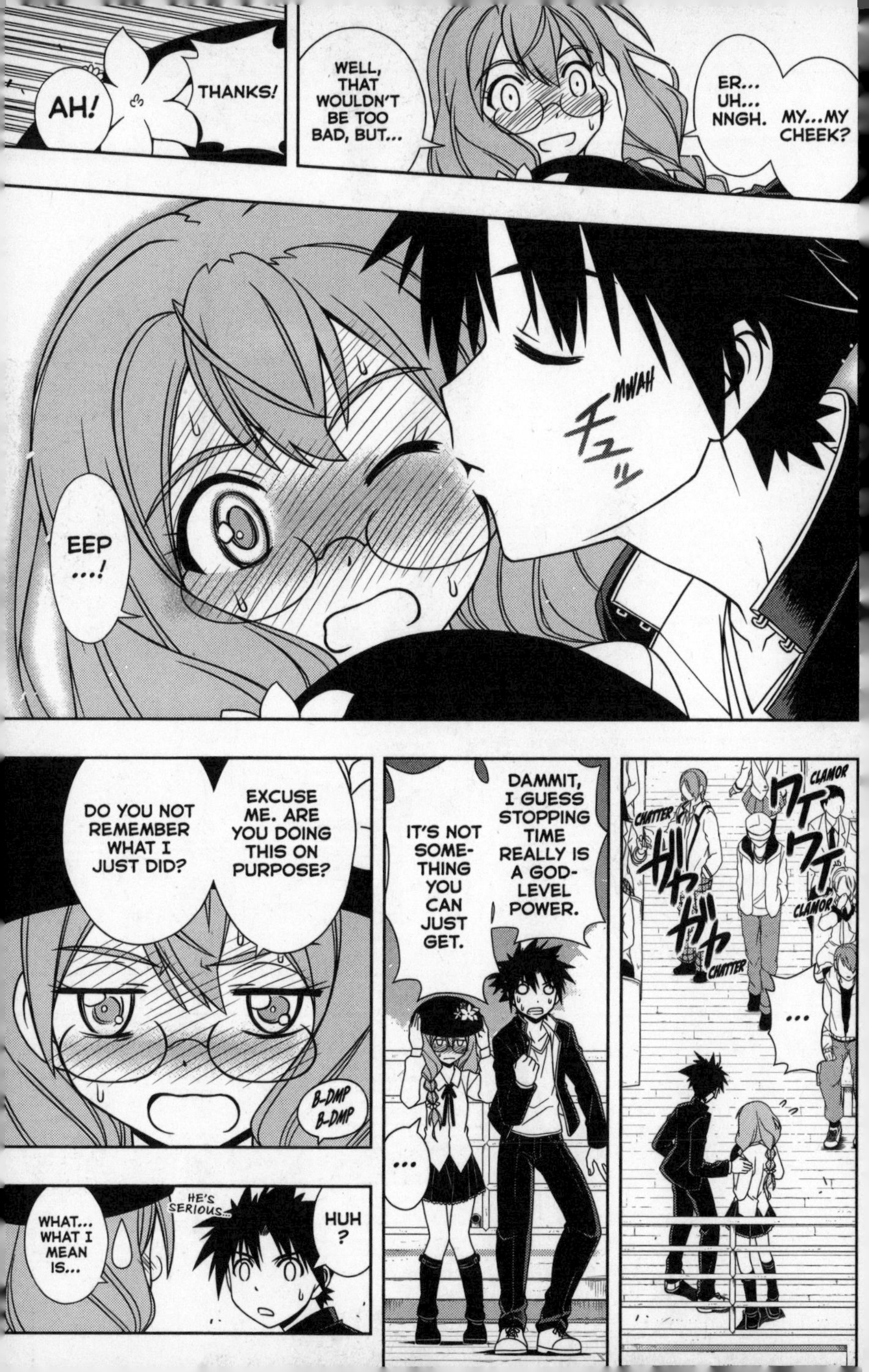
ER... UH... NNGH.
MY...MY CHEEK?
WELL, THAT WOULDN'T BE TOO BAD, BUT...
THANKS!
AH!
MWAH
チュッ
EEP ...!
CLAMOR
ワイワイ
CHATTER
ガヤガヤ
CLAMOR
CHATTER
...
DAMMIT, I GUESS STOPPING TIME REALLY IS A GOD-LEVEL POWER.
IT'S NOT SOME-THING YOU CAN JUST GET.
...
EXCUSE ME. ARE YOU DOING THIS ON PURPOSE?
DO YOU NOT REMEMBER WHAT I JUST DID?
B-DMP B-DMP
HUH ?
HE'S SERIOUS...
WHAT... WHAT I MEAN IS...

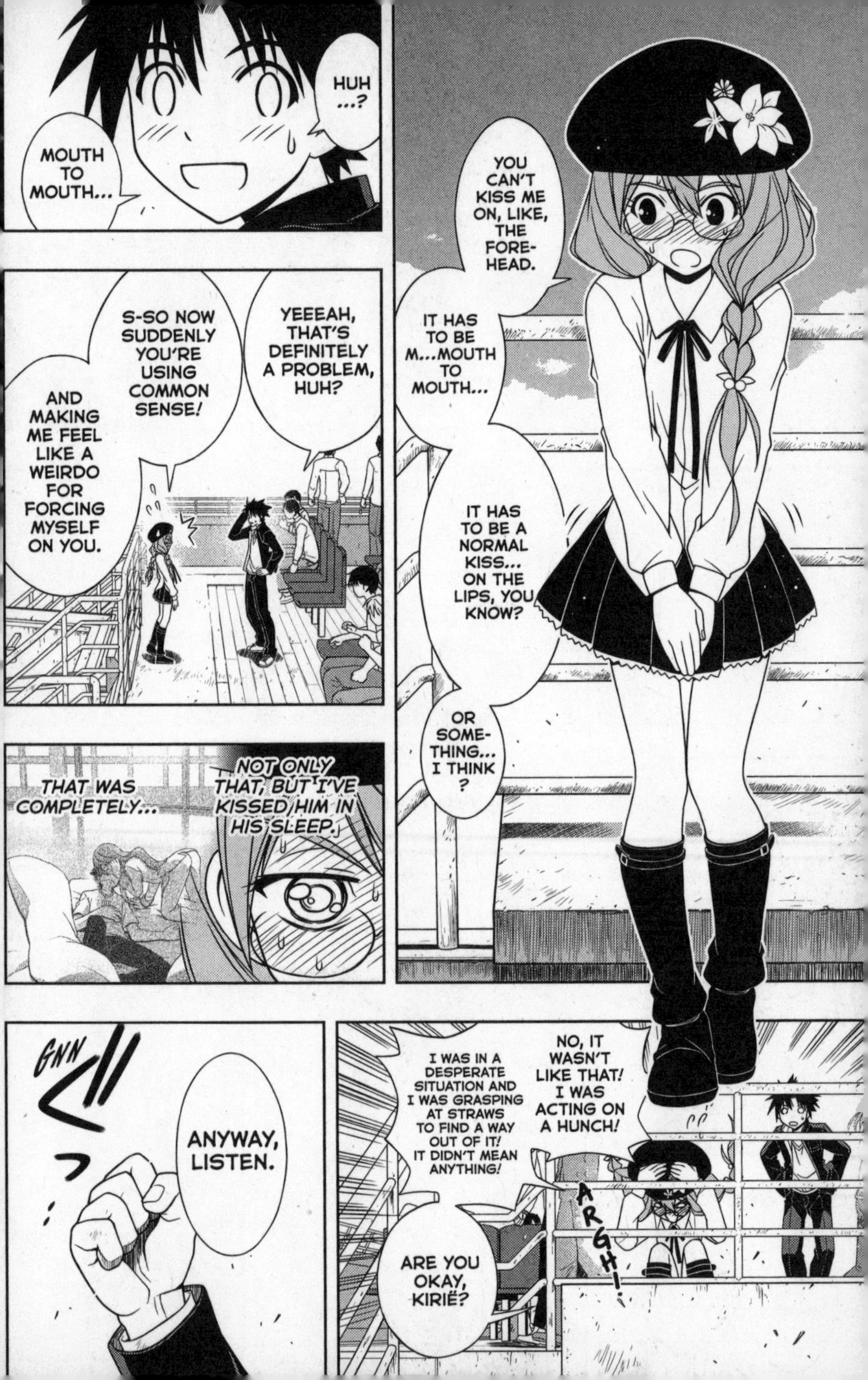
YOU CAN'T KISS ME ON, LIKE, THE FORE-HEAD.
IT HAS TO BE M...MOUTH TO MOUTH...
IT HAS TO BE A NORMAL KISS... ON THE LIPS, YOU KNOW?
OR SOME-THING... I THINK?
HUH ...?
MOUTH TO MOUTH...
YEEEAH, THAT'S DEFINITELY A PROBLEM, HUH?
S-SO NOW SUDDENLY YOU'RE USING COMMON SENSE!
AND MAKING ME FEEL LIKE A WEIRDO FOR FORCING MYSELF ON YOU.
NOT ONLY THAT, BUT I'VE KISSED HIM IN HIS SLEEP.
THAT WAS COMPLETELY...
NO, IT WASN'T LIKE THAT! I WAS ACTING ON A HUNCH!
I WAS IN A DESPERATE SITUATION AND I WAS GRASPING AT STRAWS TO FIND A WAY OUT OF IT! IT DIDN'T MEAN ANYTHING!
ARGH!
ARE YOU OKAY, KIRIË?
GNN
ANYWAY, LISTEN.

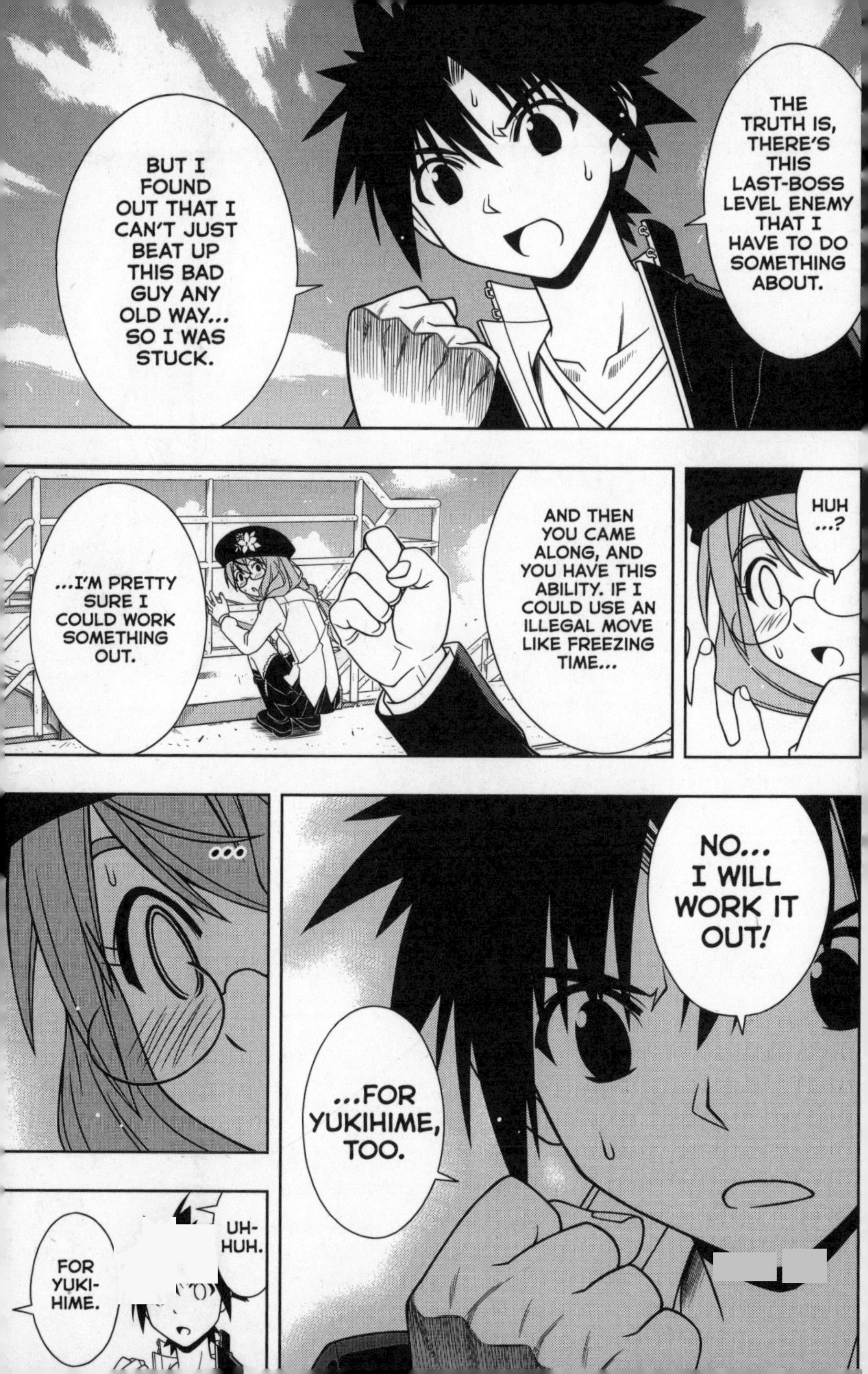
THE TRUTH IS, THERE'S THIS LAST-BOSS LEVEL ENEMY THAT I HAVE TO DO SOMETHING ABOUT.
BUT I FOUND OUT THAT I CAN'T JUST BEAT UP THIS BAD GUY ANY OLD WAY... SO I WAS STUCK.
HUH ...?
AND THEN YOU CAME ALONG, AND YOU HAVE THIS ABILITY. IF I COULD USE AN ILLEGAL MOVE LIKE FREEZING TIME...
...I'M PRETTY SURE I COULD WORK SOMETHING OUT.
NO... I WILL WORK IT OUT!
...FOR YUKIHIME, TOO.
UH-HUH.
FOR YUKI-HIME.

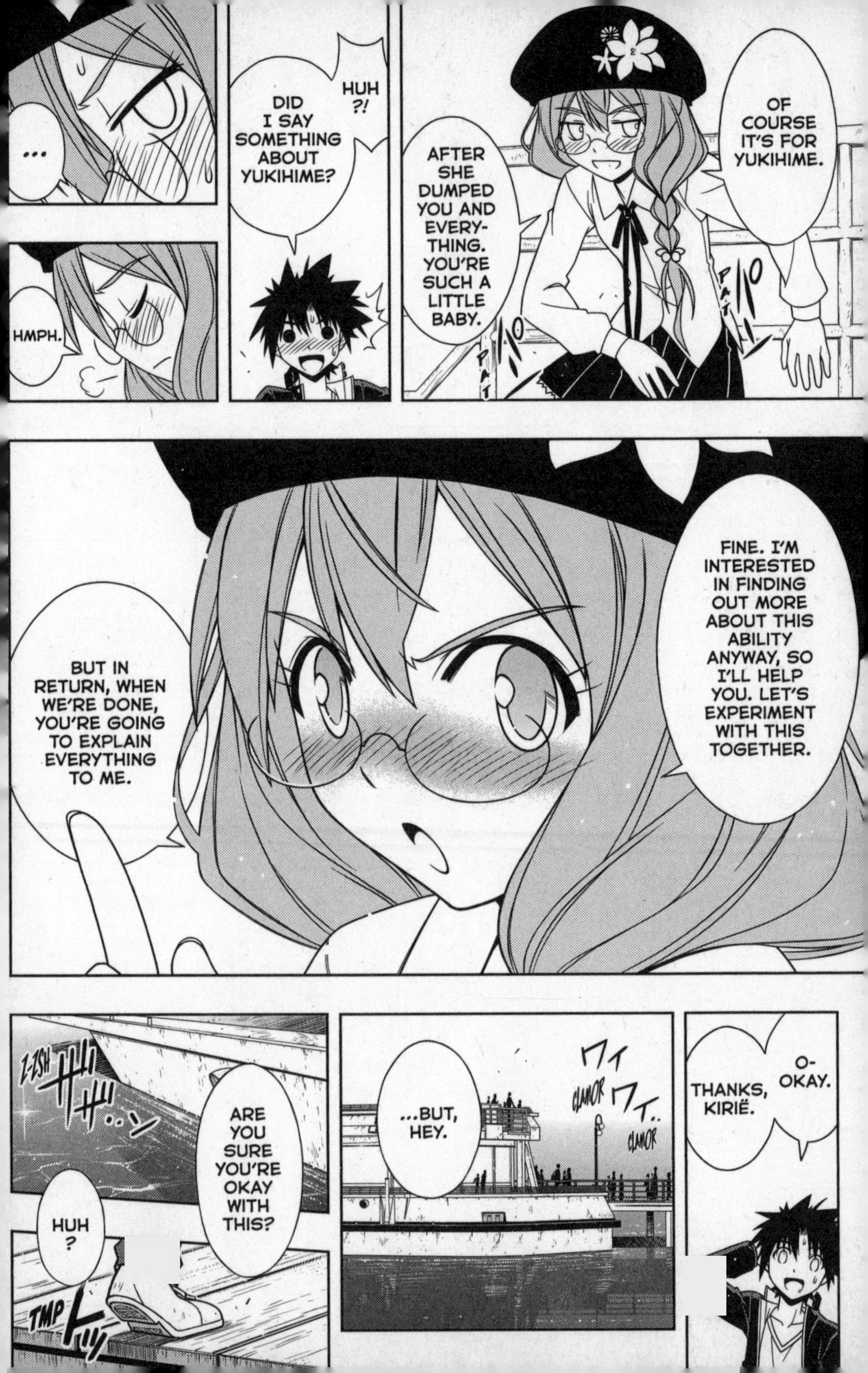
OF COURSE IT'S FOR YUKIHIME.
AFTER SHE DUMPED YOU AND EVERYTHING. YOU'RE SUCH A LITTLE BABY.
PAT
PAT
HUH ?!
DID I SAY SOMETHING ABOUT YUKIHIME?
...
HMPH.
FINE. I'M INTERESTED IN FINDING OUT MORE ABOUT THIS ABILITY ANYWAY, SO I'LL HELP YOU. LET'S EXPERIMENT WITH THIS TOGETHER.
BUT IN RETURN, WHEN WE'RE DONE, YOU'RE GOING TO EXPLAIN EVERYTHING TO ME.
O- OKAY.
THANKS, KIRIË.
ワイ ワイ
CLAMOR
CLAMOR
...BUT, HEY.
Z-ZSH
ARE YOU SURE YOU'RE OKAY WITH THIS?
HUH ?
TMP

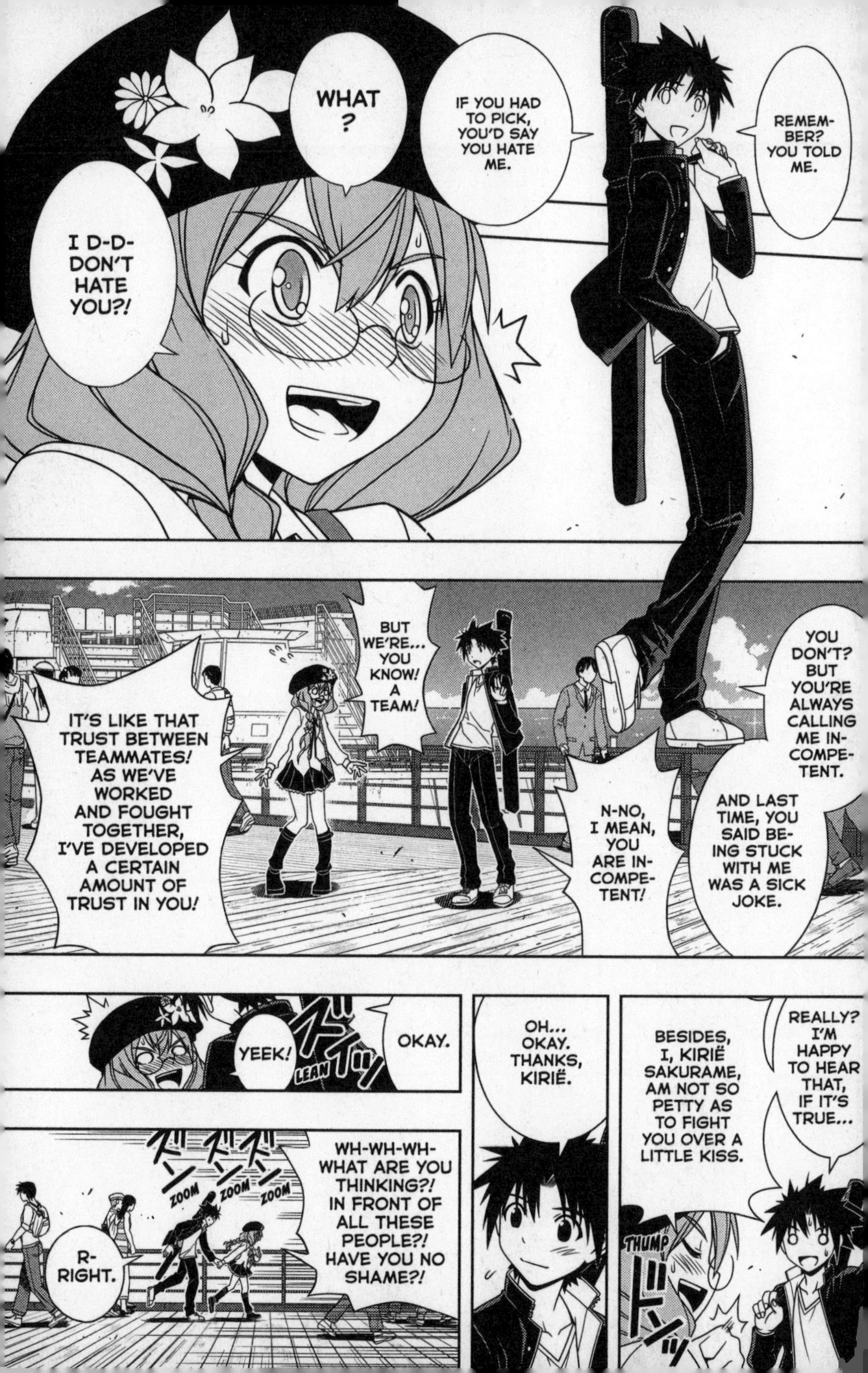
REMEMBER? YOU TOLD ME.
IF YOU HAD TO PICK, YOU'D SAY YOU HATE ME.
WHAT?
I D-D-DON'T HATE YOU?!
YOU DON'T? BUT YOU'RE ALWAYS CALLING ME INCOMPETENT.
AND LAST TIME, YOU SAID BEING STUCK WITH ME WAS A SICK JOKE.
N-NO, I MEAN, YOU ARE INCOMPETENT!
BUT WE'RE... YOU KNOW! A TEAM!
IT'S LIKE THAT TRUST BETWEEN TEAMMATES! AS WE'VE WORKED AND FOUGHT TOGETHER, I'VE DEVELOPED A CERTAIN AMOUNT OF TRUST IN YOU!
REALLY? I'M HAPPY TO HEAR THAT, IF IT'S TRUE...
THUMP
BESIDES, I, KIRIË SAKURAME, AM NOT SO PETTY AS TO FIGHT YOU OVER A LITTLE KISS.
OH... OKAY. THANKS, KIRIË.
OKAY.
LEAN
YEEK!
WH-WH-WH-WHAT ARE YOU THINKING?! IN FRONT OF ALL THESE PEOPLE?! HAVE YOU NO SHAME?!
ZOOM
ZOOM
ZOOM
R-RIGHT.

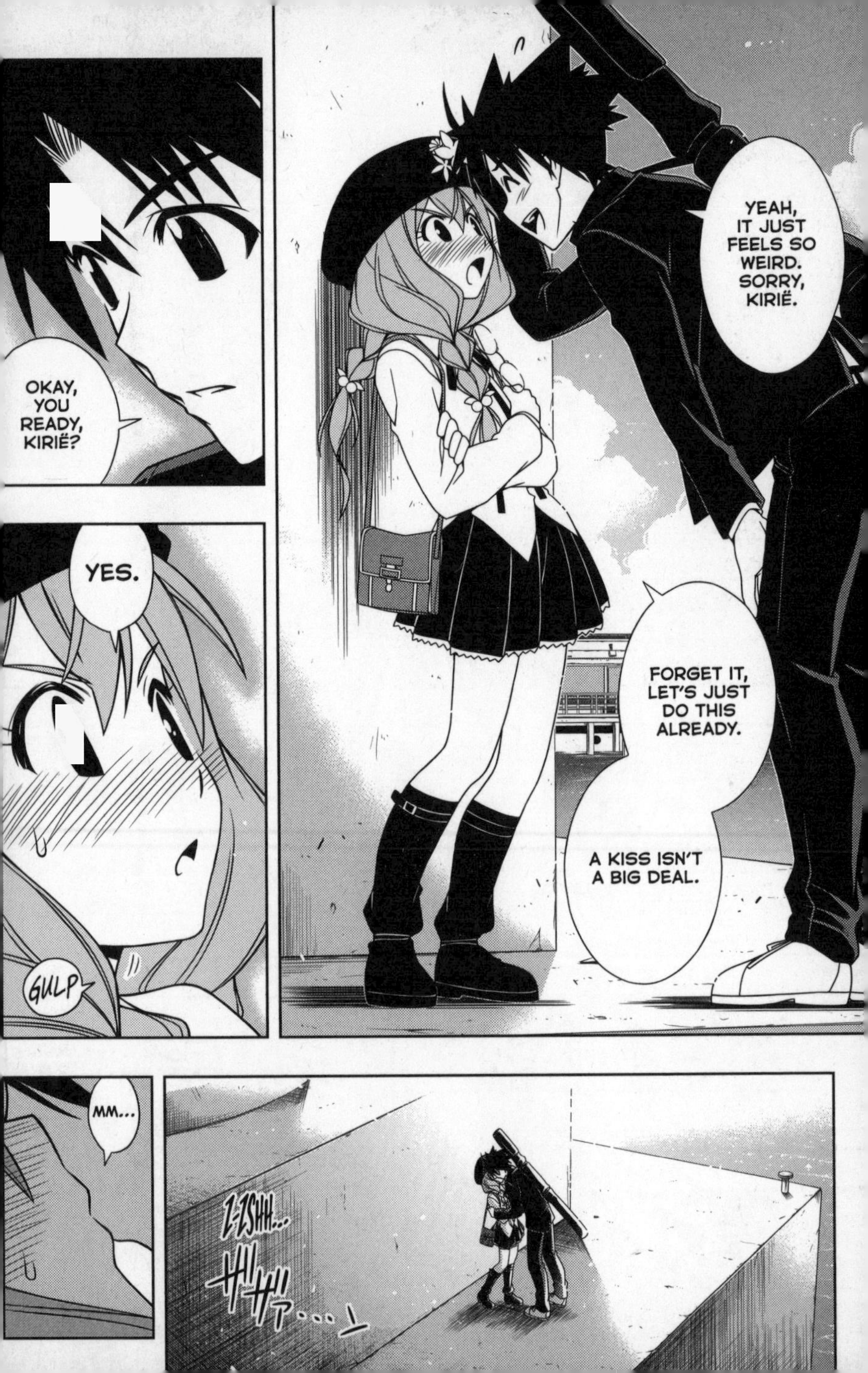
YEAH, IT JUST FEELS SO WEIRD. SORRY, KIRIË.
FORGET IT, LET'S JUST DO THIS ALREADY.
A KISS ISN'T A BIG DEAL.
OKAY, YOU READY, KIRIË?
YES.
GULP
Z-ZSHH...
MM...

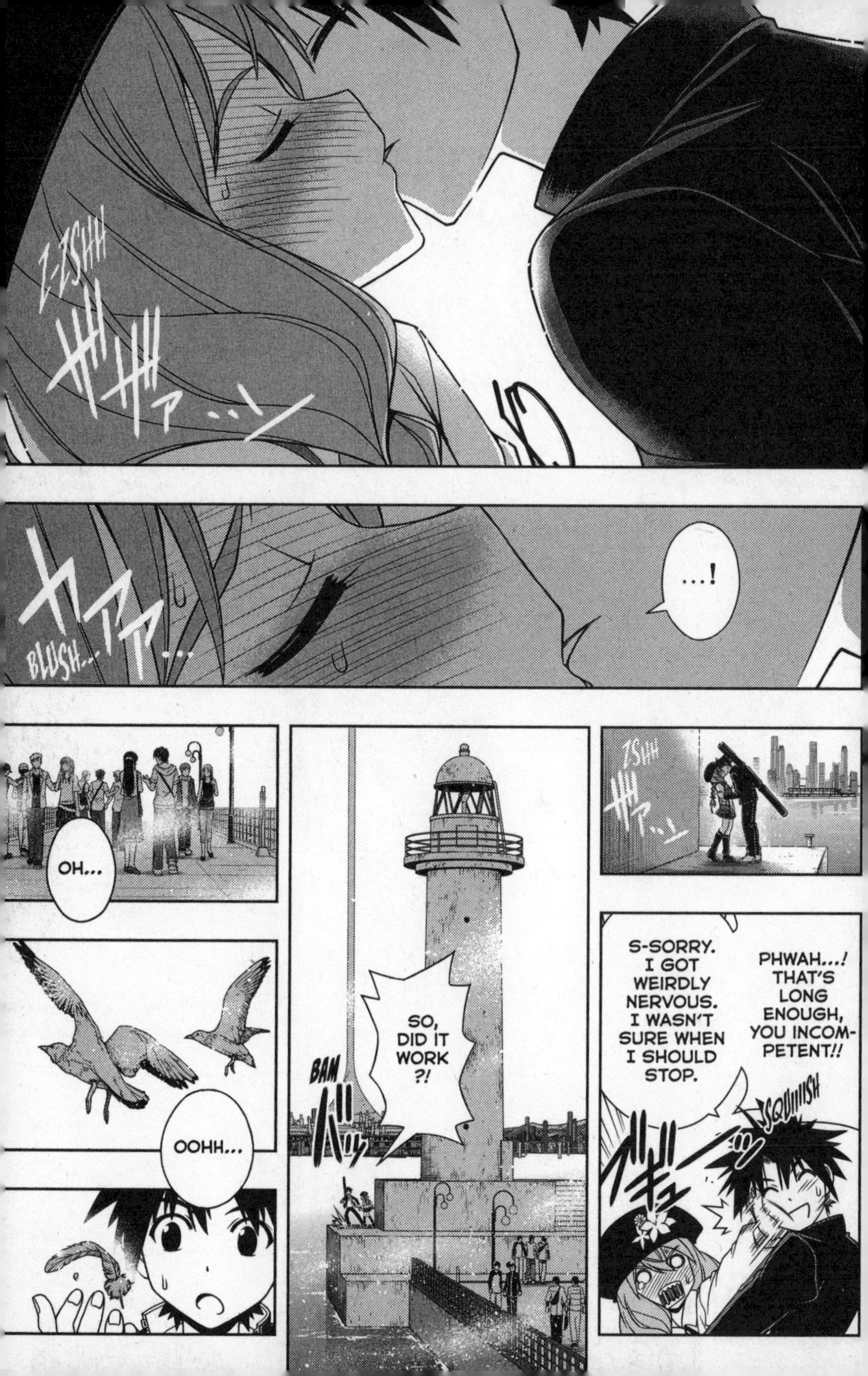
Z-ZSHH
...!
BLUSH...
ZSHH
PHWAH...! THAT'S LONG ENOUGH, YOU INCOMPETENT!!
S-SORRY. I GOT WEIRDLY NERVOUS. I WASN'T SURE WHEN I SHOULD STOP.
SQUIIIISH
SO, DID IT WORK ?!
BAM
OH...
OOHH...

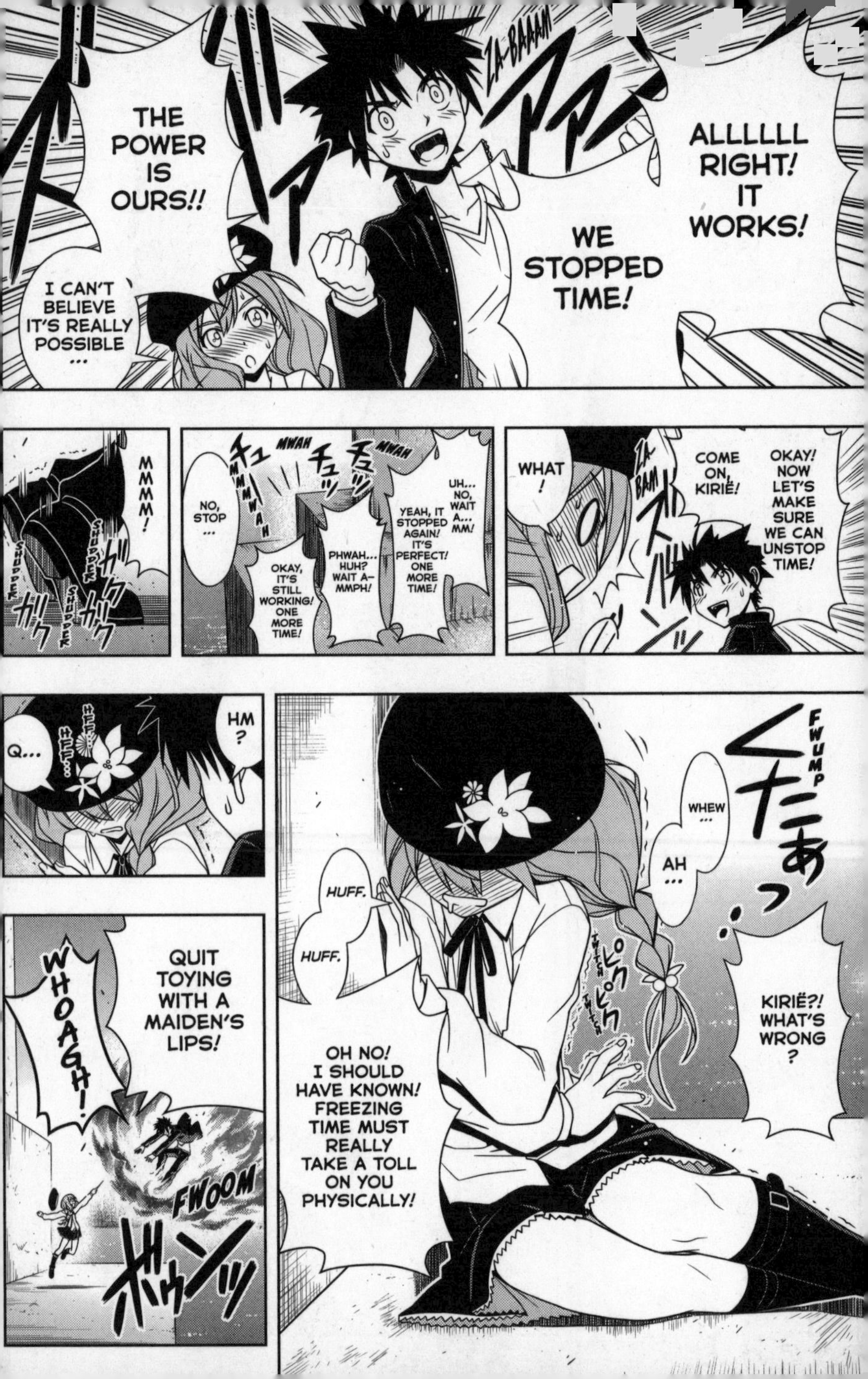
ZA-BAAAM
ALLLLLL RIGHT! IT WORKS!
WE STOPPED TIME!
THE POWER IS OURS!!
I CAN'T BELIEVE IT'S REALLY POSSIBLE...
OKAY! NOW LET'S MAKE SURE WE CAN UNSTOP TIME!
COME ON, KIRIË!
ZA-BAM
WHAT!
MWAH
MWAH
UH... NO, WAIT A... MM!
YEAH, IT STOPPED AGAIN! IT'S PERFECT! ONE MORE TIME!
PHWAH... HUH? WAIT A-MMPH!
MMMMWAH
NO, STOP...
OKAY, IT'S STILL WORKING! ONE MORE TIME!
MMMM!
SHUDDER
SHUDDER
SHUDDER
FWUMP
WHEW...
AH...
KIRIË?! WHAT'S WRONG?
TWITCH TWITCH
HUFF.
HUFF.
OH NO! I SHOULD HAVE KNOWN! FREEZING TIME MUST REALLY TAKE A TOLL ON YOU PHYSICALLY!
HM?
HFF... HFF...
Q...
QUIT TOYING WITH A MAIDEN'S LIPS!
WHOAGH!
FWOOM

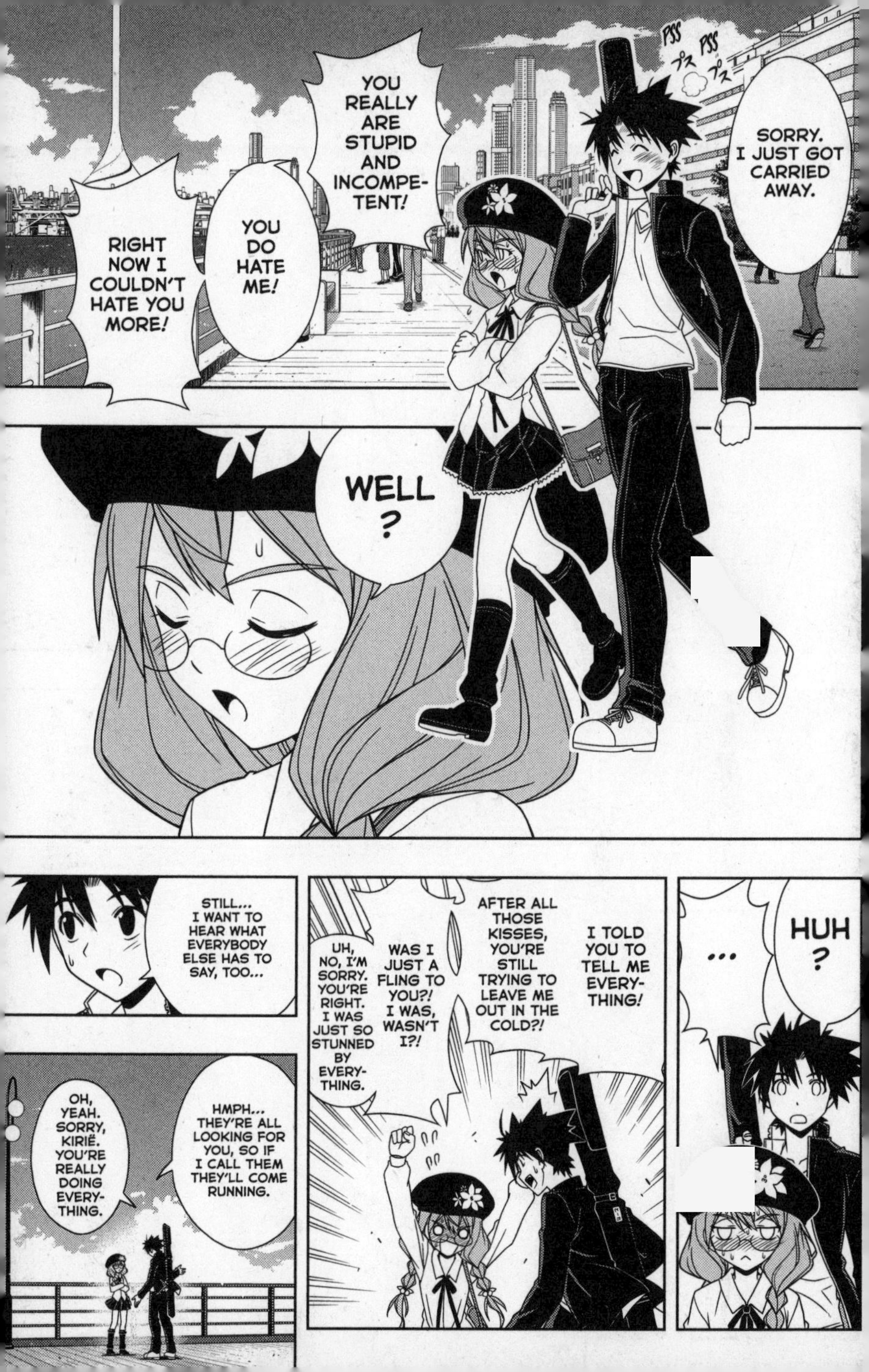
PSS PSS
プス プス
SORRY. I JUST GOT CARRIED AWAY.
YOU REALLY ARE STUPID AND INCOMPETENT!
YOU DO HATE ME!
RIGHT NOW I COULDN'T HATE YOU MORE!
WELL?
HUH?
...
I TOLD YOU TO TELL ME EVERYTHING!
AFTER ALL THOSE KISSES, YOU'RE STILL TRYING TO LEAVE ME OUT IN THE COLD?!
WAS I JUST A FLING TO YOU?! I WAS, WASN'T I?!
UH, NO, I'M SORRY. YOU'RE RIGHT. I WAS JUST SO STUNNED BY EVERYTHING.
STILL... I WANT TO HEAR WHAT EVERYBODY ELSE HAS TO SAY, TOO...
HMPH... THEY'RE ALL LOOKING FOR YOU, SO IF I CALL THEM THEY'LL COME RUNNING.
OH, YEAH. SORRY, KIRIË. YOU'RE REALLY DOING EVERYTHING.

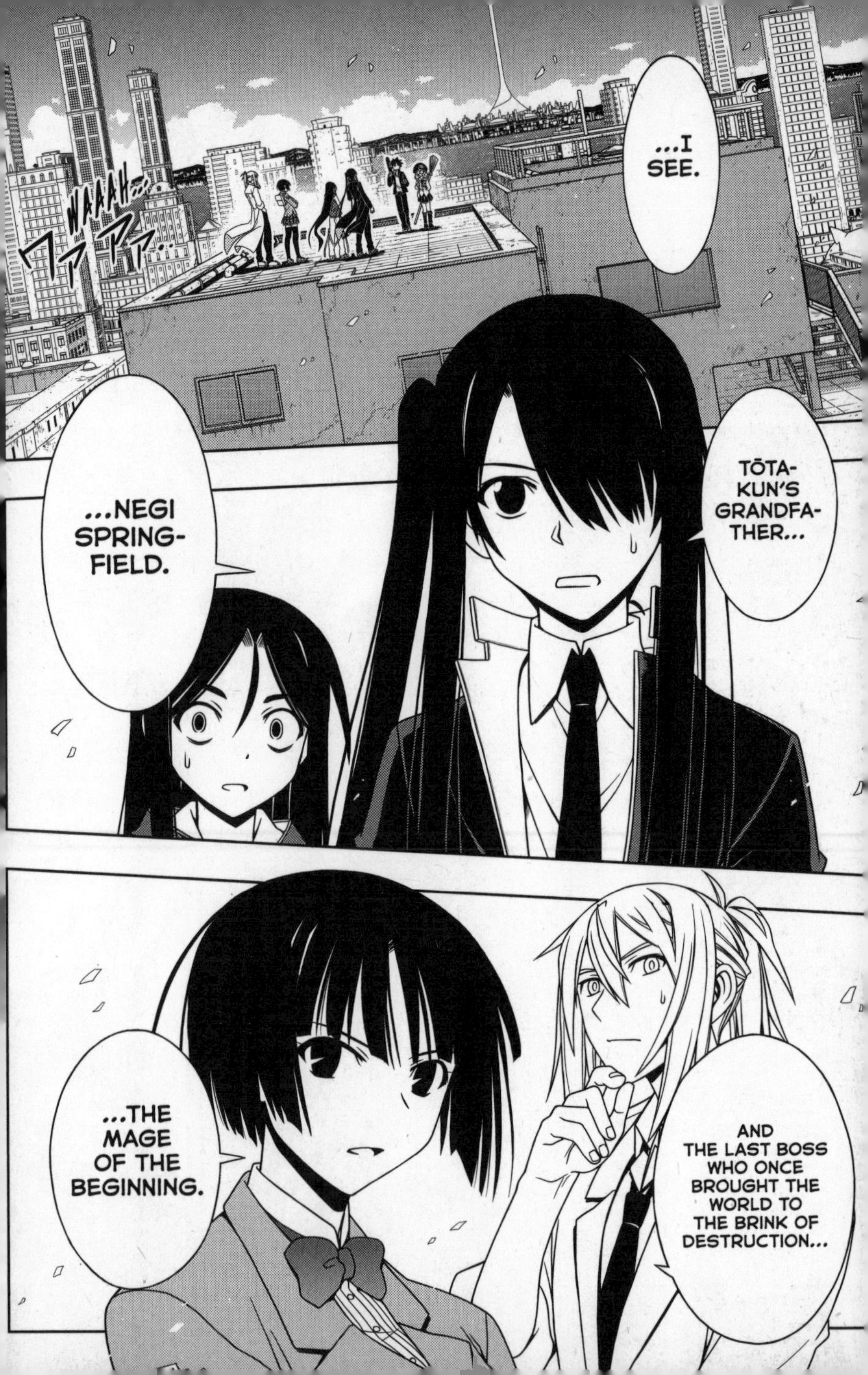
...I SEE.
WAAAH...
TŌTA-KUN'S GRANDFATHER...
...NEGI SPRINGFIELD.
AND THE LAST BOSS WHO ONCE BROUGHT THE WORLD TO THE BRINK OF DESTRUCTION...
...THE MAGE OF THE BEGINNING.

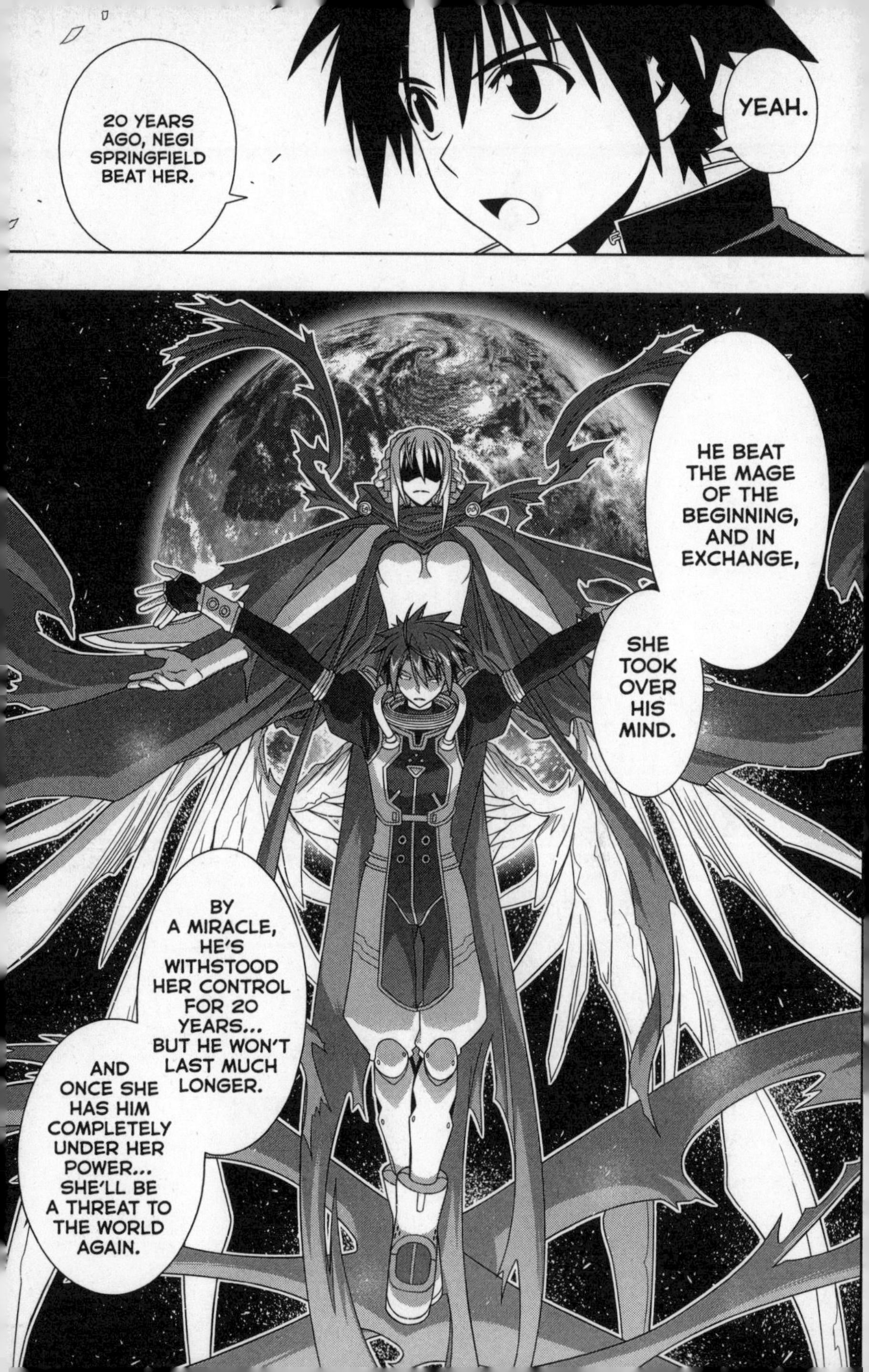
YEAH.
20 YEARS AGO, NEGI SPRINGFIELD BEAT HER.
HE BEAT THE MAGE OF THE BEGINNING, AND IN EXCHANGE,
SHE TOOK OVER HIS MIND.
BY A MIRACLE, HE'S WITHSTOOD HER CONTROL FOR 20 YEARS... BUT HE WON'T LAST MUCH LONGER.
AND ONCE SHE HAS HIM COMPLETELY UNDER HER POWER... SHE'LL BE A THREAT TO THE WORLD AGAIN.

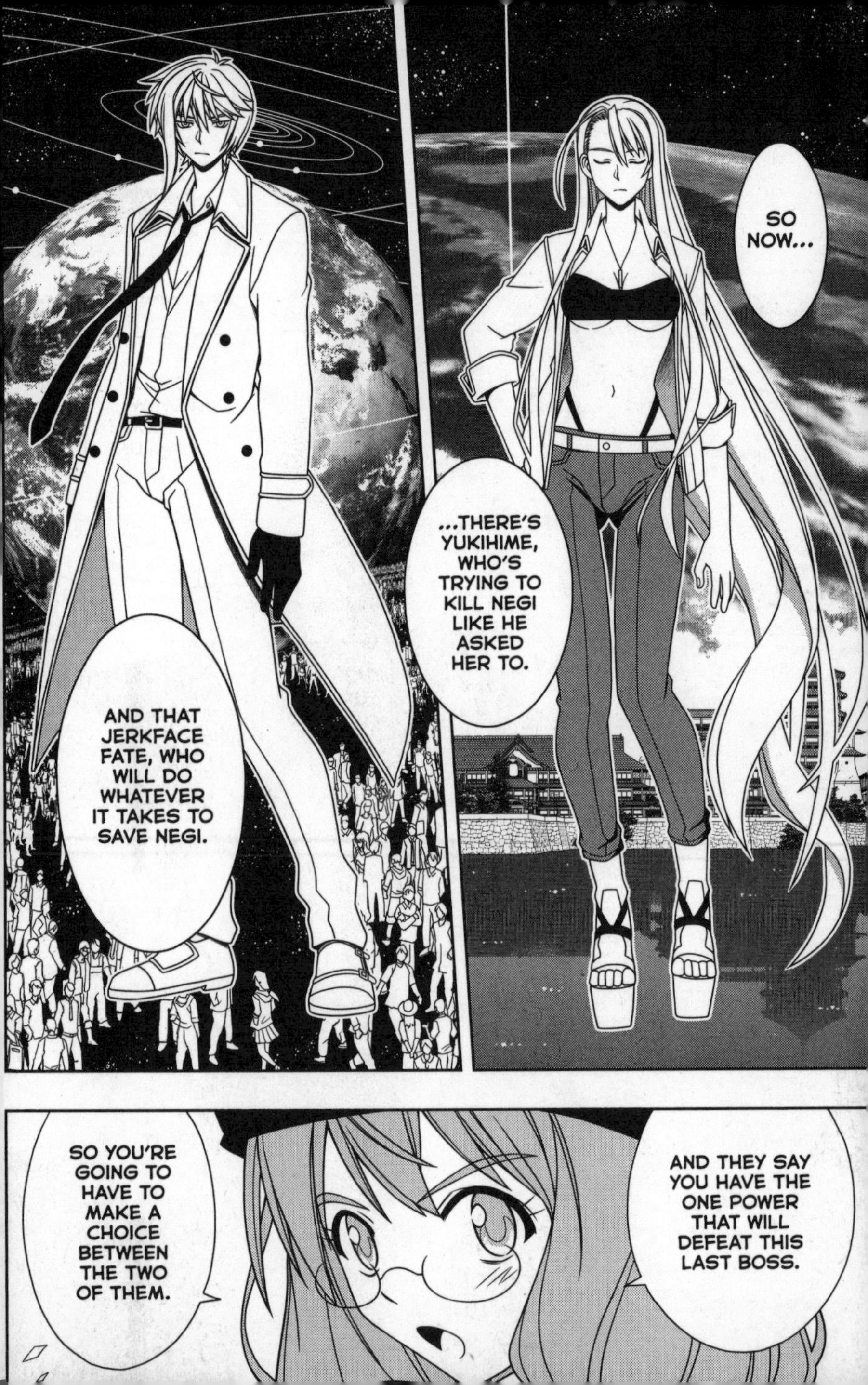
SO NOW...
...THERE'S YUKIHIME, WHO'S TRYING TO KILL NEGI LIKE HE ASKED HER TO.
AND THAT JERKFACE FATE, WHO WILL DO WHATEVER IT TAKES TO SAVE NEGI.
AND THEY SAY YOU HAVE THE ONE POWER THAT WILL DEFEAT THIS LAST BOSS.
SO YOU'RE GOING TO HAVE TO MAKE A CHOICE BETWEEN THE TWO OF THEM.

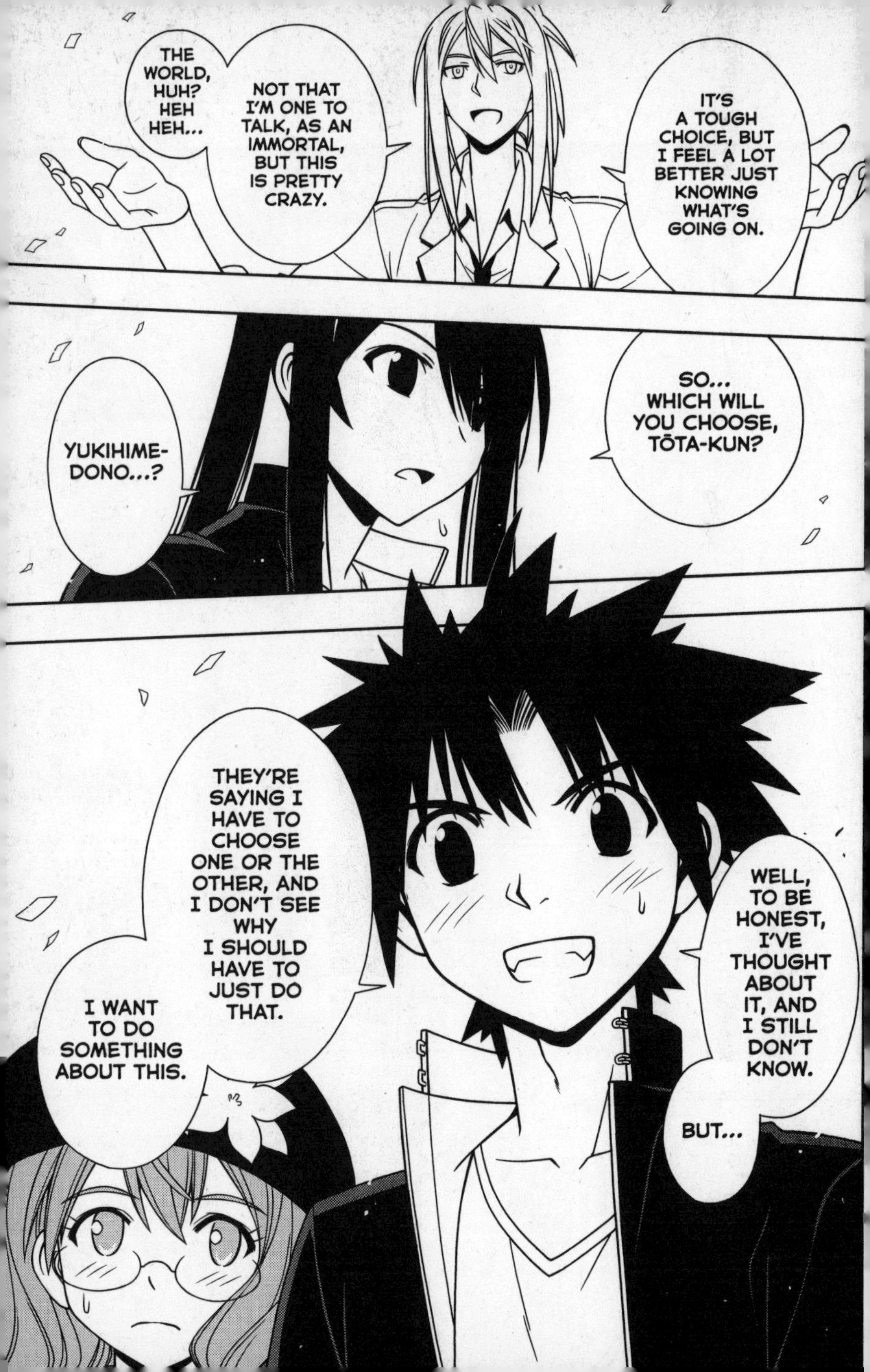
IT'S A TOUGH CHOICE, BUT I FEEL A LOT BETTER JUST KNOWING WHAT'S GOING ON.
NOT THAT I'M ONE TO TALK, AS AN IMMORTAL, BUT THIS IS PRETTY CRAZY.
THE WORLD, HUH? HEH HEH...
SO... WHICH WILL YOU CHOOSE, TŌTA-KUN?
YUKIHIME-DONO...?
WELL, TO BE HONEST, I'VE THOUGHT ABOUT IT, AND I STILL DON'T KNOW.
BUT...
THEY'RE SAYING I HAVE TO CHOOSE ONE OR THE OTHER, AND I DON'T SEE WHY I SHOULD HAVE TO JUST DO THAT.
I WANT TO DO SOMETHING ABOUT THIS.

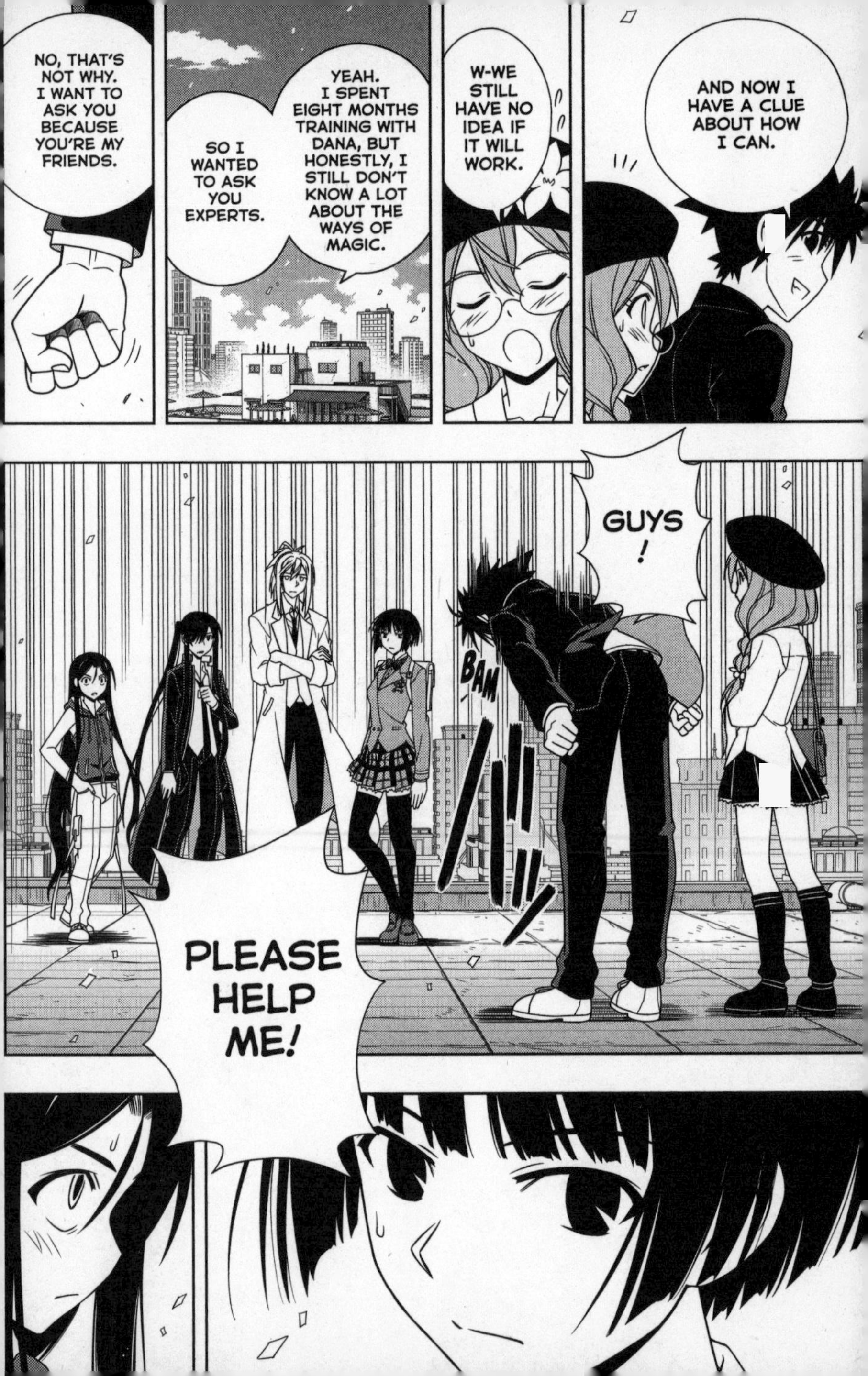
AND NOW I HAVE A CLUE ABOUT HOW I CAN.
W-WE STILL HAVE NO IDEA IF IT WILL WORK.
YEAH. I SPENT EIGHT MONTHS TRAINING WITH DANA, BUT HONESTLY, I STILL DON'T KNOW A LOT ABOUT THE WAYS OF MAGIC.
SO I WANTED TO ASK YOU EXPERTS.
NO, THAT'S NOT WHY. I WANT TO ASK YOU BECAUSE YOU'RE MY FRIENDS.
GUYS!
BAM
PLEASE HELP ME!

UQ HOLDER!

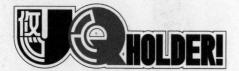

UQ HOLDER!

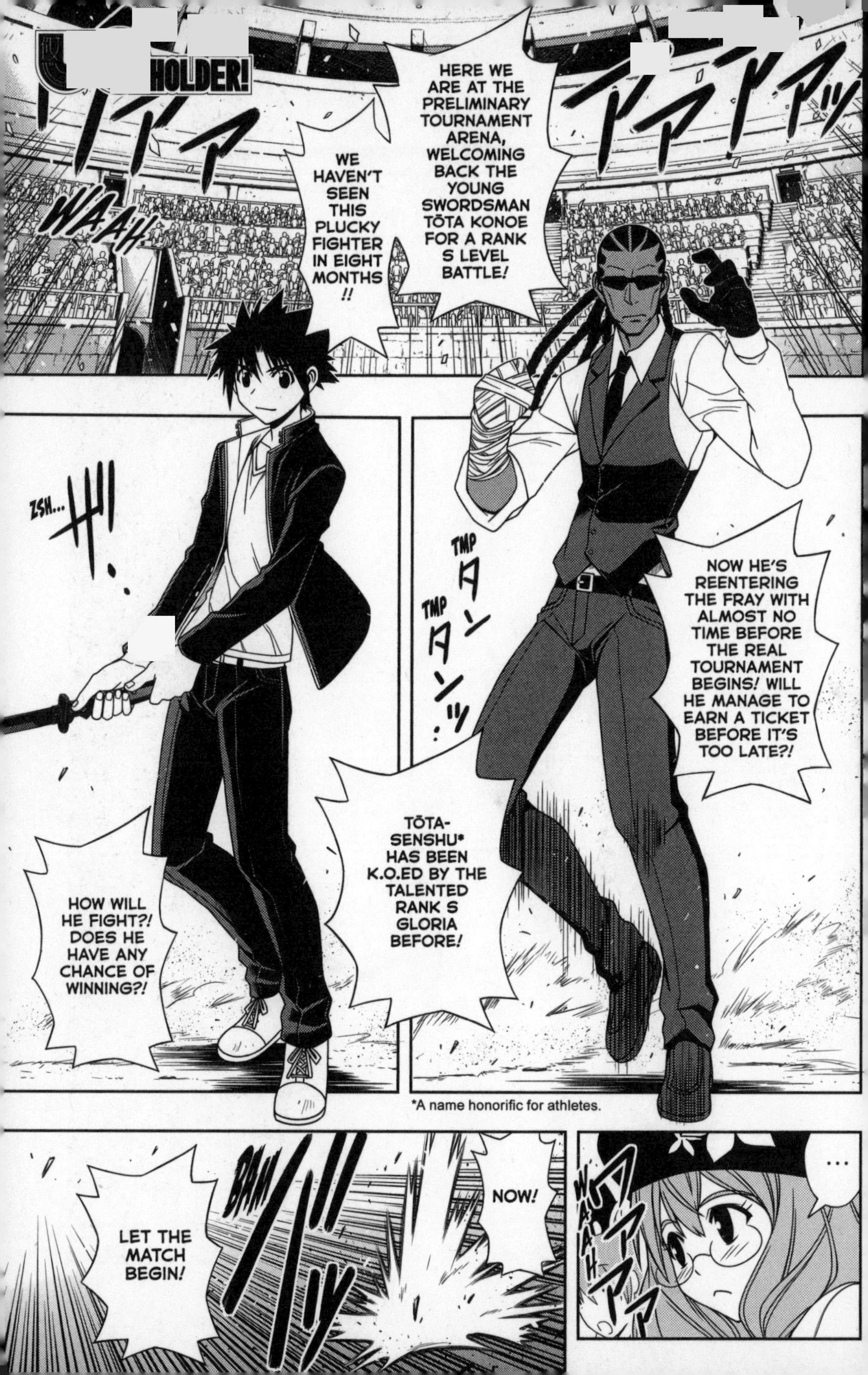
HOLDER!
アアアアッ
HERE WE ARE AT THE PRELIMINARY TOURNAMENT ARENA, WELCOMING BACK THE YOUNG SWORDSMAN TŌTA KONOE FOR A RANK S LEVEL BATTLE!
WE HAVEN'T SEEN THIS PLUCKY FIGHTER IN EIGHT MONTHS!!
WAAH
アア
NOW HE'S REENTERING THE FRAY WITH ALMOST NO TIME BEFORE THE REAL TOURNAMENT BEGINS! WILL HE MANAGE TO EARN A TICKET BEFORE IT'S TOO LATE?!
TMP タン
TMP タンッ
TŌTA-SENSHU* HAS BEEN K.O.ED BY THE TALENTED RANK S GLORIA BEFORE!
ZSH...
HOW WILL HE FIGHT?! DOES HE HAVE ANY CHANCE OF WINNING?!
...
WAAH
NOW!
BAM
LET THE MATCH BEGIN!
*A name honorific for athletes.

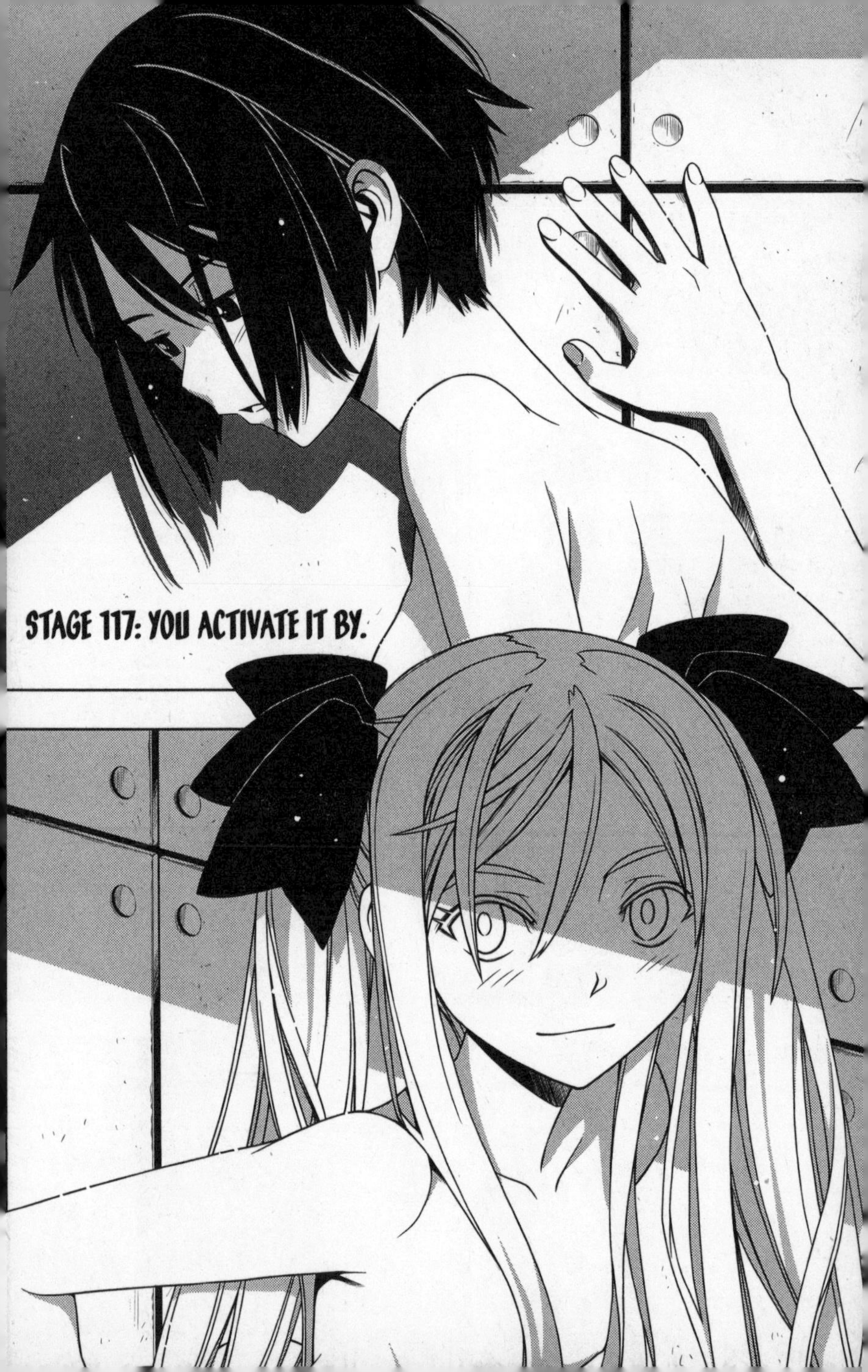
STAGE 117: YOU ACTIVATE IT BY.

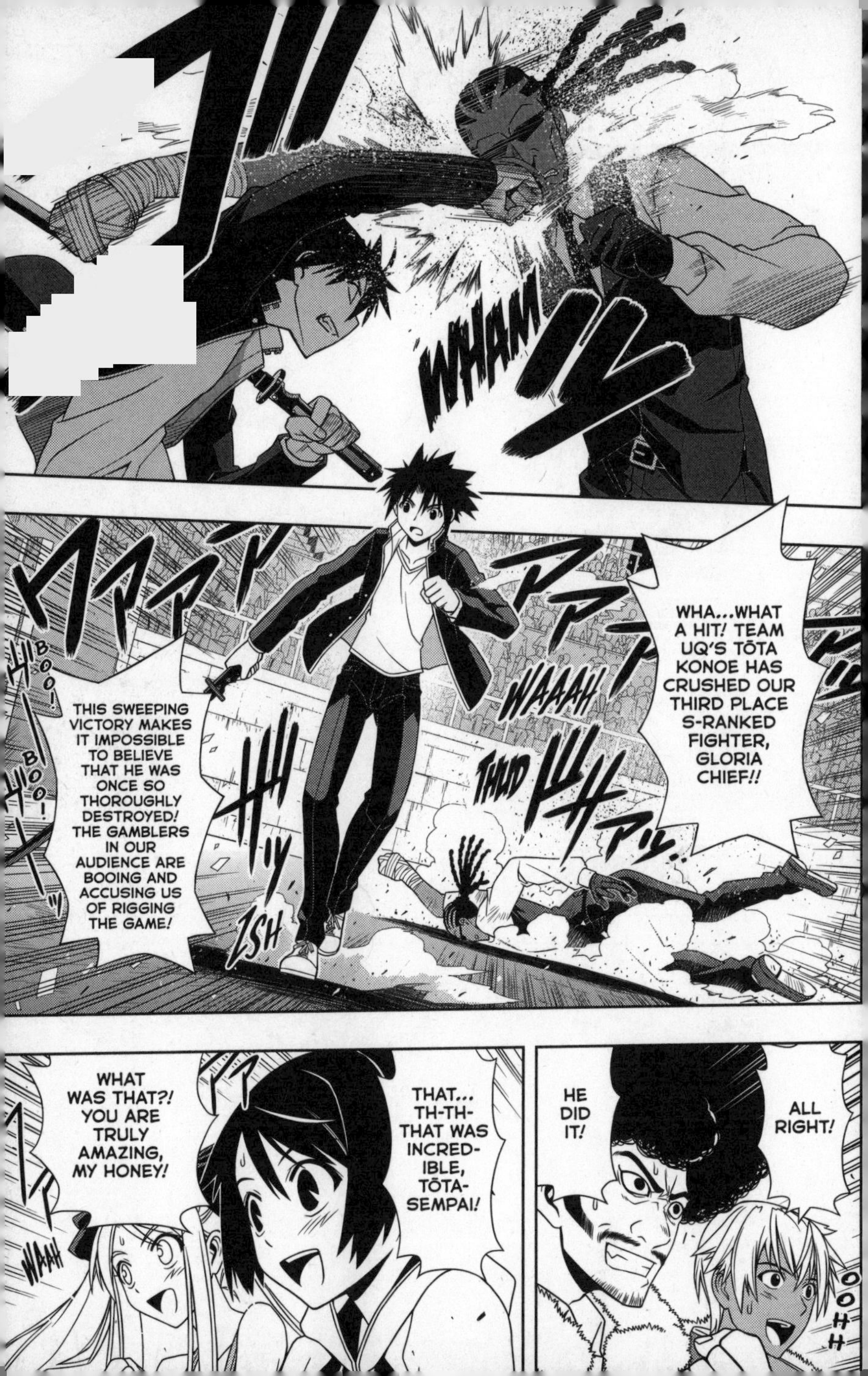
WHAM
WHA...WHAT A HIT! TEAM UQ'S TŌTA KONOE HAS CRUSHED OUR THIRD PLACE S-RANKED FIGHTER, GLORIA CHIEF!!
WAAAH
THUD
ZSH
THIS SWEEPING VICTORY MAKES IT IMPOSSIBLE TO BELIEVE THAT HE WAS ONCE SO THOROUGHLY DESTROYED! THE GAMBLERS IN OUR AUDIENCE ARE BOOING AND ACCUSING US OF RIGGING THE GAME!
BOO! BOO!
ALL RIGHT!
HE DID IT!
OOHH
THAT... TH-TH-THAT WAS INCREDIBLE, TŌTA-SEMPAI!
WHAT WAS THAT?! YOU ARE TRULY AMAZING, MY HONEY!
WAAH

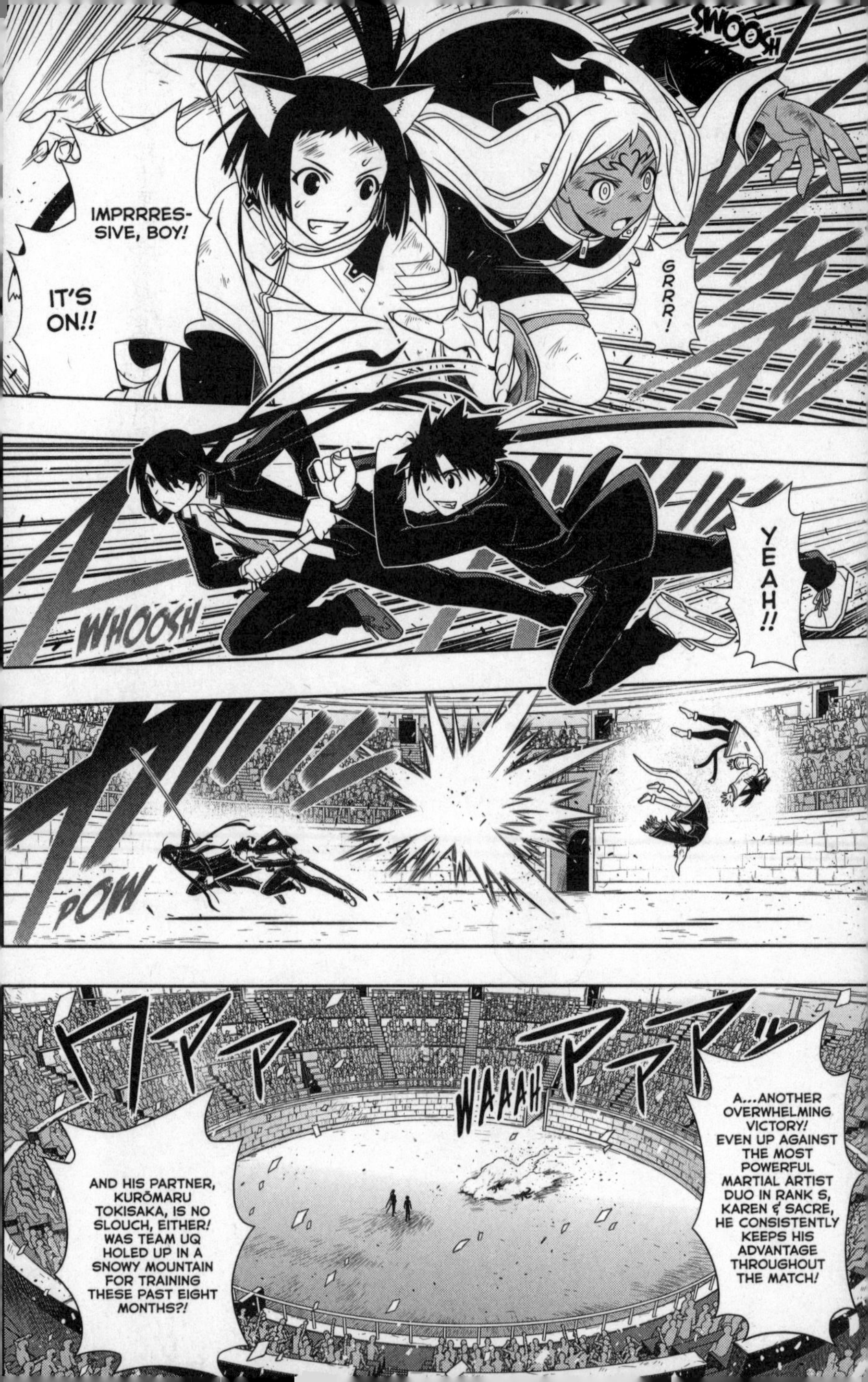
SWOOSH
GRRR!
IMPRRRES-SIVE, BOY!
IT'S ON!!
YEAH!!
WHOOSH
POW
A...ANOTHER OVERWHELMING VICTORY! EVEN UP AGAINST THE MOST POWERFUL MARTIAL ARTIST DUO IN RANK S, KAREN & SACRE, HE CONSISTENTLY KEEPS HIS ADVANTAGE THROUGHOUT THE MATCH!
WAAAH
AND HIS PARTNER, KURŌMARU TOKISAKA, IS NO SLOUCH, EITHER! WAS TEAM UQ HOLED UP IN A SNOWY MOUNTAIN FOR TRAINING THESE PAST EIGHT MONTHS?!

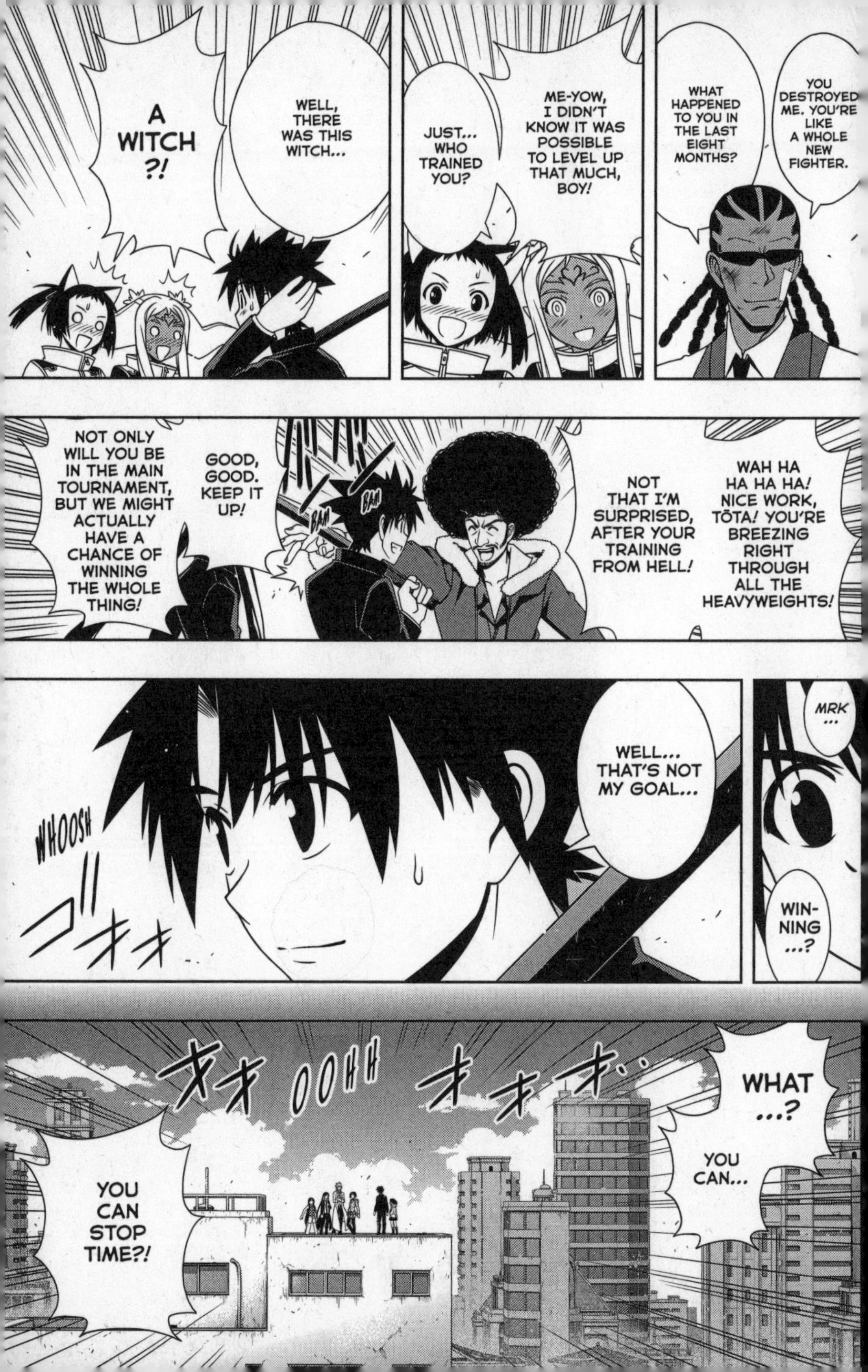
YOU DESTROYED ME. YOU'RE LIKE A WHOLE NEW FIGHTER.
WHAT HAPPENED TO YOU IN THE LAST EIGHT MONTHS?
ME-YOW, I DIDN'T KNOW IT WAS POSSIBLE TO LEVEL UP THAT MUCH, BOY!
JUST... WHO TRAINED YOU?
WELL, THERE WAS THIS WITCH...
A WITCH ?!
WAH HA HA HA HA! NICE WORK, TŌTA! YOU'RE BREEZING RIGHT THROUGH ALL THE HEAVYWEIGHTS!
NOT THAT I'M SURPRISED, AFTER YOUR TRAINING FROM HELL!
BAM
BAM
GOOD, GOOD. KEEP IT UP!
NOT ONLY WILL YOU BE IN THE MAIN TOURNAMENT, BUT WE MIGHT ACTUALLY HAVE A CHANCE OF WINNING THE WHOLE THING!
MRK...
WIN-NING...?
WELL... THAT'S NOT MY GOAL...
WHOOSH
ゴオオ
WHAT...?
YOU CAN...
オオ OOHH オォォ...
YOU CAN STOP TIME?!

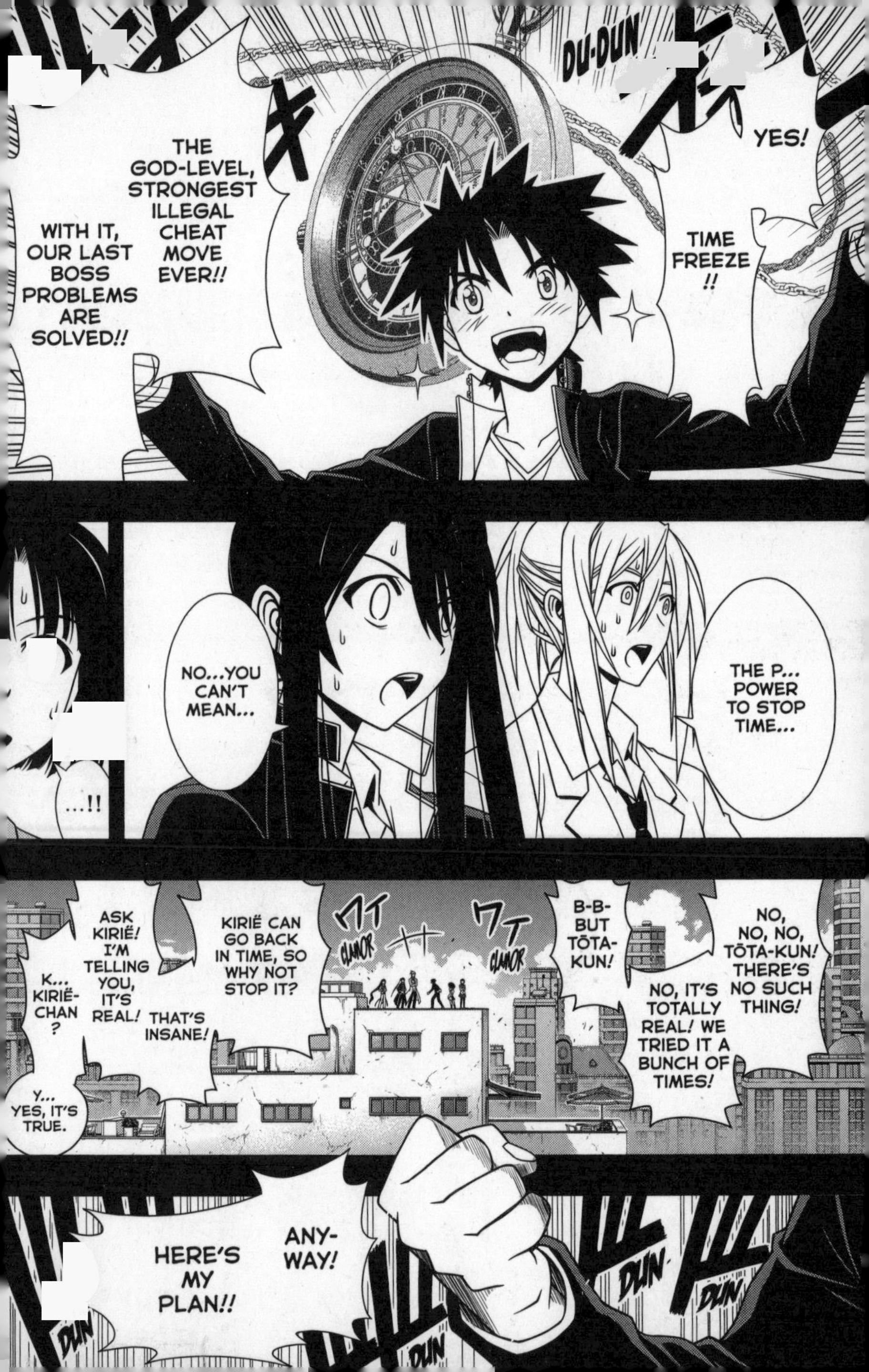
DU-DUN
YES!
TIME FREEZE !!
THE GOD-LEVEL, STRONGEST ILLEGAL CHEAT MOVE EVER!!
WITH IT, OUR LAST BOSS PROBLEMS ARE SOLVED!!
THE P... POWER TO STOP TIME...
NO...YOU CAN'T MEAN...
...!!
NO, NO, NO, TŌTA-KUN! THERE'S NO SUCH THING!
B-B-BUT TŌTA-KUN!
NO, IT'S TOTALLY REAL! WE TRIED IT A BUNCH OF TIMES!
CLAMOR
CLAMOR
KIRIË CAN GO BACK IN TIME, SO WHY NOT STOP IT?
ASK KIRIË! I'M TELLING YOU, IT'S REAL!
THAT'S INSANE!
K... KIRIË-CHAN?
Y... YES, IT'S TRUE.
DUN
DUN
ANY-WAY!
HERE'S MY PLAN!!
DUN
DUN

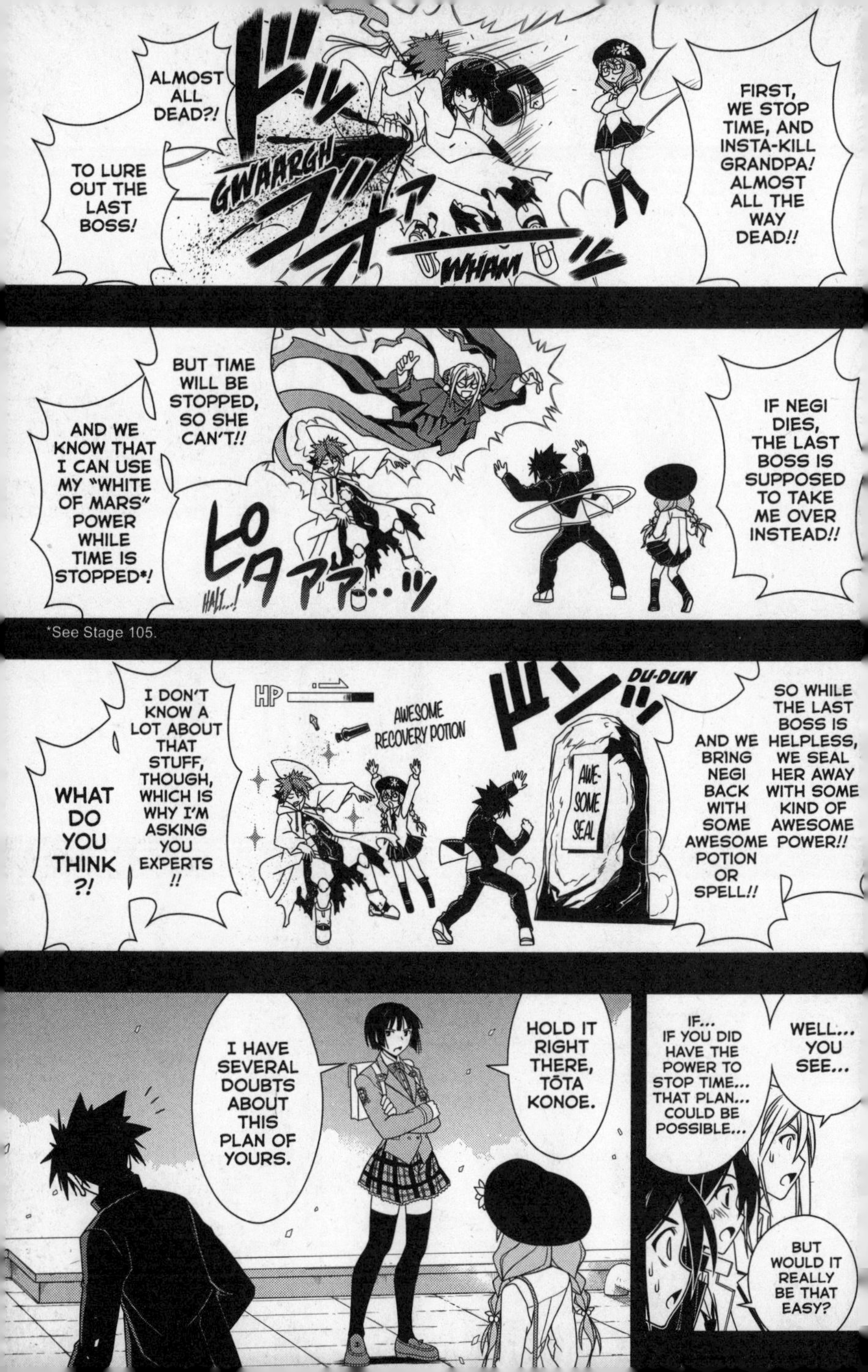
FIRST, WE STOP TIME, AND INSTA-KILL GRANDPA! ALMOST ALL THE WAY DEAD!!
ALMOST ALL DEAD?!
TO LURE OUT THE LAST BOSS!
GWAARGH
WHAM
IF NEGI DIES, THE LAST BOSS IS SUPPOSED TO TAKE ME OVER INSTEAD!!
BUT TIME WILL BE STOPPED, SO SHE CAN'T!!
AND WE KNOW THAT I CAN USE MY "WHITE OF MARS" POWER WHILE TIME IS STOPPED*!
HALT...!
DU-DUN
SO WHILE THE LAST BOSS IS HELPLESS, WE SEAL HER AWAY WITH SOME KIND OF AWESOME POWER!!
AND WE BRING NEGI BACK WITH SOME AWESOME POTION OR SPELL!!
AWE-SOME SEAL
HP
AWESOME RECOVERY POTION
I DON'T KNOW A LOT ABOUT THAT STUFF, THOUGH, WHICH IS WHY I'M ASKING YOU EXPERTS!!
WHAT DO YOU THINK?!
WELL... YOU SEE...
IF... IF YOU DID HAVE THE POWER TO STOP TIME... THAT PLAN... COULD BE POSSIBLE...
BUT WOULD IT REALLY BE THAT EASY?
HOLD IT RIGHT THERE, TŌTA KONOE.
I HAVE SEVERAL DOUBTS ABOUT THIS PLAN OF YOURS.
*See Stage 105.

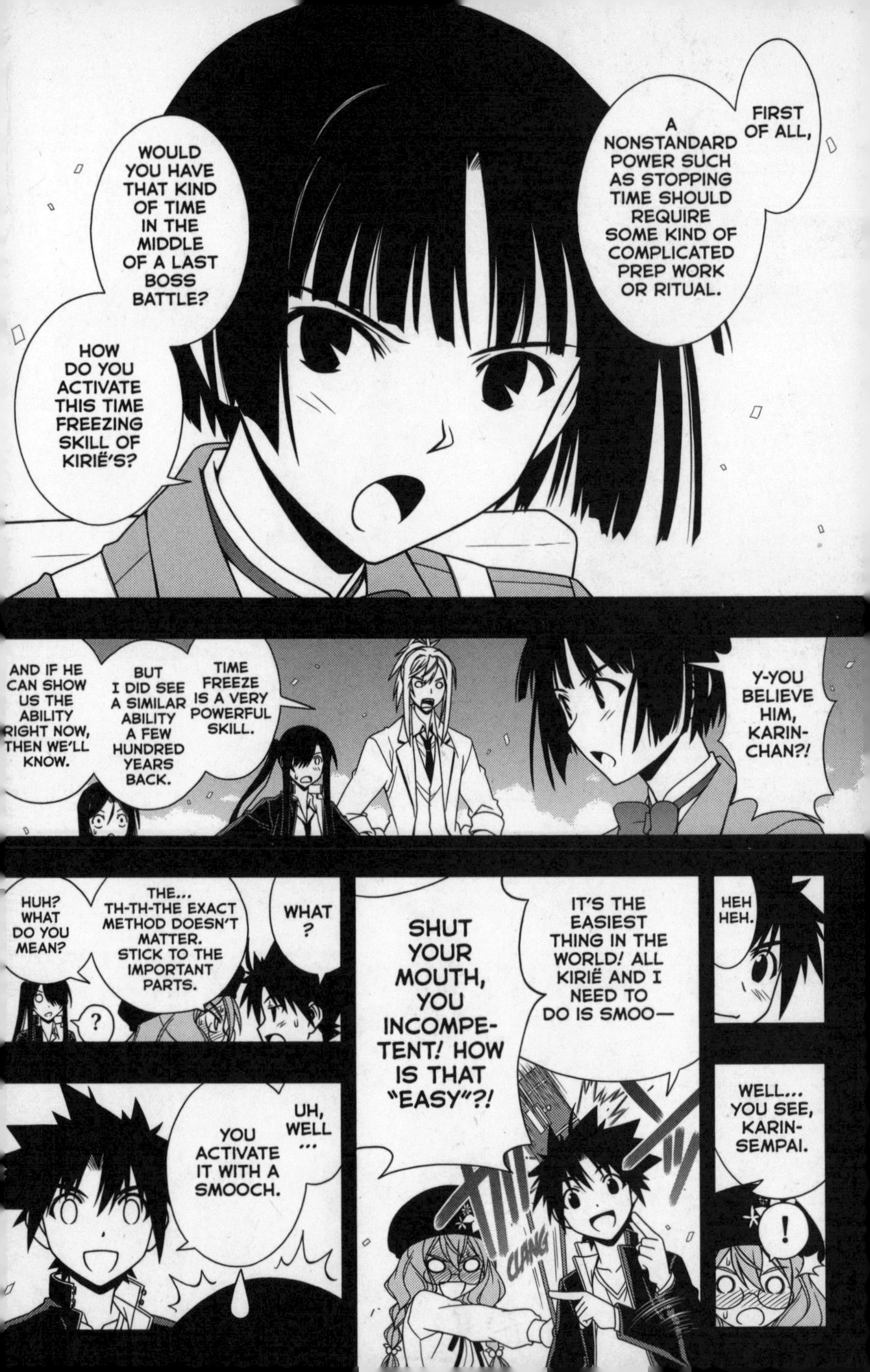
FIRST OF ALL, A NONSTANDARD POWER SUCH AS STOPPING TIME SHOULD REQUIRE SOME KIND OF COMPLICATED PREP WORK OR RITUAL.
WOULD YOU HAVE THAT KIND OF TIME IN THE MIDDLE OF A LAST BOSS BATTLE?
HOW DO YOU ACTIVATE THIS TIME FREEZING SKILL OF KIRIË'S?
Y-YOU BELIEVE HIM, KARIN-CHAN?!
TIME FREEZE IS A VERY POWERFUL SKILL.
BUT I DID SEE A SIMILAR ABILITY A FEW HUNDRED YEARS BACK.
AND IF HE CAN SHOW US THE ABILITY RIGHT NOW, THEN WE'LL KNOW.
HEH HEH.
WELL... YOU SEE, KARIN-SEMPAI.
!
IT'S THE EASIEST THING IN THE WORLD! ALL KIRIË AND I NEED TO DO IS SMOO—
SHUT YOUR MOUTH, YOU INCOMPETENT! HOW IS THAT "EASY"?!
CLANG
WHAT?
THE... TH-TH-THE EXACT METHOD DOESN'T MATTER. STICK TO THE IMPORTANT PARTS.
HUH? WHAT DO YOU MEAN?
?
UH, WELL...
YOU ACTIVATE IT WITH A SMOOCH.

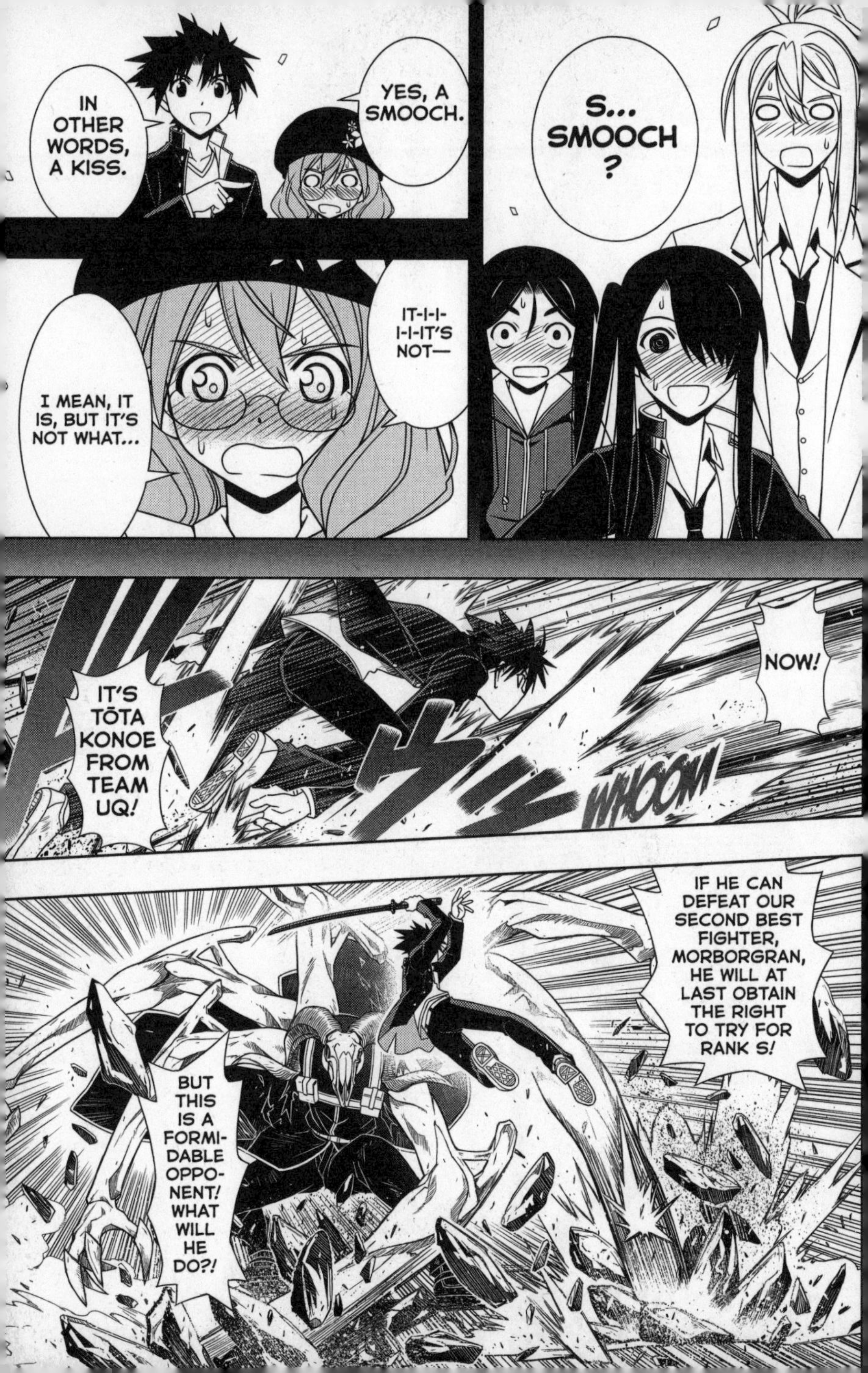
S... SMOOCH?
YES, A SMOOCH.
IN OTHER WORDS, A KISS.
IT-I-I-I-I-IT'S NOT—
I MEAN, IT IS, BUT IT'S NOT WHAT...
NOW!
WHOOM
IT'S TŌTA KONOE FROM TEAM UQ!
IF HE CAN DEFEAT OUR SECOND BEST FIGHTER, MORBORGRAN, HE WILL AT LAST OBTAIN THE RIGHT TO TRY FOR RANK S!
BUT THIS IS A FORMIDABLE OPPONENT! WHAT WILL HE DO?!

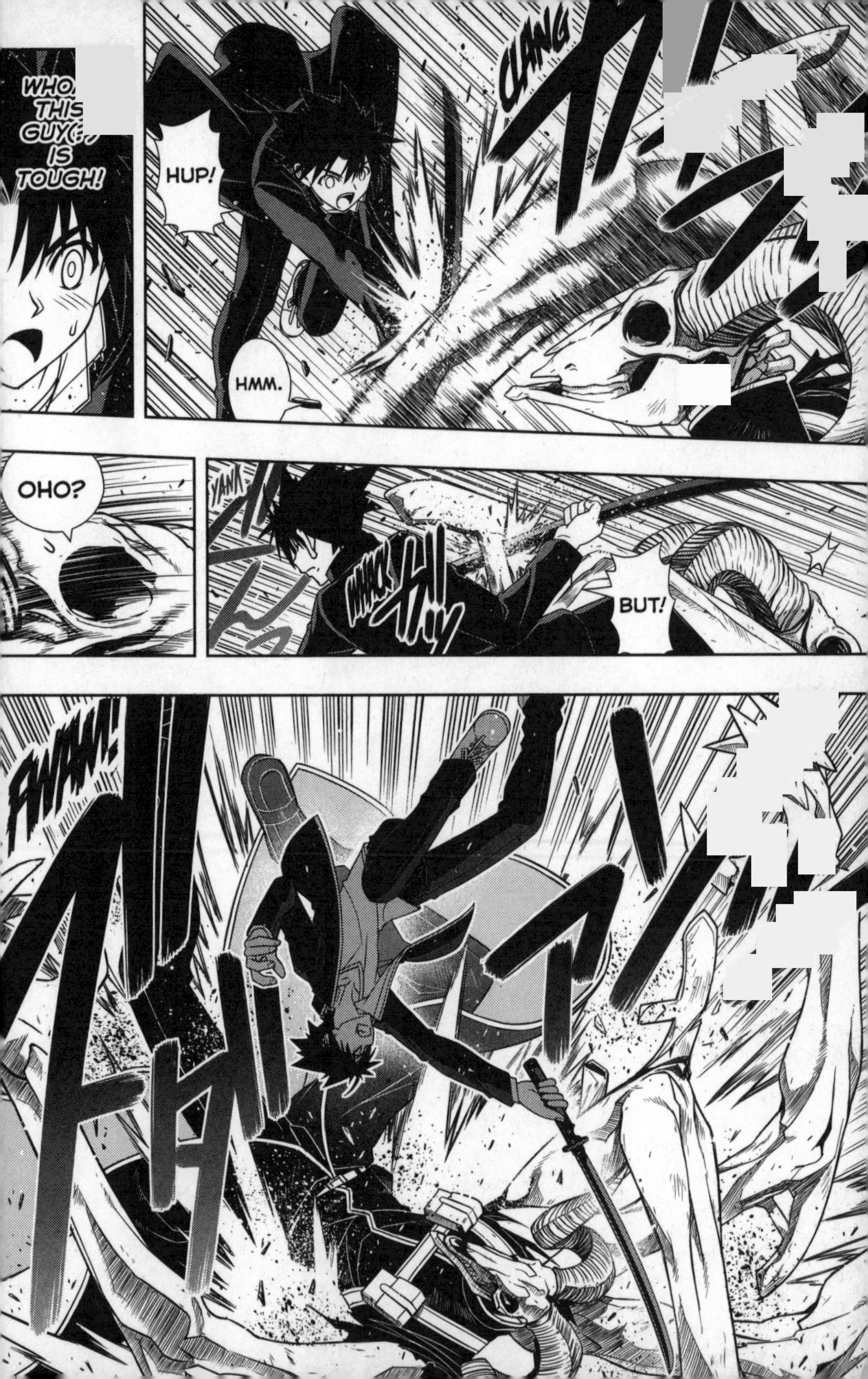
CLANG
HUP!
HMM.
WHO THIS GUY(?) IS TOUGH!
YANK
WHACK
BUT!
OHO?

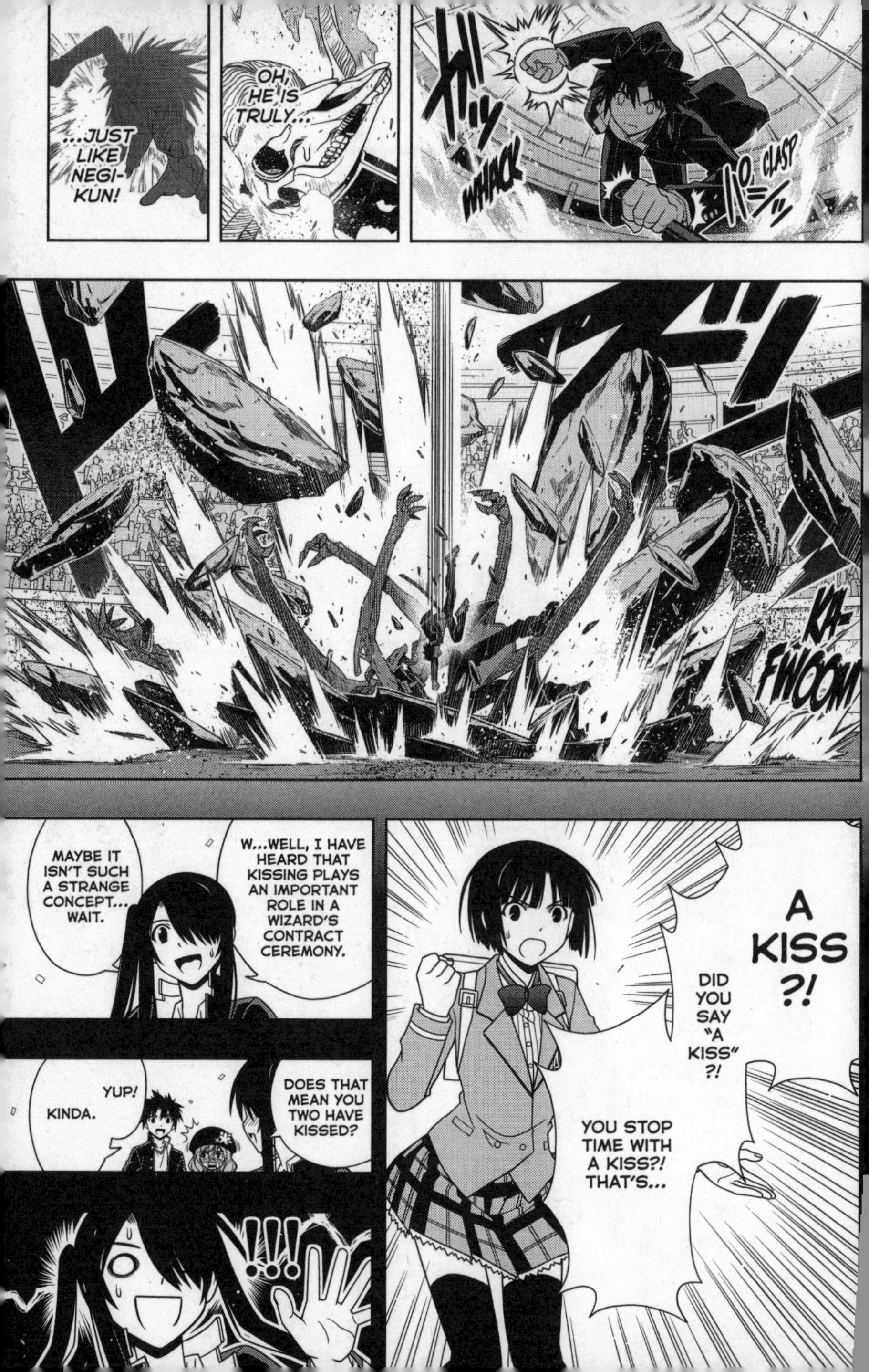
CLASP
WHACK
OH, HE IS TRULY...
...JUST LIKE NEGI-KUN!
KA-FWOOM
A KISS ?!
DID YOU SAY "A KISS" ?!
YOU STOP TIME WITH A KISS?! THAT'S...
W...WELL, I HAVE HEARD THAT KISSING PLAYS AN IMPORTANT ROLE IN A WIZARD'S CONTRACT CEREMONY.
MAYBE IT ISN'T SUCH A STRANGE CONCEPT... WAIT.
DOES THAT MEAN YOU TWO HAVE KISSED?
YUP! KINDA.
!!!

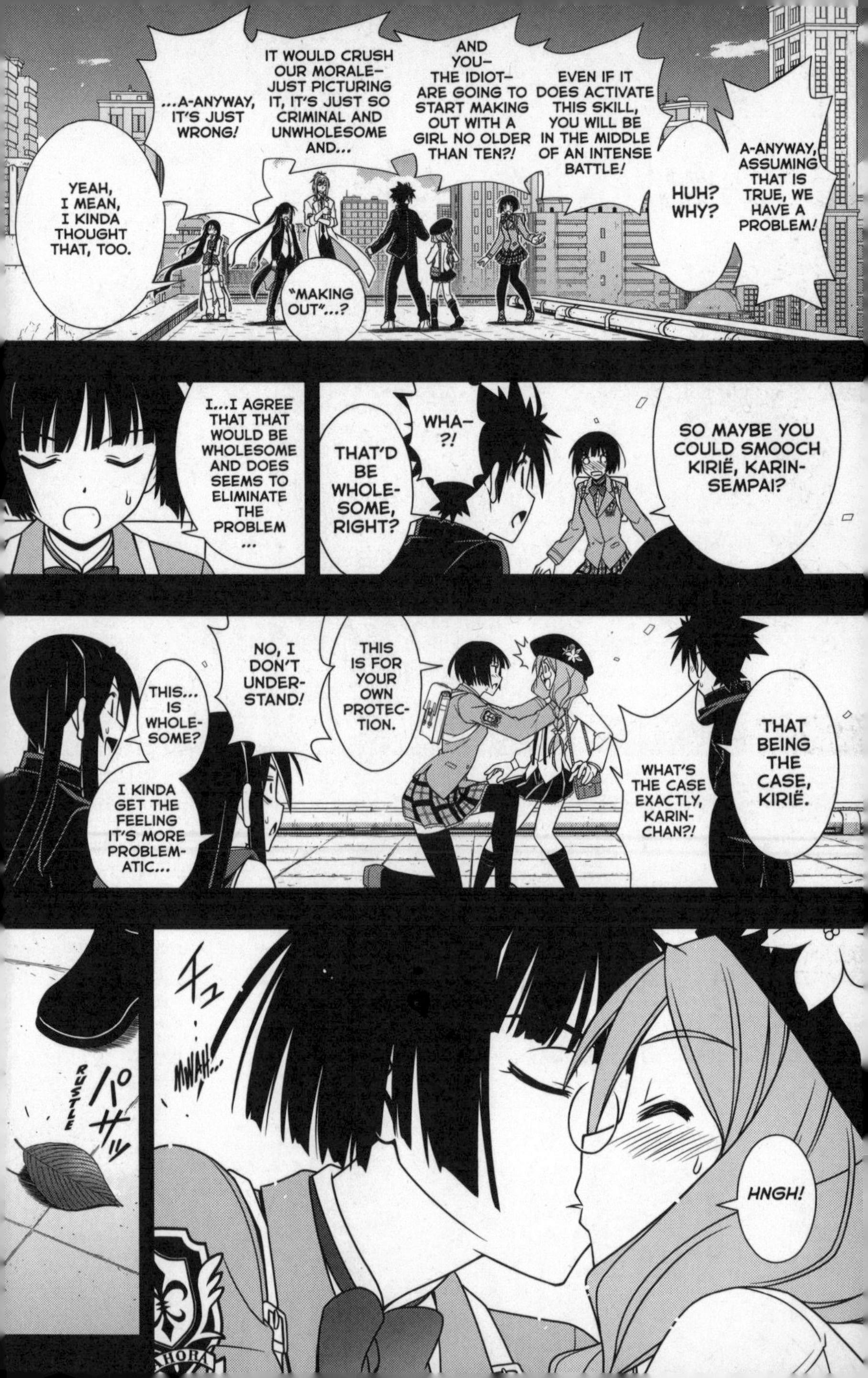
A-ANYWAY, ASSUMING THAT IS TRUE, WE HAVE A PROBLEM!
HUH? WHY?
EVEN IF IT DOES ACTIVATE THIS SKILL, YOU WILL BE IN THE MIDDLE OF AN INTENSE BATTLE!
AND YOU— THE IDIOT— ARE GOING TO START MAKING OUT WITH A GIRL NO OLDER THAN TEN?!
IT WOULD CRUSH OUR MORALE— JUST PICTURING IT, IT'S JUST SO CRIMINAL AND UNWHOLESOME AND...
...A-ANYWAY, IT'S JUST WRONG!
"MAKING OUT"...?
YEAH, I MEAN, I KINDA THOUGHT THAT, TOO.
SO MAYBE YOU COULD SMOOCH KIRIË, KARIN-SEMPAI?
WHA—?!
THAT'D BE WHOLE-SOME, RIGHT?
I...I AGREE THAT THAT WOULD BE WHOLESOME AND DOES SEEMS TO ELIMINATE THE PROBLEM ...
THAT BEING THE CASE, KIRIË.
WHAT'S THE CASE EXACTLY, KARIN-CHAN?!
THIS IS FOR YOUR OWN PROTECTION.
NO, I DON'T UNDER-STAND!
THIS... IS WHOLE-SOME?
I KINDA GET THE FEELING IT'S MORE PROBLEM-ATIC...
HNGH!
チュ
MWAH...
パサッ
RUSTLE

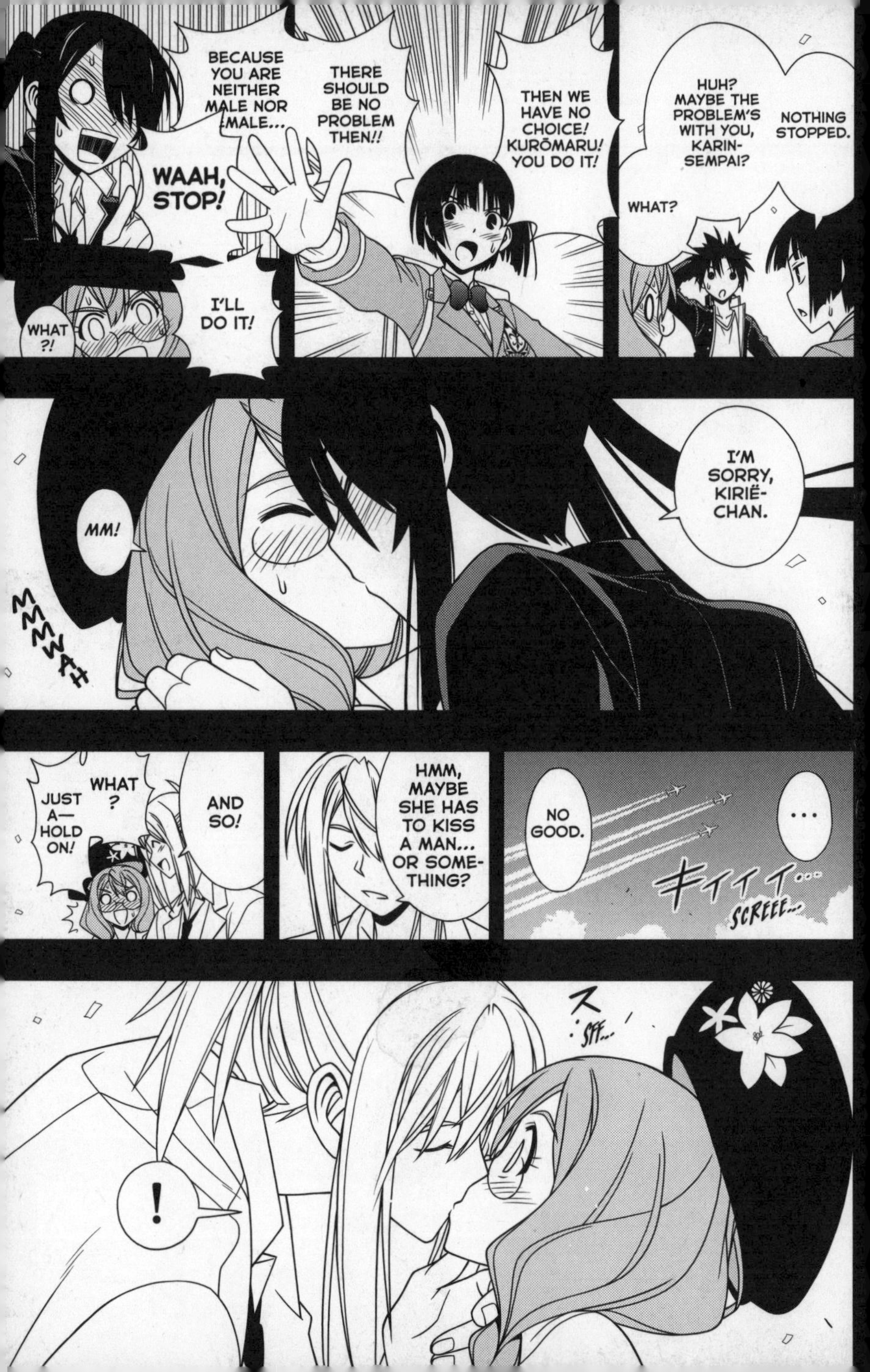
NOTHING STOPPED.
HUH? MAYBE THE PROBLEM'S WITH YOU, KARIN-SEMPAI?
WHAT?
THEN WE HAVE NO CHOICE! KURŌMARU! YOU DO IT!
THERE SHOULD BE NO PROBLEM THEN!!
BECAUSE YOU ARE NEITHER MALE NOR MALE...
WAAH, STOP!
I'LL DO IT!
WHAT ?!
I'M SORRY, KIRIË-CHAN.
MM!
MMMWAH
...
NO GOOD.
キィィィ…
SCREEEE...
HMM, MAYBE SHE HAS TO KISS A MAN... OR SOME-THING?
AND SO!
WHAT ?
JUST A— HOLD ON!
ス
SFF...
!

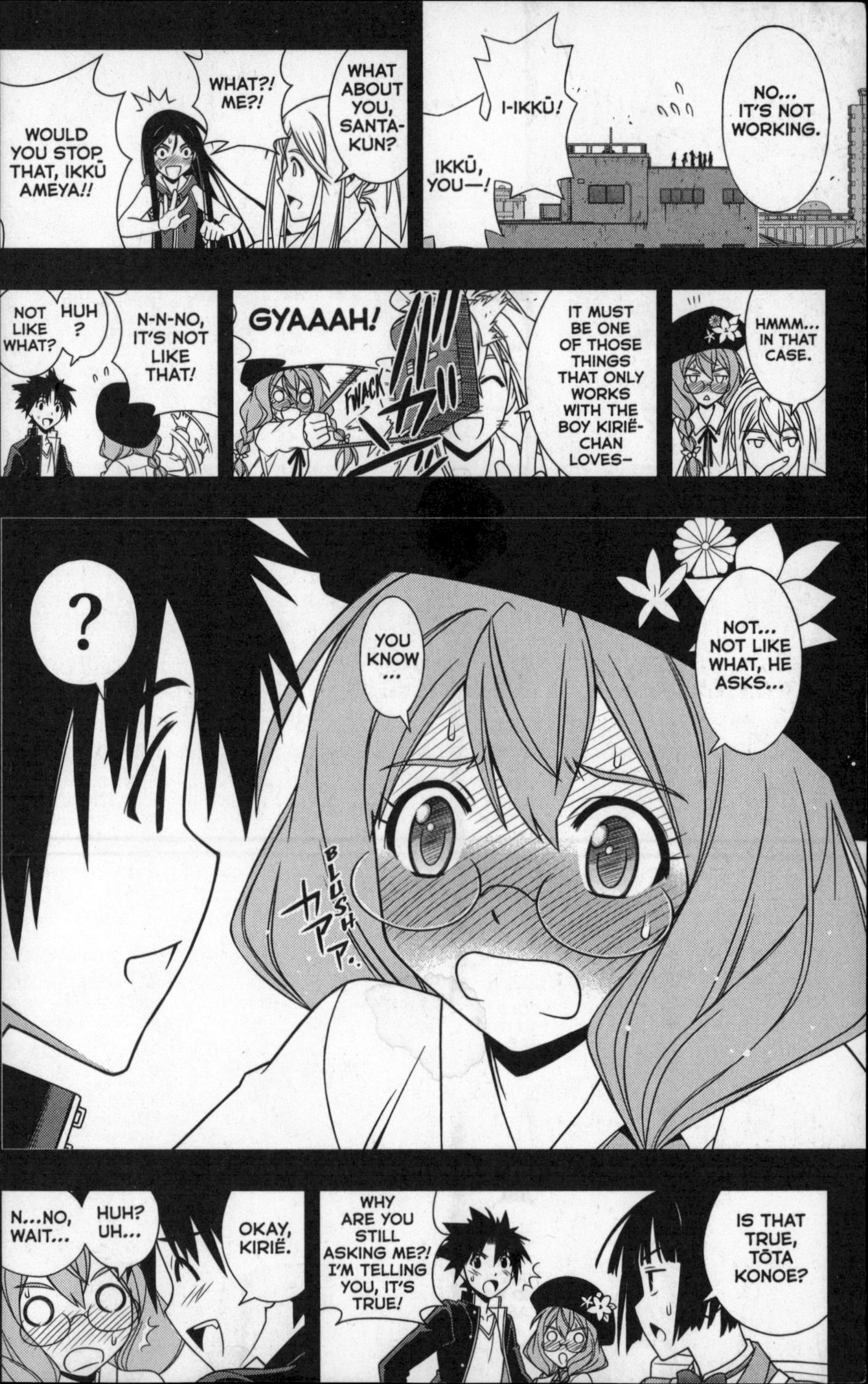
NO... IT'S NOT WORKING.
I-IKKŪ!
IKKŪ, YOU—!
WHAT ABOUT YOU, SANTA-KUN?
WHAT?! ME?!
WOULD YOU STOP THAT, IKKŪ AMEYA!!
HMMM... IN THAT CASE.
IT MUST BE ONE OF THOSE THINGS THAT ONLY WORKS WITH THE BOY KIRIË-CHAN LOVES–
GYAAAH!
FWACK
N-N-NO, IT'S NOT LIKE THAT!
HUH?
NOT LIKE WHAT?
NOT... NOT LIKE WHAT, HE ASKS...
YOU KNOW ...
BLUSH
?
IS THAT TRUE, TŌTA KONOE?
WHY ARE YOU STILL ASKING ME?! I'M TELLING YOU, IT'S TRUE!
OKAY, KIRIË.
HUH? UH...
N...NO, WAIT...

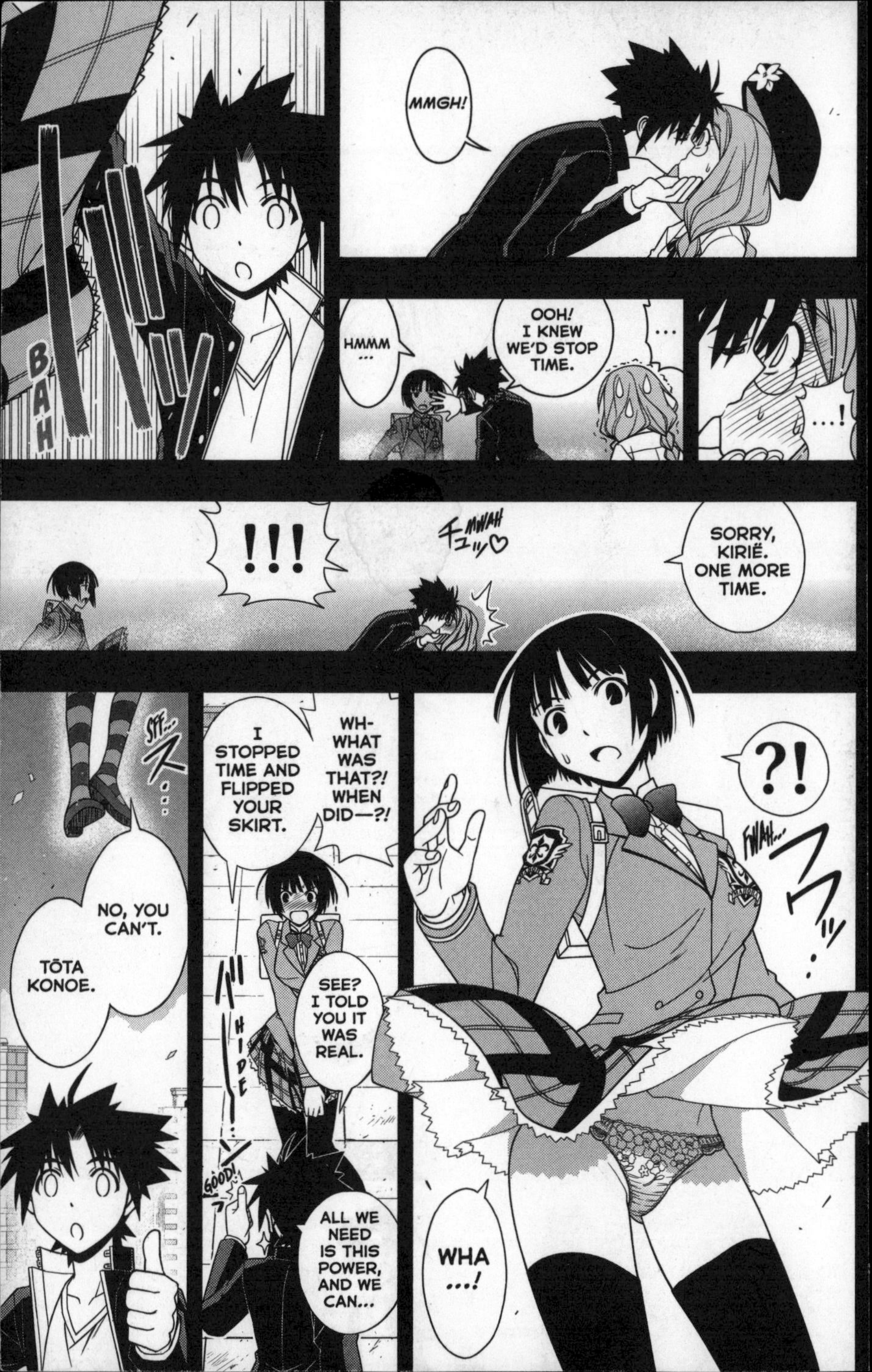
MMGH!
BAH
...!
...
OOH! I KNEW WE'D STOP TIME.
HMMM ...
SORRY, KIRIË. ONE MORE TIME.
MWAH
!!!
?!
FWAH...
WHA ...!
WH-WHAT WAS THAT?! WHEN DID—?!
I STOPPED TIME AND FLIPPED YOUR SKIRT.
SEE? I TOLD YOU IT WAS REAL.
HIDE
GOOD!
ALL WE NEED IS THIS POWER, AND WE CAN...
SFF...
NO, YOU CAN'T.
TŌTA KONOE.

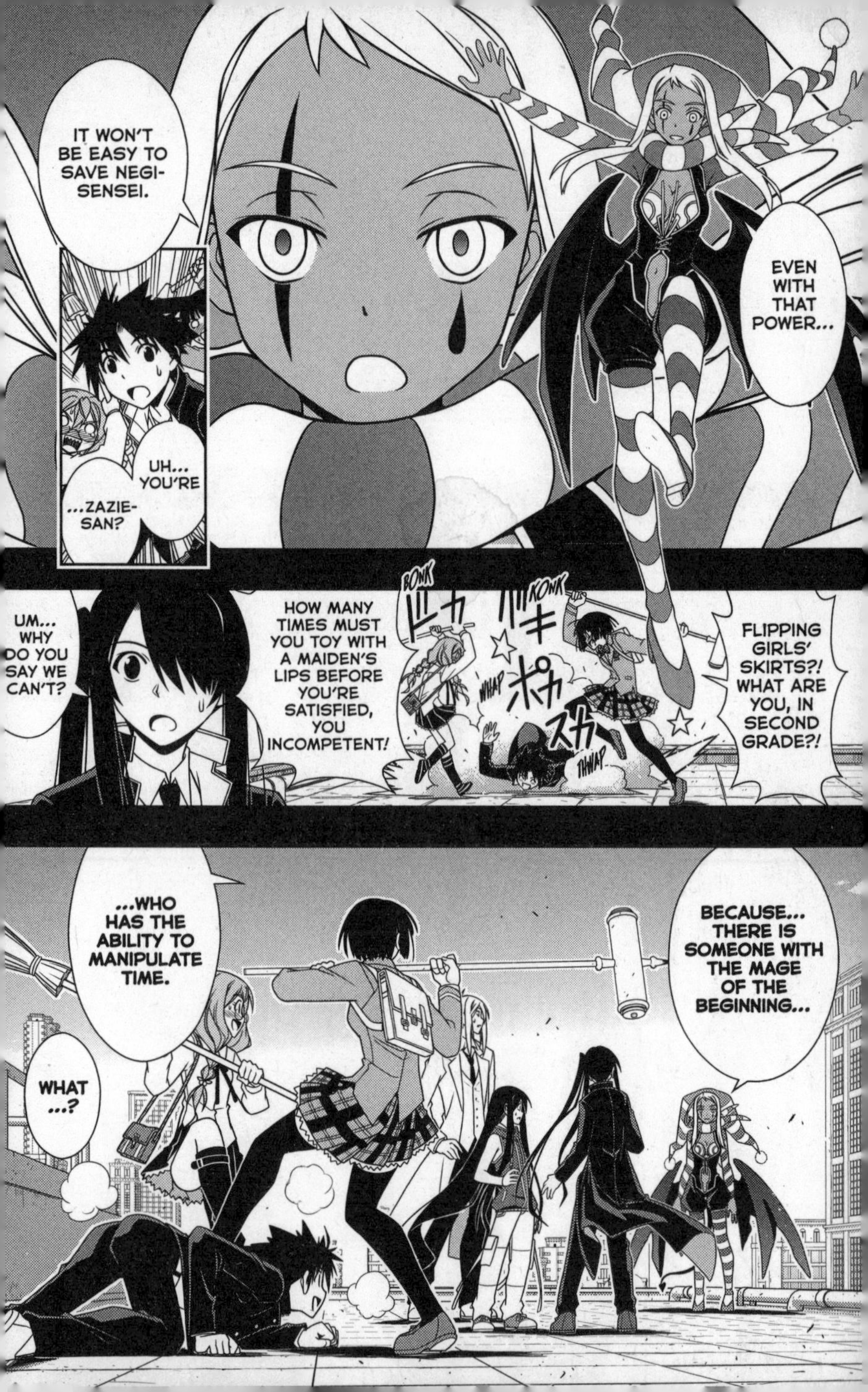
EVEN WITH THAT POWER...
IT WON'T BE EASY TO SAVE NEGI-SENSEI.
UH... YOU'RE
...ZAZIE-SAN?
FLIPPING GIRLS' SKIRTS?! WHAT ARE YOU, IN SECOND GRADE?!
KONK
バキ
BONK
ドカ
HOW MANY TIMES MUST YOU TOY WITH A MAIDEN'S LIPS BEFORE YOU'RE SATISFIED, YOU INCOMPETENT!
WHAP
ポカ
THWAP
スカ
UM... WHY DO YOU SAY WE CAN'T?
BECAUSE... THERE IS SOMEONE WITH THE MAGE OF THE BEGINNING...
...WHO HAS THE ABILITY TO MANIPULATE TIME.
WHAT ...?

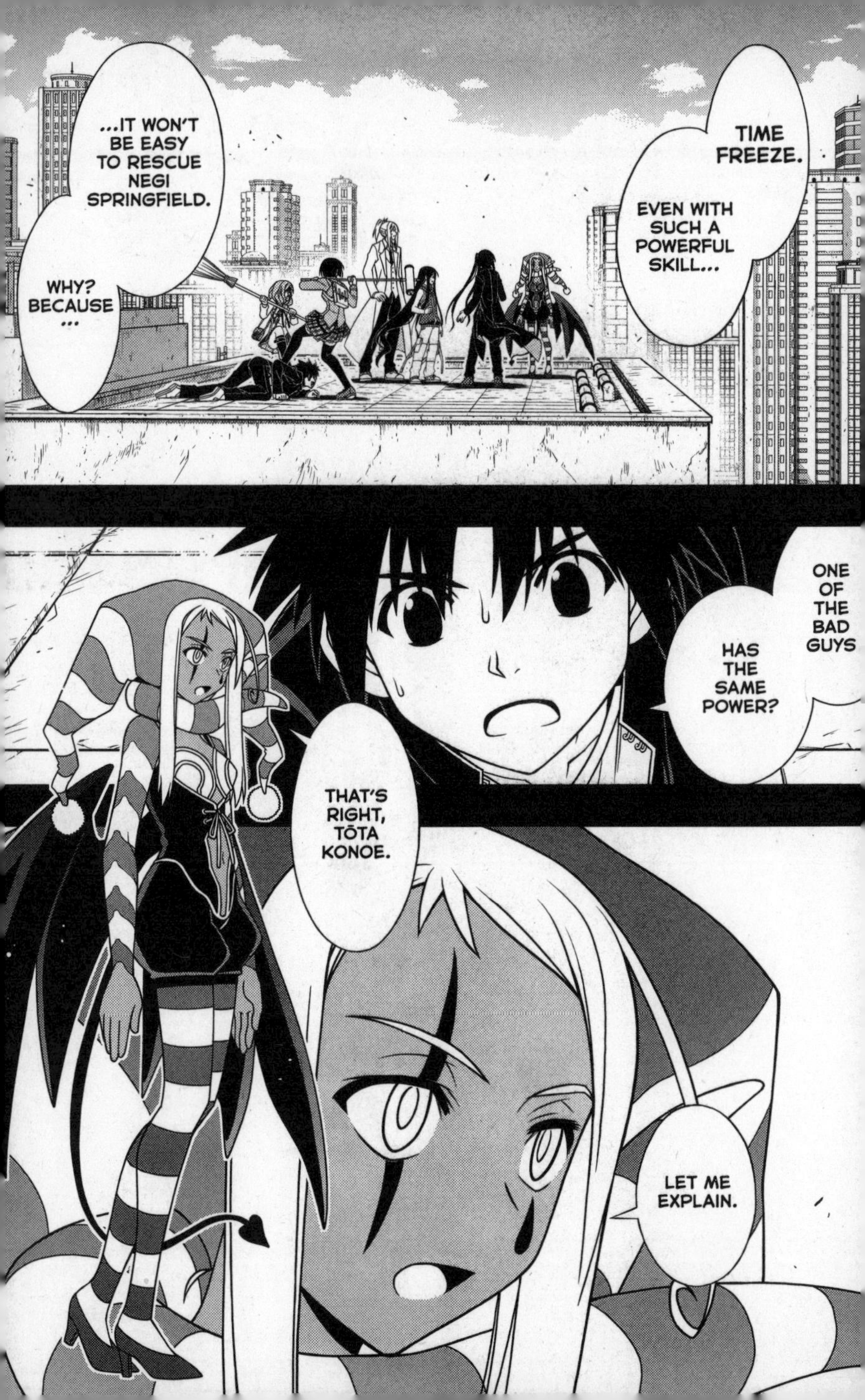
TIME FREEZE.
EVEN WITH SUCH A POWERFUL SKILL...
...IT WON'T BE EASY TO RESCUE NEGI SPRINGFIELD.
WHY? BECAUSE ...
ONE OF THE BAD GUYS
HAS THE SAME POWER?
THAT'S RIGHT, TŌTA KONOE.
LET ME EXPLAIN.

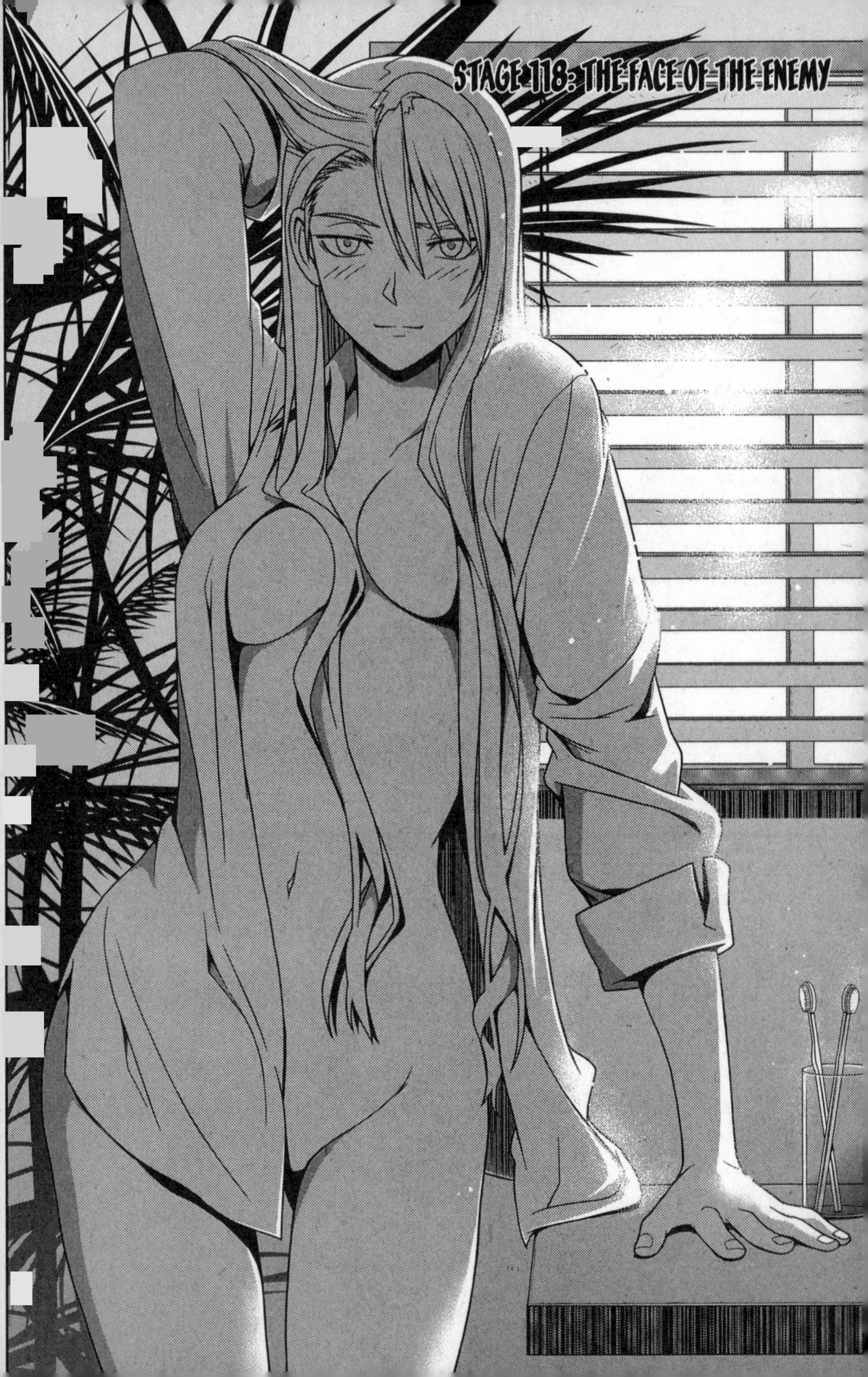
STAGE 118: THE FACE OF THE ENEMY

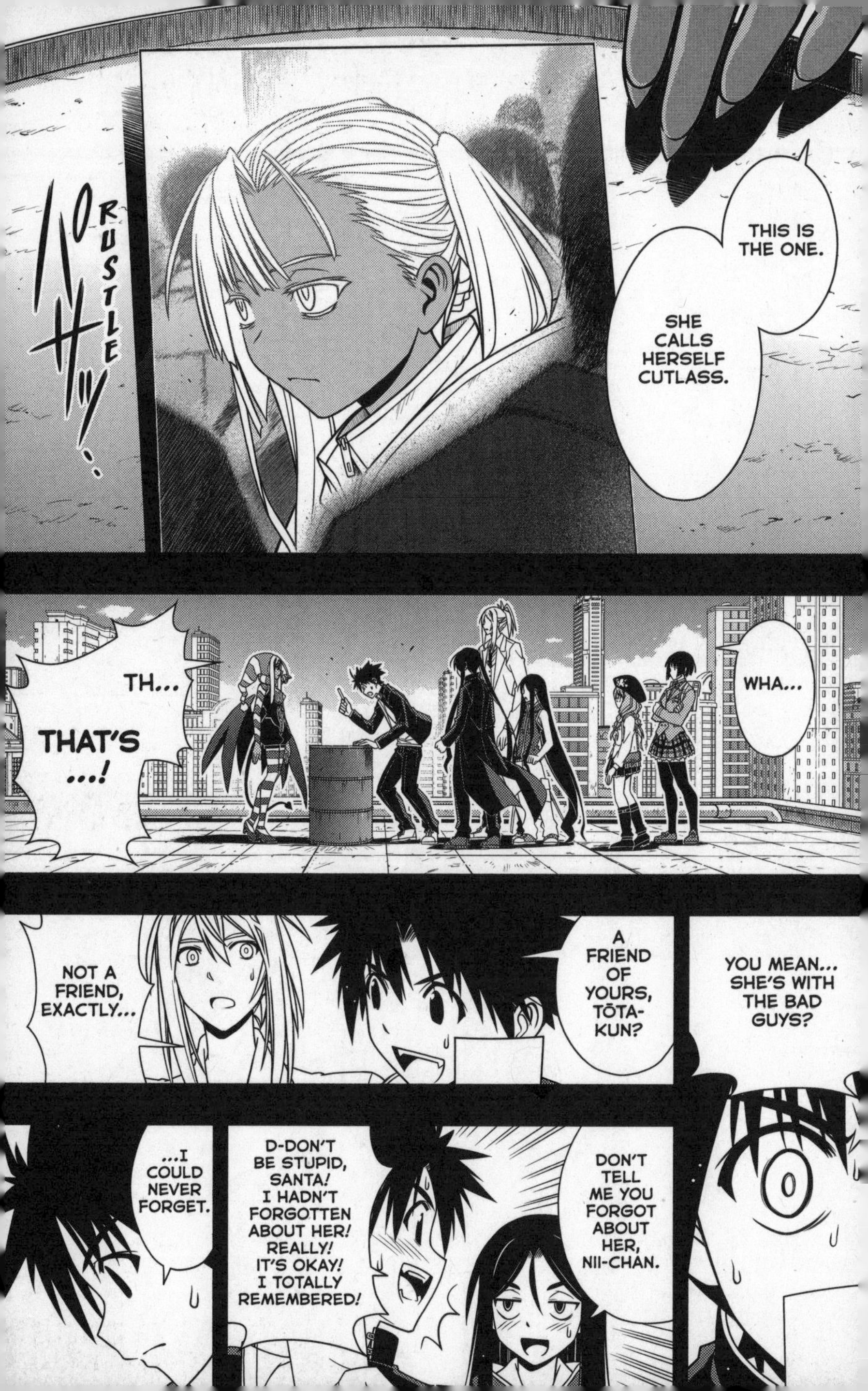
THIS IS THE ONE.
SHE CALLS HERSELF CUTLASS.
RUSTLE
WHA...
TH...
THAT'S ...!
YOU MEAN... SHE'S WITH THE BAD GUYS?
A FRIEND OF YOURS, TŌTA-KUN?
NOT A FRIEND, EXACTLY...
DON'T TELL ME YOU FORGOT ABOUT HER, NII-CHAN.
D-DON'T BE STUPID, SANTA! I HADN'T FORGOTTEN ABOUT HER! REALLY! IT'S OKAY! I TOTALLY REMEMBERED!
...I COULD NEVER FORGET.

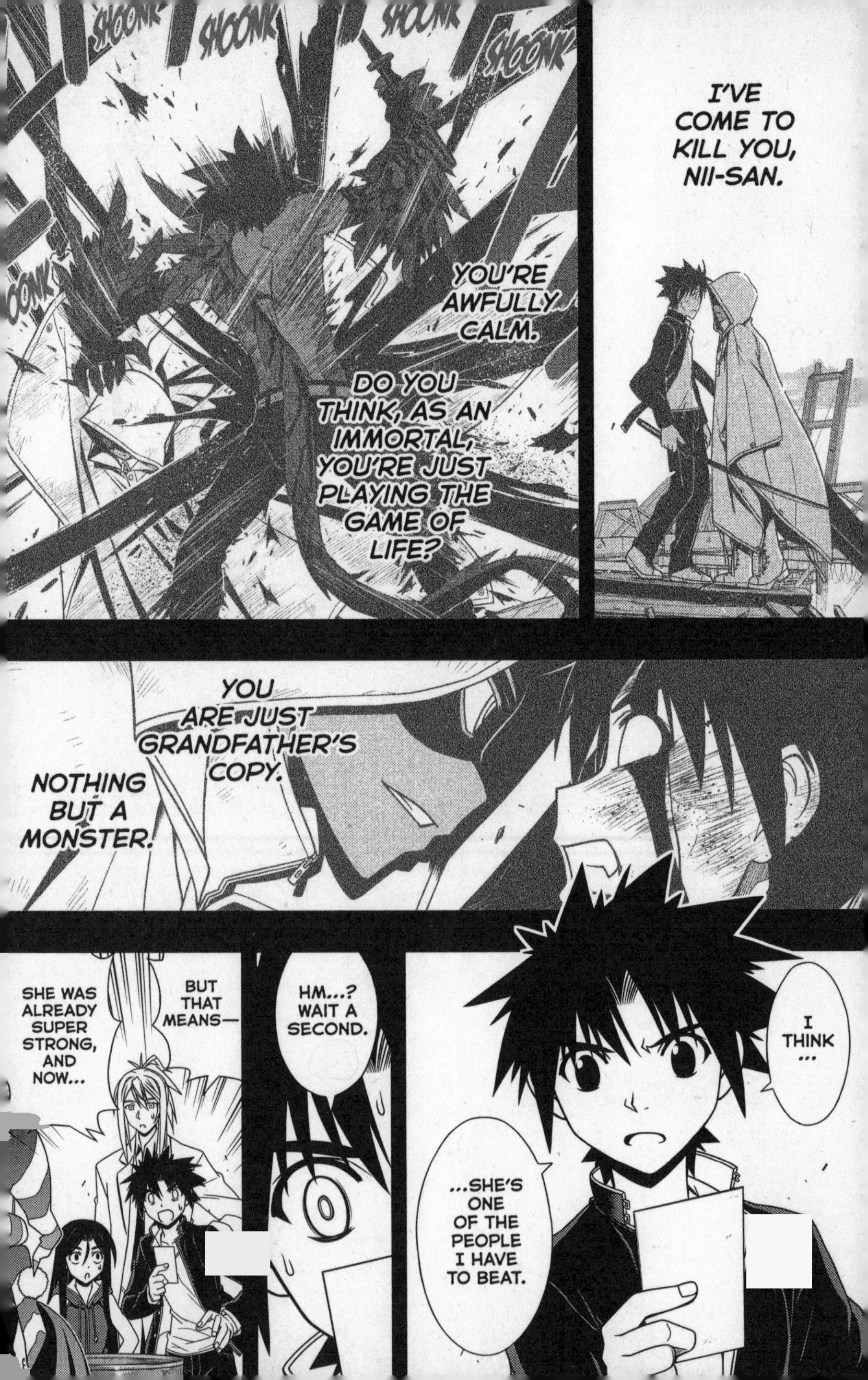
I'VE COME TO KILL YOU, NII-SAN.
SHOONK
SHOONK
SHOONK
SHOONK
YOU'RE AWFULLY CALM.
DO YOU THINK, AS AN IMMORTAL, YOU'RE JUST PLAYING THE GAME OF LIFE?
YOU ARE JUST GRANDFATHER'S COPY.
NOTHING BUT A MONSTER.
I THINK...
...SHE'S ONE OF THE PEOPLE I HAVE TO BEAT.
HM...? WAIT A SECOND.
BUT THAT MEANS—
SHE WAS ALREADY SUPER STRONG, AND NOW...

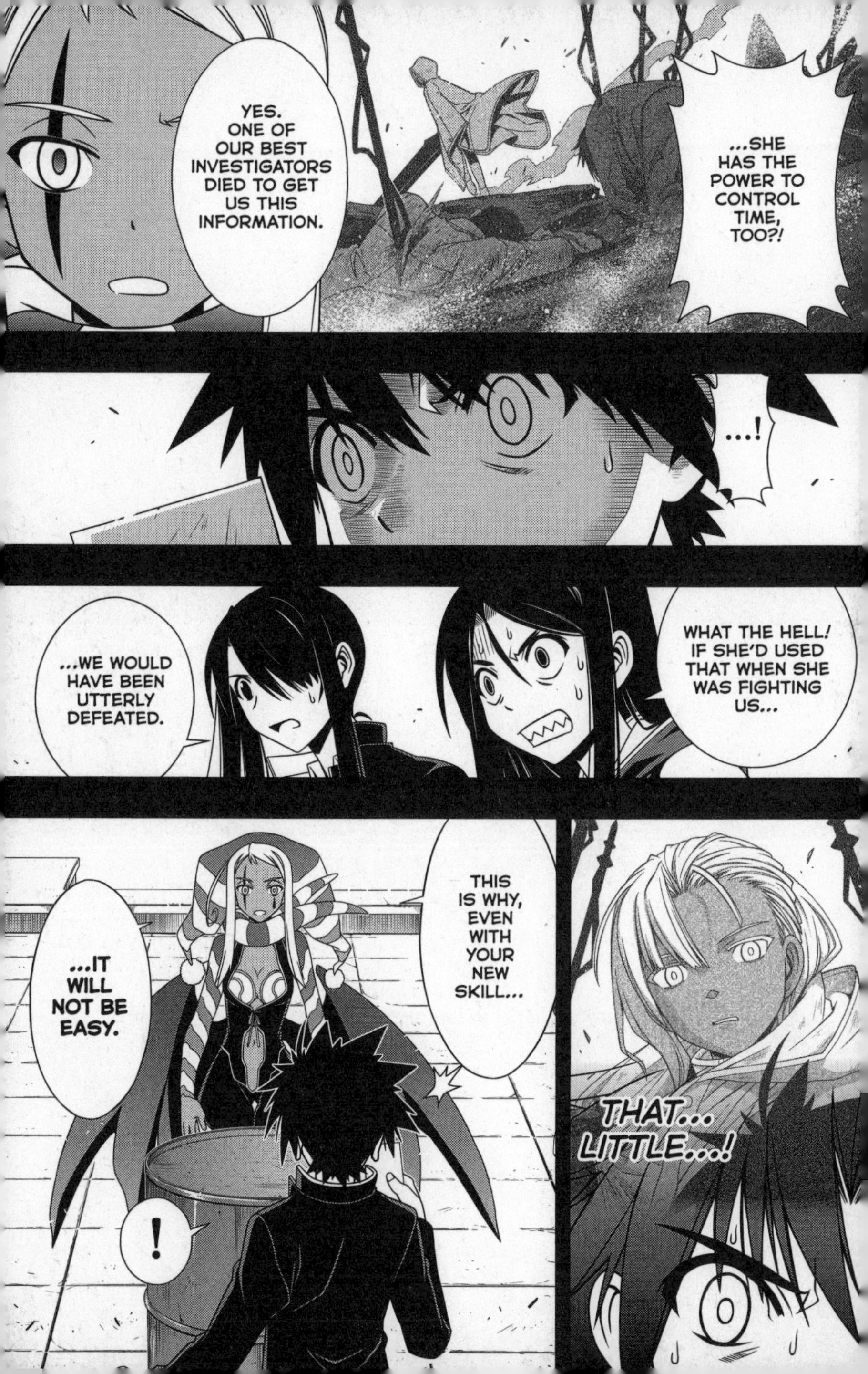
...SHE HAS THE POWER TO CONTROL TIME, TOO?!
YES. ONE OF OUR BEST INVESTIGATORS DIED TO GET US THIS INFORMATION.
...!
WHAT THE HELL! IF SHE'D USED THAT WHEN SHE WAS FIGHTING US...
...WE WOULD HAVE BEEN UTTERLY DEFEATED.
THAT... LITTLE...!
THIS IS WHY, EVEN WITH YOUR NEW SKILL...
...IT WILL NOT BE EASY.
!

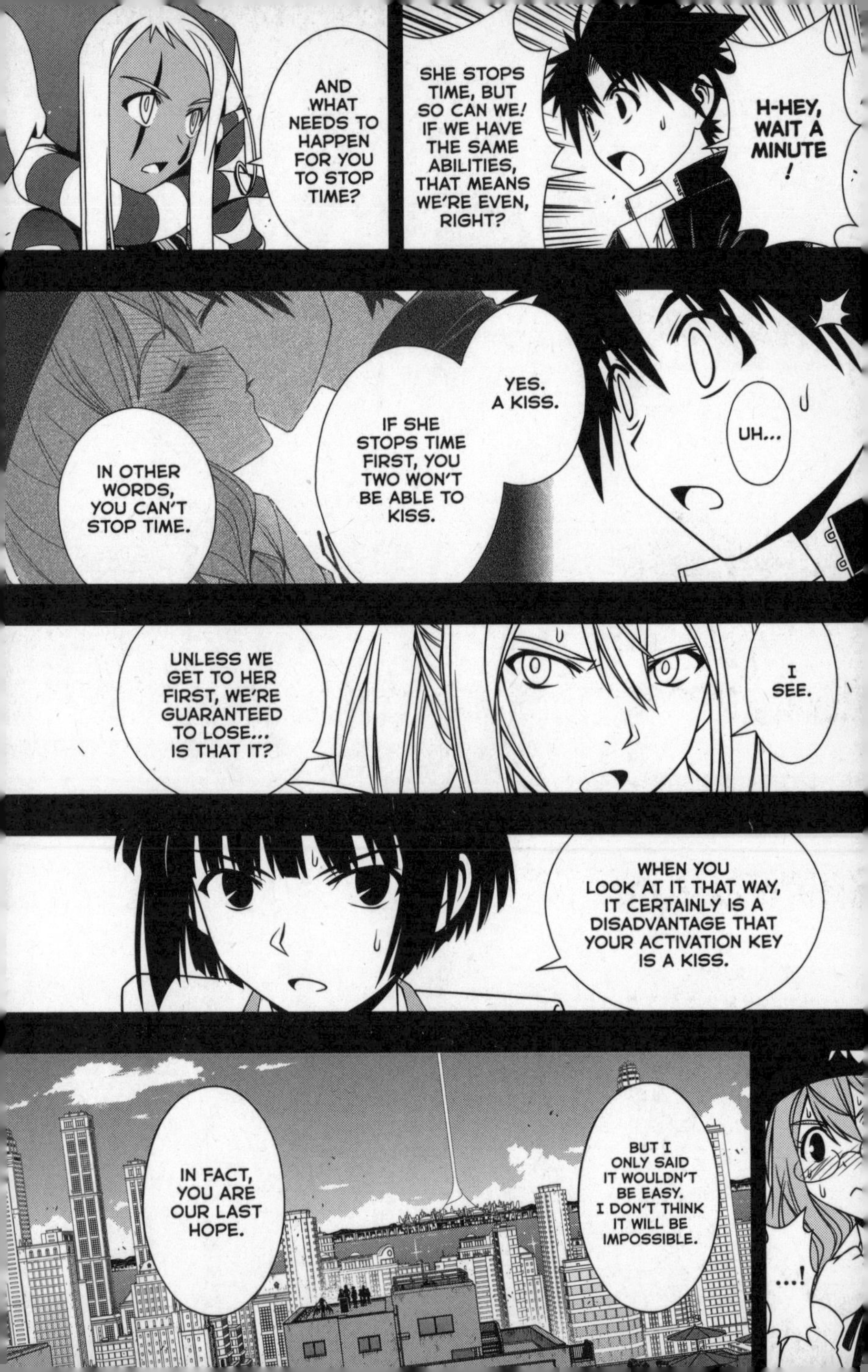
H-HEY, WAIT A MINUTE!
SHE STOPS TIME, BUT SO CAN WE! IF WE HAVE THE SAME ABILITIES, THAT MEANS WE'RE EVEN, RIGHT?
AND WHAT NEEDS TO HAPPEN FOR YOU TO STOP TIME?
UH...
YES. A KISS.
IF SHE STOPS TIME FIRST, YOU TWO WON'T BE ABLE TO KISS.
IN OTHER WORDS, YOU CAN'T STOP TIME.
I SEE.
UNLESS WE GET TO HER FIRST, WE'RE GUARANTEED TO LOSE... IS THAT IT?
WHEN YOU LOOK AT IT THAT WAY, IT CERTAINLY IS A DISADVANTAGE THAT YOUR ACTIVATION KEY IS A KISS.
...!
BUT I ONLY SAID IT WOULDN'T BE EASY. I DON'T THINK IT WILL BE IMPOSSIBLE.
IN FACT, YOU ARE OUR LAST HOPE.

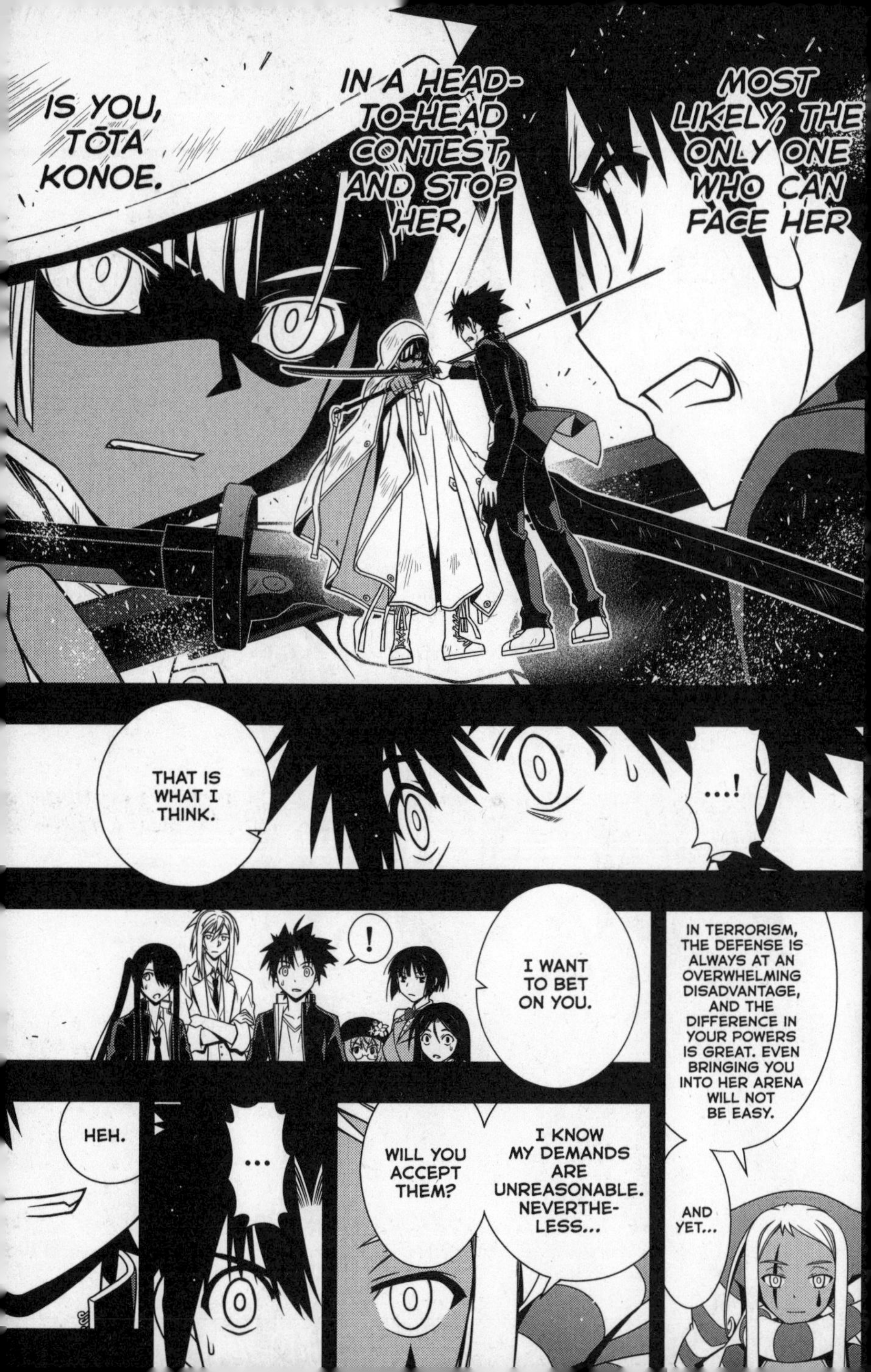
MOST LIKELY, THE ONLY ONE WHO CAN FACE HER
IN A HEAD-TO-HEAD CONTEST, AND STOP HER,
IS YOU, TŌTA KONOE.
THAT IS WHAT I THINK.
...!
IN TERRORISM, THE DEFENSE IS ALWAYS AT AN OVERWHELMING DISADVANTAGE, AND THE DIFFERENCE IN YOUR POWERS IS GREAT. EVEN BRINGING YOU INTO HER ARENA WILL NOT BE EASY.
AND YET...
I WANT TO BET ON YOU.
!
I KNOW MY DEMANDS ARE UNREASONABLE. NEVERTHE-LESS...
WILL YOU ACCEPT THEM?
...
HEH.

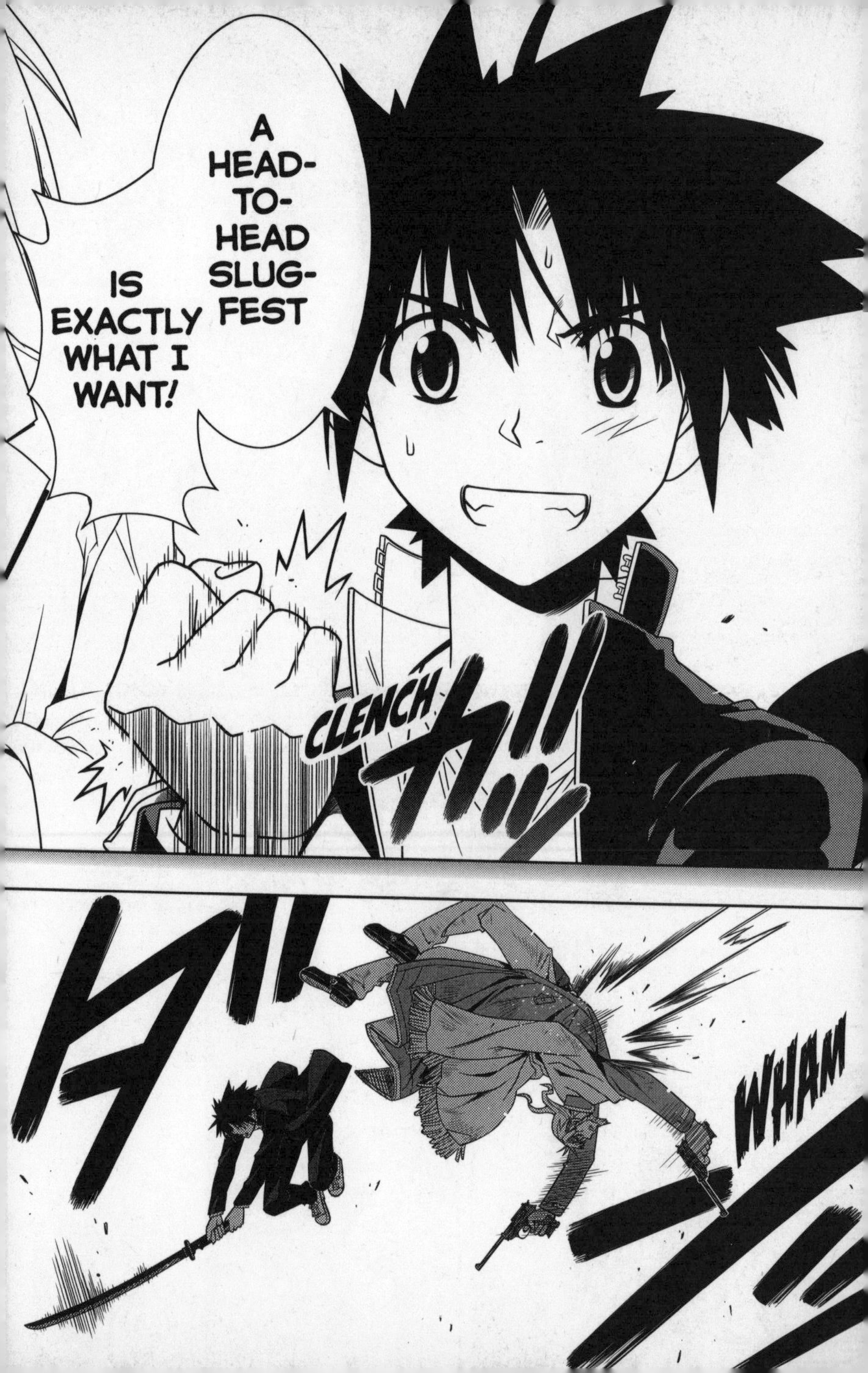
A HEAD-TO-HEAD SLUG-FEST IS EXACTLY WHAT I WANT!
CLENCH
WHAM

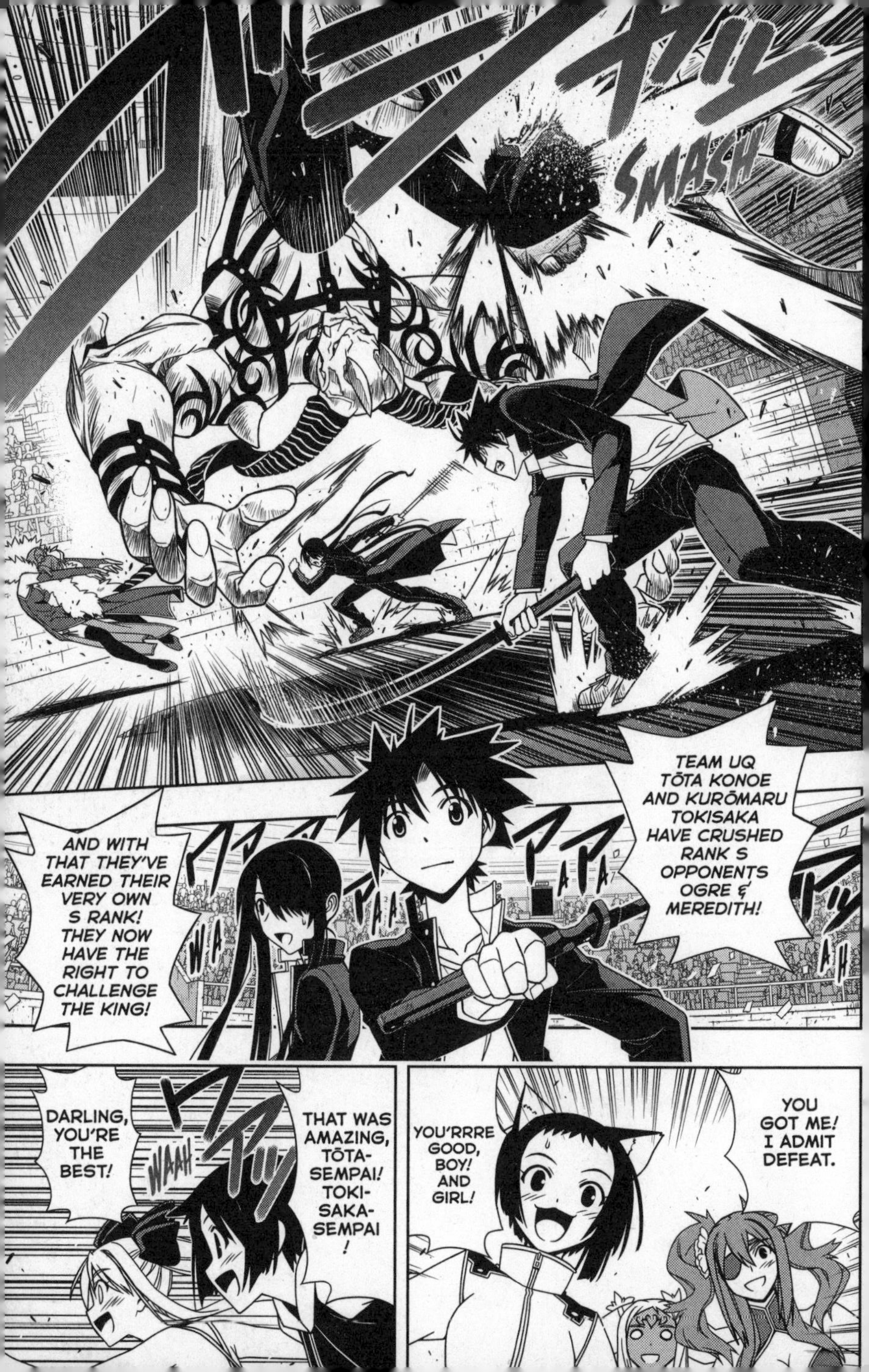
SMASH
TEAM UQ TŌTA KONOE AND KURŌMARU TOKISAKA HAVE CRUSHED RANK S OPPONENTS OGRE & MEREDITH!
AND WITH THAT THEY'VE EARNED THEIR VERY OWN S RANK! THEY NOW HAVE THE RIGHT TO CHALLENGE THE KING!
YOU GOT ME! I ADMIT DEFEAT.
YOU'RRRE GOOD, BOY! AND GIRL!
THAT WAS AMAZING, TŌTA-SEMPAI! TOKI-SAKA-SEMPAI!
WAAH
DARLING, YOU'RE THE BEST!

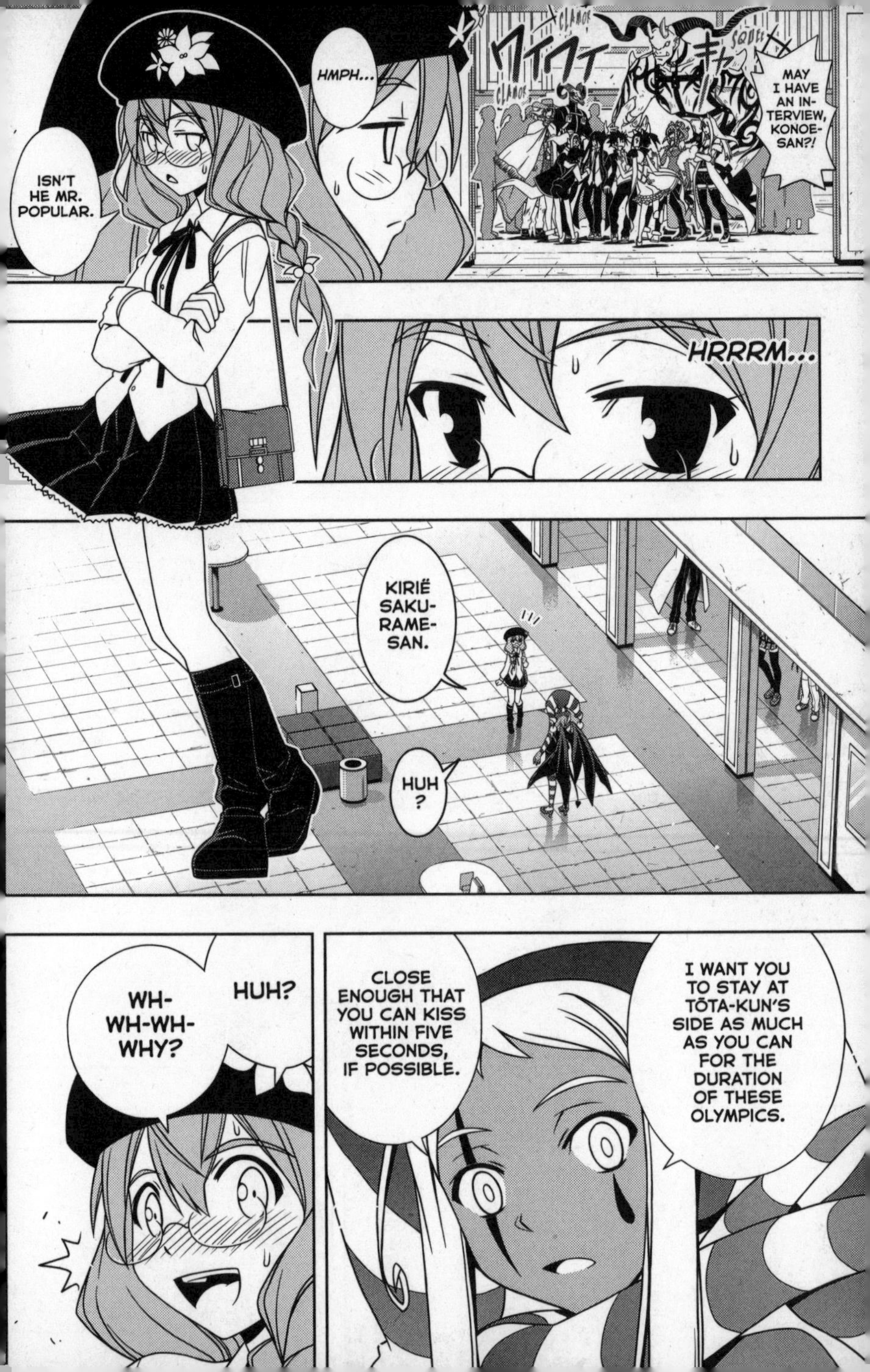
CLAMOR
ワイワイ
CLAMOR
SQUEE
MAY I HAVE AN INTERVIEW, KONOE-SAN?!
HMPH...
ISN'T HE MR. POPULAR.
HRRRM...
KIRIË SAKURAME-SAN.
HUH?
I WANT YOU TO STAY AT TŌTA-KUN'S SIDE AS MUCH AS YOU CAN FOR THE DURATION OF THESE OLYMPICS.
CLOSE ENOUGH THAT YOU CAN KISS WITHIN FIVE SECONDS, IF POSSIBLE.
HUH?
WH-WH-WH-WHY?

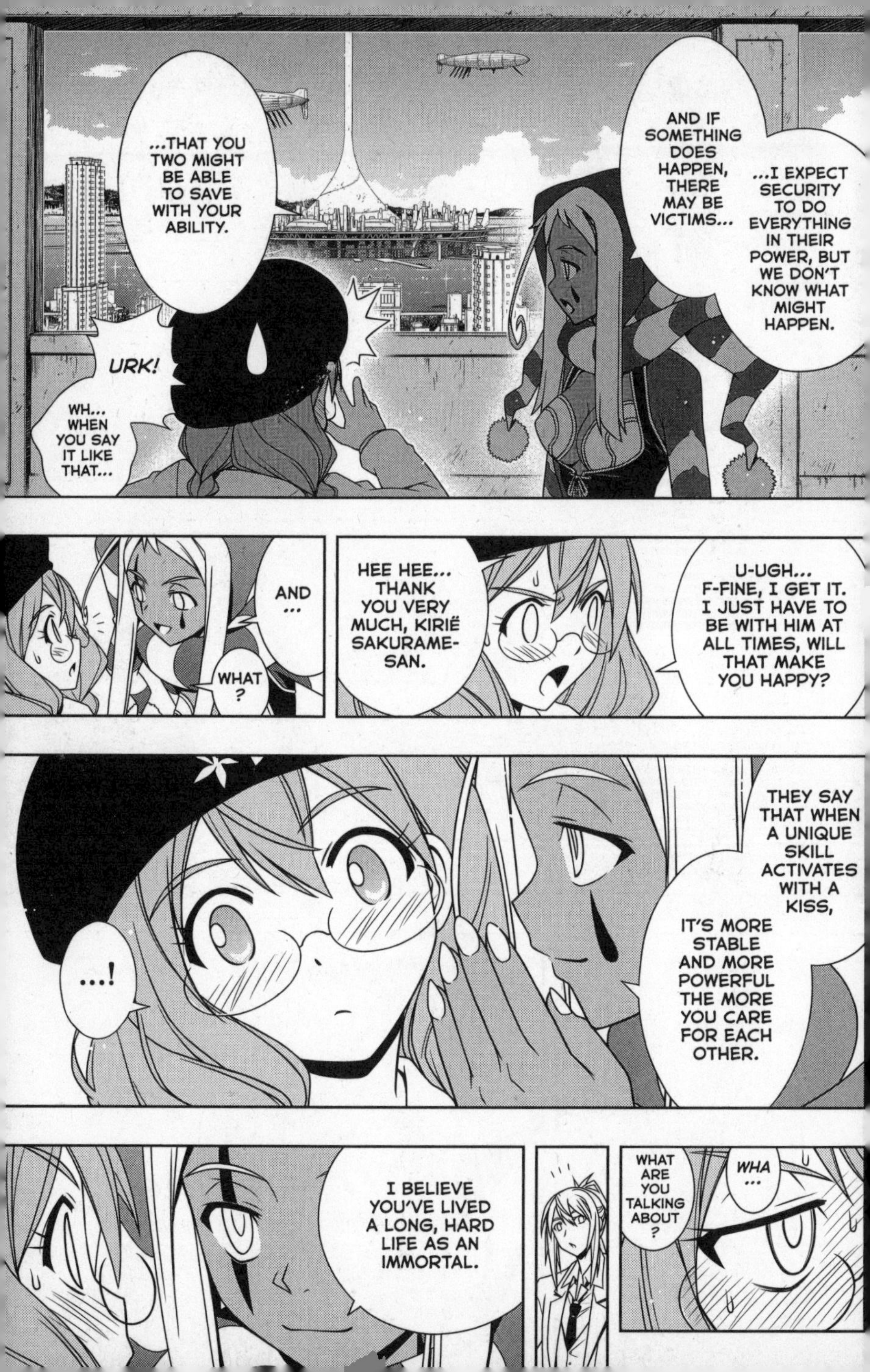
...I EXPECT SECURITY TO DO EVERYTHING IN THEIR POWER, BUT WE DON'T KNOW WHAT MIGHT HAPPEN.
AND IF SOMETHING DOES HAPPEN, THERE MAY BE VICTIMS...
...THAT YOU TWO MIGHT BE ABLE TO SAVE WITH YOUR ABILITY.
URK!
WH... WHEN YOU SAY IT LIKE THAT...
U-UGH... F-FINE, I GET IT. I JUST HAVE TO BE WITH HIM AT ALL TIMES, WILL THAT MAKE YOU HAPPY?
HEE HEE... THANK YOU VERY MUCH, KIRIË SAKURAME-SAN.
AND ...
WHAT ?
THEY SAY THAT WHEN A UNIQUE SKILL ACTIVATES WITH A KISS,
IT'S MORE STABLE AND MORE POWERFUL THE MORE YOU CARE FOR EACH OTHER.
...!
WHA ...
WHAT ARE YOU TALKING ABOUT ?
I BELIEVE YOU'VE LIVED A LONG, HARD LIFE AS AN IMMORTAL.

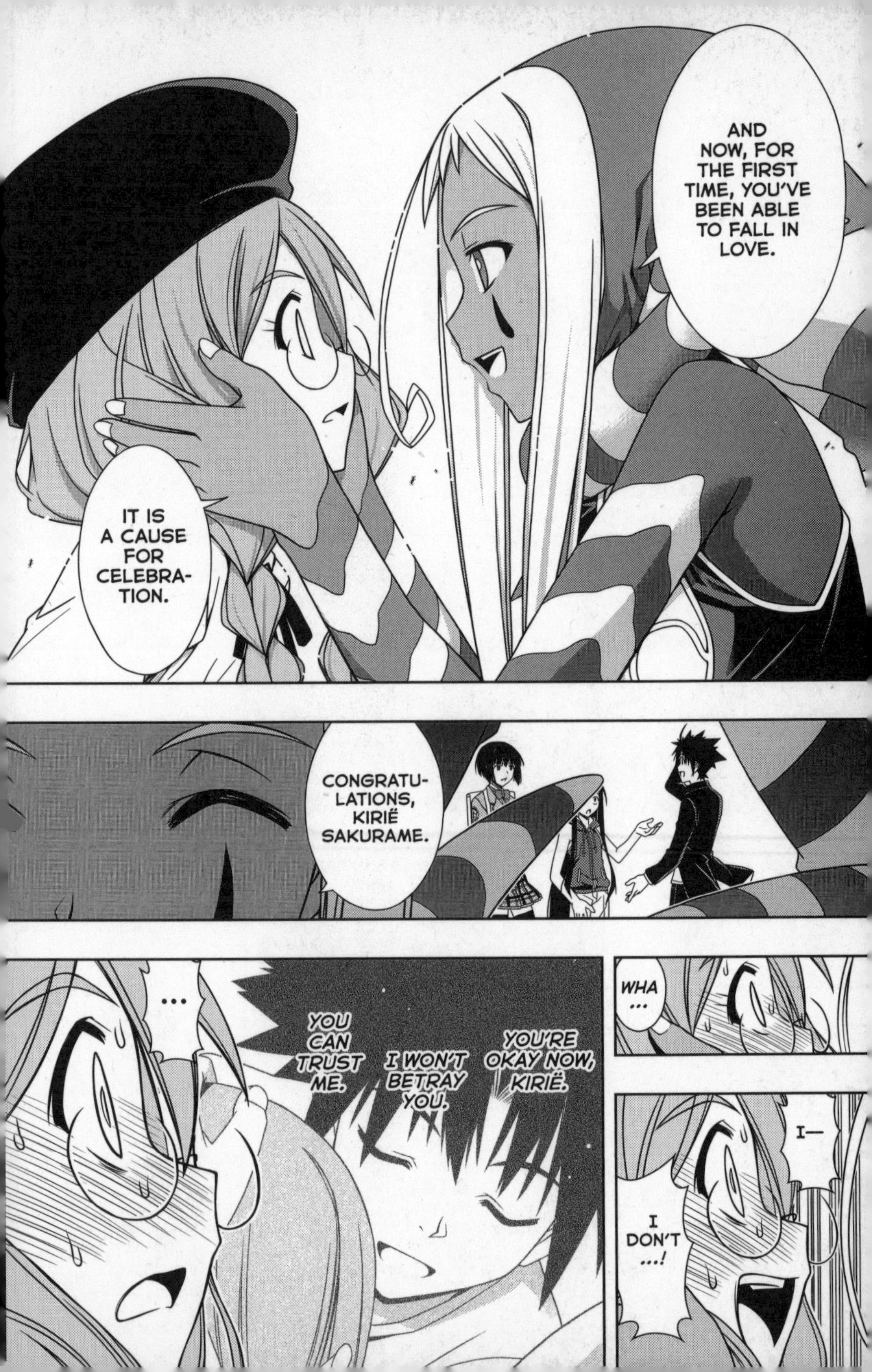
AND NOW, FOR THE FIRST TIME, YOU'VE BEEN ABLE TO FALL IN LOVE.
IT IS A CAUSE FOR CELEBRATION.
CONGRATULATIONS, KIRIË SAKURAME.
WHA ...
I—
I DON'T ...!
YOU'RE OKAY NOW, KIRIË.
I WON'T BETRAY YOU.
YOU CAN TRUST ME.
...

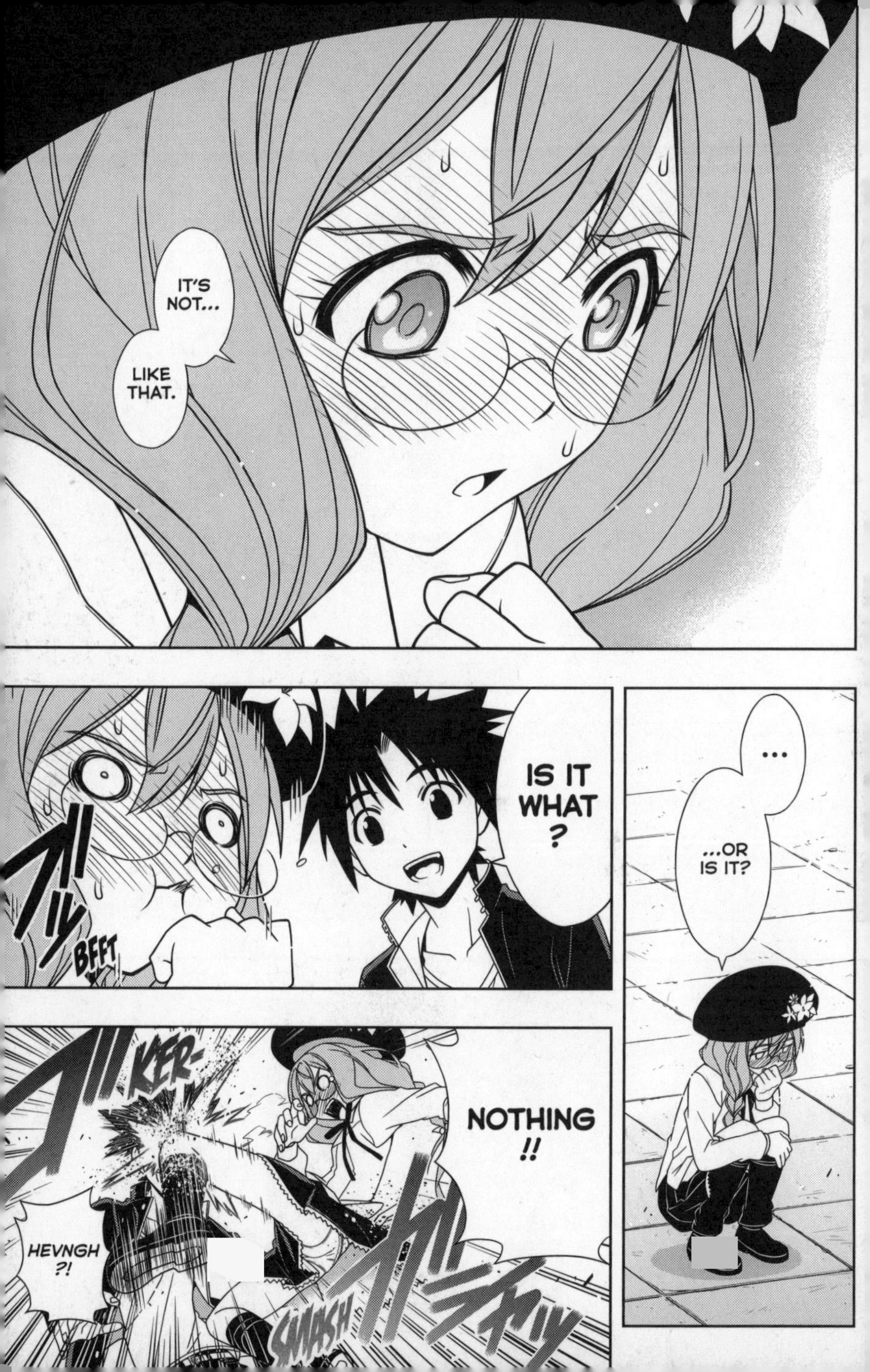
IT'S NOT...
LIKE THAT.
...
...OR IS IT?
IS IT WHAT?
BFFT
KER-
NOTHING!!
HEVNGH?!
SMASH

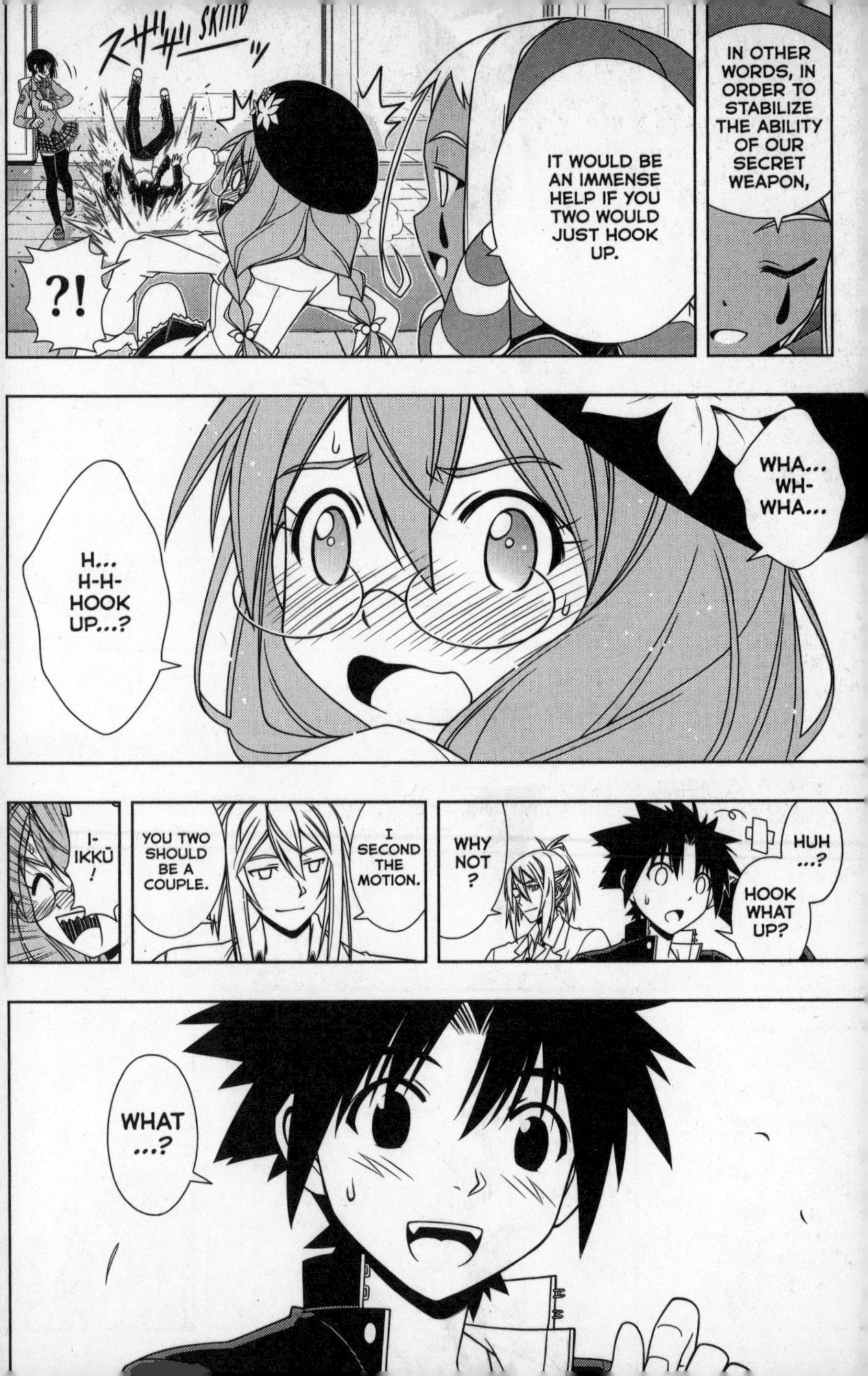
IN OTHER WORDS, IN ORDER TO STABILIZE THE ABILITY OF OUR SECRET WEAPON,
IT WOULD BE AN IMMENSE HELP IF YOU TWO WOULD JUST HOOK UP.
スザザザーッ SKIIID
?!
WHA... WH-WHA...
H... H-H-HOOK UP...?
HUH ...?
HOOK WHAT UP?
WHY NOT ?
I SECOND THE MOTION.
YOU TWO SHOULD BE A COUPLE.
I- IKKŪ !
WHAT ...?

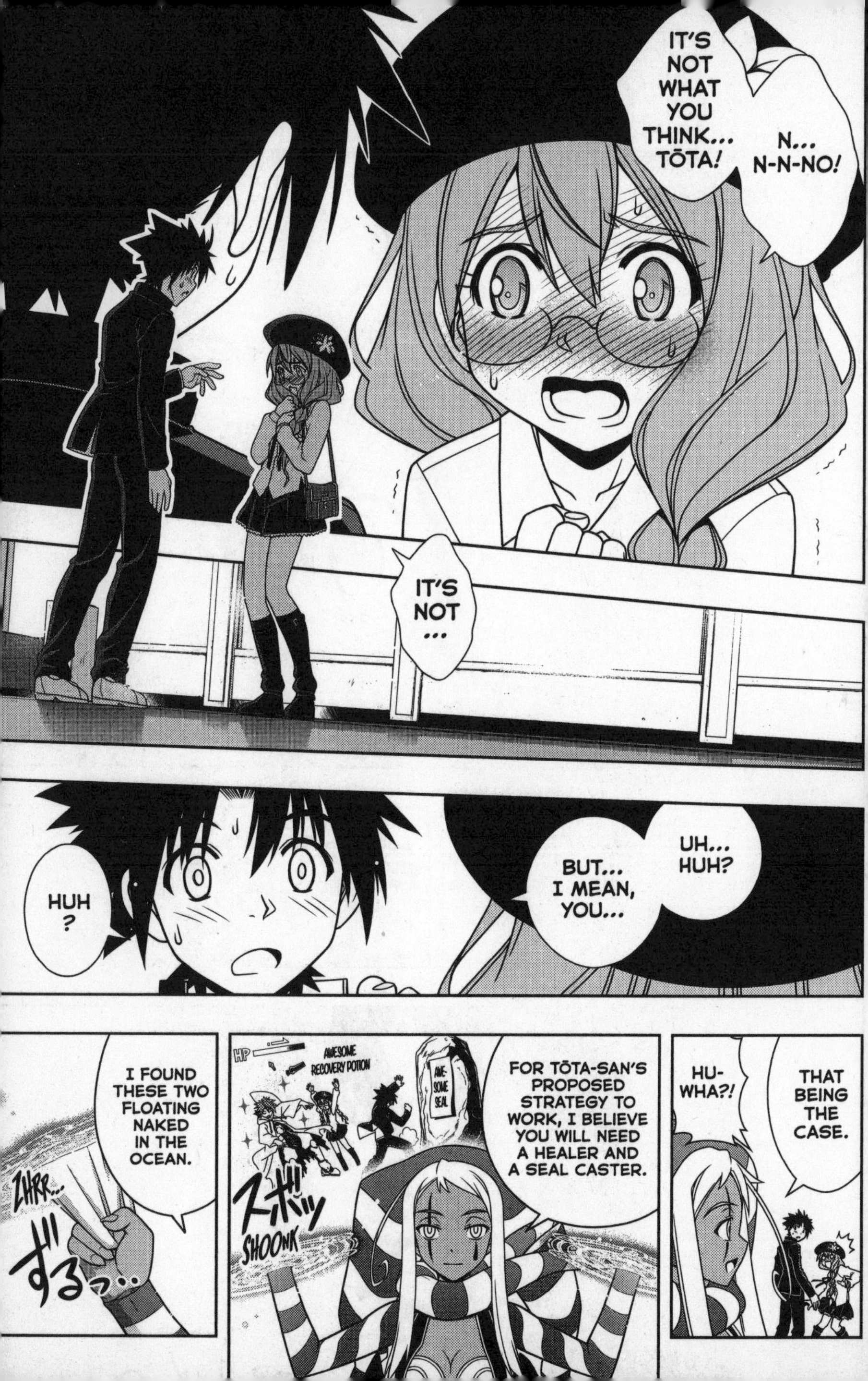
N... N-N-NO!
IT'S NOT WHAT YOU THINK... TŌTA!
IT'S NOT ...
UH... HUH?
BUT... I MEAN, YOU...
HUH ?
THAT BEING THE CASE.
HU-WHA?!
FOR TŌTA-SAN'S PROPOSED STRATEGY TO WORK, I BELIEVE YOU WILL NEED A HEALER AND A SEAL CASTER.
HP
AWESOME RECOVERY POTION
AWE-SOME SEAL
スポッ
SHOONK
I FOUND THESE TWO FLOATING NAKED IN THE OCEAN.
ZHRR...
するっ...

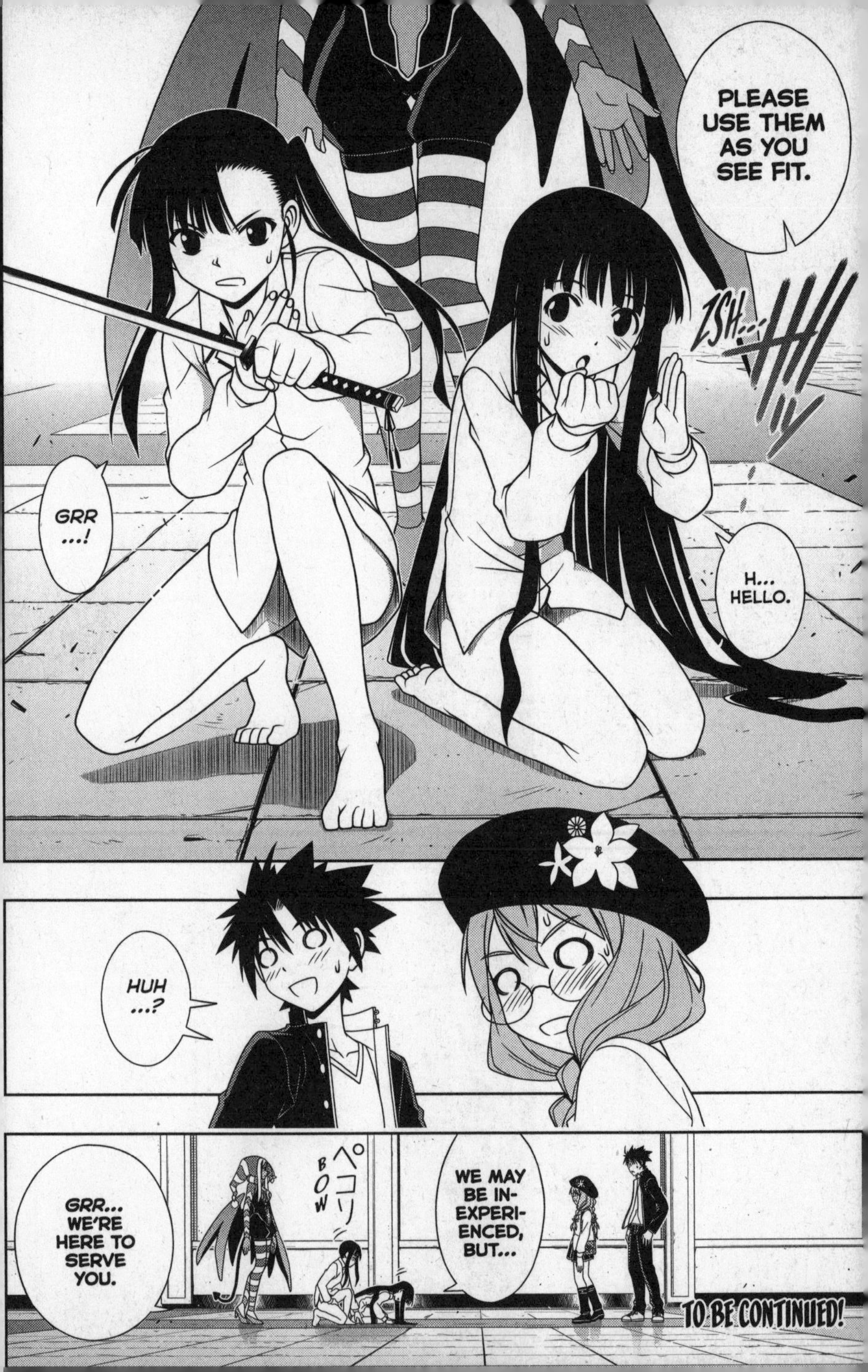
PLEASE USE THEM AS YOU SEE FIT.
ZSH...HH
H... HELLO.
GRR ...!
HUH ...?
WE MAY BE IN-EXPERI-ENCED, BUT...
ペコリ
BOW
GRR... WE'RE HERE TO SERVE YOU.
TO BE CONTINUED!

UQ HOLDER!

STAFF

Ken Akamatsu
Takashi Takemoto
Kenichi Nakamura
Keiichi Yamashita
Tohru Mitsuhashi
Susumu Kuwabara
Yuri Sasaki

Thanks to Ran Ayanaga

KC

KODANSHA COMICS

A new series from the creator of *Soul Eater*, the megahit manga and anime seen on Toonami!

"Fun and lively... a great start!"
-Adventures in Poor Taste

FIRE FORCE

By Atsushi Ohkubo

The city of Tokyo is plagued by a deadly phenomenon: spontaneous human combustion! Luckily, a special team is there to quench the inferno: The Fire Force! The fire soldiers at Special Fire Cathedral 8 are about to get a unique addition. Enter Shinra, a boy who possesses the power to run at the speed of a rocket, leaving behind the famous "devil's footprints" (and destroying his shoes in the process). Can Shinra and his colleagues discover the source of this strange epidemic before the city burns to ashes?